Immigrants—
and Immigrants

Recent Titles in
Contributions in Economics and Economic History
Series Editor: Robert Sobel

The Age of Giant Corporations: A Microeconomic History of American
Business, 1914-1970
Robert Sobel

Samuel Gompers and the Origins of the American Federation of Labor, 1848-
1896
Stuart Bruce Kaufman

Statistical View of the Trusts: A Manual of Large American Industrial and
Mining Corporations Active Around 1900
David Bunting

State and Regional Patterns in American Manufacturing, 1860-1900
Albert W. Niemi, Jr.

The American Banking Community and New Deal Banking Reforms,
1933-1935
Helen M. Burns

Gold Is Money
Hans F. Sennholz, editor

The Drive to Industrial Maturity: The U.S. Economy, 1860-1914
Harold G. Vatter

Individual Freedom: Selected Works of William H. Hutt
Svetozar Pejovich and David Klingaman, editors

Friedrich A. Sorge's *Labor Movement in the United States:* A History of the
American Working Class from Colonial Times to 1890
Philip S. Foner and Brewster Chamberlin, editors

Essays in Southern Labor History: Selected Papers, Southern Labor History
Conference, 1976
Gary M Fink and Merl E. Reed, editors

The Iron Barons: A Social Analysis of an American Urban Elite, 1874-1965
John N. Ingham

The Railroad Mergers and the Coming of Conrail
Richard Saunders

Immigrants— and Immigrants

PERSPECTIVES ON MEXICAN LABOR MIGRATION TO THE UNITED STATES

edited by Arthur F. Corwin

Contributions in Economics and Economic History, Number 17
GREENWOOD PRESS
Westport, Connecticut • London, England

Library of Congress Cataloging in Publication Data
Main entry under title:

Immigrants—and immigrants.

(Contributions in economics and economic history;
no. 17 ISSN 0084-9235)
Includes bibliographical references and index.
1. Alien labor, Mexican—United States—Addresses, essays, lectures. I. Corwin, Arthur F.
HD8081.M6I43   331.6'272'073   77-84756
ISBN 0-8371-9848-8

Library of Congress Catalog Card Number: 77-84756
ISBN: 0-8371-9848-8
ISSN: 0084-9235

First published in 1978

Greenwood Press, Inc.
51 Riverside Avenue, Westport, Connecticut 06880

Printed in the United States of America

10 9 8 7 6 5 4 3 2 1

CONTENTS

MAPS

ILLUSTRATIONS

ABOUT THE AUTHORS

Arthur F. Corwin, a Latin Americanist, formerly associated with the University of Connecticut, is the author of *Spain and the Abolition of Slavery in Cuba, 1817-1886* (University of Texas Press, 1967), and of several studies bearing on migration, such as "Mexican Emigration History, 1900-1970: Literature and Research, *"Latin American Research Review*, 8:2 (Summer 1973), 3-24. Dr. Corwin, a former member of the Faculty of Economics, University of Nuevo Leon, Mexico, 1958-1962, is presently the director of a cooperative study of Mexican labor emigration since 1900.

Abraham Hoffman, who holds a doctorate in history from the University of California, Los Angeles, has published a significant monograph on *Unwanted Mexican Americans in the Great Depression: Repatriation Pressures, 1929-1939* (University of Arizona Press, 1974). Dr. Hoffman, a member of the editorial board of the *Journal of Mexican-American History*, is also the author of several incisive articles on migration history, including "Mexican Repatriation Statistics: Some Alternatives to Carey McWilliams," *Western Historical Quarterly* 3 (1972), 391-404. Also, with a grant from the National Endowment for the Humanities, he has edited at the University of California, Berkeley, the Paul S. Taylor papers on Mexican labor in the United States.

Walter A. Fogel, Professor of Industrial Relations in the Graduate School of Management, University of California, Los Angeles, has specialized in the study of ethnic minorities in the American labor market. He was a major contributer to the UCLA Mexican American Study Project, writing *Education and Income of Mexican Americans in the Southwest* (1966) and *Mexican Americans in Southwest Labor Markets* (1967). Among his other works is *The Negro in the Meat Industry* (1970).

Lawrence A. Cardoso is a specialist in Mexican History at the University of Wyoming. His doctoral dissertation, which was submitted to the University of Connecticut, is perhaps the most complete study thus far of the socioeconomic causes of Mexican labor emigration in the period 1900-1930. This examination of Mexican archival materials and other primary sources was supported by a fellowship from the Doherty Foundation. He is also the author of "Labor Emigration to the Southwest, 1916-1920: Mexican Attitudes and Policy," *Southwestern Historical Quarterly*, 74:4 (April 1976), 400-416.

Johnny M. McCain, who has a doctorate from the University of Texas, Austin, is a specialist in borderland history at San Antonio College, where he is chairman of the Department of History. His doctoral study covered "Contract Labor as a Factor in United States—Mexican Relations, 1942-1947," and since then he has carried out extensive research on Mexican labor and settlement, and the illegal alien problem, in San Antonio and southern Texas.

Paul S. Taylor, one of the first social scientists to do empirical studies of Mexican migratory groups in the United States, has published fundamental works such as *Mexican Labor in the United States* (10 parts, University of California Press, 1928-1934), *Mexican American Frontier, Nueces County, Texas* (University of North Carolina Press, 1934), *Georgia Plan: 1732-1752* (University of California Press, 1972), and other studies concerned with labor use in historical perspective. He has frequently served as a consultant for labor matters, and his statements have appeared in congressional hearings. Although professor emeritus, Dr. Taylor is still associated with the Department of Economics, University of California, Berkeley.

Ernesto Galarza, born in Tepic, México, has not only studied the Mexican immigration experience but has lived it. After completing a basic education in California, he obtained a doctorate degree from Columbia University. In addition to other positions, he has been a Latin American affairs specialist for the Foreign Policy Association, the Pan American Union, as well as director of research and education for the National Agricultural Workers Union (AFL), and editor, labor consultant, university lecturer, and author. Among his more important publications are *Merchants of Labor: The Mexican Bracero Story* (Santa Barbara: McNally and Loftin, 1964), *Spiders in the House and Workers in the Fields* (University of Notre Dame Press, 1970) and *Barrio Boy* (University of Notre Dame Press, 1971), an autobiography.

ABOUT THE CONSULTANTS

Romeo Flores Caballero, Professor of International Relations, El Colegio de México, is the author of several interpretative studies including *La contrarre-volución en la independencia: los españoles en la vida política, social y econó-mica de México, 1804-1838* (Mexico, 1969), and a number of articles, some of which have appeared in *Historia Mexicana*. Professor Flores, who has a doc-torate in Latin American studies from the University of Texas, Austin, has served as a consultant for several Mexican-American study projects including the present cooperative book on Mexican labor emigration.

Mercedes Carreras de Velasco, another consultant, holds a master's degree in history from El Colegio de México, and is the author of an outstanding study of the Mexican side of repatriation during the Great Depression: *Los mexi-canos que devolvió la crisis de 1929-1932* (México: Secretaria de Relaciones Exteriores, 1974). She is at present a researcher in the Dirección del Archivo y Biblioteca, Secretaría de Relaciones Exteriores, and one of the directors of a documentary study of the efforts by the Mexican government to protect Mexi-can nationals in the United States during this century.

Paul S. Taylor also has served as a consultant for this collaborative book, particularly for Mexican migratory movements and settlement up to World War II.

Immigrants—
and Immigrants

1/ THE STUDY AND INTERPRETATION OF MEXICAN LABOR MIGRATION: AN INTRODUCTION

Arthur F. Corwin

> "Let us sing of our brothers who go north
> to earn their bread.
> They fly from Guanajuato, Mazatlán, and
> Irapuato, and many places more."
>
> Mexican folk ballad

Mexican Labor Studies Up to World War II

As America's "invisible minorities" emerge into the sunlight of public attention, one hears the lament that general histories of immigration to the American Commonwealth dwell heavily on European peoples and their formative influence on national development, but say comparatively little about immigration from Asia, and even less about immigration from Latin American countries, most notably Mexico. After all, some Mexican Americans say their ancestors, like the American Indians, were there to meet the good ship *Mayflower*. And they point out that since the 1920s Mexico has been the major supplier of immigrants and immigrant workers to the United States. "Our history has been suppressed."[1]

One explanation for past neglect of Mexican immigration by students of national development is that, compared to other immigrant groups, it has unique characteristics of protective coloration, and not merely that it fuses easily with earlier Hispano settler groups in the Southwest, or with present-day Puerto Ricans in Chicago, or Latin Americans in San Francisco. For many years—and even now—Mexican immigration was more in the nature of a seasonal labor trek by individuals and extended-family groups, rather than an immigrant voyage in the transoceanic sense. As a result Mexican migrants historically have played a rather inconspicuous role as a rural and industrial labor proletariat, initially undocumented, uncommitted, and, from the viewpoint of an industrial economy, unskilled. Exceptions here would be certain political and religious refugees of the revolutionary period 1912-1928, and a regular current of legal immigrants who arrive with professional or technical skills (some of them learned previously in the American economy by the enterprising "wetback"). [2]

For nearly a century the landless proletarians of rural Mexico have been seeping into border regions, and from there have been freighted or trucked by labor agents, crew leaders, or smugglers into the interior of the United States, then back again to a winter haven in Mexico, or to some "Mexiquito" in the border states. To some observers they came and went like the swallows of Capistrano. Yet always some stayed inland, often encouraged by employers or social workers. On the American side, much as in Mexico, Indo-rural folk settled in a pattern of social marginality, as in "labor camps" across the tracks, or on the urban fringe, or in the bleak industrial zones of inner cities, and like all immigrants they sought out their own kind. [3]

In what numbers? Who will ever know? A frustrating fact of Mexican immigration is that cross-border migrants—workers, tourists, shoppers, visitors, and "wetbacks," often one and the same—have never to this day been lined up and counted as shipboard immigrants were at Ellis Island. In essence this migration has been a walk-in through the nation's back door, and thus, from the viewpoint of the national community, it has seemed practically out of sight. Until World War II and the civil rights movement of the 1960s (of which the farm worker struggle forms a part, as in California and Texas), the Mexican or Chicano minority tended to maintain a low profile in the American labor market, as well as in American society and politics, in part because of ever-present deportation fears, and the deep folk loyalties of La Raza.

Although American historians ignored the early waves of transborder migration, certain social scientists, beginning with economist Victor L. Clark, were alert to the future implications of a free-flowing labor migration over the southern frontier. His "Mexican Labor in the United States" (U.S. Bureau of Labor *Bulletin 78,* September 1908, 466-522) is a firm starting point for Mexican migrant studies and labor recruitment. Clark also influenced the immense Dillingham Commission report on American immigrants (1908-1911). This joint congressional inquiry had only an incidental interest in Mexican workers as it sought to make a social-problems case against massive "cheap labor" immigration from Europe and the Orient, and to set up a selective immigration code (as happened in 1917); yet it provided valuable comparative data on early employment and wage patterns of Mexicans in the border and western states where they were commonly at work in ranching, mining, railroads, tramways, beet fields, foundaries, brickyards, and other industries. [4]

It was not until World War I and after, however, that newly established social scientists in southwestern universities, and their graduate students in sociology, social work, and education, discovered an intriguing field-work laboratory in the Mexican campesino groups that seemed to camp everywhere along the railways and roadways of the Southwest. For instance, at the University of Texas, Max S. Handman, an immigrant himself who combined economics and sociology, sought in the 1920s to distinguish between migratory groups, including political refugees, and to explain in semi-feudal terms the phenomenon of peon migration into border-state agriculture.[5] Or, another notable example, at the University of Southern California, Emory S. Bogardus, pioneered acculturation studies of Mexican groups and their social acceptance.[6]

In this period, *sin duda*, the most significant field studies of Mexicans in the American economy were carried out by Paul S. Taylor, University of California, Berkeley, an economist who has always written with an historical perspective. His ten-part work, *Mexican Labor in the United States* (Berkeley, 1928-1934), together with *A Mexican-American Frontier, Nueces County, Texas* (Chapel Hill, 1934), and *A Spanish-American Peasant Community: Arandas in Jalisco* (Berkeley, 1933), is now considered a monumental storehouse of information on the first generations of Mexican migrants in the border states, as well as in Colorado, Illinois, and Pennsylvania.[7]

Also invaluable as source books on early labor migration are two publications by Mexican anthropologist Manuel Gamio: *Mexican Immigration to the United States: A Study of Human Migration and Adjustment* (Chicago, 1930) and *The Mexican Immigrant: His Life Story* (Chicago, 1931). These factual accounts were researched in 1926-1927, with some support from the Social Science Research Council which also promoted the science of immigration studies in a nation of immigrants.

Taylor and Gamio, both conscientious practitioners of objective rules of social science, were concerned with revealing by field-work methodology, including frequent interviews, the motivations of Mexican workers, their adjustment problems, and the reasons why employers often preferred them. Nevertheless, underlying Taylor's objective data was a concern that a migrant peasantry, unable to compete for private property, or uninterested in the same, would perhaps serve, like water monopolies and political power, to subsidize giant agribusiness and facilitate corporate domination of the southwestern economy to the detriment of certain national ideals such as the family farm and the rights and dignity of labor. And Gamio's data, in fact, made a strong case not only against discrimination and exploitation of immigrant labor but against unregulated campesino migration.

In the meantime, southwestern evangelical groups had found at their doorstep, and in the same basket, a social-rescue challenge and a splendid "Americanization opportunity" in pell-mell migration over the border. This social mission, dating from the outbreak of revolutionary anarchy in Mexico in 1912, and patronizing as it may have been, nevertheless, led by the 1920s to some valuable first-hand observations on the condition of migrant families in the United States, as in the sympathetic writings of Protestant social workers such as McLean, McCombs, and others, who introduced "our little brown brother" to the American public.[8]

Gradually official interest focused on the open border. After the temporary admission of illiterate contract workers from Mexico during World War I, and following the first immigration quota act of 1921, certain congressmen, like John R. Box, were disturbed by the exemption of Mexico and other Western Hemisphere countries from the quota system. This worry was fed by multiplying reports on "wetbacks," the migrant "social problem," and the need for a border patrol, and so congressional committees began to gather data and testimony.[9] And by the end of the decade a fretting State of California began to produce its own broad surveys of Mexican labor and settlement as migrant families made a massive shift from the Texas border area westwards.[10]

The growing debate during 1924-1931 over the restriction of Mexican immigration had meanwhile generated a flood of commentaries, pro and con, by diverse spokesmen for special interest groups, and also by members of the academic community who were beginning to take sides.[11]

The Great Depression rolled back the migratory wave from Mexico and turned the attention of social scientists and social workers to domestic problems such as the dust-bowl migrants from Oklahoma, Arkansas, and Texas, who temporarily took over much of the "stoop work" in California and other states. There was a brief flurry of interest in the repatriation of Mexican labor from 1930 to 1934, by Taylor, Gamio, Bogardus, McLeon, and others, but after that the study of Mexican immigration fell upon a decade of relative neglect. And yet here and there a relevant study appeared.

The reformist New Deal administration fostered research of American labor problems, including the plight of the Mexican pecan shellers in south Texas.[12] And Varden Fuller, carrying forward the work (and concern) of Taylor, published in 1940, as part of an inquiry by Congress into depressed labor conditions, a major thesis on the formative influence of successive waves of cheap migrant labor, Oriental, poor white, and Mexican, on the rise of corporate agribusiness in California.[13]

The Literature From World War II to 1965

The decade of the 1940s was marked by increasing indignation on the part of American social and religious leaders, Protestant and Catholic, in regard to persistent discrimination against Mexican settlers whose Mexican-American sons had fought valiantly under the American flag during the Second World War. This feeling was sharpened by Mexico's threats to cut off wartime contract labor unless racial segregation was terminated. The Texas Good Neighbor Commission, hastily founded in 1943, was an outcome. Not much later, an anti-segregation campaign was carried out by Spanish-speaking leaders and war veterans, the Committee of Catholic Bishops, and other groups, In this period the term *Mexican American, or Latin American,* came into general use. [14] Also, it might be noted that in the 1940s anthropologists, such as Norman D. Humphrey and Ruth D. Tuck, wrote on the acculturation of Mexican immigrant labor in urban areas of Michigan, Minnesota, and California. [15]

Thus far we have said nothing about professional historians who wrote much about Spanish missions and conquistadors but who seemed to overlook the influence of modern Mexican migration on certain regions of the country. So it was left to a spell-binding journalist and life-long civil rights activist, Carey McWilliams, to produce a sweeping historical synthesis of Mexican migration and settlement, old and new, in the borderlands, and beyond. His *North from Mexico: The Spanish-Speaking People in the United States* (Philadelphia, 1949; reprint ed., 1968) is now considered a classic in American immigration literature. This book contains the genesis of several important concepts that have influenced nearly all subsequent writers on the Mexican minority in the United States. For example, what could be called a "frontier thesis" holds that Mexican migration northwards from colonial times to the present, recruited or not, has been a natural gravitation into familiar territory; a "labor thesis" maintains that early Hispanic settlers and incoming migrants were exploited and abused in their own native land by Anglo landgrabbers and capitalist developers, with the migrants finding themselves citizen-children and all, unwanted when jobs dried up; and, to take another example, the "hypocrisy thesis" strikes at the "fantasy heritage" of the Spanish fiestas and fictional Dons promoted by Hollywood and chambers of commerce to the near total exclusion of the Mexican heritage. Civil rightists and ethnic militants would later seize on this work as an exposé of social and economic injustice under an Anglo establishment, and thus it was destined to be a classic in ethnic-protest literature as well.

To measure the full weight of the McWilliamist labor thesis one must take into account other of his seminal works. His *Factories in the Field: The Story of Migratory Farm Labor in California* (Boston, 1939) is a brillant account of the conquest of that state by agribusiness groups, and of capitalist exploitation of stoop-labor waves. Here he made good use of material provided by Taylor, Fuller, and others, as well as his own experience as a migrant housing commissioner in California and as a legal defender of minority groups during the depression era. His thesis was reinforced by *Ill Fares the Land: Migrant and Migratory Labor in the United States* (Boston, 1942), *California: The Great Exception* (New York, 1949), and other publications. [16] Taken together his works provide a socialist indictment of corporate capitalism and laissez-faire conditions of labor enserfment, union busting, and racial segregation. This analytical framework could be applied, with some qualifications, to plantation agriculture and stoop-labor gangs in such locales as the Imperial Valley, the Lower Rio Grande Valley, the beet fields of the Midwest, or the cane fields of Hawaii and Puerto Rico.

Actually it was not until the mid-1950s and early 1960s that students of American history began to manifest a serious interest in Mexican labor immigration. In this period some of the many research gaps were filled in by dissertation writers, some of whom carried the story down to the World War II period. Some noteworthy examples were Coalson who traced the development of the migratory labor system in Texas, Martinez who looked at the Mexican side of emigration, Park who documented Mexican labor in the mines and railroads of early Arizona, and Lipshultz who studied American reaction to Mexican immigration. [17]

Meanwhile, a second exodus from Mexico was sparked by the contract labor needs of World War II. The heated debates on illegal workers and the perennial extension of the "emergency wartime program" from 1942 to 1964 (!) attracted a host of academic writers, journalists, labor leaders, social reformers, and, of course, government committees. The amount of bracero and wetback literature produced on both sides of the border in that period seems positively enormous compared with other facets of Mexican migration and settlement in the United States. Some of the more important studies bearing on policy were prepared by Jones, Rasmussen, Hancock, McClellan and Idar, and especially Galarza, who (long before César Chávez) sought to protect Mexican-American labor from unfair competition. [18]

Likewise, graduate students in the fields of economics, international relations, and history, like Carney, Tomasek, Elac, McCain, or Campbell, wrote informative studies on braceros and related wetback problems. [19] A published dissertation by Richard B. Craig, *The Bracero Program: Interest Groups and Foreign Policy* (Austin: University of Texas Press, 1971), is the most extensive analysis thus far of the politics of labor contracting. It is based on a near-exhaustive study of research literature by such writers as Hawley, Hardin, Scruggs, Copp, Padfield, and many others, as well as on government publications such as congressional hearings, or the *Report of the President's Commission on Migratory Labor in American Agriculture* (Washington, D.C., 1951).

The New Interest in Mexican Immigration Since 1965

The cooperative Mexican American Studies Project (1966-1971), supported by the Ford Foundation, and carried out at the University of California, Los Angeles, opened a new era of academic, foundation, and public interest in Mexican migration, settlement, and social adjustment. The principal publication, edited by Leo Grebler, Joan Moore, Ralph Guzman, and others, was significantly entitled, *The Mexican-American People: The Nation's Second Largest Minority* (New York: Macmillan, 1971). This heavy tome was the first major collaborative survey of the Mexican-American people carried out by social scientists. And there were important by-products, including Grebler's concise statistical and policy study, the first of its kind, on *Mexican Immigration to the United States: The Record and Its Implications* (UCLA, 1966), and his comparative treatment of the low rate of naturalization among Mexican immigrants. [20]

The efforts of federal agencies to assist underprivileged minorities starting with the anti-poverty and civil rights programs of the mid-1960s had meanwhile caused public interest to focus on the displacement effects of incoming Mexican labor, both regulated and unregulated, on such groups as the United Farm Workers headed by César Chávez and the border area Chicanos. Consequently in recent years numerous research studies have been published on border commuters ("greencarders"), illegal aliens, migrant farm labor, Chicano employment problems, and the like, by journalists, such as Dunne, by investigators under contract to government agencies, such as North; or by members of academic communities, such as Schmidt and Fogel, who were also associated with the UCLA project; by Briggs, a noted labor economist at the University of Texas; or by certain graduate students. [21]

Since 1970 congressional hearings have become a growing source of statistical and testimonial information on the impact of Mexican labor, "wet" and "dry," on various sectors of the American economy and labor market. These hearings also provide information on immigration policy, control problems faced by the Immigration and Naturalization Service, special interest groups, the use of federally funded services by illegal aliens, and reform proposals. [22]

Moreover, as a result of rather desperate efforts by the Immigration Service to focus public attention on the "invisible invasion" (with estimates of eight to eleven million illegals in 1976), and the related policy concerns of the President's Domestic Council Committee on Illegal Aliens, appointed in January 1975, various federal departments, including Justice, State, Labor, and the General Accounting Office, as well as state and local agencies, have been bringing out a shifting mosaic of fact-finding studies on illicit migration from all countries, but mainly from Mexico. Extensive reports—including a summary view of America's alien dilemma by the Domestic Council task force—seek to cover job patterns, wage levels, tax and dollar drains, social assistance costs, and reform questions, such as limited amnesty or penalties for employing illegals, foreign policy modifications, aid for underdeveloped countries, and reforms in permissive Great Society Programs. [23]

Mexican Literature on Emigration

Although Mexican scholars have given much attention to Mexico-United States relations and the unforgettable dismemberment of 1848, they have done surprisingly little research on labor emigration. Manuel Gamio was a shining contradiction; yet even his two books on Mexican laborers over the border were published only in English by the University of Chicago Press (1930-1931) and were scarcely known in Mexico until the recent interest in Mexican-American studies. Within government circles, however, there was a considerable literature of "official concern," including consular correspondence and the annual *Memorias* of the Ministry of Foreign Relations and other government departments. This literature dealt with problems generated by mass emigration, such as population and labor loss, repatriation needs, and heavy—if not hopeless—consular obligations to protect free-floating campesinos and their families (usually undocumented) from exploitation, discrimination and arbitrary deportation, and to foster mutual-aid societies among emigrants, like the *Comisiones Honoríficas*. In general, Mexican writers, such as Landa y Piña, Santibañez, Hidalgo, and Loyo, urged the government to discourage by every means possible (short of a blockade) the emigration of undocumented campesinos, and to prevent the Americanization or *pochismo* of Mexicans abroad by fostering patriotic programs of *mexicanidad*. [24]

Later, during the bracero program (1942-1964), there was an intense public feeling that braceros and *mojados* (wetbacks) in the United States were being exploited by self-serving employers and conniving officials, but few research studies of note appeared in this period, except for an occasional government survey of bracero recruits, policy statements by government officials, or an academic thesis. As in the 1920s such writings were usually polarized, some holding that labor emigration was detrimental to Mexico's developmental needs, others that it was favorable to Mexico's balance of payments, and the need to "educate" the campesinos. [25]

Since the 1960s there has been a less intense effort to dissuade emigration because officials and economic advisors realize that the country has become relatively overpopulated. The government is now more concerned with protecting Mexican access to the American labor market. Yet at the same time, as a matter of national pride and deeply rooted sentiments of Raza brotherhood, Mexican officials, consuls, and editorialists have never ceased to keep a close watch on Mexicans in the lost provinces, and to denounce any reported abuses or mass deportations, as may be appreciated in a perusal of leading newspapers such as *Excelsior* or *Novedades*. [26]

In recent years the focus of interest has also shifted toward Mexican-American affairs. Today public officials and journalists, with a grim sense of satisfaction, follow more closely the rise of Raza militancy across the border; and they show a special interest in La Huelga of Chávez, for after all, that movement flies on the one flank the black and red flag of México's revolutionary labor movement, and on the other, the national banner of the Virgin of Guadalupe. Meanwhile, hundreds of Chicano students have made the pilgrimage back to *la madre patria* and have drawn attention to their minority situation and their struggle for liberation. More important, Mexico now has well-funded research centers, linked to El Colegio de México, the National University, the Instituto Nacional de Antropología e Historia, and other institutions. Increasingly there have been cooperative exchanges between these institutions and the Mexican-American studies movement in the United States. In addition, the Mexican and American governments, in a shared concern about a common border have agreed to study the problem of controlling illegal aliens and the drug traffic, and to seek new ways of cooperation.

As a result of the foregoing factors, a substantial body of research literature on Mexican labor emigration is at last beginning to appear in the Spanish language. McWilliams' *North from Mexico* was translated and published in 1968, and Gamio's *The Mexican Immigrant* in 1969. Articles by Anglo-American and Mexican-American scholars have been appearing in such periodicals as *Historia Mexicana*, and original books have appeared in such series as Sep-Setentas; for example, David Maciel, Patricia Bueno, and others, *Aztlán: historia del pueblo chicano, 1849-1910* (Mexico, 1975).

Equally significant, Mexican scholars, who have published many works on labor conditions in Mexico, have begun to bring out original research on emigration and repatriation; for instance, Mercedes Carreras de Velasco, *Los Mexicanos que devolvió la crisis 1929-1932* (México: Colección del Archivo Histórico Diplomatico Mexicano, Secretariá de Relaciones Exteriores, 1974), and two volumes by historian Moisés González Navarro that bear heavily on labor emigration policy and attitudes: *Población y sociedad en México, 1900-1970* (México: UNAM, 1974). Another notable example would be Jorge Bustamante, a sociologist associated as much with Raza study centers in the United States as with El Colegio de México. His work, in fact, reflects increasing Raza collaboration on both sides of the border, as well as his own "participant-observer" impressions (while helping to research the wetback phenomenon as a graduate student at the University of Notre Dame, he entered as a *mojado*, and has since spent considerable time in border research). [27] Bustamante, who has been an advisor to the Mexican government on emigration policy, is also an exponent of Mexico's aggressive Third World view of United States-Mexico relations.

Ethnic Studies and Interpretations

In the late 1960s, and following a pattern of federal and foundation support for black studies, Mexican-American curricula and research centers began to proliferate, particularly in southwestern universities, but also in some midwestern locales, such as Notre Dame University. This, in turn, has led to a veritable cascade of publications, including new academic journals concerned exclusively with Raza topics and founded by graduate students, like the *Journal of Mexican American History* (University of California, Santa Barbara [since 1970]), *Aztlán, International Journal of Chicano Studies and Research* (formerly *Chicano Journal of the Social Sciences and the Arts*) (University of California, Los Angeles [since 1970]), or the *Chicano Law Review*, first printed in

1974 at UCLA, and again the work of graduate students who, in this case, have a special interest in protecting Mexican emigrants. [28]

The new academic concern with minorities has led to many other publications, some of questionable value, by various schools of "Anglo," "Mexican-American," and "Chicano" interpretations. The term *Chicano* had meanwhile surfaced in Mexican labor settlements, commonly called *barrios* or *colonias*. Much of the minority literature, of course, has a cathartic function, yet, at the same time, scholars in ethnic studies have been filling in, refining, and even correcting the grand interpretive design laid out by McWilliams. For instance, Abraham Hoffman's *Unwanted Mexican Americans in the Great Depression: Repatriation Pressures, 1929-1939* (Tucson: University of Arizona Press, 1974), is a carefully documented piece of research on Mexican labor repatriation in the 1930s, and another published thesis by Mark Reisler, *By the Sweat of Their Brow: Mexican Immigrant Labor in the United States, 1900-1940* (Greenwood Press, 1976), appears to be in some respects a definitive history of the first wave of Mexican labor.

Also, some general surveys have pushed beyond McWilliams' research, such as history texts by Matt S. Meier and Feliciano Rivera that stress the labor emigration experience: *The Chicanos: A History of Mexican Americans* (New York: Hill and Wang, 1972); and *Readings on La Raza* (New York: Hill and Wang, 1974). Other major surveys by Stoddard and Cardoso, among others, have looked closely at the socioeconomic background of Mexican out-migration. [29]

Until the sudden emergence of minority studies, and the recruitment of ethnic scholars, there was actually little "input" from Mexicans and Mexican-Americans in the study and interpretation of Raza migration, settlement, and acculturation, with the exception of Gamio, Martínez, Galarza, and a few others. Now a new generation of writers in search of umbilical roots and cultural autonomy have moved rapidly, and with a sense of mission, into these fields.

One preliminary revisionist task that Raza writers have set for themselves is the preparation of new textbooks and annotated bibliographies that would be fitting for Mexican-American and other students in the social sciences and history. [30] Fact-gathering projects have been designed to collect archival data in the United States and Mexico, as well as oral history from Mexican settlers and Raza leaders, for so few of them have written of their experiences. Usually it was the Anglo-American—or *gabacho*—who wrote about La Huelga or La Causa, or picked up the immigrant story, as in Eugene Nelson's *Pablo Cruz and the American Dream* (Salt Lake City: Peregrine Smith, 1975). Now, however, the spirit of ethnic liberation has inspired Mexican Americans not only to work on biography but to write autobiography, a significant forerunner being *Barrio Boy* (Notre Dame, 1971), by Ernesto Galarza, who came as a youngster to the United States. Furthermore, the nature of transborder migration and insights into the "wetback subculture" have been graphically presented in a new

genre of Chicano novel, such as Richard Vásquez' *Chicano* (New York: Dou-
bleday, 1970) or Raymond Barrio's *The Plum Pickers* (Richmond, Calif.: Ven-
tura Press, 1969).

Raza research, whether by a conservative "Mexican-American School" or a
more militant "Chicano school," has been directed, not only toward the gathering of sources, but also toward the wiping-out of racial stereotypes from a
heap of establishment literature and films. Such efforts would include a reas-
sessment of certain myths such as the "docile peon," the "Mexican social
problem," or Anglo-American views of acculturation.[31] Foremost in these revisionist efforts has been the Chicano Studies Center at the University of California, Los Angeles. Through the Center's publications, including *Aztlán, International Journal of Chicano Studies Research* and a monograph series, Chicano scholars such as Juan Gómez-Quiñones, Carlos Cortes, and Jesús Cha-
varría have already done much to rewrite Mexican labor and settlement history, and to demolish the common assumption that Raza workers, documented or not, rarely participated in organized labor movements. See, for example,
Luís L. Arroyo and Victor B. Nelson Cisneros, eds., "Special Issue on Labor
History and the Chicano," *Aztlán* 6:2 (Summer 1975), 137-325.

Naturally, the unsavory stereotype of the "wetback" had to be undone, for
this image bears heavily on the immigrants' status in national society. According to one vanguard study, *Los Mojados: The Wetback Story* by sociologists
Julian Samora, Jorge Bustamante, and Gilbert Cárdenas, wetbacks are properly understood not as "illegals" or "sneaks," but as a reservoir of needed
workers for which the Immigration Service has historically served, innocently
or not, as an on-and-off valve control, letting in "cheap labor" and deporting it
as "illicit," according to economic cycles.

The work of McWilliams—one is tempted to say McWilliamismo—has
been an inspiration for much revisionist effort. But McWilliams, an "old left
liberal" influenced by the labor-depressed 1930s and the capitalist crisis of
that time, has been found wanting by "new left" revisionists, who, inspired by
Marxist-Lenist concepts, seek to shoehorn minority studies into the spreading
Third World ideology of colonialism, internal and external. Activist scholarship in black, brown, and yellow studies has found in internal colonialism a
handy but perhaps simplistic explanation of complex phenomena in American
society (the Metropolis, in Marxist terms), such as the persistent social marginality of certain ethnic groups even in such metropolitan areas as Los Angeles,
San Antonio, and New York, as well as in rural New Mexico and migrant
camps across the country. Herein also is found the root cause of class alienation, institutionalized discrimination, and a gamut of "poverty indicators."

Along this line of Third World interpretations, practitioners of ethnic
studies, like sociologists Joan Moore and Robert Blauner, have distinguished
between three general categories of minorities: (1) "Conquest minorities,"
such as the American Indians, Puerto Ricans, native Hawaiians, and original

Mexican settlers of the Southwest, who have been forced by territorial conquest into a minority status and a colonial relationship to the dominant society. (2) Blacks and to some extent Oriental "coolie laborers" who were subjected to "forced immigration" and caste exclusion, as are the Chicanos. (3) European immigrants who, by contrast, made a "voluntary entry" into American society and into a labor market relatively open to them.[32]

Militant Raza scholarship in the United States and Mexico has given such Third World concepts a special twist and projected them back to a preindustrial period of frontier conflict and agrarian imperialism in the Southwest. For instance, in a reevaluation of borderland history, *Occupied America: The Chicano's Struggle toward Liberation* (San Francisco: Canfield, 1972), Rodolfo Acuña insisted that later generations of Mexican immigrants were strained through an institutionalized structure of territorial conquest, caste discrimination, and labor exploitation dating from the Anglo-Saxon seizure of Texas and other provinces of northern Mexico.

Similarly, sociologist Rodolfo Álvarez of the University of California, Los Angeles, in "The Psycho-Historical and Socioeconomic Development of the Chicano Community in the United States," *Social Science Quarterly* 53 (March 1973), 920-942, has asserted that the Mexican-American minority was the creation of an imperial conquest. Therefore brown liberation and self-discovery has been a painful evolution ranging from the first Mexican settlers in the borderlands, who were overwhelmed by Anglo expansionists, through the migrant labor generations, to the present American-born Chicano generations that struggle against economic marginality and totally reject Anglo assimilation. In this effort to redo the literature on minorities and to achieve cultural autonomy, the writer correctly affirms that at last the Raza movement has "its own certified savants."

External forms of colonialism have likewise provided Raza scholars on both sides of the "arbitrary line" with an *apologia* that links the sensitive subject of "wetback migration" with capitalist expansion and labor exploitation abroad. Since Third World migration is predominantly "undocumented immigration," allegedly carrying the "stigma of illegality," neo-Marxism provides a ready-made explanation: Third World peoples are driven to emigrate to the American metropolis by economic imperialism, or by regressive colonial structures maintained in Mexico, the Philippines, Taiwan, and elsewhere by international corporations such as Standard Oil, Anderson Clayton, Anaconda, and the like; or alternatively, Third World peoples are brought in clandestinely or legally to serve capitalist groups under a system of quasi-government collusion.[33]

Such revisionist literature, in saying little about the self-serving drives of emigrant adventurers and the predatory types who have always lived on selling emigration and false hopes, seems to foster, unintentionally, counter-stereotypes, equally suspect, such as the masochistic innocence of Third World folk: What indignities will they not suffer to come to America?

Other Raza variations of Third Worldism are also quite *sui generis*, such as: (1) Mexico, since the dictator Porfirio Díaz (1876-1911), has been an exemplary economic colony of foreign capitalists, but especially Gringo capitalists. (2) On both sides of the line, American employers have used La Raza as a surplus-labor pool. During American economic recessions, as in 1921, 1929-1939, 1947, 1954, 1973-1976, Mexican workers and dependents have been made the scapegoats of American unemployment and welfare problems, and have been hustled back to Mexico as "repatriates" or put on social assistance to avoid class warfare (as with the blacks). The voluntary departure cycle maintained by the Immigration Service for hundreds of thousands of illegals each year is interpreted by Raza writers and Mexican officials as an informal bracero program to provide cheap labor without the supervision of labor standards. (3) Chicanos are forced to migrate northward because American imperialists took half of Mexico in 1848, leaving no territory to absorb the demographic vitality (vigor *demográfico*) of La Raza. [34] (By 1976 Mexico's population had passed 63 million, not counting several million emigrants.) Whatever the circumstances of entry, Raza workers and dependents are entitled to a full share of "surplus value" expropriated by Gringo capitalists from migrant labor and Mexican territorial resources. (5) Raza folk are not immigrants to America del Norte and do not intend, like other immigrant groups, to jump into the "melting pot." [35] More like Puerto Rican nationalists, who feel their Borinquen was seized in 1898, Chicano militants consider themselves not voluntary citizens but refugees of imperialism. (6) Under the Aztlán mythology fostered by Chicano ideologues, the "spiritual decendants of the Aztecas" are coming to recover the original homeland in the American Southwest. [36] (This homeland is totally without archeological confirmation, and of course, American Indian groups dispute the claim.)

In view of conflicting "tribal claims" for compensation and the need to legitimate "undocumented immigration" (or justify amnesty proposals), it seems that a Raza variation of Marxist-Leninist thought offers the broadest claim on the Anglo-American establishment—a claim that would not only cover the 75,000, or more, Spanish speaking in the Southwest in 1848, but the millions of migratory folk who have since trekked in from Mexico. Whether in Mexico or in Aztlán del Norte neo-Marxists and nationalists agree that compared with any other immigrant group, La Raza has been the most exploited caste in American economic development. This thesis—a quasi-official one in Mexico—is best expressed by Bustamante, who holds that nearly everywhere, but particularly in the Anglo Southwest, Mexicans provided the main proletarian labor force. This labor force, he contends, supplanted Oriental coolies, American Indians, Filipinos, Italians, Slavs, and other immigrant labor, as

well as blacks and even Mexican Americans, in agriculture, the railroad industry, mines, industrial sweat shops, and the maintenance, construction, and service industries, including domestic service, while the unpaid surplus value of
Raza labor subsidized the expansion of American corporate wealth and power,
even in Mexico itself, and served to maintain a privileged standard of living
and education for the Anglo bourgeoisie and its children. [37] It follows from this
key theme of Chicano labor history that Anglo America owes the Mexican
working class something—at least a more "humane" immigration policy. [38]

Leaving out ideological concept, other revisionists, like North, Villalpando,
Cornelius, Cárdenas, and Piore, have questioned the restrictionists' usual as-
sumptions that illegal aliens from Third World countries pay little in taxes,
generate high social assistance costs, displace native workers, adversely affect
the nation's balance of payments, or always seek permanent settlement. [39] An
excellent résumé of contradictory findings and bewildering proposals to solve
America's alien dilemma, by armchair social scientists and government committees, is given by Joyce Vialet, *Illegal Aliens: Analysis and Background*
(Washington, D.C.: Congressional Research Service, Library of Congress,
1977).

The foregoing pages merely abbreviate the exploding research and literature on Mexican labor and settlement. Persistent readers would find more, including suggested research needs, in the studies indicated in the notes, in the
"reprints" of unpublished dissertations by R and E Research Associates (4843
Mission St., San Francisco, Ca., 94112); and, for the broader migratory vistas,
in Paul Meadows and others, *Recent Immigration to the United States: The
Literature of the Social Sciences* (Washington, D.C.: Research Institute on Immigration and Ethnic Studies, Smithsonian Institution, 1976), and in Thomas
Weaver and Theodore E. Downing, eds., *Mexican Migration* (Tucson: Bureau
of Ethnic Research, University of Arizona, 1976).

Actually organizations of professional investigators, academicians, and militant scholars have just begun to work a bonanza of possibilities for subsidized
research on America's illegal alien dilemma: for instance, The Association of
Borderland Scholars, founded in 1976 by sociologist Ellwyn S. Stoddard, University of Texas at El Paso; The Mexico-United States Border Research Program, initiated in 1977 and coordinated by Stanley R. Ross, Latin Americanist, University of Texas at Austin, and by Horacio Flores de la Peña, Centro de
Investigación y Docencia Económica, Mexico City; numerous research centers
at American, and increasingly Mexican, academic institutions; or private
agencies doing contract work for perplexed public officials, like Transcentury
Corporation's Center for Labor and Migration Studies, directed by David S.
North, and centered in Washington, D.C. The future promises a flood of publications and position papers of mixed quality, which will undoubtedly raise
more questions than answers. Desperate immigration officers complain that

the last thing we need is more research, but just as immigration begets immigration so research begets research.

To this point perhaps enough has been said to suggest that the United States' and Mexico's sharing of a common—and still disputed—land border is a geopolitical fact that, like Alsace-Lorraine, readily sets transborder migration off from all other immigrations to America, and that this subject naturally lends itself to polemical treatment. After all, in the history of United States and Mexican relations, "the first illegal aliens were the Anglos."[40]

About This Book

The children of the Spanish Conquest began walking to what is now the American Southwest even before the founding of Jamestown in 1607. Yet these mestizo settlers of the colonial and Mexican eras numbered only in the hundreds. The migration of several million Mexicans over the southwestern border, our main concern here, has been a twentieth-century phenomenon. The present book, an outcome of a cooperative project that involved researchers in the United States and Mexico, is not intended to be a complete history of Mexican migration or of Mexican labor in the American economy, but rather an interpretative survey of the causes and consequences of this migratory movement, with special emphasis on control problems and policy responses in both countries during the past 60 years, and particularly since the mid-1960s. No attempt has been made to cover a small migration of political or religious refugees from Mexico or the domestic history of the Chicano descendants of Mexican settlers in the United States, although, here and there, where it seemed relevant, acculturation matters have been touched upon.

Sources for this volume include materials up to approximately 1950 from the diplomatic and consular correspondence in the National Archives, Washington, D.C.; the archives of the Secretaría de Relaciones Exteriores, Mexico City; nonrestricted immigration files of a more current date; and special collections such as the papers of Carey McWilliams in the Los Angeles Public Library.

Important published sources include the *Annual Report* of the United States Immigration and Naturalization Service (INS), congressional hearings, the *Congressional Record*, and government agency reports; and on the Mexican side, the *Memorias* of the Ministry of Relaciones Exteriores, and of Gobernación (internal affairs), as well as the *Diario Oficial* which publishes laws, decrees, and circulars. In addition to a variety of newspapers in both countries, such as the *New York Times* and *Excelsior*, many published reports of Mexican labor migration by social workers, journalists, and social scientists were used, especially field reports by Paul S. Taylor, Manuel Gamio, Ernesto Galarza, Julian Samora, David S. North, Vernon Briggs, Jr., and others.

Moreover, first-hand observations and interviews by the principal investigator, Arthur F. Corwin, with immigration and consular officials, employers, migrant workers, and other knowledgeable persons on both sides of the border have contributed to an understanding of the dynamics of present-day migratory movements, both legal and surreptitious, and related policy questions. In this respect special thanks are due to the following persons: Robert J. Seitz, Public Information Officer, Western Region; James F. Greene, Deputy Commissioner of Immigration and Naturalization, Central Office; Harlan B. Carter, former Chief of the Border Patrol and former Regional Commissioner of Immigration; Leonard W. Gilman, also a former Regional Commissioner of the Western Region; Joseph Sureck, District Director of Immigration, Los Angeles; William T. Toney, former Deputy Chief Patrol Agent, Del Rio Sector of the U.S. Border Patrol; Charles J. Feary, former Deputy Chief Patrol Agent, Laredo; John W. Holland, former District Director of Immigration, San Antonio; Joe Staley, present Director, San Antonio; Herman C. Moore, former Chief Patrol Agent, El Paso; Donald Brown, District Director, Phoenix; Donald C. Coppock, former Deputy Associate Commissioner, Central Office; Ralph Farb, Office of General Counsel, Central Office; Charles Beechie, former District Director of Immigration, Mexico City; Sam Karp, former Chief, Visa Section, and Don Lautz, Consul, American Embassy, Mexico City; Edward Kreuser, American Consul, Monterrey; Judge Fletcher Rawls and John R. Peavey of McAllen, Texas, both in border inspection before 1920; Clyde C. Colbert, Laredo, and Albert Del Guercio, both early members of the Border Patrol; Joseph M. Swing, former Commissioner of Immigration (1954-1960); and many other veterans and retirees in the immigration and consular services, as well as persons associated with the judiciary committees in Congress.

Also of special assistance were Mrs. Fred W. Neale, San Antonio; Conley C. Kemper, former Coordinator of Migrant Labor, Texas Good Neighbor Commission, Austin; Robert C. Jones, Director, Villa Jones International Cultural Center, Oaxtepec, Mexico; and Ernest G. Garrison, former border patrolman, San Antonio, whose satirical cartoons of the "wetback game" were for many years posted on Immigration Service bulletin boards. Moreover, Matt S. Meier, University of Santa Clara, provided bibliographical resources; Donald L. Zelman, Tarleton State University, Stephenville, Texas, shared research findings on Mexican labor settlement in southern California; Joseph B. Fichandler carried out cooperative research in Mexico City and Washington, D.C.; Larry García y Griego helped trace nineteenth-century Mexican migration; Dr. Varden Fuller suggested perspectives on the impact of Mexican labor on California agribusiness; and Charles E. Hancock Bureau of Land Management, Reno, assisted with research questionnaires for farm and ranch labor.

I wish, furthermore, to acknowledge the assistance of Juan Barona Lobato, Asuntos de Trabajadores Migratorios, Secretaria de Relaciones Exteriores;

Jorge Aguilar Saldaña, Director, Servicio Consular de México; Professor Martín Quirarte, former chargé, historical section, Foreign Relations archives; Consul Guillermo Váldez, Denver; Consul Ernestina Fernández Picazo, Corpus Christi; Consul Hector Jara, Laredo; José Ramos Gallegos, Canciller, Mexican Consulate, San Antonio; and other members of Mexico's consular corps in such cities as Dallas, Kansas City, San Francisco, and Phoenix.

Financial support for cooperative research on Mexican labor migration and settlement in the United States was received principally from the National Endowment for the Humanities, Washington, D.C., during the period 1970-1974. Also, in that time assistance was given by the University of Connecticut through faculty research grants, as well as by the American Council of Learned Societies, and Project Hope of Washington, D.C., and Laredo. In addition, a grant from the Weatherhead Foundation made possible the updating of information on recent migratory affairs. Among persons who facilitated grants-in-aid were: William R. Emerson and David Wallace, National Endowment for the Humanities; Stuart F. Wilson, Coordinator of Research Services, University of Connecticut; John J. Owen, Associate Director, University of Connecticut Foundation; and Bill Walsh, Jr., of Project Hope.

Finally, it should be noted that some paragraphs of a previous study by Arthur F. Corwin, namely, "Causes of Mexican Emigration to the United States: A Summary View," in *Perspectives in American History*, Charles Warren Center for Studies in American History, Harvard University, 7 (1974), 557-635, have been incorporated into this book.

Notes

1. See interview statements in Stan Steiner, *La Raza: The Mexican Americans* (New York: Harper and Row, 1969).

2. See Arthur F. Corwin, "Causes of Mexican Emigration to the United States: A Summary View," in the annual *Perspectives in American History* 7 (1973), published by Charles Warren Center for Studies in American History, Harvard University (Cambridge, 1974), pp. 557-635.

3. Among notable studies in community marginality are: William Madsen, *The Mexican Americans of South Texas* (New York: Holt, Rinehart and Winston, 1964) and Arthur J. Rubel, *Across the Tracks: Mexican Americans in a Texas City* (Austin: University of Texas Press, 1966). See also Rudolph O. De la Garza et al, *Chicanos and Native Americans: The Territorial Minorities* (Englewood Cliffs, N.J.: Prentice Hall, 1973).

4. U.S. Congress, Senate, *Reports of the Immigration Commission (Dillingham Committee) . . . 61st. Cong., 3d Sess.* (1911), particularly volumes 1, 24, and 25.

5. "The Mexican Immigrant in Texas," *Southwestern Political and Social Science Quarterly* 8 (June 1926), 33-41; or "Economic Reasons for the Coming of the Mexican Immigrant," *American Journal of Sociology* 35 (January 1930), 601-605.

6. Examples: "Second Generation Mexicans," *Sociology and Social Research* 13 (1929), 276-283; "Racial Distance Changes in the United States During the Past Thirty

Years," *Sociology and Social Research* 44 (1959), 127-135; and *The Mexican in the United States* (Los Angeles, 1934).

7. See Abraham Hoffman's tribute: "An Unusual Monument: Paul S. Taylor's *Mexican Labor in the United States* Monograph Series," *Pacific Historical Review* 55 (May 1976), 255-270.

8. Robert N. McLean, *That Mexican! As He Really Is, North and South of the Rio Grande* (New York, 1928); Vernon McCombs, *From Over the Border: A Study of Mexicans in the United States* (New York, 1926); likewise, Rev. G. L. Cady et al., *National Conference Concerning Mexicans and Spanish Americans in the United States. Report of Commission on International and Interracial Factors in the Problems of Mexicans in the United States* (El Paso, 1926); or the journal of Protestant social concern, *Survey Graphic*, for the years 1912-1932.

9. For example, U.S. Congress, House Committee on Immigration and Naturalization, *Hearings, Temporary Admission of Illiterate Mexican Laborers, 66th Cong., 1st Sess.* (1920); *Hearings, Seasonal Agricultural Laborers from Mexico, 69th Cong., 1st Sess.* (1926); or *Hearings, Immigration from Countries of the Western Hemisphere, 70th Cong., 1st Sess.* (1928).

10. *Mexicans in California: Report of Governor C.C. Young's Mexican Fact-Finding Committee* (Sacramento: State of California, 1930). Also important, Constantine Panunzio and the Heller Committee, *How Mexicans Earn and Live: A Study of the Income and Expenditures of One Hundred Mexican Families in San Diego, California* (Berkeley, 1933).

11. Examples: Charles P. Howland, "Mexican Immigration," *Survey of American Foreign Relations* (published for the Council of Foreign Relations by Yale University Press, 1931), pp. 202-233; Robert F. Foerster, *The Racial Problems Involved in Immigration from Latin America and the West Indies to the United States. A Report Submitted to the Secretary of Labor* (Washington, D.C., 1925); or, Roy L. Garis, *Immigration Restriction: A Study of the Opposition to and Regulation of Immigration into the United States* (New York, 1927). The literature of the restrictionist debate is covered by Lipshultz, note 19, and in the works of Hoffman and Reisler cited earlier in this chapter.

12. Selden C. Menefee and Orin Cassmore, *The Pecan Shellers of San Antonio* (Washington, D.C.: Works Project Administration, 1940); see also Menefee's *Mexican Migratory Workers in South Texas* (Washington, D.C.: Works Project Administration, 1941).

13. "The Supply of Agricultural Labor as a Factor in the Evolution of Farm Organization in California," in U.S. Congress, Senate Subcommittee on Education and Labor, *Hearings, Violations of Free Speech and Rights of Labor, 74th Cong., Part 54* (1940), 19777-19898.

14. See Pauline Kibbe's informative account of discrimination and erratic progress in improving race relations: *Latin Americans in Texas* (Albuquerque, 1946).

15. For instance, Humphrey, "The Cultural Background of the Mexican Immigrant," *Rural Sociology* 8 (1948), 239-255; or Tuck, *Not With the First: Mexican Americans in a Southwest City* (New York: Harcourt, Brace, 1946).

16. See Joseph P. Navarro, "The Contributions of Carey McWilliams to American Ethnic History," *The Journal of Mexican American History* 2 (Fall 1971), 1-19; and

Carey McWilliams, "Once a Well-Kept Secret," *Pacific Historical Review* 42 (August 1973), 309-318.

17. George O. Coalson, "The Development of the Migratory Farm Labor System in Texas, 1900-1954" (Ph.D. thesis, University of Oklahoma, 1955); John R. Martínez, "Mexican Emigration to the United States, 1910-1930" (Ph.D. thesis, Berkeley: University of California, 1957); Joseph F. Park, "The History of Mexican Labor in Arizona During the Territorial Period" (M.A. thesis, Tucson: University of Arizona, 1961); and Robert F. Lipshultz, "American Attitudes Toward Mexican Immigration, 1924-1952" (Master's thesis, University of Chicago, 1962).

18. Robert C. Jones, *Mexican War Workers in the United States: The Mexico-United States Manpower Recruitment Program and Its Operation* (Washington, D.C.: Pan American Union, 1945); Wayne D. Rasmussen, *A History of the Emergency Farm Labor Supply Program, 1943-1947* (Mimeographed, Washington, D.C.: U.S. Department of Agriculture Monograph No. 13, 1951); Richard H. Hancock, *The Role of the Bracero in the Economic and Cultural Dynamic of Mexico: A Case Study of Chihuahua* (Stanford University, Hispanic American Studies, 1959); Andrew C. McLellan and Ed Idar, *What Price Wetbacks?* (Austin: Texas State Federation of Labor and American G.I. Forum, 1954); and Ernesto Galarza, *Merchants of Labor: The Mexican Bracero Story* (Santa Barbara: McNally and Loftin, 1964).

19. John P. Carney, "Postwar Mexican Migration: 1945-1955, with Particular Reference to the Policies and Practices of the United States Government Concerning Its Control" (Ph.D. thesis, Los Angeles: University of Southern California, 1957); Robert D. Tomasek, "The Political and Economic Implications of Mexican Labor in the United States" (Ph.D. thesis, Ann Arbor: University of Michigan, 1958); John C. Elac, "The Employment of Mexican Workers in United States Agriculture, 1900-1960: A Binational Economic Analysis" (Ph.D. thesis, Los Angeles: University of California, 1961); Johnny M. McCain, "Contract Labor as a Factor in United States-Mexican Relations, 1942-1947" (Ph.D. thesis, Austin: University of Texas, 1970); and Howard L. Campbell, "Bracero Migration and the Mexican Economy, 1951-1964" (Ph.D. thesis, Washington, D.C.: American University, 1972).

20. "The Naturalization of the Mexican Immigrant to the United States," *International Migration Review* 1 (Fall 1966), 17-32.

21. John G. Dunne, *Delano: The Story of the California Grape Strike* (New York: Farrar, Straus and Giroux, 1967); David S. North, *The Border Crossers: People Who Live in Mexico and Work in the United States* (Washington, D.C.: Transcentury Corporation, 1970); Fred H. Schmidt, *Spanish Surnamed American Employment in the Southwest*, prepared for the Colorado Civil Rights Commission (Washington, D.C.: Equal Employment Opportunity Commission, 1970); Walter Fogel, *Mexican Americans in Southwest Labor Markets*, Mexican American Study Project, Advance Report 10 (Los Angeles: University of California, 1967); Lamar B. Jones, "Mexican American Labor Problem in Texas" (Ph.D. thesis, Austin: University of Texas, 1965); Vernon D. Briggs, Jr., *Chicanos and Rural Poverty* (Baltimore: Johns Hopkins University Press, 1973); and a cooperative work by Briggs, Fogel, and Schmidt, *The Chicano Worker* (Austin: University of Texas Press, 1977).

22. Noteworthy examples: U.S. Congress, House Judiciary Committee, *Illegal Aliens, Hearings before Subcommittee No. 1 . . . 92d Cong., 1st and 2d Sess.* (5 parts,

1971-1972), commonly known as the "Rodino Hearings"; and Senate Judiciary Committee, *Immigration 1976. Hearings before the Subcommittee on Immigration and Naturalization, 94th Cong., 2d Sess., March-April, 1976* (1976).

23. A sampling: David S. North and Marion F. Houstun, *The Character and Role of Illegal Aliens in the U.S. Labor Market*, prepared under contract by Linton and Company (Washington, D.C.: U.S. Department of Labor, Employment and Training Administration, 1976); U.S. General Accounting Office, Comptroller General, *Need to Reduce Public Expenditures for Newly Arrived Immigrants and Correct Inequity in Current Immigration Law* (Washington, D.C., 1975); U.S. General Accounting Office, Comptroller General, *Immigration-Need to Reassess U.S. Policy* (1976); California State Social Welfare Board, "Position Statement: Aliens in California" (Sacramento: Department of Social Welfare, 1973); State of Illinois, Legislative Investigative Commission, "Illinois Study on Illegal Aliens" (Springfield, 1971); and Domestic Council Committee on Illegal Aliens, *Preliminary Report* (Washington, D.C.: Department of Justice, December 1976). The latter also contains a current bibliography of studies and legislative discussions of illegal aliens and policy questions.

24. For example, in 1928, Andrés Landa y Piña, head of the Department of Migration, prepared for the Secretaría de Relaciones Exteriores "La migración y protección de Mexicanos en el extranjero," later published as *El Servicio de Migración en México* (1930); Enrique S. Santibañez, Consul General in San Antonio in the 1920s, wrote a series of articles for *Excelsior*, a leading national newspaper, explaining the nature of Mexican labor emigration and protectionist problems, later published as *Ensayo acerca de la inmigración mexicana en los Estados Unidos* (San Antonio, 1930); Alfonso Fabila's *El problema de la emigración de obreros y campesinos* (México, 1928), written in Los Angeles and distributed by the Mexican government, was a characteristic warning to La Raza not to seek El Dorado over the border where Mexican families surely faced hard labor, discrimination, and unbearable Americanization pressures from the public schools. For writings by Gilberto Loyo and others, see Arthur F. Corwin, "Mexican Emigration History: Literature and Research," *Latin American Research Review 8* (Summer 1973), 3-24.

25. Some of the more important examples: México, Secretaría de Trabjo, Dirección de Previsión Social, *Los braceros* (Mexico, 1946); Gloria R. Vargas y Campo, "El problema del bracero mexicano" (Thesis, México: UNAM, 1964); Stella Leal Carrillo, "Importancia económica y social de la población mexicana en Estados Unidos de America" (Thesis, México: UNAM, 1963); or José L. Salinas, *La immigración de braceros, visión objetiva de un problema* (Guanajuato, 1955).

26. The Secretaría de Trabajo y Hacienda Pública has since the late 1920s kept a file of newspaper clippings on Mexicans in the United States, in the Biblioteca Lerdo de Tejada, Mexico City. For example, see assessment of Mexican labor exploitation by Chicano pyschologists Juan J. Sánchez and Saúl Solache, associated with UCLA, reported in *Excelsior*, January 10, 1977, pp. 1,11.

27. "Espaldas mojadas: Informe de un observador participante," *Revista de la Universidad de México* 26 (Marzo 1973), 3 ff.

28. For example, a special issue on American immigration policy and history by Michael Asimow et al., in *Chicano Law Review* 2 (Summer 1975), 129 pp.

29. Ellwyn S. Stoddard, *Mexican Americans* (New York: Random House, 1973), and Lawrence A. Cardoso, "Mexican Emigration to the United States, 1900 to 1930: An

Analysis of Socio-economic Causes" (Ph.D. thesis, Storrs: University of Connecticut, 1973).

30. Some noteworthy bibliographical compilations are: Ernie Barrios et al., *Bibliografía de Aztlán: An Annotated Chicano Bibliography* (San Diego: California State University, Centro de Estudios Chicanos, 1971); Luis G. Nogales, *The Mexican American, a Selected and Annotated Bibliography* (Rev. ed., Stanford University Press, 1971); or, Juan Gómez Quiñones and Alberto Camarillo, *Selected Bibliography for Chicano Studies* (Los Angeles: University of California, Mexican-American Studies Center, 1975). See also Matt S. Meier and Feliciano Rivera, *Bibliography for Chicano History* (San Francisco: R and E Research Associates, 1972).

31. See Cecil Robinson, *With the Ears of Strangers: The Mexican in American Literature* (Tucson: University of Arizona Press, 1961); Manuel P. Servín (ed.), *The Mexican Americans: An Awakening Minority* (Beverly Hills: Glencoe Press, 1970); Octavio I. Romano, "The Anthropology and Sociology of the Mexican Americans," *El Grito, A Journal of Contemporary Mexican American Thought* 2 (Fall 1968), 13-26; Nick C. Vaca, "The Mexican Americans in the Social Sciences, 1912-1970, Part I: 1912-1935," *El Grito, A Journal of Contemporary Mexican American Thought* 3 (Spring 1970, 3-24), "Part II: 1936-1970." 4(Fall 1970), 17-51; and similar articles in *Aztlán*. Revisionism is considered further in A. F. Corwin, "Mexican-American History: An Assessment," *Pacific Historical Review* 42 (August 1973), 269-308.

32. Moore, "Colonialism: The Case of the Mexican American," *Social Problems* 17 (Spring 1970), 463-471; and Blauner, *Racial Oppression in America* (New York: Harper and Row, 1972). For other perspectives on territorial conquest and social marginality, see De la Garza et al., note three; and Manuel P. Servin (ed.), "Early Southwestern Minorities," *Journal of the West* 14 (October 1975), special issue on Indians, Mexican-Americans, and women.

33. For instance, National Catholic Conference of Catholic Bishops Committee for the Bicentennial, *Liberty and Justice for All* (Washington, D.C., 1975), particularly sections by Third World priests, pp. 37-58; and declarations made by delegates to the Second United States-Mexico Meeting on Migration, held in Mexico City, April 21-24, 1975, under the auspices of the U.S. Catholic Conference and the Mexican Episcopate. See *Excelsior*, April 22-25, 1975.

34. A. F. Corwin, *Contemporary Mexican Attitudes Toward Population, Poverty, and Public Opinion* (Latin American Monograph 25, Gainesville: University of Florida, 1963).

35. Characteristically the Anglo "kiss of death" is abhorred by such Raza writers as Armando B. Rendón, *Chicano Manifesto, the History and Aspirations of the Second Largest Minority in America* (New York: Macmillan, 1971).

36. Aztlán (literally, the place of the Aztecs) is variously defined as a spiritual or cultural regeneration of Raza groups in the United States; or as a political "reconquista" of the lost provinces; or simply as a quest for social justice. For literary expressions of Aztlán see periodicals like *El Grito*, or such compilations as Philip D. Ortega (ed.), *We Are Chicanos: An Anthology of Mexican American Literature*; for political expressions see United Farm Workers, *El Malcriado* (Delano), or periodicals by the reborn generation such as *La Raza Nueva* (San Antonio), and *La Raza* (Los Angeles); and for Mexican-American and Latin American lobby groups and programs see National Council of La Raza, *Agenda* (Washington, D.C.).

37. For example, Jorge A. Bustamante, "The Historical Context of the Undocumented Immigration from Mexico to the United States," *Aztlán* 3 (Fall 1972), 257-282; or his "Commodity Migrants: A Structural Analysis of Mexican Immigration to the United States," paper prepared for the Conference on Contemporary Dilemmas of the Mexican-United States Border, sponsored by the Weatherhead Foundation, San Antonio, April 14-18, 1975.

38. Statements by various Mexican, Chicano, and Anglo-American scholars and government officials and consultants at symposium and workshop on "Immigration and Public Policy: The Humanistic Imperative," sponsored by Chicano Training Center, held at University of Houston, April 15-16, 1977.

39. North and Houstoun, *The Character and Role of Illegal Aliens*; Manuel Vic Villalpando and others associated with the San Diego County Immigration Council, *A Study of the Socioeconomic Impact of Illegal Aliens on the County of San Diego* (County of San Diego Human Resources Agency, January 1977); Wayne A. Cornelius, with Juan Díez-Cañedo, *Mexican Migration to the United States: The View from Rural Sending Communities* (Cambridge, Mass.: Center for International Studies, Massachusetts Institute of Technology, 1976); Gilbert Cárdenas, "United States Immigration Policy toward Mexico: An Historical Perspective," *Chicano Law Review*, UCLA, 2 (Summer 1975), 66-91; and Michael J. Piore, "Illegal Immigration to the United States: Some Observations and Policy Suggestions," in *Illegal Aliens: An Assessment of the Issues* (Washington, D.C.: National Council on Employment Policy, October 1976).

40. Mauricio Mazón, "Illegal Alien Surrogates: A Psychohistorical Interpretation of Group Stereotyping in Time of Economic Stress," *Aztlán* 6:2 (Summer 1975), 320.

2/ EARLY MEXICAN LABOR MIGRATION: A FRONTIER SKETCH, 1848–1900
Arthur F. Corwin

No sooner had Mexico relinquished the northern territories when news of a major gold strike near Sacramento, California, electrified the western world. As Leonard Pitt, author of *The Decline of the Californios*, described it:

After a century of slow population growth, during which the arrival of twenty-five cholos or fifty Americans seemed a momentous occasion, suddenly and without warning California faced one of the swiftest, largest, and most varied folk migrations of all time.... 100,000 newcomers in the single year 1849—80,000 Yankees, 8,000 Mexicans, 5,000 South Americans, and several thousand miscellaneous Europeans.[1]

Altogether in the two years 1849 and 1850 probably around twenty thousand Mexicans, many of them experienced miners, rushed to Alta California, mostly overland from the silver regions of Sonora and Zacatecas. It seems that in that brief time more people left Mexico, at least temporarily, for what is today the American Southwest than during the entire Spanish and Mexican eras.

In an episode that illustrates recurring anti-alien feeling in California labor history, most of the Mexican miners, who usually worked in peon gangs for a *patrón*, were, sooner or later, driven out of the mine fields by Anglo-American and other immigrant groups. Californios, Chilenos, and other Latin Americans often received similar treatment.[2] Some of the Mexicans abandoned California, some returned seasonally for several years, some began working for

American *patrones*, who then, like later railroad and agribusiness employers, protected them, and others moved into coastal communities where, as in Los Angeles, they soon established "Sonora towns" and "little Mexicos" (Mexiquitos). They were joined by California vaqueros, peons, and seasonal Indian laborers displaced by the collapse of the mission and rancho system. As gringos greedily took over northern California, Spanish-speaking groups tended to congregate in southern California where the old order was not totally "overwhelmed" until the boom of the 1880s in agriculture, railways, real estate, and tourism.[3]

The Spanish-California rancho elites that had usually kept aloof from Mexican half-castes, or "cholos" (earlier sent as settlers by a desperate Spain and Mexico), and "mission Indians" found themselves rapidly losing status in the eyes of the Yankee argonauts, who rarely bothered in the gold-fever atmosphere to distinguish one group from another. The newly arrived Americanos, their prejudices inflamed by cries of the Alamo and Goliad and the recent Mexican war, as well as the Mexican *patrón* custom of bringing in peon labor gangs, tended to lump all the Spanish speakers together as alien interlopers(!) and "greasers." When Mexican and Latin-American miners were driven into the coastal towns, they mixed imperceptibly with the natives. This served to

THE TERRITORIAL CESSION OF 1848

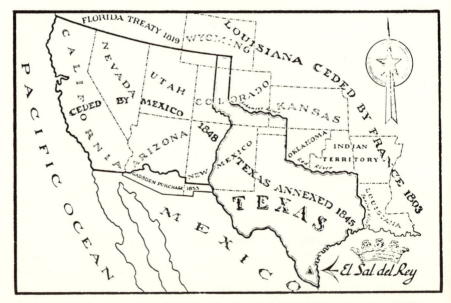

From Wallace Hawkins, *El Sal del Rey* (Austin: Texas State Historical Association, 1947), p. 22. Reproduced by permission of the Texas State Historical Association.

break down the old and somewhat artificial line between "Spanish Californians" and "Mexicans," and the fusion went on continuously thereafter.[4] But to proud Spanish Californios, like Hugo Reed, the whole lot of forty-niners and the Anglo-Saxon vigilante committees that sprang up to preserve "law and order" were a plague on a beautiful land:

Vagabonds from every quarter of the globe. Scoundrels from nowhere, rascals from Oregon, pickpockets from New York, accomplished gentlemen from Europe, interlopers from Lima and Chile, Mexican thieves, gamblers of no particular spot, and assassins manufactured in Hell for the express purpose of converting highways and biways into theatres of blood; then, last but not least, Judge Lynch with a thousand arms, thousand sightless eyes, and five-hundred lying tongues.[5]

In the long view of California history, said Pitt, the Mexican miners represented merely one link in a chain of migrants who moved into the Spanish borderlands after 1848. "They foreshadowed the coming of the wetbacks and the braceros in the twentieth century."[6] After 1850 Mexican miners and adventurers, principally from Sonora, Chihuahua, Sinaloa, Durango and Zacatecas, continued to filter into California, and then into the mines of Nevada and southern Arizona in the late 1850s, and some even showed up in Colorado mining camps in the 1860s. In the meantime, the frontier populations of the two countries were moving closer together. As Americans moved toward the Pacific Coast, ranchers and miners in Mexico were cautiously pushing northward against desert and Indian barriers, particularly after the strongman Porfirio Díaz brought internal peace to Mexico (1876-1910), and the American and Mexican governments, beginning around 1880, cooperated in the pursuit and punishment of Indian, Mexican, and Anglo border raiders and cattle thieves.[7]

From northern Sonora it was relatively easy (once the Indian menace had been reduced) to cross over to mines, lumber mills, railway spurs, and ranches in southern Arizona, where native Indians and refugee Yaquis were also a part of the labor force. Soon both sides of the border constituted one economic region. A two-way migration resulted between Arizona settlements like Tucson, Tubac, Douglas, Tombstone, Bisbee, and Naco, and Sonoran towns and rancherias, especially after American companies in the 1880s began to develop mines in Sonora, most notably at Cananea, just forty-five miles south of the Arizona line. Cananea, a major holding of the American Cananea Consolidated Copper Company (later owned by Anaconda), had around 20,000 inhabitants in 1900, being then the largest mining town in the border area.[8]

The migration of Sonoran miners and seasonal workers into Arizona was partly reflected in the census reports. In 1860 the Mexico-born numbered 963, exceeding the 941 Arizona-born; over 80 percent of the latter were of Hispano-Mexican descent, including the missionized Indians around the old Bac mission near Tucson. In 1870 the equivalent figures were 4,364 and 1,245. By 1880 the reported Mexico-born reached 9,330, and by 1900, 14,172.[9] By 1900 the railroads (mainly the Southern Pacific) were also pumping in immigrant labor from southern and central Europe, while the Sonoran mines tended to absorb some of the Mexican labor. Sonora was thinly populated, having but 222,000 reported inhabitants in 1900, when the state of Chihuahua had perhaps 100,000 more, and the territory of Baja California probably less than 10,000 residents in all.

Technology, meanwhile, was laying the groundwork for a continuous flow of emigration from the more populous areas of central Mexico. The completion of a transborder railway system in the 1880s joined the heartland to the United States and practically eliminated historic barriers to Hispano-Mexican migration northward. The Iron Horse leaped over hostile deserts and barren plains. The steam engine and other mechanical innovations, such as the windmill and the repeating rifle, facilitated settlement on the arid lands of the border states and the Great Plains. We can savor the meaning of these inventions from Webb's sweeping view of frontier stagnation before the age of technology:

Let us imagine ourselves standing among the buffalo Indians of the southern escarpment of the High Plains in the year 1600. By that time the Spaniards had taken Mexico and had thrown their advance guard northward among the mountains as far as Santa Fe. On the east they were in Florida. A century later we find them in eastern Texas on the French border. A half-century more: Santa Fe stands far to the west; San Antonio, Nacogdoches, and San Saba appear on the east. But if a Spaniard wanted to go from San Antonio to Santa Fe ... he went hundreds of miles out of the direct way, thus avoiding the open Plains country.

Fifty years go by, and bring us to 1800; and still we find that the Spaniards traveled with no more freedom across the Plains. In 1821, when Spain lost her possessions, the situation had not changed. There were Spanish settlements on both sides of the Plains [including California missions]. For twenty-seven more years Mexico exercised nominal jurisdiction over the region without altering the status left by Spain. The result is that there exist on the Great Plains today but few reminders of Spanish ownership. Here and there a place name of creeks, lakes, and hills—nothing more.[10]

Finally in the second half of the nineteenth century, technology and Anglo-Mexican cooperation in pacifying a wild frontier opened new channels of Hispano-Mexican migration over the plains of Chihuahua, Coahuila, Nuevo Leon, and Tamaulipas that sloped toward the Rio Grande and the sprawling Texas border line. In south Texas, unlike any other border section, Mexican pastoral settlement already projected like a peninsula over the disputed boundary. And this area—the lower Rio Grande valley—was fated to become a principal migratory funnel into the United States, along with the railway "pipeline" from central Mexico to El Paso, completed in 1884. As Paul S. Taylor has shown in *A Mexican-American Frontier*, Anglo-American cattle and sheep ranchers who pushed into southwest Texas began, as early as the 1850s, to employ migrants from nearby Mexican ranches and from the border states of Tamaulipas, Nuevo Leon, and Coahuila, and employed them increasingly as the sheep and cattle industries began to thrive. These early migrants worked as vaqueros, sheepherders, shearers, handymen, and domestics.[11]

As railroads encouraged migration and economic development, migrant peon families from Mexico's Central Plateau moved increasingly into wide-open border towns (on both sides) in search of work, excitement, and better access to duty-free industrial goods, forming thus the beginnings of a seasonal labor reservoir that would later supply, through the railway network, common labor to many states of the Union. By the 1890s El Paso, Eagle Pass, and Laredo were important recruiting centers and labor agents were sending "border Mexicans" inland as cotton pickers, as track workers, and as grubbers to clear the land for farming and pasture. By 1900 railroads had spread this labor throughout the border states, and by the first years of this century, Mexicans were working in irrigation agriculture nearly everywhere in the Southwest as pickers, planters, and packers for the emerging vegetable and citrus industries, as in the so-called magic valleys of Texas, New Mexico, Arizona, and California. By then hardly an Anglo rancher or farmer in the borderlands was without his "meskins."

From the first contacts Anglo-American entrepreneurs encouraged migrant families to settle on or near their farms and ranches, some of which had been carved out of Spanish-Mexican land grants. This was especially true of the southwest Texas channel. To a remarkable degree Anglo-Texan frontiersmen, some with roots in the slaveholding South, adapted themselves to a semifeudal agricultural pattern similar to that practiced by the old California dons, the New Mexico *Ricos*, and the *hacendados* of Mexico itself. This phenomenon may still be seen on Texas farms and ranches. For instance, the great King Ranch for many years has contained colonies of Mexican families; the Callaghan and Johnson ranches, the Bentsen farms, and other large holdings have Mexican peon families at hand. In many other instances migratory families were encouraged to settle as sharecroppers and seasonal workers in nearby shanty towns, making casual labor available at the snap of a finger but freeing the *patron*, the crew leader or contractor, from any *noblesse oblige* responsibilities. Such camps were reminiscent of the slave shacks of the Deep South and of the Spanish colonial policy of conveniently establishing native labor in nearby "Indian towns" or "mission towns." So by the opening of the present century one found dozens of migrant labor colonies alongside such towns as Del Rio, Eagle Pass, Laredo, McAllen, and Brownsville, and soon after, San Antonio, Corpus Christi, Asherton, Carrizo Springs, Uvalde, Ozona, Encinal, Cotulla, Mirando City, Hebronville, Falfurrias, Raymondville, Pearsall, Dilley, Castroville, Mercedes, San Benito, Harlingen, Mathis, Robstown, Beeville, Falls City, and elsewhere.[12] By 1910 this design was rapidly spreading to other border states, such as California, as employers searched for a mobile and cheap supply of "stoop labor."

As Mexican workers, as well as adventurers and vagabonds, moved into the Southwest, incidents of racial conflict and social discrimination soared, and not merely in Texas and California, as McWilliams made quite clear in his pioneer survey *North from Mexico*. [13] Mexicans were commonly hounded out of communities by Texas and Arizona rangers and assorted deputy sheriffs and vigilante groups, although Mexican *desperados* seemed to have inflicted a fair share of border "atrocities." [14] Yet the Mexican resident population increased steadily in the border states, for all the while southwestern *patrones*, including Mexican Americans, continued to welcome Mexican labor (so long as it wasn't unionized) even as native American and immigrant workers, as well as early labor organizations such as the Western Federation of Miners and the Railway Brotherhood, continued to resent them.

Transborder migration went unrecorded for many years. By 1900, as Burma pointed out, cycles of seasonal migration were already fixed in border areas and railroads were spreading the pattern to the interior. Migrants, most combining track and harvest work, went north in the spring, often Indian-style with their families, and in the fall returned to Mexico or to labor camps near the border. [15] No one has yet discovered a divining rod for determining how many of them actually remained on the American side. Mexican officials never kept consistent migration records until the founding of the nation's Migration Service around 1909, and even then the few Mexican officials in border towns paid little attention to migratory families.

The United States did not attempt to maintain full records of customs or migration movements on the Mexican land border until port-of-entry stations were set up there in 1894. [16] Before that date "Mexican immigrants," as reported by the Commissioner General of Immigration, were only those who arrived at American seaports. This was generally true until 1908. American immigration inspectors at border ports like Nogales, El Paso, or Laredo paid little attention to migrant workers, casual border visitors, or recruiting agents who swarmed around border towns practicing their trade in spite of the American law of 1885 against importing contract labor. In any case, not much could be done about an unguarded frontier. [17]

Thus we have only anemic and virtually useless figures for Mexican immigration in the period 1850-1900: [18]

1851-1860	3,078
1861-1870	2,191
1871-1880	5,162
1881-1890	1,913
1891-1900	971

Moreover, no immigration records for Mexico were kept for the years 1886-1893, and for other years some of the recorded immigrants were not Mexican but persons whose last residence was Mexico.

Actually the only official counts that may serve to sketch in the Mexican settlement story before 1900 are decennial census reports. With all their vacuities such reports at least confirm the fact that the Mexican immigrant population grew remarkably in the period 1848-1900. (See Table 1.)[19]

To appreciate the significance of the figures in Table 1, one should recall the frontier situation of 1848. By the Treaty of Guadalupe Hidalgo, Mexico ceded a territory that would in time include the states of Texas, New Mexico, Arizona, and California, and parts of Colorado, Nevada, and Utah. At that time, the total Hispanicized population, which included but a few hundred Mexican "immigrants," was probably between 75,000 and 80,000, distributed roughly as follows:

1. 60,000 in Mexico, mainly in the northern enclave centering around Santa Fe and Taos in the upper Rio Grande basin with Santa Fe, the largest *pueblo*, having around 3,000 residents.
2. 8,000 to 10,000 in California along the narrow coastal mission belt from San Diego north to San Francisco, again, the population consisting principally of creoles, mestizos, and missionized Indians, with Los Angeles, the largest town, having nearly 1,500 residents.
3. 5,000 to 6,000 in Texas of a similar ethnic mix, found mostly in the old mission area along the San Antonio River, and along the lower Rio Grande from Laredo south, with San Antonio de Bexar, by far the largest settlement, having perhaps 2,600 Spanish-speakers.
4. 800 to 1,000 in Arizona border country around Tucson and Tubac.

Table 1 Mexican Foreign-Born Population in the United States

Census	Mexico-born	Decennial Increase
1850	13,317	
1860	27,466	14,149
1870	42,435	14,969
1880	68,399	25,964
1890	77,853	8,454
1900	103,410	25,557

Source: U.S. Office of the Census, *Seventh Census of the United States, 1850* (1853), xxvii; *Eighth Census* (1864), 622; *Ninth Census* (1872), I, 341; *Tenth Census* (1883), 495; *Compendium of the Eleventh Census* (1894); and *Twelfth Census . . . Population* (1910), I, clxxiv.

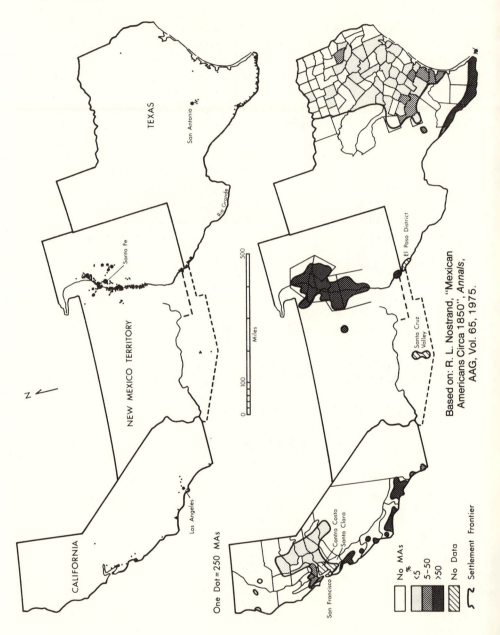

One Dot = 250 MAs

Miles

0   100   500

Based on: R. L. Nostrand, "Mexican
Americans Circa 1850", *Annals,*
AAG, Vol. 65, 1975.

No MAs
%
<5
5–50
>50
No Data
Settlement Frontier

TEXAS

San Antonio

Rio Grande

Santa Fe

NEW MEXICO TERRITORY

CALIFORNIA

Los Angeles

El Paso District

Santa Cruz
Valley

Santa Clara
Contra Costa

San Francisco

N

MEXICAN AMERICANS
CIRCA 1850

RICHARD L. NOSTRAND

University of Oklahoma

After the Mexican War southwestern Mexicans became Mexican Americans. at least nominally. This map shows distributional and proportional patterns at that critical moment in the Mexican American's experience.

In 1850 Mexican Americans were scattered between the Pacific and Gulf coasts. yet three-fourths of the more than 80.000 total lived in the upper Rio Grande basin area. Their proportions relative to non-Mexican Americans were uniformly high only in eastern New Mexico Territory. where some counties were nearly purely Mexican American. Elsewhere. the infiltration of non-Mexican Americans during the Mexican era had. for the most part. reduced this people to minority status: only one-fifth of the total population was Mexican American in 1850.

Data for this reconstruction were derived from the 1850 population census schedules for California. New Mexico Territory. and Texas and from supplementary estimates. In the schedules Mexican Americans were identified as persons 1) who had Spanish given and/or Spanish surnames: 2) who were born in the Southwest. Louisiana. Missouri. Mexico. or Spain: 3) who were not Indian as determined by "color." place of residence. or nativity: and 4) who were apparently permanent residents judging from the places where they were enumerated. The 1850 census probably underenumerated Mexican Americans. and the enumerated total (74.302) is probably less valid than are the distributional and proportional relationships.

Dots representing 6.000 Mexican Americans in the El Paso District. the Santa Cruz Valley. and the three counties fronting San Francisco Bay are based on the supplementary estimates. The settlement frontier in California is modified from S. A. Galpin. "Population-California." the first of ten maps in Plate XXXVI b in Francis A. Walker. compiler. *Statistical Atlas of the United States based on the Results of the Ninth Census 1870* (New York: Julius Bien. Lithographer. 1874): in New Mexico Territory it drew upon the J. W. Abert and W. G. Peck map of 1846-47 reproduced as Map No. 2 (in pocket) in Annie Heloise Abel. ed.. *The Official Correspondence of James S. Calhoun while Indian Agent at Santa Fé and Superintendent of Indian Affairs in New Mexico* (Washington: Government Printing Office. 1915). and D. W. Meinig. *Southwest: Three Peoples in Geographical Change 1600-1970* (New York. Oxford University Press. 1971). pp. 27-32: and in Texas it is after Terry G. Jordan. "Population Origins in Texas. 1850." *Geographical Review.* Vol. 59 (1969). p. 102. County boundaries in California are from Owen C. Coy. *California County Boundaries: A Study of the Division of the State into Counties and the Subsequent Changes in their Boundaries* (Berkeley: California Historical Survey Commission. 1923). p. 3: in New Mexico Territory they are from the Abert-Peck map and Charles F. Coan. "The County Boundaries of New Mexico." *Southwestern Political Science Quarterly.* Vol. 3 (1922-23). p. 253: and in Texas they are from "Texas Counties. 1850." Map. No. 1691 in the Texas State Archives. Austin.

Historical Geography Newsletter, Vol. 5, No. 2 (Fall 1975)
Map Supplement No. 1

Most numerous were aboriginal Indians, numbering perhaps 160,000 to 200,000, and controlling most of the territorial cession. [20]

The federal census of 1850 reported 74,302 people of Mexican origin in the United States, but because of the California gold rush and other factors, a more reasonable figure would run somewhere between 80,000 and 90,000. [21]

Although the full dimensions of the Mexico-born population and the Chicano descendants in the United States cannot be ascertained from official data, that population was probably as large in 1900 as the native Hispano-Mexican population of the Southwest, which by then may have increased to around 170,000, including perhaps 100,000 in New Mexico alone. [22] More precise figures are impossible because census takers counted Mexican-American natives as Caucasians, providing no special ethnic category as with Negroes, Orientals, and American Indians, perhaps in deference to the *gente de razón* in the border states, who stressed Castillian or European origins and often intermarried with Anglo-Americans.

What remains beyond doubt is that by 1900 a populous "Mexican peninsula" had been established in south Texas that would shape the thrust of twentieth-century Mexican migration into the interior of the United States. The rapid buildup of Mexico-born settlers in Texas is indicated by the census counts in Table 2.

In 1900 foreign-born Mexicans in Texas were almost three-fourths of the total recorded Mexico-born population in the United States, as shown in Table 3. To the figures in the table one might add a guesswork figure of from 235,000 to 245,000 or more for groups of Spanish speakers not counted or identified as such by census takers, like unregistered settlers, second-generation groups, and natives tracing their ancestry back to 1848 or before. Such an addition would suggest a more realistic total of perhaps 335,000 to 350,000 Hispano-Mexican (or Chicano) people in the United States around 1900. Some Chicano researchers, like Martínez, would run the estimate much higher, from a low of

Table 2   Texas Census Counts for 1850-1900

Census	Total Foreign-Born Mexicans
1850	4,459
1860	12,443
1870	23,020
1880	43,161
1890	51,559
1900	71,062

Source: Census figures from U.S. sources provided by the Institute of Texas Cultures, San Antonio, October 31, 1974.

Table 3   Mexico-Born Population by State, 1900

State	*Mexico-born*
California	8,086
Arizona	14,172
New Mexico	6,649
Colorado	274
Texas	71,062
Other	3,150
Total	103,393

Source: U.S. Bureau of the Census, *Twelfth Census of the United States, 1900: Population* (1901), I, clxxiv.

381,000 to a high of 552,000.[23] However, such conjectures make little allowance for a high percentage of the Hispano-Mexicans being seasonal migrant workers who resided as Mexican nationals in Mexico during the off-season.

If one looks back over the second half of the nineteenth century, it is apparent that a pronounced migratory drift from Mexico into the border states was underway before 1900; it would not be until the present century, however, that one could properly speak of mass Mexican migration to this country. But that is another story.

Notes

1. Leonard Pitt, *The Decline of the Californios: A Social History of the Spanish-Speaking Californians, 1846-1890* (Berkeley: University of California Press, 1968), p. 52.

2. Richard H. Morefield, "The Mexican Adaptation in American California, 1846-1875" (Master's thesis, Berkeley: University of California, 1955), pp. 3-31. See also W. P. Morrell, *The Gold Rushes* (New York, 1941); and Robert F. Heizer and Alan J. Almquist, *The Other Californians: Prejudice and Discrimination Under Spain, Mexico and the United States to 1920* (Berkeley: University of California Press, 1971).

3. Carey McWilliams, *Southern California Country: An Island on the Land* (New York, 1946).

4. Pitt, *The Decline of the Californios*, p. 53. See also Cecil Robinson's informative *With the Ears of Strangers: The Mexican in American Literature* (Tucson: University of Arizona Press, 1963).

5. Hugo Reed to Abel Stearns, April 22, 1849, quoted by Pitt, *The Decline of the Californios*, p. 52. The fate of the Californio elite is also suggested by Myrtle M. McKittrick's *Vallejo Son of California* (Portland, Ore., 1944).

6. Pitt, *The Decline of the Californios*, p. 67.

7. J. Fred Rippy, *The United States and Mexico* (New York, 1928); and R. D.

Gregg, *The Influence of Border Troubles on Relations Between the United States and Mexico, 1876-1910* (Baltimore, 1937).

8. C. L. Sonnichsen, "Colonel William C. Greene and the Strike at Cananea, Sonora, 1906," *Arizona and the West* 13 (Winter 1971), 343-368.

9. Joseph F. Park, "The History of Mexican Labor in Arizona During the Territorial Period" (Master's thesis, Tucson: University of Arizona, 1961), pp. 119, 138, 147. For the significant Mexican role in Arizona mining, see Manuel P. Servin and Robert L. Spude, "Historical Conditions of Early Mexican Labor in the United States: Arizona— A Neglected Story," *The Journal of Mexican American History* 5 (1975), 43-56.

10. Walter Prescott Webb, *The Great Plains* (New York, 1931), pp. 83-84.

11. Paul S. Taylor, *A Mexican-American Frontier: Nueces County, Texas* (Chapel Hill, 1934). Also relevant is Val W. Lehman's *Forgotten Legions: Sheep in the Rio Grande Plain of Texas* (El Paso: University of Texas Press, 1969), which also covers the emerging cattle industry.

12. Poverty conditions of high-fertility Texas *colonias*, which send surplus population to many states as migrant workers, have been the object in recent years of socioeconomic surveys, for example, W. K. Upham and David E. Wright, "Poverty Among the Spanish Americans of Texas: Low-Income Families in a Minority Group" (Report 66-2, Department of Agricultural Economics and Sociology, College Station: Texas A & M University, 1966); or Harley L. Browning and S.D. McLemore, *A Statistical Profile of the Spanish-Surname Population of Texas* (Bureau of Business Research, Austin: University of Texas, 1964).

13. Carey McWilliams, *North from Mexico: The Spanish-Speaking People in the United States*, originally published in 1948 (Westport, Conn.: Greenwood Press, 1968).

14. Border incidents of violence have been enumerated for one area by pioneer settler Frank C. Pierce, *A Brief History of the Lower Rio Grande Valley* (Menasha, Wisc., 1917), ch. 11; and celebrated in such literary works as Américo Paredes' account of Chicano resistance hero Gregorio Cortes, *"With His Pistol in His Hand"—A Border Ballad and Its Hero* (Austin: University of Texas Press, 1958). More details would be found in various record groups in the National Archives, Washington, D.C., and in the consular archives, Secretaría de Relaciones Exteriores, Mexico City. See also note 7.

15. John H. Burma, *Spanish-Speaking Groups in the United States* (Durham, 1954), p. 40.

16. Darrel H. Smith and H. Guy Herring, *The Bureau of Immigration: Its History, Activities and Organization* (Baltimore, 1924), p. 7. For more details on the lack of immigration controls on land borders see Larry García y Griego, "Los Primeros Pasos al Norte: Mexican Migration to the United States, 1848-1929" (Senior thesis, B.A., Princeton University, April 1973).

17. Occasional references to complaints arising from American immigration officers' attempts to enforce immigration laws and head tax provisions, as in the 1880s and after, on Mexican migrant workers passing through border towns, are found in Record Group 85, Records of the United States Immigration and Naturalization Service, National Archives; and in Mexican consular correspondence, Archivo Histórico de la Secretaría de Relaciones Exteriores.

18. U.S. Immigration and Naturalization Service, *Annual Report*, Table 13: Immigration by Country, for Decades, 1820-1973.

19. See García y Griego, "Los Primeros Pasos al Norte."

20. Principal sources for 1848 estimates are Hubert H. Bancroft's *Works* on the Pacific Coast states, Arizona, New Mexico, the north Mexico states, and Texas (San Francisco, 1882-1889) for which Bancroft and a team of researchers examined original sources; U.S. Census Office, *Seventh Census of the United States* (1850); James M. Cutts, *The Conquest of California and New Mexico* (1848; reprinted, Albuquerque, 1965), containing Mexican electoral estimates of northern Mexico provinces in 1844 (pp. 11-12); D. W. Meinig, *Southwest: Three Peoples in Geographical Change 1600-1970* (New York: Oxford University Press, 1971); and Richard L. Nostrand, "The Hispanic-American Borderlands: A Regional Geography" (Ph.D. thesis, Los Angeles: University of California, 1968), pp. 116, 137-139, 146.

21. Richard L. Nostrand, "Mexican Americans circa 1850," *Annals of the Association of American Geographers* 65:3 (September 1975), 378-390; and Oscar J. Martínez, "On the Size of the Chicano Population: New Estimates, 1850-1900," *Aztlán, International Journal of Chicano Studies Research* 6:1 (Spring 1975), 43-67. As Nostrand and Martínez make clear in their detailed analyses, the federal census of Mexican-origin groups in 1850 is suspect for undercounts. It reported 6,678 Mexican Americans in California, of whom 2,697 resided in Los Angeles, a refuge for native Californios, Mexicans, and Latin Americans driven out of the minefields of northern California. The census found 5,456 Mexico-born persons in California, principally Sonoran gold rushers. But how many remained uncounted? How many returned to Mexico? How many Mexican settlers were overlooked elsewhere in border areas?

In his article Nostrand made additions for California, Texas, and New Mexico, arriving at an estimated 80,302 for the Southwest, and 82,500 for all the United States, compared to the total 1850 census finding of 74,302. Martínez, allowing for a possible 40 percent undercount in California, Arizona, and Texas, and 20 percent in New Mexico, projected a much higher range of 87,000 to 118,000 for the Chicano population in 1850. The number of native Mexicans in the lost territories who removed permanently to Mexican territory after the treaty of 1848 is not known, but, all in all, the figure seems negligible, particularly since the Gadsden Purchase of 1854 annexed a good part of the repatriate settlements, as in the Mesilla-El Paso area.

22. A. M. Espinosa, "New Mexico," *The Catholic Encyclopedia* (1911), XI, 4.

23. Martínez, "On the Size of the Chicano Population," p. 48, 56.

3/ VAMOS AL NORTE: CAUSES OF MASS MEXICAN MIGRATION TO THE UNITED STATES

Arthur F. Corwin and Lawrence A. Cardoso

> One of the main causes of the revolution was the condition of the working man in Mexico. In many of the states it amounted almost to slavery.
>
> Enrique D. Ruíz,
> Mexican Consul General, 1923[1]

Mexican transborder migration in this century can be conveniently divided into two phenomenal waves, the first from approximately 1900 to 1930, when the Great Depression cut it short; the second, touched off by World War II, continues undiminished to this day. Since land, often held in common, was the ancient basis of the Indo-peasant's livelihood, its importance can scarcely be exaggerated, especially when one considers that the land base of the peasantry was rapidly shrinking as the twentieth century approached.

During the regime of General Porfirio Díaz (1876-1911), misguided colonization and land development laws allowed land speculators, Mexican and foreign, to seize millions of hectares of farm and pastoral land, including communal holdings of many peasant villages that had remained intact as a customary or "squatter's right" during the Spanish and early republican periods. Also, vast stretches of the public domain were gobbled up by surveyors, land companies, politicians, and shrewd hacienda owners. The land grab forced even more of the rural peasantry into peonage on great haciendas and ranchos.

Peonage—particularly debt peonage—was nearly universal among the landless peasantry. Owners and administrators of property operated small provision stores, the hated *tiendas de raya*, and by this means advanced food, seed, and supplies to dependent peon families. Because of static wages and the manipulation of accounts, the illiterate peon rarely could pay off a debt, and through ancient custom, which had the force of law, sons inherited the debts of their fathers, unless, of course, they chose to run away. An arbitrary system of control in the hands of creole and mestizo overlords who lacked any tradition of *noblesse oblige* was another good reason for stealing away in the night. Andrés Molina Enríquez's classic indictment of the evils of the Porfirian hacienda, first published in 1909, accused the owners and administrators of exercizing "the absolute domination of a feudal lord" with the power to chastize and even execute with impunity the recalcitrant worker.[2] Others attributed peasant flight to *caciquismo*, a system of "conquest government" dating from Aztec and Castillian times (and still functioning in rural Mexico), whereby local political bosses and "Indian Chiefs" (*caciques*) hold despotic control over the village peasantry.[3]

Perhaps the most important "push" factor was simply abject poverty, commonly known in Mexico as *la miseria rural*. The condition of semi-starvation may be seen in the relation between wages and food costs. At no time in the thirty years preceding the Revolution of 1910 did the average daily pay for common farm labor exceed $.25 a day in U. S. currency. During that period the American dollar, based on the gold standard, equaled two silver pesos, and the costs of staples such as corn and beans more than doubled in Mexico.[4] Little wonder that the debt-ridden *campesinos*, in economist Jesús Silva Herzog's words, suffered the primeval wants of food, clothing, and shelter.[5]

According to Walter E. Weyl's revealing study of labor conditions in Mexico, published in 1902, daily wages in Mexican currency for agricultural labor in selected states in 1893 were reported as shown in Table 1. Commenting on the given approximations, Weyl noted that in general wages were lowest in the states situated on the heavily populated Central Plateau states, two exceptions being Vera Cruz and the northeast border state of Tamaulipas.[6]

Mining work was more remunerative than farm or pastoral labor, yet here also mine wages tended to follow the same inverse proportion to population density; for example, wages were markedly higher in Chihuahua, Sonora, or Durango, and lower in populous states of the Central Plateau such as Guanajuato, then as now a principal source of migratory labor for other states of Mexico and the United States. Table 2 gives estimated daily mine wages, in Mexican currency, for selected states and occupations in 1899.

In some ways the very benevolence of the Porfirian regime contributed to the plight of the peon class. Until the latter part of the nineteenth century, population growth was painfully slow because of a high mortality rate, but with advances in public health, especially in the use of mass vaccination and domestic peace under a paternal dictatorship, the population leaped from about 9 million in 1876 to almost 15 million in 1910. By the latter date about 80 percent of the people lived in rural areas, and about 5 percent of Mexican families owned 90 percent of the nation's land.[7] It is hardly surprising, therefore, that a rapid population increase within a semifeudal subsistence economy could only contribute to the deprivation and displacement of the peasantry.

Table 1   Population Densities and Wages for Selected Occupations
in Certain Mexican States, 1893

State	Overseers	Herders	Peons	Population per sq. mile
Aguascalientes	$.25– .37	$.13– .20	$.13– .25	35.1
Coahuila	.37– .50	.37– .50	.25– .75	3.7
Durango	.31– .62	.31– .50	.25– .37	7.7
Chihuahua	.50– .75	.50– .75	.37– .62	3.0
Guanajuato	.27– .62	.25– .37	.18– .25	92.1
Federal District	.50	.50	.37– .40	
Hidalgo	.18– .50	.18– .50	.18– .50	61.6
Jalisco	.25– .50	.25– .50	.25– .50	34.8
México	.25– .50	.18– .50	.18– .50	90.7
Michoacán	.25– .50	.25– .50	.18– .75	38.8
Morelos	.50	.50	.37–1.00	57.6
Nuevo León	.25–1.00	.25– .75	.18– .50	13.1
Puebla	.37– .50	.25– .60	.18– .50	80.2
San Luís Potosí	.40	.20	.18– .25	22.5
Sonora	.50–1.75	.37–1.00	.37–1.00	2.4
Tamaulipas	.18– .25	.18– .25	.18– .25	6.3
Vera Cruz	.37–1.00	.37–1.00	.18– .37	29.3
Zacatecas	.25–1.00	.25– .75	.18– .50	18.2

Source: Adapted from figures ascribed to official sources in Walter E. Weyl, "Labor Conditions in Mexico," *Bulletin of the Department of Labor* 38 (January 1902), 38-39.

The figures given in Table 3, incomplete as they may be, suggest the nature of the out-migration phenomenon: In certain areas of Mexico the combination of population growth, land shortage, and depressed wages led to the rapid emergence of a migratory labor class, most notably in the densely populated states of the Central Plateau such as Guanajuato, Jalisco, Zacatecas, and San Luís Potosí. By the 1890s increasing numbers of displaced peasants were wandering over Mexico in search of work. Many moved into cities like Guadalajara, San Luís Potosí, Monterrey, and Mexico City itself, while many others headed for north Mexico, where there was a labor shortage. In northern states such as Tamaulipas, Coahuila, Chihuahua, and Sonora, the development of railroads, mining, and ranching, spurred by American and other foreign investors during the permissive Porfirian era, created a rising demand for migrant labor at high wages, for these states, semi-desert in nature, had a population density generally less than five persons per square kilometer compared with a range of twenty to sixty in the central states. As a result landless peons began to gravitate toward the northern frontier in such numbers that by the turn of the

Table 2   Daily Mine Wages for Selected Occupations, 1899

State	Ore breakers	Drillers and Pickmen	Furnacemen	Peons
Coahuila	$ .75	$ .75−1.00	$ .75	$ .50− .75
Chihuahua	1.50	.51−2.50	1.50	1.00−1.50
Durango	.50−1.50	.40−1.50	.75−1.00	.37−1.00
Guanajuato	.18− .50	.50		.18− .37
Guerrero	.37	.50− .75	.37	.37
Hidalgo	.31− .75	.31−1.00		.25− .50
Michoacán	.50−1.00	.50−1.00	.37−1.00	.37− .75
Nuevo León	.50−1.00	1.00−2.00	.66−1.00	.50− .75
Querétaro	.50	.50−1.00		.25− .37
San Luís Potosí	.25− .66	1.00−1.60	.50	.25− .50
Sonora	1.00−2.00	.45−1.00	1.00−2.00	.45−2.00
Zacatecas	.50−1.75	.70−1.00	.70−1.50	.37− .50

Source: Adapted from figures ascribed to official sources in Walter E. Weyl, "Labor Conditions in Mexico," *Bulletin of the Department of Labor* 38 (January 1902), 38-39.

century hacienda owners and newspaper editorialists were complaining loudly of a serious labor storage.[8]

Table 3   Emigrants from Native States, 1900-1910

State	1900		1910	
	I	II	I	II
Guanajuato	77,263	8.86	102,696	9.75
Hidalgo	39,513	4.53	56,455	5.36
Jalisco	98,408	11.29	97,386	9.25
México	151,037	17.32	142,169	13.50
Michoacán	30,522	3.50	48,802	4.64
Puebla	64,260	7.37	66,825	6.35
San Luís Potosí	68,298	7.83	83,011	7.89
Zacatecas	84,970	9.74	112,949	10.73

Source: Moisés González Navarro, *La vida social en el Porfiriato*, in *Historia moderna de México*, ed. Daniel Cosío Villegas (Mexico, 1957), IV, 27. See also Sumner Cushing, "The Distribution of Population in Mexico," *Geographical Review* 2 (April 1921), 227-242.

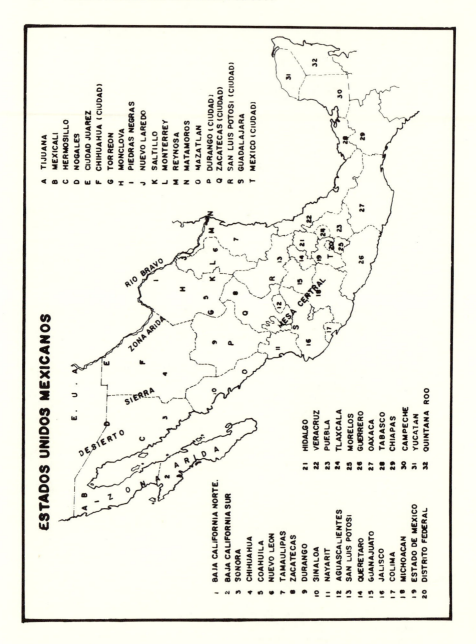

ESTADOS UNIDOS MEXICANOS

1 BAJA CALIFORNIA NORTE.
2 BAJA CALIFORNIA SUR
3 SONORA
4 CHIHUAHUA
5 COAHUILA
6 NUEVO LEON
7 TAMAULIPAS
8 ZACATECAS
9 DURANGO
10 SINALOA
11 NAYARIT
12 AGUASCALIENTES
13 SAN LUIS POTOSI
14 QUERETARO
15 GUANAJUATO
16 JALISCO
17 COLIMA
18 MICHOACAN
19 ESTADO DE MEXICO
20 DISTRITO FEDERAL

21 HIDALGO
22 VERACRUZ
23 PUEBLA
24 TLAXCALA
25 MORELOS
26 GUERRERO
27 OAXACA
28 TABASCO
29 CHIAPAS
30 CAMPECHE
31 YUCATAN
32 QUINTANA ROO

A TIJUANA
B MEXICALI
C HERMOSILLO
D NOGALES
E CIUDAD JUAREZ
F CHIHUAHUA (CIUDAD)
G TORREON
H MONCLOVA
I PIEDRAS NEGRAS
J NUEVO LAREDO
K SALTILLO
L MONTERREY
M REYNOSA
N MATAMOROS
O MAZATLAN
P DURANGO (CIUDAD)
Q ZACATECAS (CIUDAD)
R SAN LUIS POTOSI (CIUDAD)
S GUADALAJARA
T MEXICO (CIUDAD)

Commonly migrants were seen walking, Indian-fashion, hundreds of miles to the northern border in search of a fabulous dollar-a-day wage and adventure. Reportedly, others sold their last pig and the crossbeams of their humble cottage or borrowed the money to buy a rail ticket from Jalisco or Guanajuato to El Paso or Nogales. The emigrants could not be dissuaded from crossing the line by the somber warnings of border officials. They gave little thought to work contracts, and one observer said they doubted all reports of deceptions and bad treatment in the United States. Anyway, could it possibly be worse there than conditions at home?[9]

The roots of Mexico's migratory labor flow, however, are not found exclusively in peonage conditions perpetuated by the Díaz dictatorship. This is an oversimplification propagated by many post-revolutionary writers. The fact is that there were scattered all over Mexico, small, semi-tribal groups, or extended families, who lived collectively in primitive huts, still to be seen in many parts of the country, and called *rancherías* by the Spaniards. The inhabitants of these mobile villages foraged for seasonal work as their ancestors had foraged for food or game, making shelters of any material available. The ranchería was actually a subculture containing many vestigial characteristics of pre-agricultural tribes which had remained on the margins of the economy since the Spanish conquest in 1521 and were little affected one way or another by a change in landed property. They often became "squatter camps" near missions, mines, haciendas, plantations, railway junctions, and cities, or wherever there were sources of seasonal employment.

Out of the rancherías and squatter camps of Sonora came many of the first migratory workers in the Anglo-American borderlands; for example, during the California gold rush in the late 1840s, during the mining boom in Arizona in the 1860s and after, and during the construction of the Southern Pacific Railroad in the 1880s. In the Southwest the ranchería migrant from Mexico mixed easily with native Indian laborers from southwestern rancherías and with native New Mexicans and Arizonians.[10]

Another source of migratory labor flowed from small farm properties or from ranches privately owned by creole and mestizo colonist families. Unlike the ranchería casual laborers or hacienda peons, small peasant proprietors and rancheros and their sons valued private property, and often migrated hundreds of miles in search of outside income in order to buy land near their home village in the Central Plateau or in the northern provinces.[11] From such villages in the frontier states of Nuevo León, Tamaulipas, and Coahuila came migrant workers to south Texas sheep and cattle ranches as early as the 1870s and before. As irrigated agriculture developed there, some of these seasonal workers, unlike other "landless peasants," became sharecroppers with part ownership in farm animals, equipment, and the harvest itself. Some acquired farm properties in Texas; others returned to Mexico for that purpose.[12]

Among Mexican emigrants there were always some small shopkeepers, artisans, and workers who had acquired skills in mining, ranching, and railway work, but, as often happens when such people move to another country, many ended up in common labor for such reasons as language deficiency, lack of capital, or nativist opposition, but principally because a more industrialized economy has little place for village trades and crafts. Furthermore, the widespread entrepreneurial practice of hiring immigrant labor in gangs under a paternalistic contracting system, and relatedly, the pronounced preference of migrant folk or *la raza* to live and work among their own kind worked against the upward mobility of Mexican emigrant labor in the United States.[13]

Nevertheless, as Victor S. Clark, the first to study methodically the nature of Mexican labor migration, pointed out in his study of 1908, the early transborder migrant was typically from the peon labor class.

The term "pelado," by which those migrating to Texas are known, signifies literally the man who has been stripped, a sort of intensified "sans culottes," and indicates that the Mexicans crossing the lower Rio Grande come largely from the migratory labor class of their own country. In California the Mexican laborers are known as "cholos," a word borrowed from Peru, where it applies to a certain type of Indian. . . . Probably most of the laborers entering the United States from El Paso or westward, with the exception of a few miners from Sonora and Chihuahua, were originally in peonage, though they may have escaped from this relation some time before migrating to the north.

Mexicans of either of these classes are Indians, with a slight infusion of white blood. They are Indians in physique, temperament, character, and mentality. A person familiar with Mexico can tell the state or district a laborer hails from by the old tribal peculiarities of his underlying Indian stock. It is said that Mexicans have been unwittingly admitted to Indian schools in the United States. . . . And yet in almost any large group of Mexican laborers individuals are encountered who, in different surroundings, would easily pass for Europeans.[14]

As Clark emphasized, seasonal labor along the border was a long-standing phenomenon, but the emerging novelty was the massive out-migration from the Central Plateau of the Indo-peasantry who previously had no contact with Anglo-Americans:

The Mexicans who cross the border to work are either making their first trip to the United States or are making a second or third seasonal visit from the interior of Mexico or are of that big class of American-Mexican frontier residents who reside intermittently in either country. These last are less apt to travel widely or work regularly, except during cotton-picking time in Texas and in Oklahoma; their migratory habits are not of recent origin, and they are not vacating old industries in Mexico to enter new occupations in the United States. The immigrant of interest is the one who has recently appeared in the field, coming from the central part of the Republic, leaving his ancestral home and callings, and ready to venture almost anywhere in search of work.

These immigrants appear at the border in sombrero, serape, and sandals, which, before crossing the river, they usually exchange for a suit of "American" clothing, shoes, and a less conspicuous hat. In fact, at Juarez and at El Paso a thriving trade of old clothes has sprung up to meet this demand.[15]

Although the migratory phenomenon in Mexico has historically deep and complex roots, it was, above all, railroad technology that enabled the Mexican population to move en masse through the hostile desert regions of the north and gave the so-called Mexican casual his remarkable mobility. Railways bridged the Great Western Desert that had separated the population centers of the two countries. In 1884 the great rail center of El Paso, leading to all points including Los Angeles and Chicago, was connected with Chihuahua City, which in turn was linked to the Central Plateau and Mexico City. Nogales, Arizona, leading into the Southern Pacific line, was connected with Hermosillo, Sonora, in 1882, and soon after, San Antonio and Corpus Christi were connected with Monterrey, Mexico, by way of Laredo, and spur lines grew like the roots of a plant. Clark observed that railroads carried the central Mexican villager a thousand miles from his home to within sight of the border, and there American employers, "with a gold wage, have little difficulty in attracting him across that not very formidable dividing line.[16] Because of its direct railway communication with the "swarming states" of central Mexico, El Paso was the most important distributing point (and still is) for Mexican Labor. Said Clark:

> Of the border cities mentioned El Paso is the only one that is a real labor depot. San Antonio is probably the most important distributing point of Mexican labor for Texas proper. Kansas City, Missouri is given as their destination by many arrivals at El Paso, and that city is resorted to by them as an employment center. Los Angeles serves the same purpose for Southern California, and has a large colony from Old Mexico. Tucson, Arizona, and Trinidad and Denver, Colorado, have agents that handle a fairly large number of Mexican laborers.[17]

Wages in the Texas border region were then $1.00 to $1.25 per day for unskilled labor on railroads, as high as $1.75 in other border states such as California, and even higher farther inland. Section hands on north Mexican railways deserted by the hundreds for higher wages across the border. Mexican miners did the same, and then agricultural workers. Soon Mexican pick-and-shovel gangs were found in nearly every railroad town and mining camp in the Southwest, and working down the rail lines these gangs, usually with return transportation guaranteed, made their way to California citrus groves, Colorado beet fields, Texas cotton plantations, and railway service centers such as Laramie, Kansas City and Chicago, working for daily wages that ran from $.50 to $2.00 or more, at a time when a dollar equaled two pesos.[18]

In many cases the employer and employees were already acquainted. American mining and railroad companies in Mexico brought many of their trained gangs over the border to work with the same company on the American side. Mexican miners, for example, were shifted from American-owned mines in northern Sonora to American mines in southern Arizona, and the Southern Pacific transferred track crews and foremen from its Mexican subsidiaries to its southwestern lines, more so after Chinese coolie labor began to dwindle following the Exclusion Act of 1882. [19]

The economic development of the American Southwest coincided with the northward drift of Mexico's population. Railroads, using Mexican and other immigrant labor, integrated the Southwest into the nation's industrial economy. Mining shifted from precious metals to industrial minerals such as copper and coal, as in New Mexico, Arizona, Colorado, Utah, and Oklahoma. Copper mines in the west increased from three in 1869 to 180 in 1909, and coal mining, heavily using Mexican labor, boomed in those states. Citrus and cotton cultivation in California, Arizona, and the lower Rio Grande Valley of Texas flourished because of rail facilities, cheap labor, and desert irrigation projects encouraged by the federal Newlands Act of 1902. [20]

Increasingly, after the shutoff of Oriental migration in 1882 and 1907, southwestern farm and plantation owners saw the day-haul laborers, or *jornaleros*, of Mexico as the ideal solution to cyclic labor needs on large holdings. Dating back to Spanish and Mexican rule, the southwestern river valleys, unlike the family and tenant farm pattern prevailing elsewhere, were dominated by large blocs of land and irrigation rights. Moreover, borderland climate permitted nearly a year-round production of crops. In California, where by 1900 farming operations on 1,000 acres or more accounted for nearly 60 percent of all farm acreage, lettuce could be shipped from the San Joaquin Valley in the north from March to December and from the southern Imperial Valley from December through March. The "winter garden" districts of Texas and Arizona were similar in their land use patterns. [21] It thus happened that the migratory habits of the Mexican *campesino* fit neatly with the needs of southwestern agribusiness.

Mexicans of the "casual labor" class worked in family groups, could live in the corner of a field, putting up their own huts, were easily managed by labor contractors and crew leaders, were not ambitious to acquire American land, and accepted lower wages than other groups (yet never hesitated to leave for higher wages elsewhere). It was further alleged by growers that Mexican help would not remain permanently in the country and cause a social problem as had the Oriental coolies. The *Pacific Fruit Grower*, a voice of western agribusiness, was pleased to note in 1907 that Mexicans were "plentiful, generally peaceable, and . . . satisfied with very low social conditions." [22] A broad immigration study, carried out in 1908 by a congressional commission, found a surprising number of Mexican immigrants in southwestern industries, and expressed concern about an emergent social problem. The members of the Dillingham Commission believed the Mexican to be "less desirable as a citizen than as a laborer," but added hopefully: "The permanent additions to the population, however, are much smaller than the number who immigrate for work." [23]

Mexican labor mobility was likewise vital to the foundation and maintenance of the beet sugar industry in Colorado, Kansas, California, Nebraska, and other states. The first Mexicans were brought into the South Platte Valley of Colorado in 1903, and by 1909 Mexicans numbered more than 2,600, making up over 40 percent of the field crews in the area. In the beet fields of Colorado, as elsewhere in the West, other immigrant groups, such as Italians, Slavs, Russians, or Irish, found they could move up from farm worker or tenant to owner and employer through the use of Mexican migrants. [24] In California reportedly more than 1,000 Mexican nationals worked in beets in 1908. The cotton industry in the Imperial Valley was soon just as dependent on Mexican labor. As one grower put it: "We mean to get Mexicans for the work and get all we need." And so they did. [25] The continuous expansion of citrus and truck-gardening industries in southern California, Arizona, and Texas also meant the need for more labor from Mexico. [26]

The south Texas region was a striking example of the close link between agricultural prosperity and the availability of migrants. With the completion of the St. Louis, Brownsville, and Mexico Railroad in 1904, Texas planters and investors could tap the supply of Mexican labor through the border port of Matamoros, and also Reynosa, while at the same time shipping produce direct to eastern markets. [27] According to Paul S. Taylor, before 1904 Nueces County, which included the city of Corpus Christi, exported sheep and cattle, using Mexican shepherds and *vaqueros*. But economic transformation followed quickly. New farms, some of them purchased by midwesterners who seized on peon labor as eagerly as any southern planter, sprang up to produce fruits, vegetables, cotton, and pecans. Cotton production jumped from 498 bales ginned in 1899 to 8,566 bales in 1910. By the latter year almost 3,000 Mexicans worked in Nueces County. They cleared land and leveled it, planted, tended, and harvested the crops. Around 60 percent of this labor force came from the states of the Central Plateau. [28]

In mining, as in agriculture, Mexican workers took jobs which other groups refused, such as chopping timbers, picking and shoveling ore, and doing general cleanup work. The coal and iron industries of southern Colorado, centered around Trinidad and Pueblo, imported Mexican nationals and Spanish-Americans from New Mexico. By 1905 there were over 10,000 miners of Mexican origin, many with families, living in that area; a similar pattern of labor settlement developed in northern New Mexico around the coal mines of Raton and Gallup. [29] Railroads served as a bridge to mining jobs, since, typically, track workers jumped contracts for higher pay. Mine wages for common labor ranged as high as $2.46 per day compared to $1.00 or $2.00 for track work. Understandably, in the copper and smelting industries close to the border, as

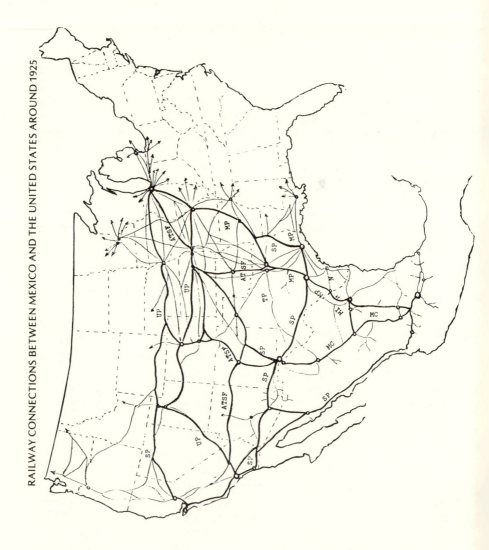

RAILWAY CONNECTIONS BETWEEN MEXICO AND THE UNITED STATES AROUND 1925

"ACROSS THE TRACKS"

No immigrant group in American history has been so intimately tied to railroads as the Mexican. Railways were in fact the arteries of Mexican migration. The network shown here roughly coincides not only with the migratory paths since the 1880s but also with the territorial pattern of Mexican settlement in the United States - a pattern that has endured to the present day. By 1930 colonies of Mexican migrant families could be found in nearly every large town and city along these routes. Migrants worked along the railroads while frequently shifting from one seasonal job to another in mines, agriculture, tramways, packing houses, construction, factories, odd jobs, and perhaps back to railways again, always some settling down permanently. Cars and trucks, commonly used in the 1920s, served to accentuate the remarkable mobility of the Mexican "casual." All U. S. railroads indicated here used Mexican labor, often providing housing or boxcar apartments along the company's right-of-way, or encouraging settlement nearby, thus tending to fix the Mexican colony "across the tracks." Principal users were the Southern Pacific and the Santa Fe which continually pumped Mexicans into the United States to compensate for frequent turnover of track workers.

SP	Southern Pacific. To El Paso, 1881. Its Mexican Line completed 1882-1912. Direct to California 1923.
ATSF	Atchison Topeka and Sante Fe. Linked to Al Paso in 1881.
MP	Missouri Pacific. To Laredo in 1880s.
TM	Texas Mexican. Corpus Christi to Laredo 1881.
TP	Texas Pacific. To El Paso, 1881.
SBM	St. Louis, Brownsville and Mexico, 1904.
UP	Union Pacific. Chicago to San Francisco, 1869.
MC	Mexican Central, or Norte de Mexico, to El Paso, 1882-1884.
N	National Railway. To Laredo, 1882, and to Brownsville, 1904.
MI	Mexican International To Eagle Pass, 1882.

in southern Arizona, almost 100 percent of the common labor force was of Mexican origin.[30] Moreover, to promote economic development of their right-of-ways and freight volume, railroads frequently allowed growers and mine operators "to borrow" their Mexican workers in the off-season, railway officials knowing that more could easily be recruited on the border.[31]

More than any other influence, it was the railroads that fixed the early settlement patterns of Mexican workers and their families. By 1909 Mexican emigrants comprised most of the track-maintenance crews and over 10 percent of the workshop crews on southwestern railways, principally the Southern Pacific, and the Atchison, Topeka and Santa Fe, and by that date Mexican workers were commonly hired by other railroads such as the Union Pacific and the Rock Island. The fact that Los Angeles had a Mexican emigrant community of about 15,000 in 1908 was in part due to railway employment policies. Elsewhere, the "Mexican town" across the tracks could be traced, as in Albuquerque, San Bernardino, Dallas, Denver, Salt Lake City, Oklahoma City, Kansas City, Topeka, Omaha, or Chicago, and in countless smaller communities, to employment, transportation, and housing facilities provided by railroads to Mexican workers, who, increasingly after 1910, were used by railway management to counter unionization efforts and labor strikes by such groups as the Industrial Workers of the World, and, later, the American Federation of Labor. But, as we have seen, railroad colonies served more than railroads. They were conduits to the inner cities and to many sectors of the labor market. Since the railroads tended to maintain a pool of surplus workers, because of rapid turnovers, railway colonies in larger cities often became recruiting centers for contractors seeking other types of labor.[32] All the while, rail workers naturally drifted toward nearby, and better-paying, jobs in meat-packing plants, flour mills, warehouses, and other industries located close to the tracks, much as they drifted into nearby mines and foundries. Thus railway management was continually pumping in fresh supplies of Mexican workers, and sometimes their families, hopefully to create employment stability.[33]

American companies set up recruiting centers along the Mexican border before 1900. Clark noted that Mexican migrants arrived there penniless, "but with the moral certainty of securing immediate employment."[34] At the border migrants were met by company contractors, or *enganchadores*, who regularly supplied railroads with track workers, or migrants were signed up through labor agencies that supplied common labor for a variety of jobs. Supplying provisions and food during the worker's term of employment was a profitable business for large contractors; "indeed, this is their main source of revenue . . . to furnish labor in return for the privilege of keeping the commissary." Clark added that the commissary practice was a kind of modified debt peonage not unlike the old hacienda store.[35]

Railway employers usually transported labor recruits without charge, and offered a free return ticket to a worker who completed his contract. Other employers paid the passage one way but usually deducted the amount from wages. Labor agents paid subsistence during travel, and this too was taken out of wages, unless, of course, the worker jumped contract, which was frequently the case. Contract workers were sent as far as 2,000 miles from El Paso. According to Clark, one of the larger labor agencies in the first eight months of 1907 sent Mexican laborers through the railway arteries as follows: "To the Chicago, Rock Island and Pacific Railway, 3,523; to the El Paso and Southwestern System, 1,593; to the Fort Worth and Denver City Railway, 973; and to the Pecos Valley and Northeastern Railway, 421." [36]

Recruiters on the Mexican side, known as *enganchistas*, or hookers, lured displaced or restless people to the border contracting offices. Most enganchistas were hardly a cut above the peon class, but they were familiar with company needs, and many of them were bilingual residents of the border towns. In Mexico, according to Clark, they worked "principally among the city and tramp labor population," partly because in rural areas hacienda owners were hostile to them. [37]

American employers themselves, or their foremen, often engaged in direct recruiting despite the Alien Contract Labor Law of 1885, which outlawed such activity. It was not unusual for a group of planters from Texas, Oklahoma, or Colorado to send a manager or foreman to the Rio Grande to pick up a party of one hundred or more men and their families. [38] Furthermore, cities near the border openly advertised for Mexican labor. [39] Here an oversight in the 1885 law was exploited. So long as an alien worker arrived in the United States without a contract in his hand, and so long as he was hired on the American side of the line there was, technically, no violation of the law. Little wonder that labor agents urged Mexican migrants to step over the line to sign up. [40]

Given the push and pull factors at work on both sides of the border, the mass migration of Mexican labor to the southwestern states, and from there to the interior of the United States through railroad arteries, seems in retrospect to have been inevitable. Revolutionary upheaval in Mexico from 1910 to 1920, contrary to conventional interpretation, must therefore be understood not as the primary cause of mass emigration but as a catalyst—albeit an important one—of an exodus already underway.

Perhaps the Revolution gave its most important impulse to rural migration by uprooting and setting in motion thousands of panic-stricken families. The semifeudal bonds between master and peon were snapped as the latter joined the insurgents or fled the countryside as revolutionary chieftains, such as Emiliano Zapata, decreed the abolition of peonage and the distribution of land in territories under their control. [41] Along with displaced peons, land owners and overseers fled to the cities or across the border to escape possible reprisals. Food production dropped as fields were left unplanted or domestic animals and laborers were requisitioned by marauding bands of revolutionary or government troops. Each time anarchy broke out in the period from 1910 to 1920, refugees, including defeated troops, headed for the safety of the border. In one instance, American border authorities granted asylum to over 8,000 persons. [42]

Here social services in the United States played an important role in attracting émigrés. Private and public charity agencies organized relief services to aid poverty-stricken families. Organizations such as the Red Cross and Protestant missions set up soup kitchens, gave out clothing, and arranged for lodging and even employment. Thus many emigrants were encouraged to stay and send for others. In the meantime, Mexican laborers and their American employers had already discovered that social service agencies could help subsidize the migrant labor cycle. Families of seasonal workers, who normally would have returned to winter in Mexico or the immediate border area, found that they could winter in cities like Los Angeles, San Antonio, Kansas City, or Chicago with a little help from community relief agencies, public and private. Sometimes, the Mexican government itself contributed to this subsidy pattern. [43]

The entry of the United States into World War I in 1917 increased the demand for Mexican labor and opened up a broader spectrum of job opportunities, including factory work. With low-cost immigrant labor from Europe shut off by the Immigration Act of 1917 and wartime conditions, and with millions of Americans in uniform, more American employers turned to Mexican labor. Although the law of 1917 for the first time established general immigration restrictions on the Mexican border, employers were quick to ask the Secretary of Labor to exempt Mexican contract workers from literacy tests and the eight-dollar head tax. [44] Some 72,000 workers came legally into the United States under the wartime exemptions of 1917-1921, but even more significantly the labor demands of the war and the shutoff of other sources of labor led directly to the so-called wetback invasion of the 1920s. *Coyotes*, or smugglers of wetback labor, and enganchistas had no difficulty guiding a migrant family past an occasional immigration inspector. Other wetbacks found their own way to border employment agencies. [45] The establishment of the Border Patrol in 1924 diverted but did not stop the flow of *mojados* into the United States.

Following World War I, and because of a rise in labor militancy, Mexican nationals, south Texas Mexicans, and southern blacks were increasingly imported as *esquiroles*, or strikebreakers. As with the anti-Oriental feeling in California, much of the long-standing anti-Mexican feeling of other immigrant groups and native Americans can be traced to the importation of "alien scab labor." [46]

All the while the primary pull factor was the great disparity in wages. Anthropologist Manuel Gamio, who studied Mexican migrants in the United States in 1926 and 1927, estimated that the average wage earned was six times that for similar work in Mexico. The emigrant worker not only earned enough to meet his elemental needs, but he was able to spend money on education and luxuries. Mexican "repatriates" commonly returned home with farm animals, farm implements, radios, and even cars, and this said more than a thousand words. [47]

A brief comparison of wages (see Table 4) not only suggests the commanding attraction of American jobs but also helps explain why some migrant workers were moving from border areas saturated with Mexican labor to places as distant as Chicago, Illinois, Gary, Indiana, and Bethlehem, Pennsylvania, where Paul S. Taylor found them in the late 1920s. [48]

Mexican migration to the United States virtually stopped during the Great Depression of the 1930s. Public hostility rose against alien labor and unemployed native workers eagerly grabbed for jobs previously held only by Mexicans. In the period from 1931 to 1934 more than 350,000 Mexicans were repatriated, and during the remainder of the decade Mexican emigrants generally found themselves unwelcome. The Depression had ended an exodus to the United States. This is shown in U.S. figures, imperfect as they may be: from 1901 to 1930 about 728,000 Mexican immigrants were legally admitted to the United States, but in the decade from 1931 to 1940 only some 23,000 Mexican immigrants were admitted. The number of unregistered migrants who settled on the United States side of the border during the 1901-1930 period was probable over a million, but many of these returned during the crisis of the Depression, some attracted by the repatriation efforts of the Mexican government. [49]

World War II clearly marks the beginning of a second exodus of Mexican emigrants. Here the bracero program was as important a catalyst as the Revolution of 1910 in the first exodus. Under the emergency contract-labor program initiated in 1942 and prolonged until December 1964, more than 4.5

Table 4   Average Daily Wages for a Common Laborer in U.S. Currency

Year	Agriculture			Industry, Rails, Mines, Factories	
	Mexico	*U.S. Border*	*U.S. Interior*	*Mexico*	*U.S. General*
1900	$.20–.25	$ .50– .75	$ .75–1.00	$.40– .50	$1.00–2.00
1910	.20–.25	.50–1.00	1.00–1.50	.50– .75	1.25–2.50
1920	.20–.25	1.00–2.00	1.50–2.50	.50– .75	3.00–4.00
1930*	.25–.40	1.50–2.50	2.00–3.00	.50–1.00	3.50–5.00

*Before the impact of the 1929 stockmarket crash

Source: Based on a composition of data from Clark, "Mexican Labor"; Gamio, *Mexican Immigration*; Taylor, *Mexican Labor in the United States*; Paul H. Douglas, *Real Wages in the United States, 1890-1926* (Boston, 1930); *U.S. consular correspondence from Mexico.* National Archives, Record Group 59, File 811.111/Mexico, 1910-1929; Mexican consular correspondence in AHSRE, files IV/350 to IV/560.

million temporary workers were admitted to the United States. Some worked on the railroads up to 1946, but most worked in agriculture and food processing. Some braceros were recontracted several times, but possibly 1.5 million of the total admitted were distinct persons who, for the most part, had never been in the United States before 1942, and who for the first time had a taste of the high wages and adventure that old repatriates had talked about in the plazas and taverns of Mexico. Even before the first braceros had tried the program, the first recruiting center in Mexico City's National Stadium was swamped with applicants.[50]

During World War II braceros found themselves fervently welcomed as war workers and allies in nearly half of the states of the union. The first reports of high wages and generally good treatment by gringo employers under contract agreements spread throughout Mexico, erasing any memory of hostile attitudes during the Depression. In a short time swarms of eager migrants began bypassing the provincial recruiting centers and making their own way to the border. A second exodus was underway.[51]

Postwar prosperity, Cold War considerations, and a growing dependence on imported Mexican labor by American growers led not merely to perennial renewal of the so-called emergency program but to rapid expansion under U.S. Public Law 71 in 1951.[52] By then bracero contracting had risen from some 53,000 in 1943 to over 190,000, eventually reaching a peak of over 447,000 in 1959. Many American employers who had trained braceros for certain jobs sought to keep them as permanent workers on immigrant visas. Under a permissive visa policy thousands of braceros were brought in as "sorely needed" semiskilled or skilled immigrants. Soon these immigrated workers began sending for relatives, and legal immigration from Mexico, which was negligible in the 1930s and early 1940s, began to rise. By 1955 it approached 50,000 a year, and it moved steadily upwards, topping 71,500 in fiscal 1974, then dropping to 62,205 in fiscal 1975, a year of economic crisis.[53] Thus the bracero program helped prime a new current of legal immigration.

The contract-labor program had an even more significant impact on the emergence of wetbackism. Many employers encouraged braceros to return illegally, and for his part the bracero, like earlier migrants, soon learned that it was an easy matter to skip a contract or return to the United States surreptitiously. Countless thousands of other "line jumpers" sought to avoid an uncertain fate at the contracting centers and the usual payoffs to local Mexican officials and go-betweens. By 1946 the bracero-control structure was literally swept aside by hordes of wetbacks, families and all, migrating into the border states and setting up primitive rancherías and shanty towns as in the lower Rio Grande Valley.[54]

A comparison of the number of wetback apprehensions with the number of braceros legally contracted during the period 1946-1954 suggests the dimensions of the control problem. (See Table 5.)

Table 5   Mexicans Deported and Contracted as Braceros, 1946-1954

Year	Deportation of Mexican illegals	Braceros contracted
1942	5,100	4,203
1943	8,860	53,098
1944	29,176	62,170
1945	69,111	49,494
1946	101,478	32,043
1947	199,282	19,630
1948	203,945	35,345
1949	293,000	107,000
1950	480,000	67,500
1951	509,040	190,745
1952	528,815	197,100
1953	885,587	201,380
1954	1,058,000	309,033
Total	4,371,394	1,328,741

Source: Ernesto Galarza, *Merchants of Labor: The Mexican Bracero Story* (Santa Barbara, 1964), pp. 59, 70, 79. Deportation figures vary somewhat.

Although figures for wetback deportations (like braceros contracted) include many "repeaters," on the other hand, those who got away were obviously not registered. Little wonder that by 1954 a U.S. Border Patrol officer could denounce the wetback phenomenon as "the greatest peacetime invasion complacently suffered by a country under open, flagrant, contemptuous violation of its laws." [55]

The great deportation drives of the summer of 1954 broke the back of the so-called wetback invasion by herding over the border more than a million mojados, including women and children. Thereafter apprehensions dropped steadily to an annual average of less than 50,000 by the final years of the bracero program. Bracero contracting expanded in the period from 1955 to 1960 to an average annual figure of 400,000, in part to absorb some of the "illegals." But the number gradually decreased, as congressional and labor opposition grew, to about 180,000 in 1964, the final year of the program. [56] Even so the wetback equation was by no means solved. In the bracero era perhaps 2 million Mexican nationals, besides legal braceros, had acquired a taste for higher wages and adventure on the American side and had learned the tricks of getting around. Once contracting ended, a latent wetbackism reasserted itself. Apprehensions of wetbacks—many of them habitual repeaters—zoomed upward from 55,349 in fiscal 1965 to 781,438 in fiscal 1976. Then a swarm of "amnesty seekers" followed in fiscal 1977, sending total apprehensions to 1,042,215. Of this number 95 percent, or 954,778, were Mexicans. [57] Now, however, mojados are no longer found predominantly in agricultural labor, but, like other groups of illegal aliens, in a great variety of jobs, skilled and unskilled.

The Mexican government was at first embarrassed and then troubled at the undignified rush of braceros and mojados for American jobs. During the war emergency the government had hoped to ration workers to the American economy as the figures for the 1940s show. Mexican officials wished to avoid another repatriation problem like that of the 1930s, and they were disturbed to see campesinos desert agrarian reform projects that had become, like Zapata, the very symbol of revolutionary rebirth. Also, anxious to industrialize, Mexican leaders opposed the loan of industrial labor, excepting some semiskilled railway workers during the war. [58] Yet industrial workers, along with campesinos and assorted adventurers, dropped everything in order to join the "bracero gold rush."

As in the 1920s and before, Mexican nationalists demanded that the government take positive steps to terminate the shame of bracerismo and the mojado exodus. But the irony was that the more the government tried to protect braceros, and regulate contracting conditions, the more American employers preferred wetbacks. [59] As in World War I and the 1920s the government seriously considered prohibiting the exit of all Mexicans without valid passports and contracts, and provisions to that effect were actually incorporated into Mexican migration law. [60] Yet these provisions were at no time rigorously enforced because Mexican officials realized they could not fight seductive wages in the United States with purely negative measures.

Actually, the second exodus was propelled by conditions quite similar to those that caused the northward migration of 1890-1930. Despite some real improvements in rural life, reports and surveys of the 1940s found that the benefits of economic progress had scarcely touched several million farm laborers and small peasant proprietors. Typically, one study of 1945 concluded that many agrarian reform efforts had been a "lamentable waste."[61] Many peasants had, indeed, received plots of land, but without water, credit facilities, or an agricultural extension service. In many cases the recipients reverted to pre-Columbian subsistence farming.

The National Revolutionary Party had struggled through successive administrations, to improve agrarian life in a country that has been classified as more than 50 percent arid land. In the period from 1926 to 1940, 4 to 8 percent of the national budget was invested in irrigation, and from 1941 to 1960 a remarkable 10 to 13 percent. From 1917 to 1965 more than 131.6 million acres, or 27 percent of the national territory, was given to more than 2.6 million families. In the Cárdenas period alone (1934-1940) more than 44 million acres were distributed to about 775,000 campesino families. Since the 1940s relatively heavy investments have been made in developing agricultural credit, banking, education, and transportation facilities. Yet, according to one authority, the total amount of arable land in Mexico as of 1955 was less than 49.4 million acres. Of that amount about 2 million acres had a year-round supply of rainfall, and about 6.2 million acres were under irrigation (compared to 10.6 million acres in the American Southwest). The remaining acreage was classified as seasonal farmland dependent on a sometimes uncertain rainfall.[62]

The average size of a land grant during the period 1917 to 1965 was approximately 57 acres, but in most cases this was partly arid land or pastoral land. Where irrigated plots were given, they averaged from 24 to 48 acres per family, but usually only half or less of this acreage received an allotment of water.[63]

At the same time the government's investments in public health have led to a population explosion of the most serious dimensions since the 1940s. In 1930 the population of Mexico was about 17 million people; in 1940, 19.5 million; in 1950, 25 million; in 1960, 35 million; in 1970, 48.5 million, and in 1975, 61 million with a projection of 90 to 100 million in 1990. In January 1973 the government took the first firm steps to make contraception facilities available for lower-income groups through the public health service, but it is too early to say what the results might be. Meanwhile, however, millions of campesinos and rancheria groups are without land, and *ejidatarios*, or communal farmers, who received plots of land have subdivided their land among their sons and grandsons, and small proprietors have often done the same. Thus agrarian reforms have scarcely kept pace with the population growth.[64] One critic has concluded that Mexico today suffers not so much from feudal latifundia as formerly but from minifundia, for "almost 90 percent of agricultural holdings are minifundia."[65]

According to the census of 1960, there were 1.3 million small landowners whose holdings averaged less than 12.5 acres in size. Communal property held by some 1.5 million ejidatarios were scarcely any larger.[66] As a result of minifundia, the low productivity of farm cooperatives, and population pressures, many peasant proprietors have sold or leased their property to neighbors or to agribusiness corporations, some of them American subsidiaries; and commonly ejido shareholders (who are forbidden to sell or abandon their land allotments) rent their share.

Villagers that abandon agriculture, or merely seek to supplement farm or other income, have now for generations, as in the *Mesa Central*, sought jobs in Mexican cities or in the United States, where the annual rise in summer employment happens to dovetail into the winter agriwork cycle in Mexico.[67] Come April the annual migration (dreaded by the U.S. Border Patrol) begins, and by October the backflow. Likewise, this pattern has been transferred to *Mexiquitos* in American border states, supplemented by public assistance.

Low wages continue to play the fundamental expulsive role. In the war years, 1941-1945, wages rose in Mexico, but still rural laborers, or *jornaleros*, could do no better than $.40 to $.60 a day (in U.S. currency), and inflation shrunk real wages. In Mexico's urban areas pay for the unskilled averaged less than $1 a day, as incoming migrants depressed wage levels. By contrast, wartime contract labor over the border was guaranteed $.50 an hour, and soon after $.75. But when wetbacks and their families poured over the line after 1947, they depressed "stoop labor" pay to as low as $.15 an hour in south Texas and $.25 an hour in California's Imperial Valley. Yet by hundreds of thousands they came. [68]

During the 1950s wages increased in Mexico hand in hand with the cost of living, and there were real gains in public health and education. Yet the hard facts of a subsistence economy remained much the same. Researchers lamented that, around 1960, 77 percent of all Mexican families (then about 27.5 million people) had monthly incomes of $80 or less, and 50 percent less than $50 a month. [69] Even allowing for the lower cost of living in Mexico, such figures spell out mass poverty. In the 1960s common labor in rural areas received about $1.00 to $1.25 per day, and in urban areas from $1.50 to $1.80. But in small shops, agriwork, and domestic service, these minimum wages were rarely paid, and in many cases people were employed only part-time.

Presently Mexico suffers from a growing problem of subemployment in both rural and urban areas. The redundancy of employment in a semi-industrialized economy characterized by subsistence agriculture in many regions, excessive population growth, and chronic urban marginality, is suggested by Table 6.

One student of *sub-empleo*, writing in 1965, has suggested that from 2 to 4 million agriculturists were redundant. [70] Persistent migration from rural areas has, in turn, created a major problem in urban underemployment. In the towns and cities of Mexico, displaced migrant families are underemployed in numerous personal service and mini-retail activities that, as Oscar Lewis found in his studies of the culture of poverty, consume the energies of an entire family from dawn to dusk. [71] This bustle of marginal activities (suggestive of an Indian marketplace) includes street vendors, domestics, shoeshine boys, street hawkers, ticket sellers, beggars, prostitutes, and hustlers. Some of these types were described by Friar Sahagún over 400 years ago. [72] Some economists maintain that most of the persons employed in the so-called services sector of

Table 6   Occupational Structure of Mexico for 1940-1970

(figures represent millions of persons)

Employment	1940	1950	1960	1970
agriculture, livestock, and forestry,	3.8	4.8	6.3	8.3
services	1.3	2.1	3.7	6.3
industry	.9	1.3	2.0	3.1
Total labor force	6.0	8.2	12.0	17.7

Source: Bonilla Sánchez in Rodolfo Stavenhagen et al., *Neolatifundismo y explotación Emiliano Zapata a Anderson Clayton & Co.* (Mexico, 1968), pp. 162-163.

the national economy—a group that swelled from 3.7 million to 6.3 million from 1960 to 1970—are simply displaced rural folk performing tasks that are perhaps traditional yet unproductive and regressive from the viewpoint of a modern industrial economy. [73] Perhaps half of Mexico's potential labor force is subemployed. In addition, there are the unemployed who may have numbered over 5 million in 1976. [74]

In spite of the foregoing account, it would be misleading to attribute the present high level of Mexican transborder migration to poverty or subsistence living. This explanation is a standard one offered to any committee in the United States or Mexico seeking to investigate the Mexican migration problem. In fact, however, some sectors of the Mexican population are emigrating more than ever before precisely because living conditions have improved along with economic opportunities. Mexico is in many ways a dual society and economy. Vestigial Indian cultures may still passively resist modernization, but within modern Mexico general social and economic improvements have brought about a "revolution of expectations," just as one sees in other parts of the western world. Many would-be emigrants possess industrial or managerial skills, sometimes acquired in American subsidiaries in Mexico. They are receptive to emigration even as well-paid railroad workers and miners were before 1910. A machinist receiving the handsome wage of $.80 (U.S.) an hour might be inclined to emigrate on learning that the same work pays $6.00 an hour in Los Angeles or Dallas. The motive force in such a case would not be poverty but rather a drive more and more common among Mexico's emigrants: the desire for economic improvement. This trend suggests that even if poverty were completely abolished in Mexico, it would not relieve the migration pressures on the American border. [75]

In the past fifty or sixty years some pull factors on the American side have remained much the same. In the 1920s Juan García could say, "If you are out of work in this country, somebody feeds you; if you are out of work in Mexico, nobody cares." [76] An oversimplification, yet Ramón and his family in the 1970s might feel much the same way:

Call him Ramón. . . . He, his wife and their six children, have little to look forward to this Christmas. Both parents are unemployed. The family has no real home, and they . . . fear any unexpected knock on the door. Ramón and his family are only one of many such families . . . in the Valley. Technically, they are criminals, but in the season of giving, charity sometimes has a way to circumvent the law books.

The Interfaith Center . . . tries to give each family a turkey dinner on Christmas Day, and also collects canned goods, and non-perishable foods, clothing, toys, and household articles for distribution to families in need. Prospective donors and families in need may contact the Center at . . . . [77]

More tangible are the income transfers of an industrial welfare state, such as unemployment compensation, social security, or pensions. For years such income has also been collected by many perennial repatriates. who qualify by doing an annual work period over the line, and then customarily winter, like snow birds, in Mexico, retiring there eventually on such benefits. In fact, the village economy often hangs on such income.[78]

Above all there has always been an eloquent difference in wage levels. By 1974 the Echeverría government (1970-1976), seeking to redistribute national income and discourage emigration, raised the daily minimum wage for common labor from $1.85 to $3.00 (U.S.), in rural areas and from $2.50 to $4.00 in urban areas, with a high of $4.50 to $5.50 in the border zone.[79] In 1976 wages were again hiked, this time 40 percent to meet rampant inflation, so that unskilled workers were entitled, theoretically, to around $5.25 per day and up to $7.00 on the border fringe. However, minimum wages have never been enforced for migrant and marginal groups. In September 1976, the peso, for the first time since 1954, was devalued from 12.5 per dollar to nearly twenty-two. American wages thus seemed all the more attractive as Mexico started another round of raising wages to avoid nationwide huelgas.

In the United States up to 1974 farm workers usually started at a federal minimum of $1.65 an hour (plus incentive pay), but common labor in construction, manufacturing, and food processing made from $2.00 to $4.50 an hour, the higher wages found inland. For skilled work the same approximate differences held. Moreover, American employers paid overtime for shifts exceeding eight hours a day, and that was not usually the case in Mexico. In 1974 Congress raised the federal minimum to $2.00 an hour, and escalated it to $2.50 by 1976 and to $2.65 by 1978. In that period common labor not covered by federal law was paid anywhere from $1.80 to $2.50 an hour.

Other pull factors have meanwhile become an established promotional business. A mere phone call to labor agencies like Benavides and Benavides, American Crystal, Great Western, Gonzáles, or Cavazos, operating at border ports-of-entry, will, as in the 1920s, propel any available recruits to, say, Missoula, Montana. Operators of border-town trucks, taxis, and mini-buses solicit as always men, women, and children (some turned down at visa offices) for regular back-road runs to San Francisco, Portland, Denver, Dallas or Chicago, with custom service to any crossroad in America. And "innocent campesinos" are still drawn to the boundary line, more so now by border development programs. In the border zone, *enganchistas*, *coyotes*, and *polleros* flourish as always; so do travel agencies that live off cut-rate tourist excursions, now by air direct to the United States or via Puerto Rico or Canada; so do innkeepers, job foremen, and purveyors of false documents; so do predatory lawyers, consultants, and public notaries who work "immigrant hardship cases."[80] Thus, smuggling aliens, some of them carrying drug packets to pay their passage, has become a billion-dollar enterprise, and to such a degree that the chain of collaborators, stretching from Boston to Mexico City, will continue mechanically to pump in gullible aliens no matter what the economic situation may be in the United States.

Furthermore, American employers, including Mexican-Americans, have always welcomed, *con un abrazo*, low-cost labor regardless of legal status, and there is not yet a law to castigate the employer of illegal aliens. Bilingual social services, including a vast spread of welfare programs, food stamps, and immigrant aid groups, are more available than ever before to native and alien alike. Chicano militants and civil rights workers have established a virtual protectorate over the Mexican barrios in the United States, in many cases making them off limits to immigration officers. And, in general, the legal immigrants can now more readily meet the standards imposed by American immigration acts, especially if they have close relatives in the United States.[81] All the while there is the pervasive reality of border proximity and the outstretched hands of friends and relatives on the American side, constant invitations to step across the line.

Finally, the sweeping offers of amnesty for several million illegal aliens made by the administration of President Jimmy Carter, inaugurated in January 1977, promised to set off a third phenomenal wave of Mexican transborder migration.

Notes

1. "Consul General . . . Statement of Conditions," *The El Paso Times*, September 17, 1923, in "Enrique R. Ruíz, su expediente personal," 21-4-1 (III)/1/131/5429, Archivo Histórico de la Secretaría de Relaciones Exteriores, Mexico City. Hereafter cited as AHSRE with appropriate file number.

2. Andrés Molina Enríquez, *Los grandes problemas nacionales* (Mexico, 1909); George M. McBride, *The Land Systems of Mexico* (New York, 1923).

3. Moisés González Navarro, *La colonización en México, 1877-1910* (México, 1960), 132-136.

4. Fernando González Roa and José Covarrubias, *El problema rural de México* (Mexico, 1917), 180.

5. Jesús Silva Herzog, *El agrarismo mexicano y la reforma agraria* (2nd ed.; Mexico, 1959), 128.

6. Adapted from figures ascribed to official sources in Walter E. Weyl, "Labor Conditions in Mexico," *Bulletin of the Department of Labor* 38 (January 1902), 39.

7. McBride, *The Land Systems of Mexico*, 154.

8. González Navarro, *La vida social*, 26-27; and his *La colonización*, 124-136.

9. Ibid.; also by González Navarro, *Población y sociedad en México, 1900-1970* (2 vols.; Mexico, 1974), II, 179.

10. On the mixed use of coolie, Indian, Mexican, and other immigrant labor in mining and railway construction see U.S. Congress, Senate, *Reports of the Immigration Commission: Japanese and Other Immigrant Races in the Pacific Coast and Rocky Mountain States: Diversified Industries*, 61st Cong., 2nd Sess. (Washington, 1911), part 25, 11-21 ff; Joseph F. Park, "The History of Mexican Labor in Arizona during the Territorial Period" (Master's thesis in history, University of Arizona, 1961).

11. See Paul S. Taylor's study of a village where small proprietorship was common:

A Spanish-Mexican Peasant Community, Arandas in Jalisco Mexico (Berkeley, 1933).

12. Paul S. Taylor, *A Mexican-American Frontier.*

13. This pattern may be discerned, for example, in studies of immigrant settlement in railway colonies, as in Judith Fincher Laird, "Argentine, Kansas: The Evolution of a Mexican-American Community, 1905-1940" (Ph.D. thesis, University of Kansas, 1975); or in a series of articles by Bill Wright on Topeka's colony of Mexican railworkers, again, on the Santa Fe Railroad, entitled "Heritage of the Colony," *Topeka Daily Capitol,* December 17-22, 1961.

14. Victor S. Clark, "Mexican Labor in the United States," *Bulletin of the Department of Labor* 78 (September 1908), 466-467. This is an invaluable account of labor recruiting and labor distribution.

15. Ibid., 467.

16. Ibid., 470.

17. Ibid., 474.

18. Ibid., 470-475; U.S. Congress, Senate, *Abstracts of Reports of the Immigration Commission,* 61st Cong., Senate Document no. 747 (1911), 682-694.

19. Park, "The History of Mexican Labor in Arizona;" Carey McWilliams, *North from Mexico* (New York, 1968), 168-169.

20. Orris Herfindahl, "Development of the Major Mining Industries in the United States from 1839 to 1909," in National Bureau of Economic Research, *Employment and Productivity in the United States after 1800* (New York, 1966), 316; Alfred Eichner, *The Emergence of Oligopoly: Sugar Refining as a Case Study* (Baltimore, 1969); E.J. Foscue, "Agricultural History of the Lower Rio Grande Valley," *Agricultural History* 8 (March 1934), 124-137; Gerald Nash, *The American West in the Twentieth Century* (Englewood Cliffs, N.J., 1973).

21. Varden Fuller, "The Supply of Agricultural Labor in California," in U.S. Congress, Senate, *Hearings before a Subcommittee of the Committee on Education and Labor, Violations of Free Speech and Rights of Labor,* 76th Cong., 3rd. Sess. (1940), 19778, 19883; Carey McWilliams, *Factories in the Fields* (Boston, 1939). See also Paul S. Taylor, *A Mexican-American Frontier*; and his *Mexican Labor in the United States: Dimmit County, Winter Garden District, South Texas* (Berkeley, 1930).

22. Fuller, "The Supply of Agricultural Labor," 19861.

23. U.S. Congress, Senate *Reports of the Immigration Commission,* II, 690-691.

24. U.S. Congress, Senate, *Immigrant Races in Agriculture,* vol. 24, pt. 3, 2-39. See also James Michener's dramatic account of Colorado's development in *Centennial* (New York, 1974), chap. 12.

25. Paul S. Taylor, *Mexican Labor in the United States: Imperial Valley* (Berkeley, 1928), 12.

26. For the growth of agricultural production in California see Fuller, "The Supply of Agricultural Labor," and Nash, *The American West.*

27. For economic transformation in south Texas see Foscue, "Agricultural History," and Frank C. Pierce, *A Brief History of the Lower Rio Grande Valley* (Menasha, Wisconsin, 1917), 128-231.

28. Taylor, *A Mexican-American Frontier,* 84-85, 92, 95.

29. Clark, "Mexican Labor," 477, 487, 496, 519; U.S. Congress, Senate, *Reports of the Immigration Commission. . . Immigrant Races in. . . Diversified Industries,* vol. 25.

30. Ibid., 128-131, 190-191, 194; Park, "The History of Mexican Labor," 205-233.

31. N. Ray and Gladys Gilmore, "Bracero in California," *Pacific Historical Review* 32 (August 1963), 268.

32. Ruth Tuck, *Not with the Fist: Mexican Americans in a Southwest City* (New York, 1946), 38; Louis and Richard Parry, *A History of the Los Angeles Labor Movement* (Berkeley, 1963), 71; Paul S. Taylor, *Mexican Labor in the United States: Chicago and the Calumet Region* (Berkeley, 1932), 27.

33. Laird, "Argentine, Kansas," chap. 4.

34. Clark, "Mexican Labor," 475.

35. Ibid.

36. Ibid., 476.

37. Ibid.

38. Ibid.

39. Taylor, *A Mexican-American Frontier*, 105.

40. González Navarro, *Población y sociedad*, II, 207-208; Clark, "Mexican Labor," 469-476.

41. The agrarian revolutionaries decreed the end of debt peonage. See Manuel González Ramírez (ed.), *Fuentes para la historia de la Revolución mexicana* (4 vols.; Mexico, 1954-1957), I, passim.

42. On one occasion the whole village of Villa Acuña fled to Del Rio, Texas, as the troops of General Orozco advanced. Mexican consul, Del Rio, to Secretary of Foreign Relations, September 23, 1912, AHSRE, 16-8-90. On another occasion some 5,000 defeated federal troops, plus camp followers and hundreds of civilian refugees crossed in a body at Presidio, Texas. Commissioner General of Immigration, *Annual Report, 1914*, 34.

43. For example, the Mexican government provided $5,000 in aid to seasonal migrants stranded in Fort Worth. E.R. Cockrell, mayor of Fort Worth, to President Álvaro Obregón, May 18, 1921, Obregón papers, Archivo General de la Nación, Mexico City, file 822-M-1.

44. U.S. Department of Labor, "Results of Admission of Mexican Laborers Under Departmental Orders for Employment in Agricultural Pursuits," *Monthly Labor Review* 11 (November 1920), 1095-1097. Mark Reisler, *By the Sweat of Their Brow: Mexican Immigrant Labor in the United States, 1900-1940* (Westport, Conn., 1976), chap. 2, summarizes the World War I temporary labor program.

45. See the account of the Mexican consul in San Antonio, Enrique Santibañez, *Ensayo acerca de la inmigración mexicana en los Estados Unidos* (San Antonio, 1930).

46. Taylor, *Mexican Labor in the United States: Chicago and the Calumet Region*, 109-115; Laird, "Argentine, Kansas," chap. 4; interviews with old timers in the Mexican colony, Topeka, Kansas, February 27, 1976.

47. See Manuel Gamio's description of items taken back to Mexico by returning migrants: *Mexican Immigration to the United States* (Chicago, 1930), 41.

48. See Taylor's series of ten studies, *Mexican Labor in the United States* (1928-1934); Reisler, *By the Sweat of Their Brow.*

49. Moisés González Navarro, "Efectos sociales de la crisis de 1929, "*Historia Mexicana* 10 (abril-julio 1970), 536-558; Mercedes Carreras de Velasco, *Los mexicanos que devolvió la crisis 1929-1932* (Mexico, 1974); Abraham Hoffman, *Unwanted Mexican Americans in the Great Depression: Repatriation Pressures, 1929-1939* (Tucson, 1974).

50. Ernesto Galarza, *Merchants of Labor*, 52.

51. The welcome prepared for the vanguard of braceros by the War Food Administration and American grower associations is indicated by Philip G. Bruton, Director, Office of Labor, War Food Administration, to J.W. Carrigan, Division of Mexican Affairs, State Department, October 3, 1944, National Archives, RG 59, 811. 504/10-344 (1940-1944). The influence of the bracero program on the illegal alien flow is noted by Julian Samora, with Jorge Bustamante and Gilberto Cardenas, *Los Mojados: The Wetback Story* (Notre Dame, 1971), 43-46; Otey M. Scruggs, "The United States, Mexico and the Wetbacks, 1942-1947," *Pacific Historical Review* 30 (May 1961), 149-164; Eleanor M. Hadley, "A Critical Analysis of the Wetback Problem," *Law and Contemporary Problems* 21 (1956), 334-357.

52. See Richard D. Craig, *The Bracero Program: Interest Groups and Foreign Policy* (Austin, 1971).

53. United States Immigration and Naturalization Service (INS), *Annual Report, 1976*, Table 8.

54. See the graphically illustrated *What Price Wetbacks?* (Austin: American G.I. Forum and the Texas Federation of Labor, 1953) by Ed Idar and Andrew C. McClellan.

55. Ibid., 59 (quote); *INS Reporter* 2 (January 1954), 39.

56. Craig, *The Bracero Program.*

57. INS, *Annual Report*, Table 27B.

58. Information on Mexican attitudes and policy toward braceros can be found in National Archives, RG 59, State Decimal File 1940-1945, 811.504/Mexico; Craig, *The Bracero Program*, 16-23, 58-61; González Navarro, *Población y sociedad*, II, chaps. 10-11.

59. Craig, *The Bracero Program*, 60-61, 126; Galarza, *Merchants of Labor*, chap. 7, "The Wetback Obligato"; U.S. President, *Report of the President's Commission on Migratory Labor in American Agriculture* (Washington, 1951), 50, 53-54.

60. González Navarro, *Población y sociedad*, II, 194-223.

61. Salvador Lira López et al., "La pobreza rural en México," (mimeographed report, Mexico, 1945), 34. For other critical opinions of agrarian reform see Gilberto Loyo, *3 breves estudios* (Mexico, 1970), 36-39; Jesús Silva Herzog, *Un ensayo sobre la revolución mejicana* (Mexico, 1946).

62. Adolfo Orive Alba, *La política de irrigación en México* (Mexico, 1960), 42. Other sources of data on Mexican investment in agricultural reform and productivity are: Roger D. Hansen, *The Politics of Mexican Development* (Baltimore, 1971), 58-65, 77-83, 86-88; Pablo González Casanova, *Democracy in Mexico* (New York, 1970), 48, 114-115, 223; and for the period up to 1945 see Nathan L. Whetten, *Rural Mexico* (Chicago, 1948).

63. Interviews by Arthur F. Corwin with Eduardo Chávez, director of irrigation and colonization development in the lower Rio Grande Valley, 1935-1940, Mexico City, July 15, 1971; and interviews with repatriates settled in agrarian colonies in the border states of Nuevo León and Tamaulipas, August 23, December 20 and 24, 1970.

64. Orive Alba, *La política de irrigación*, 174-175. For population data and enduring poverty see González Casanova, *Democracy in Mexico*, 74-79.

65. Rodolfo Stavenhagen et al., *Neolatifundismo y explotación de Emiliano Zapata a Anderson Clayton & Co.* (Mexico, 1968), 10.

66. Fernando Paz Sánchez, in ibid., 83-84.

67. Arturo Bonilla Sánchez, in ibid., 150; González Casanova, *Democracy in Mexico*, 114.

68. U.S. President, *Report of the President's Commission on Western Hemisphere Immigration* (Washington, 1968), 71-72, 78-80; Galarza, *Merchants of Labor*, 30.

69. González Casanova, *Democracy in Mexico*, 104-106, 139-140. See also Ifigenia Martínez de Navarrete, *La distribución del ingreso y el desarrollo económico de México* (Mexico, 1960); Ana María Flores, *La magnitud del hambre en México* (Mexico, 1961); Hansen, *The Politics of Mexican Development*; James Wilkie, *The Mexican Revolution: Federal Expenditure and Social Change since 1940* (Berkeley, 1970). For a study of the concentration of wealth in the hands of corporations and powerful families see Alonso Aguilar M. and Fernando Carmona, *México: riqueza y miseria* (Mexico, 1972).

70. From Bonilla Sánchez in Stavenhagen et al., *Neolatifundismo*, 129.

71. Oscar Lewis, *The Children of Sánchez* (New York, 1961); and his *Pedro Martínez: A Mexican Peasant and His Family* (New York, 1964).

72. Fray Bernardino de Sahagún, *Historia general de las cosas de la Nueva España*, ed. Angel M. Garibay (4 vols.; Mexico, 1956), III, 130-151.

73. Bonilla Sánchez in Stavenhagen et al., *Neolatifundismo*, 162-163; González Casanova, *Democracy in Mexico*, 72, 84-85. See also the cooperative study rich in data profiles on Mexican migration, internal and external, in Thomas Weaver and Theodore E. Dowing (eds.), *Mexican Migration* (Tucson: Bureau of Ethnic Research, University of Arizona, 1976).

74. Problems of population pressures, unemployment, subemployment, and growing urban crisis, as quantified by Mexican sociologists, demographers, economists, and government planners, are a frequent front page topic in Mexican newspapers, such as *El Universal*, Mexico City, June 2, 1972; *El Diario de Monterrey*, February 6, 1976; *La Tribuna de Monterrey*, February 25, 1976, or *Excelsior*, Mexico City, February 18-21, 1976; December 30-31, 1976.

75. On this point see Alejandro Portes, "Return of the Wetback," *Society*, 11, (March-April, 1974), 40-46.

76. Quoted by social worker Robert N. McLean, *That Mexican!* p. 125.

77. "Help Wanted," *Van Nuys* (California) *News*, December 18, 1975.

78. Wayne A. Cornelius, with Juan Díez-Cañedo, *Mexican Migration to the United States: The View from Rural Sending Communities* (Cambridge, Mass.: Center for International Studies, Massachusetts Institute of Technology, 1976); and his "Illegal Mexican Migration to the United States: A Summary of Recent Research Findings and Policy Implications," a briefing paper (Cambridge, Mass.: Department of Political Science, M.I.T., April, 1977); also binational study by Weaver and Downing, eds., *Mexican Migration*; moreover, interviews by A. F. Corwin with Mexican priests and laymen doing emigration advisory service in villages of central Mexico, Segundo Encuentro Mexicano Estadounidense de Migraciones, under auspices of United States Catholic Conference and Mexican Episcopate, Mexico City, April 21-24, 1975.

79. For disparities in income distribution in Mexico in recent years see Armando Labra, "La concentración del ingreso en México: un enfoque sectorial," in *Cuestiones económicas nacionales* (Mexico, 1971); Ifigenia M. de Navarrete, "La distribución del ingreso en México, tendencia y perspectivas," *El Perfil de México en 1980* (Mexico, 1970); Aguilar and Carmona, *México: riqueza y miseria*. For an example of wages fixed by the Comisión Nacional de los Salarios Mínimos for various occupations see *Excelsior*, January 2, 1974.

80. Texas Bureau of Labor Statistics, *Report on Migratory Labor: Movements and Licensed Texas Labor Agents* (Austin, 1974); and Domestic Council Committee on Il-

legal Aliens, *Preliminary Report* (Washington, D.C.: Department of Justice, December 1976), pp. 72-73.

81. Interviews with American consuls in Mexico City, August 15, 1970; Ciudad Juárez, August 23, 1972; Monterrey, March 12-13, and December 30, 1974, and February 17, 1976. Other factors working against control of mass immigration from Mexico and other countries have been outlined by the Commissioner of Immigration, Leonard F. Chapman, Jr., in "Illegal Aliens: Time to Call a Halt!", *Reader's Digest* 109 (October 1976), 188-192.

4/ WETBACKISM SINCE 1964: A CATALOGUE OF FACTORS

Arthur F. Corwin and Johnny M. McCain

> Did you hear how they are mistreating that poor old wetback in Chicago? Well, he can't go home this year for Christmas because *la migra* has run out of funds again.
>
> Chicano humor

The present "alien invasion" from Third World countries, but principally Mexico, has been underway since approximately 1964, and, in the opinion of high-ranking immigration officials, it has been the most difficult enforcement problem federal authorities have faced in their efforts to uphold the national immigration laws and standards first generally established in 1917. Since the mid-1960s a confluence of factors has seemed to undermine the best efforts of the U.S. Immigration and Naturalization Service (INS) to maintain effective alien control on the Mexican border and in the interior of the country. We will here summarize some of these factors.[1]

Ending of the Cooperative Bracero Program

The abolition of the Mexican contract-labor program in December 1964 had two principal effects on alien control. On the Mexican side of the border there was after that date the usual accumulation of several hundred thousand restless ex-braceros and "deported wetbacks," who, accustomed to work in the United States and unable to qualify for legal immigration, simply reverted to the customary method of illicit entry. Equally important, the government of Mexico after 1964 ceased its feeble efforts to control the migration of non-contract labor, for there was no binational agreement by which Mexican officials might feel obligated to protect contract workers from wetback competition.

Massing of Subemployed Millions in Mexico's Border Zone

American immigration officials see no relief in sight from "wetback pressures." Not only has Mexico's population zoomed from 17 million in 1930 to nearly 64 million in 1976, but it may double in the next twenty years. Concern about the surplus peasantry swarming into the cities led the Echevarría government (1970-1976) to begin cautiously contraceptive services for proletarian mothers via the national health service starting in 1972; and the Population Law of February 6, 1974, committing the country to the goal of population planning, has been followed by a bold propaganda campaign to change the *macho* value system. However, it may be many years before the large family ceases to be a national custom. Moreover, the latest population law reaffirms Mexico's historic policy of encouraging settlement along the northern frontier.[2]

Since World War II Mexico's border population has been doubling about every ten years. As late as 1940 Matamoros, Reynosa, Piedras Negras, Nogales, and other gateway cities were dusty border towns of 15,000 or less. At that date Ciudad Juárez had scarcely 55,000 inhabitants, Mexicali about 45,000, Nuevo Laredo perhaps 30,000 and Tijuana fewer than 25,000. By 1975, counting the floating or squatter populations, Piedras Negras and Nogales had over 80,000 each, Reynosa and Nuevo Laredo nearly 180,000 each, Matamoros nearly 220,000, Mexicali over 400,000, Tijuana better than 700,000, and Ciudad Juárez close to 650,000. At that time Mexico's border-strip population was approaching 5 million, usually in a rather promiscuous form of "twin city," like Ciudad Juárez and El Paso, or Nuevo Laredo and Laredo.[3]

Aside from border-crossing opportunities, the main reason for the rapid concentration of subemployed along Mexico's northern fringe is the so-called free zone—a ribbon of territory on the Mexican side, 30 kilometers wide that runs along the common border. Within this strip the Mexican government has for over a century given special exemptions to border residents, originally to settle the frontier and secure it against gringo expansionists. Later, concessions and franchises were given to border merchants and businessmen to promote tourism and trade with the United States.

In 1965, to compensate for the closing of the bracero program and to improve the Good Neighbor image, Mexico launched a border development program that sought to clean up the border, attract more tourists, and entice both Mexican and American industries, through tax exemptions, inport-export privileges, and controlled labor unions, to settling there.[4] As a result of new jobs created in the zone—about fifty thousand have been created thus far by American subsidiary plants—and the availability of jobs, legal and illegal, on the American side, plus the circulation of tourist and trade dollars and the fixing of higher minimum wages there, real wages have been notably higher in the zone. Furthermore, the ability of border residents, unlike other Mexican nationals, to bring in American cars, household utilities, clothing, and groceries at low import duties or none at all—maybe just a little *mordida*—is another strong incentive for moving to the border, as is the dream of becoming a "border commuter" in the American labor market.

However, most border migrants—many of them unattached adventurers—end up jobless or holding menial jobs at best. For one thing, as in Puerto Rico and Taiwan, female labor is usually preferred in satellite industries. For another, new waves of job-hungry migrants displace earlier ones, who then displace border Mexican Americans, and so on. Currently there is probably a fluid population of over 1½ million jobless and subemployed men and women along Mexico's border, together with several hundred thousand restless and school-free teenagers who make a daily sport of border-crossing. This amorphous population literally has its nose pushed against the border window, and has nothing to do all day but "look for cracks in the border-control system."[5]

New-Style Wetbacks

Today what is being called the "new wetback invasion" is better described as an infiltration of new-style migrants. This migration is virtually invisible to the general public. The new "wets" are not the ragged peons or "stoop labor" of yesteryear, who in rubber-tired *huaraches* plodded over the back trails or rambled down the highways in broken-down trucks with women and little *chamacos*, looking for farm and ranch work. Today's *mojados* exemplify the increasing modernization of Mexico, the improved methodology of alien smugglers, and the grapevine knowledge that the Border Patrol has shut many doors to farm jobs in the border Southwest. Now more than ever illegals head for better wages and easier work in cities, towns, farms, and ranches far from the border regions. Later they may send for family members.[6] Many such workers collect unemployment compensation during the slack season, and family members may collect welfare or food stamps—a pattern now common among America's working class. Others are commuters who keep their families in Mexico. They hold regular seasonal jobs and, each spring, make an annual payoff to a familiar smuggler, labor agent, or job foreman. During the winter season many collect jobless benefits through a United States address.

Now the illegal alien more commonly "invests money." When, for example, a welder with a Mexican wage of $.75 an hour (U.S. currency) gets a letter from a *primo* in Chicago or New York saying that he can make $6 or $8 a hour on a night-shift welding crew, he may decide to take his savings and jump the line. Illegals frequently pay—sometimes by installments taken out of paychecks—as much as $400 to be smuggled to a distant American city, and more if the package deal includes a union job, identification papers, and housing arrangements. Not only is the new-style wetback "documented," but he has learned, with the help of Raza *compadres*, that employment, or food stamps, or social assistance from public and private agencies, usually requires nothing more than the giving of a local address.[7]

The new wetback is not so wet. He may walk calmly through a port of entry flashing a document, most commonly the border-crossing card (Form I-186) that permits a temporary visit of seventy-two hours in a 25-mile-wide American zone that "leaks like a sieve." There are presently over a million such cards circulating in Mexico's border zone.[8] Moreover, advised to dress like typical Americanos, or Chicanos, the "sophisticated alien" finds protective coloration in cities like Dallas, Houston, Chicago, Los Angeles, Kansas City, Toledo, and New York, or wherever he or she, and often the family, can "disappear" into Mexican-American or Puerto Rican *barrios* or *colonias*. Even the most rustic *compesinos* can learn, after repeated non-penalty expulsions, how to make it in the spreading "wetback subculture."[9]

La Huelga and Border Patrol vigilance of agrilabor have influenced the new wetbackism. Since 1964 California's César Chávez has sought to unionize migrant farm labor under the banners of the Aztec eagle and *la Virgin de Guadalupe*, with subsidies from the American Federation of Labor. The Huelga movement has opposed border commuters (particularly nonunion ones), who with "greencards" live in Mexico and work in the United States. (In one suit brought by the United Farm Workers the Supreme Court ruled, on November 24, 1974, that greencarders may legally commute to American jobs on a daily but not on a seasonal basis.) Similarly, Chávez has denounced wetbacks (particularly nonunion ones), alleging that illegals and growers with the connivance of *la migra* (Immigration Service), undermine wages and unionization. Many illegals are now in the ranks of the UFW, or in the rival Teamsters Union. Nevertheless, one side effect of such protests has been to divert part of the wetback stream from the Rio Grande Valley or California valleys into other channels of employment.[10]

Rising Labor Costs

Employers are naturally inclined to prefer the "wetback obligato," to use Ernesto Galarza's phrase. An alien without papers tends to be docile and work for less and can be turned over to immigration authorities if there is trouble. But since 1964 this standard explanation no longer fits the full, complex pattern of alien infiltration from Mexico and other countries into so many fissures of the American economy. Here one must give some weight to the universal complaints of employers that union demands in industry and agriculture, and government income-support programs, have kept the cost of American labor artificially high and maintained unreliable labor. And can one brush aside the observations that rising taxes, inflation, and high minimum wages have been pushing American industries, of many shapes and sizes, to a desperate search for cost-cutting measures? More so than in the early 1960s, businessmen have been inclined to move labor operations to Taiwan, Hong Kong, Puerto Rico, Mexico, and elsewhere or to import low-cost tractable labor, legal or illegal.[11]

War on Poverty and Welfare

In 1964 President Johnson's war to end the paradox of poverty in what some reformers were calling "a shamefully affluent society" went into high gear. Dozens of bilingual government agencies and special outreach commandoes, such as VISTA Volunteers and eager young legal-aid lawyers, began assiduously recruiting case loads of "poverty folk" for social service programs. Several million native Americans were recruited from unskilled, semiskilled, and seasonal labor jobs, or no jobs at all, to join overlapping programs that seemed to offer a grab bag of benefits in housing, health, food stamps, training for pay, welfare assistance, legal service, and the like, with special allowances for large families. After 1964 many poverty folk apparently discovered that, considering all the benefits, cooperation with poverty fighters and the new political patronage was often better than working for pay, especially in physically demanding jobs. Others found that they could be more more selective about jobs. Migratory-labor families, accustomed to seasonal work, have been induced to settle down, usually out of the labor market, in order to stay with social assistance, or to undergo training for higher-paying industrial jobs that somehow never materialize, or to keep their children in special school programs like Head Start, Upward Bound, Horizons Unlimited, Bilingual Education, or a dozen other educational, diet, and health programs.[12]

One unforeseen result of Great Society programs was the creation of a "labor vacuum" that in its extent and its federally subsidized nature seems unique in American history. Increasingly, the casual observer in the inner cities of New York, Chicago, Washington, D.C., San Francisco, Miami, and elsewhere, saw Jamaicans, Haitians, Dominicans, Chinese, Filipinos, French Canadians, and Mexicans, among others, with or without papers, employed as bellhops, kitchen help, taxi drivers, warehouse workers, gardeners, maids, factory hands, hospital orderlies, or in more skilled work. Commonly employers complained that in the midst of high unemployment and job-training programs the natives, and even socially assisted "illegals," were turning down jobs at the going wage.

Like all richly developed nations, the United States needs someone to do the "dirty work," whether dishwashing or doctoring, editorialized *Time* magazine in its bicentennial survey of the new Third World immigration.[13] Perhaps so. In any case, anti-poverty programs had a catalytic effect on Mexican immigration. The "little Mexicos," or *colonias* of immigrated Mexicans and Mexican Americans, that served as "labor pools" translated to the American side of the border, especially after the immigration law of 1917 ceased, to provide the "usual quotas" of either migratory farm laborers or semiskilled workers for industrial and service jobs. The resulting labor shortage was filled, increasingly after 1965, by overflooded labor pools on the Mexican side of the border. This might be described as the "suction effect" of Great Society programs.

There was little sustained protest from unemployed native Americans. Buffered by anti-poverty agencies, as they had not been in the 1950s, when a great cry was raised against wetbacks, they were often more concerned about welfare and ethnic rights, unemployment compensation, and other forms of social security than about jobs or stricter alien control. By 1977 the unemployment rate seemed fixed at around 7 percent, and there were over 18 million Americans on food stamps and nearly 9 million youngsters on aid-to-dependent-children. The federal government was then spending close to $160 billion on health, education, and welfare.

There is more. "Getting the poor involved in anti-poverty programs" was a major goal of the Great Society. To some degree this has been accomplished, but with surprising distortions. Illegal aliens soon constituted an important part of the clientele of a self-perpetuating anti-poverty bureaucracy. For instance, from the beginning the Migrant Councils, like the Illinois or Iowa Migrant Councils, designed mainly to assist Mexican-American agrilaborers and their families, felt a *raza* obligation to provide immigration, employment, and social service counseling for legal and illegal aliens alike. Also, private agencies fighting poverty have latched onto federally funded programs in their conscience-bound efforts to assist the disadvantaged. Examples would be the Catholic Bishops' Committee in San Antonio, the Cardinals' Committee in Chicago, The Denver Catholic Community Service, the U.S. Catholic Conference in El Paso, the United Farm Workers Organizing Committee, and similar private groups that sponsor immigration services, headed by militant Chicanos committed to the "liberation of La Raza from Anglo exploitation" and from harassment by the hated *migra* and the local police. To promote immigration and civil rights test cases, some of these service groups may plant Spanish-surnamed citizens among apprehended aliens. Another sign of the times would be city governments, like that of Los Angeles, San Antonio, or Houston, which, because of the growing importance of the Chicano vote, channel funds from the Model Cities Program to private agencies (like One-Stop Immigration) that help *mojados* legalize their status.[14]

Ethnic Rights and Alien Control

Ethnic militancy, supported since the mid-1960s by the War on Poverty and the civil rights movement, is, in fact, inseparable from the present illegal alien phenomenon. Now more than ever certain ethnic groups manifest an ambivalence that in its political effects serves to favor migration, particularly from such "folk countries" as Mexico, Dominican Republic, Jamaica, Haiti, and, one might add, the Free State of Puerto Rico. Before the Great Society era most minority leaders felt that jobs and new-found national identity were threatened by massive immigration of "paisanos" from poverty-stricken countries. Generally ethnic leaders did not then protest the efforts of the Immigration Service and the Labor Department to uphold immigration laws and American wage standards. Today, however, the new-style ethnic leadership is inclined to see any vigorous attempts by federal agencies to keep "soul brothers" out as a WASP plot to keep down the dark-skinned races or as a pretext for racial discrimination.

In the 1940s and 1950s Mexican-American organizations, like the American G.I. Forum and the League of United Latin American Citizens, were conspicuous leaders in demanding wetback control.[15] Today many such leaders have gone "Chicano"—a term that originated in the wetback barrios of the border states in the 1920s. The *mojado* is no longer seen as a threat, but as a racial and political reinforcement. And Chicano liberationists find they no longer need or want the jobs taken by Mexican newcomers. There is a peculiar symbiosis here; federal programs and "wet labor" literally have freed many "professional ethnics" to devote their full energies to the political culture of "underprivileged minorities" and to assail all forms of real or imagined discrimination and exploitation, including, of course, immigration control.

Chicano nationalism, sprouting in barrios across the country, and reinforced by mass immigration, works for the political "reconquest of the Southwest by the Mexican race," that is, *la raza*, and the spiritual restoration of the mythical Aztlán, or the original homeland of the Aztecs. Characteristically, Chicano leaders call for an open border with Mexico in reparation for the unjust conquest of "Chicano territory," and insist on the ancient and unalienable right of the Indo-Americans—the first Americans—to migrate where they please, over any "artificial boundary," in search of Aztlán, or for liberation from colonialist exploitation imposed on Third World countries, like Mexico, by American corporate capitalism. Naturally liberation also means removing the deportation menace from the *colonias*, and accordingly Raza leaders have set up court challenges and workshops to implement "Aztlán immigration policy," including broad amnesty plans.[16]

Political climates have been so changed by ethnic populism that immigration-enforcement officials operate under severe handicaps; in fact, they have lost control of the situation, especially in the "Latino barrios," and have been reduced to pleading their cases like any other client group in the Great Society. Only ambivalent support can be expected from traditional Mexican-American leadership, for so many Chicano settlers, legal and illegal, have poured into the border states and beyond since World War II that the old "Spanish-American" leaders (some of whose ancestors go back to 1920 or even 1848) have been overwhelmed. The new leadership must appeal to the immigrant population and the Chicano youth wave (as in Mexico itself, a high percentage of the Raza population).

Chicano politicians, like Kiko de la Garza and Edward Roybal, demand a per capita share of federal funds for all Raza members, documented or not, protest census undercounts as a kind of "Anglo plot," and look to a grand alliance of all Latino groups in which illegals are commonly found. The more militant leaders, like Reies López Tijerina, seek to recover old land grants (tax-free), promote federal rural assistance for the victims of 1848, and lead a Pan Latin mestizo movement.

The Indo-Hispano citizen is caught in a somewhat tortuous situation but considers his few losses to the so-called "wetback" . . . as insignificant compared to his gains in terms of thawing out his frozen and suppressed language and culture. So . . . we don't see them as a threat—not to our jobs, not to our wives, not to our culture.[17]

Equity Claims

Long lines of Mexican nationals waiting in vain for certification from the Labor Department, as "needed workers," see others, seemingly less qualified, given special consideration because of equity acquired while working or residing as an illegal. Why wait when one can walk to the United States?[18]

If any alien can just manage to get inside the country and join kinfolk or find a potentially permanent job, it seems that he or she has immigration policy and social-rescue agencies pulling on his or her side. In the parlance of immigration lawyers and counselors, the resident illegal is considered to be "building up equity." With the added help of the employer, the resident illegal can often meet the labor certification and public-charge tests. The admission might have been charged against the annual allotment of 120,000 non-preference immigrants for the Western Hemisphere, in accord with the act of 1965. More likely, he or she would have close relatives legally in the United States and thus could have been admitted in the "immediate relative" group, for which there is no fixed limit, or as the parent of a "citizen child," he could have been admitted without labor certification. The citizen child loophole was not closed until an immigration reform bill became Public Law 94-571 on October 20, 1976. (See chapter 6 on American immigration policy.)

For some years the INS had a special Mexican Equity Visa program (MEV), which gave admission priority to "family hardship cases," mostly arising from illegal entry, and the Service still has a small "Family Unit" program. More important, with help from such agencies as the International Institute of Los Angeles, the Legal Aid Society of Denver, the immigrant-aid network of the U.S. Catholic Conference, and Chicano mutual-help groups like CASA (Centro de Accion Social Autónomo), founded in California by political activist Bert Corona, and its counterpart TU CASA, founded in San Antonio by Mario Cantu, hundreds of family heads and individuals are legitimated each year. Thus the "equity visa" appears to reward those taking a shortcut to the United States and to encourage surreptitious entries in a never-ending spiral. Moreover, the equity system raises many false and costly hopes often exploited by a whole species of immigrant counselors and shyster attorneys in Mexico and in Chicano barrios. Little wonder that Chicano militants have been demanding blanket amnesty for all illegals who feel they have some equity. [20]

Abuse of Border-Crossing Cards

Short of a valid immigrant visa, what the new-style wetbacks treasure most of all is a border-crossing card, (I-186). This *mica*, as it is called in Mexico, bears a photo of the holder and serves as a multiple-entry tourist visa for any number of seventy-two-hour visits to a twenty-five-mile-wide border zone. It is good indefinitely unless revoked for reason of abuse such as accepting employment while on a temporary visitor pass. [21] Once in a border town, however, the border crosser can apply to the immigration office for a permit to go inland, perhaps to visit relatives in Los Angeles or Dallas, or to buy parts for a machine or special medicines for a sick person. Increasingly immigration inspectors are under public relations pressures to concede such requests, for under reciprocity arrangements with Mexico they are expected to honor the *mica* as a local passport, and the solicitant may have connections with Mexican-American groups. In the words of an inspector:

So we don't check out these requests as closely as we should even though we think this man or that woman is ready to streak for Gary, Indiana, just as soon one gets by the Border Patrol station. Anyway, they can easily make private arrangements with the taxi drivers around here to be taken inland, or they'll walk it. [22]

Not only are there more than a million border-crossing cards in the hands of residents and transients in Mexico's border zone, but the backlog of applications runs into the hundreds of thousands. According to veteran immigration inspectors these cards represent an enormous gap in documentary control. For one thing, there is no consistent return control on the I-186, or on the temporary permit (Form SW-434) to visit the interior of a border state, or on Form I-94 which authorizes a visit beyond the border state. Such permits are given "in good faith," for the INS does not have the means to check out possible overstays. The border-crossing card itself could be revoked if the Service should discover an abuse. But once in the United States the illegal resident or worker usually sends it to friends or relatives in Mexico for safekeeping. [23] If one is apprehended, the standard reply, under a pseudonym, is that he or she crossed the border unseen. The deportee is then classified as an EWI (entered without inspection) and returned to Mexico under the non-penalty voluntary departure arrangement, and the card can be used again. In fiscal 1973, for example, 542,244 out of a total of 576,823 Mexican illegals apprehended were listed as "EWIs," but immigration officers were aware that many of them actually used a crossing card. Yet how could they prove it? [24]

Under border reciprocity American officials have, in effect, surrendered control over an important part of the procedure for determining the applicant's qualifications. As it is, Mexican migration officials for many years have been authorized to issue a local passport (FM-13) to any citizen who can establish a six-months or more residency in a border community. There has always been a notorious traffic in this "local passport" (*tarjeta local*).

Commonly an applicant who cannot get a Mexican federal or state passport in the interior, or a consular visa, moves to the border, and shortly has the FM-13 in hand. [25] With this and a couple of specious letters showing permanent employment in a Mexican border town, he or she then applies to the nearest American immigration office for the border-crossing card, I-186. American officials must then determine if the FM-13 has been properly issued.

Until 1970, when Congress began to investigate illegal-alien questions, many American consular officers took the FM-13 at face value and issued visitors' visas in a wholesale manner. Now there is a more conscientious consular effort to check out an applicant's background. Still immigration officers complain that inexperienced, "come-and-go" consuls accept applications with excessive leniency, leaving to port inspectors the problem of rejecting consular approval, as well as questioning the good word of Mexican officials, including municipal authorities who, in some cases, as in Nuevo Laredo, certify the residential requirements of the *mica* applicant. This is a touchy matter that calls into question the whole spirit of border cooperation, reciprocity, integrity, and national sensitivities. Lacking manpower to check it all out, the Immigration Service has tended to be permissive. [26]

The Consular Connection

American consuls abroad receive little special training in the handling of migratory situations, country by country. Expertise in visa work receives relatively little recognition from the State Department, and morale tends to be low. As soon as a visa officer has acquired experience, it seems he is transferred to another continent. His stay in any post is rarely more than two years. [27] The most serious difficulty is the lack of personnel for determining the validity of an avalanche of applications for visas and visitor cards. [28] The American Consulate in Monterrey, which is responsible for a district covering nearly a third of Mexico and handles more visa applications than any other American office except Manila, is a case in point. In fiscal 1973 and again in 1974, the Monterrey consulate issued over 20,000 immigrant visas and twice as many non-immigrant visas. Yet only three persons were examining applicants, occasionally digging at a fraud problem that may have involved a remote mountain village. Said a visa official, "If the State Department wants it any other way they'll just have to put more people on the job." [29]

Another consul explained it this way:

Today nearly all of the applicants for an immigrant visa are connected with what was originally an illegal entry. They come to our waiting room with all their papers put in order by an immigration counselor, some of them shady characters, who usually know all the angles and technicalities of the law. They expect a visa right away, and they show birth certificates, letters from employers, papers for a "citizen child," or marriage to an American citizen, testimonials of good character, skilled-labor experience, and so on. All such statements are for sale in Mexico and the United States, and there is the question of deportation records and false names, or maybe a wife and children in Mexico not yet revealed. Then there is the matter of tourist visas and border-crossing cards. We often suspect that these will be used to take a job, but can we prove intention? The tourist applicant shows us money, maybe it's "spot money" loaned for the occasion. Or, he shows us a letter that he is permanently employed in Mexico and has every reason to return to his job, maybe it's a fake. There is no way we can check all this out, although we do our best.[30]

On September 12, 1973, Joshua Eilberg, Chairman of the House Immigration Subcommittee, commented on the effect of rising work loads and overworked consuls: "Thousands of illegal aliens come into this country every year because consular officials are making only cursory investigations of visa applicants. This is not the fault of the men in the consulates, but of the State Department which refuses to send enough trained personnel abroad to do this kind of work."[31] The trend since the early 1960s has been in the direction of more visa work and less personnel, as the figures in Table 1 suggest.

The State Department and its foreign service in Mexico have taken some steps to reduce the incidence of false papers. For instance, they are insisting that Mexican certificates of birth, marriage, and residence be issued or notarized by the state archives of vital statistics, rather than by the village registries, which have often been open to bribes or special pleading.[32] The State Department also managed to remove in the summer of 1974 the much-lamented Article I of the United States-Mexico Consular Agreement of November 12, 1953, whereby Mexican federal, state, and city officials, and all personnel in government subsidiaries, including schoolteachers, railway workers, and a

Table 1

	Immigrant Visas Issued	*Non-immigrant Visas Issued*	*Consular Officers*
1962	273,190	775,027	536
1972	293,966	2,290,576	494

Source: U.S. Congress, *Review of the Administration of the Immigration and Nationality Act, Hearings before the Subcommittee on Immigration, Citizenship, and International Law*, 93rd Cong., 1 Sess. (1973), pp. 176-178.

host of minor office workers, and members of their families, could cross the border without a visa examination on a reciprocity basis with American federal officials. "Hopefully, this will put an end to all those underpaid public officials from Mexico who seek employment in Illinois." [33] Furthermore, since 1975 consular personnel in Mexico has increased slightly, mainly because of American public outcry over American youths held in Mexican jails on drug charges.

Border Inspection Split

The only persons professionally trained for migrant inspection are officers of the Immigration Service. As trainees they undergo fourteen weeks of formal instruction at the Immigration Border Patrol Academy at Port Isabel, Texas, customarily followed by an "apprenticeship" in the Border Patrol, whereby experience is gained in recognizing "wetback types" and fake credentials. Some officers then transfer to immigration inspection, and some to the Customs Service, under the U.S. Treasury. As a rule those with Border Patrol training have been the best watchdogs on the border. Although most customs officers have lacked such training, they have been doing a major part of the immigrant inspection work at ports of entry for many years because the INS has lacked manpower. At major ports like El Paso and San Isidro, traffic lanes checked by customs officers, and even by Agricultural and Public Health officers, have been considered "soft spots" by professional guides, who have a perfect understanding of inspection procedures. [34] They also understand that the principal concern of customs personnel is not illegal entry or false documents per se but contraband goods. One result has been much flashing of documents on the border and very uneven scrutiny. Another result has been infighting between underfunded immigration officials and better-funded customs people over the control of funds, personnel, procedures, and even over the disposition of illegal aliens and contraband. Only since 1973 have federal administrators made a serious attempt to study, test, and reform border inspection procedures. Increasingly government reports have strongly urged that border inspection efforts be managed by a single agency. [35]

Hospitality Leaks

Another inspectional fissure has been local reciprocity by quasi-feudal border provinces. On border fiesta days held by twin cities, like Laredo and Nuevo Laredo, Mexican families and transients by the tens of thousands have been allowed to cross the bridge without inspection, especially during the George Washington's Birthday celebration, which lasts three days. Illegal aliens from all over Mexico await these "open port" days. Once across the bridge they can lie low in rooming houses or with Chicano *parientes*; when the Border Patrol relaxes its vigilance on roads leading into "federal territory," they strike out for the interior. *¿Quién es Jorge Washington?*

Also, since about 1952 pregnant women on "shopping missions" have not been stopped from crossing over to a border town and, in the words of an immigrant inspector, "leaving a little basket at Uncle Sam's doorstep," that is, a citizen child born in a "gringo hospital," sometimes in a charity ward. [36] Some of the advantages of such a birth are that the child can be placed with friends or relatives on the American side and attend public schools free; later the child can choose to work or live in the United States and bring in a Mexican spouse. Until reform law P.L. 94-571 was passed on October 20, 1976, immigrant workers received special visa preferences for having a citizen child, usually born while the parents were clandestinely in the United States. For others, the citizen child is a long-term investment. At age twenty-one the citizen child (and there is a huge crop, according to immigration officers) can fulfill kinship obligations by legally bringing in his or her parents under the "immediate relative" priorities of American immigration law.

Actually many "American births" never occur on the American side. Midwives of Mexican descent in Texas border counties for years have made a business of registering "Mexican-American births" at the local court house, although the child was born on the other side. Another practice, less frequent, has been to baptize "visitor children" in American churches and then offer a baptismal certificate as proof of native birth, as is the custom in rural Mexico. [37]

One-Sided Border Watch

Apparently the only times that the two "good neighbors" have cooperated effectively in border control were during the days of Geronimo and Indian raiders and during certain phases of the bracero program (1942-1964). Otherwise guides and flatboats have continued to ply their trade within sight of Mexican border migration offices. Leaving the country without proper documentation and the recruiting of persons within Mexico have been punishable offenses for years under Mexican population and migration laws, but such provisions have been used primarily by migration and customs officers to shake down outgoing or incoming wetbacks (*mojados*), as well as hookers (*enganchistas*), fixers (*coyotes*), boatmen (*pateros*), and guides (*polleros*). [38]

In accordance with fixed policy the Secretary of Internal Affairs (*Gobernación*) has, off and on since 1915, sought to dissuade migrants from leaving the country, especially if they lacked a protective labor contract. In 1974 the Echeverría government, which had sought in vain to establish a new bracero contract program, again charged Mexican border authorities to watch for undocumented migrants and to discourage their exit; and the Population Law of that year again provided for fines and imprisonment for contractors and smugglers operating in Mexico, including those transporting alien workers, such as Guatemalans, across the country. [39] In fact, both governments, following the recommendations of twin interagency commissions on surreptitious labor migration established by executive orders in 1972, have taken cooperative measures, particularly in regard to deportation procedures, but not in regard to a joint border patrol.

Actually, the Mexican government has never, in its concern for an economic safety valve, imposed penalties on undocumented workers. Mexican officials have cooperated in massive non-penalty deportations, allowing bus, train, and air lifts to return a portion of *mojados* to Mexico's interior at American or deportee expense. However, all such forms of cooperation are delicately strung and hang on the cultivation of *compadre* relations with supersensitive Mexican officials.

Lack of Interagency Cooperation

Aside from the Immigration Service, almost no American agencies, federal, state, or municipal, have been obligated by law to check for and report illegal aliens. Since the INS and the consular visa service are hopelessly under-manned, this situation has led to a unique form of foreign aid. Not only do Third World poverty folk have easy access to the labor market, but whether legally admitted residents or not, they have easy access to public assistance. A common joke in New York City, Miami, or Los Angeles is the first sentence of Berlitz English that the new immigrant learns on arrival: "Where is the welfare office?"

After the Supreme Court decision of June 14, 1971 (*Graham v Richardson*, 403 U.S. 365), the Social Security Amendments of 1972 (P.L. 92-603; 86 Stat. 1329), and subsequent regulations, illegal aliens (but not legal ones) were barred from participation in such federal programs as Supplemental Security Income for the Aged, Blind, and Disabled, Aid to Families with Dependent Children, Medicaid-Medicare, and food stamps. Later, the Unemployment Compensation Amendments of October 20, 1976 (P.L. 94-566), also excluded illegals.

Actually, up until the revised HEW regulations of 1974, there were no clear distinctions in the claims made on a vast spread of social assistance and em-ployment programs by native residents, legal aliens, and illegal ones. Federal war-on-poverty guidelines instructed all agencies using federal funds to adhere only to the criteria of need and local residence. [40]

Moreover, HEW regulations served only as imprecise guidelines so that aliens or "equity cases" residing "under color of law" could still be entitled to public assistance. Moreover, immigrant investigators still face the same replies from social agencies as from employers: "We are not an enforcement agency." "Clients are a confidential matter." Such responses come from state and local welfare administrations, Office of Economic Opportunity, Model Cities, Head Start, legal services for the poor, public health and hospital services, food commodity and food stamp programs, employment services of the Departments of Agriculture and Labor, migrant labor councils, coop and commune experiments with federal funding, employment training such as Job Corps and SER, and the public schools. The same applies to the private sector: industrial employers, labor unions, church-run charities, United Fund, immigrant-protection societies, American Civil Liberties Union, migrant ministries, Community Service Organization, Catholic Campaign for Human Development, Mexican-American Legal Defense Fund, and many others. [41]

The federal regulations of 1974 inspired several states, such as Arizona, and the attorney general of Texas (February 5, 1975), to rule against illegals on welfare, and moved the State of California to authorize welfare, health, and employment personnel to report suspect immigrant applications to INS authorities. But, typically, a California state judge opined (December 1974) that local officials need not ascertain the legal status of an alien before granting eligibility for assistance. Meanwhile, merely informing alien applicants of a possible check by the INS has caused some withdrawals and tax savings. (For the controversy on socioeconomic costs, see Chapter 10.)

The historic public-charge clause in immigration law provides that legal aliens who end up on public assistance within five years of admission are deportable unless there is cost reimbursement. But affidavits of support have never been legally binding and are cheerfully signed by sponsors—a growing racket. And due to another loophole in the law, the INS cannot apply the public-charge provision unless the welfare department initiates a demand for repayment, a very rare occurrence.

Furthermore, the law allows the immigrant to recur to public assistance due to certain post-admission circumstances such as unexpected job loss or disability. This allowance bears heavily on the amnesty movement for several million Third World illegals, who have minimal job skills, are functionally illiterate in English, and often have extended families to support. Virtually no legal or legalized alien has been deported since the depression-struck 1930s under the public-charge proviso, but some state and local welfare offices, overrun by newly arrived immigrants, like Westchester County, New York, would like to pass on a multimillion dollar tax bill to the federal government. (A vast viewing audience saw this situation graphically portrayed in a CBS television documentary, "How Many Aliens on Welfare?", produced by Martin Phillips, on *60 Minutes*, May 21, 1977.)

In another matter of great import, the universal use of social security cards as "job passports," cooperation with the Social Security Administration has been trifling. The SSA Amendments of 1972 require that all applicants establish their citizenship or alien status and that a card number be assigned to each incoming immigrant, and provide that willful fraud be punished by a fine of $1,000 and/or imprisonment up to one year, and, further, that the INS be notified if records indicate illegal employment. Yet one arm of the federal octopus always works against another. The Privacy Act of 1974 virtually nullified inter-agency cooperation. Still social security numbers are now used, with congressional approval, to track down absent fathers of families on welfare, in spite of the "police state!" outcry and even though social security cards are now stamped: "For social security purposes only—not for identification." The upset authors of the "Rodino bill," H.R. 8713, would have specifically authorized cooperation between the fantastic HEW conglomerate and the INS.

At the insistence of the Immigration Service, the Internal Revenue Service has investigated unpaid taxes, but most employers of illegals are careful to deduct taxes from all paychecks. Although this is done primarily as a "cover," some revisionist researchers argue that undocumented workers are deserving taxpayers. (See Chapter 10.)

Top immigration officials in congressional hearings, a major study of illegal workers by North and Houstoun (prepared for the Department of Labor), and the President's Domestic Council Committee on Illegal Aliens (set up in January 1975) have all strongly urged a plan of federal cooperation on illegal aliens, including possibly an interagency task force, coordinated at the cabinet level, to enforce immigration laws, minimum wages, safety standards, tax deductions, and social assistance regulations. [42]

State and local law enforcement agencies usually assist INS officers, and of course, countless tips are received from paid informants and anonymous sources. However, other federal agencies, better funded than the INS, seek to protect underprivileged minorities from "oppression" by such "racist enforcement agencies" as the Border Patrol, the Texas Rangers, the Deputy Sheriffs of Los Angeles County, or the Chicago police. Currently the Immigration Service is plastered with class-action suits and injunctions sponsored by federally funded migrant councils and civil libertarians, the purpose of which, simply stated, is to remove immigration vigilance from highways, streets, social agencies, and job sites as an offensive and discriminatory imposition on the civil rights of brown-skinned Americans and legal resident aliens. Chicano militants, like Chávez, have wildly charged that the hated *Patrulla* shoots down illegal aliens. [43]

Protests by ethnic leaders and legal-aid lawyers have, in fact, created a hornet's nest of outrage against "totalitarian alien raids," such as that which netted around 11,500 illegals in Los Angeles from May 23 to June 20, 1973. [44] This may have been the last sweep of its kind, for Chicano barrios have been made practically off limits by judicial decisions, for instance, *Illinois Migrant Council v. Alva A. Pilliod et al.* (No. 74C311), by which a U.S. district court judge issued, on July 29, 1975, a preliminary injunction against questioning suspected aliens on the streets or in public places. This injunction, yet to be tested, could hold for the entire country.

Other decisions reduced Border Patrol checkpoints in California and

Arizona, and seriously impaired a long-standing authority to question and search vehicles for suspected aliens and smugglers, on the grounds of violating the Fourth Amendment, as decided in *United States v. Baca* (S.D. Cal., 1973), *United States v. Almedia-Sánchez* (R 13 U.S. 266, 1973), or *United States v. Brignoni-Ponce* (422 U.S. 873, 876). The Supreme Court has been very divided, but in *United States v. Martinez-Fuerte et al.* (No. 74-1560, July 6, 1976), a majority at least upheld the legality of questioning. Most checkpoints were restored in border areas, but the ultimate fate of such control points seems still in doubt.

Mother America

Undoubtedly court decisions, as well as legislative reluctance to face square-ly the alien dilemma, have been influenced by symbolic interpretations of American liberties and due process guarantees. As immigration officers see it, aliens from Latin America and elsewhere have on their side, if not the Virgin of Guadalupe (Patroness of the Americas), the mother image of the Statue of Liberty. Representative of countless emotional protests against immigration control is a letter of January 9, 1973, to the U.S. Attorney General, by the presi-dent of a New York lawyers association in behalf of its many clients:

Dear Sir: Inscribed at the base of the Statue of Liberty, the words of Emma Lazarus proclaim to the world—"Give me your tired, your poor, your huddled masses yearning to breathe free. Send these the tempest tossed to me. I lift my torch beyond the sea."

This Association, dedicated to the fair administration of our immigration laws, firmly believes that these stirring words best describe the immigration philosophy of the United States as a "Nation of Immigrants."

We regret that recent practices of the Immigration and Naturalization Service have given us serious cause to doubt that our Government also subscribes to the philosophy set forth by Miss Lazarus. . . .

We vigorously protest . . . and urge you to intervene. [45]

In a word, federal authorities, if they would uphold immigration standards fixed by law, find themselves working against a sacred image which can be easily invoked to cover any group of "refugees."

To Fence or Not to Fence?

For some years there has been some high chain-link fencing near Yuma, San Isidro, Nogales, and El Paso—a mere 24 miles in all. Yet, incredibly, there has been none from El Paso southeast to Brownsville, a 1,000-mile stretch that has always served as the main overland "wetback funnel" into the United States. Skeleton crews of border guards point out that fencing in strategic locations, particularly where twin cities merge, as at Brownsville and Matamoros, would not solve the escalating problem of entry by false documents or concealed motives, but it would facilitate control of line jumping, drug smuggling, and petty thievery, which absorbs a good part of the scarce border guard's energy. [46]

Actually, most objections to fencing come from the American side, as in Texas where for generations employers have been accustomed to "Mexican help." And there is the peculiar circular argument of immigration officials pointing to gaping holes in any fence: "A fence would cut down on patrol-force needs but we don't have enough men to watch the fence." [47]

During the Bracero Program (1942-1964) it was proposed that the United States-Mexico Boundary Commission, or some other agency, should build more fencing. But congressmen generally oppose a fence on the boundaries of American Democracy (but not ocean moats) as an abhorrent idea altogether: "Why can't they behave like Canadians?" [48] Likewise, border chambers of commerce, notably in south Texas, and binational business fraternity groups like to talk of "open borders," "twin cities," and "gateways," and insist that fence control would positively offend Mexico. Such opposition led to the removal of immigration "watch towers" in certain Texas border towns. [49]

Mexican officials and editorialists routinely denounce fencing, but the official position is that the United States has a sovereign right to fence its side of the border. Actually some Mexican officials have wondered why *Tío Sam*, who dutifully keeps escorting millions of *mojados* back to the starting line, did not years ago build a fencing system, like the one for livestock across most of the border. [50] Some border residents have also wondered about it: "How would a fence differ much in principle from miles of border sand strips dragged smooth by the Border Patrol and watched carefully for footprints?" [51]

Given the rapid buildup of population pressures in Mexico's border development zone it seems inevitable that some form of fence control would impinge on the rhetoric of the Good Neighbor. In 1973 the American government began quietly extending the use of electronic detectors, first used in Vietnam, at crossing points frequently used by wets and dope smugglers. [52] There were at first Mexican protests, but after inspecting the system, high Mexican officials made no further public objections. [53] The INS has sought to cover about 350 miles of border strips with "sensors," but these are no better than the force available to watch the strips. At night electronic dashboards light up like tilted pinball machines, and patrolmen, when available, dash out to intercept. But the older border-smuggling business has made its adjustments too, sending out decoy groups, setting off false alarms, and even stealing detectors, while the main body of infiltrators crosses somewhere else. [54] Thus far sensors have had little deterrent effect.

No Effective Prosecution of Alien Smugglers

According to the Immigration and Nationality Act of June 27, 1952 (Sec. 274), any person who knowingly brings in an illegal alien, or knowingly induces, conceals, or harbors an illegal alien, "shall be guilty of a felony, and upon conviction thereof shall be punished by a fine not to exceed $2,000 or by imprisonment for a term not to exceed five years or both." In fiscal 1975 the Border Patrol located 6,860 alien smugglers, most of them Mexicans and Mexican Americans. However, alien smuggling has never been effectively prosecuted. Amazingly the INS has not yet been authorized to confiscate vehicles used by alien smugglers unless they are found carrying contraband as well. [55] Prosecution has also been frustrated because smuggled aliens—following the "wetback code"—rarely testify against one who aided them, and so the Attorney General's office has dropped most prosecution efforts. [56]

In cases of successful prosecution most federal or district judges have been gullible and indulgent. Typically, prosecution results were like those described for the following Denver case:

We all worked hard to prepare this case. And what sentences did these two smugglers get for hauling in 38 persons in a horse trailer at $200 each? The district judge gave the one five days and a $500 fine, first offense. He gave the other, probably not a first offender, a $2,000 fine, and four months in jail, but immediately ordered a work-release so that this person could pay the fine, and also return the money taken from the Mexican nationals. Sad to say, the six persons who agreed to testify suffered most for they spent three months in jail waiting for the trial to come up. And, of course, we had to pay the full cost of their maintenance in the county jail at about $13 dollars a day. [57]

For years the average sentence for first and second offenders has been a fine of $150 to $2,000, often suspended in part. Smuggling rings, and increasingly labor racketeers, engaged in a multimillion dollar "cheap-labor" business can easily afford to lose a driver now and then, put up money to cover bonds and minor fines for other "pawns," and each time learn to profit from mistakes. Once in a while, however, the Immigration Service has busted a major ring, at least temporarily, as in Los Angeles in 1973:

Described by newspapers as a $3 Million-a-year smuggling ring, the operation, known as "Las Hueras" or "The Blondes," was allegedly led by three Los Angeles women. Aliens would be contacted in Tijuana, Mexico, and for $225 transported through the U.S. port of entry, and temporarily housed at private homes and motels to await eventual relocation in Los Angeles. The ring brought as many as 50 aliens into the United States each day. As the result of the Service probe, 25 indictments were returned charging conspiracy to smuggle, harbor, and transport illegal aliens. [58]

Meanwhile, prosecution of alien smugglers has been made even more difficult and costly by a court decision of 1975 requiring that all smuggled aliens intercepted in a shipment be held as material witnesses, a condition that a penurious Immigration Service can hardly meet. On the other hand, several current House bills would authorize confiscation of smugglers' vehicles.

Insufficient Prosecution of Illegal Aliens

Since 1929 American immigration law has provided for penalties against illegal entry by individuals:

Any alien who after March 4, 1929, enters the United States at any time or place other than as designated by immigration officials or eludes examination or inspection by immigration officials, or obtains entry to the United States by a willfully false or misleading representation or the willful concealing of material fact, shall be guilty of a misdemeanor and, on conviction, shall be punished by imprisonment for not more than one year or by a fine of not more than $1000, or by both.[59]

By the Immigration and Nationality Act of 1952 (Sec. 275), a second offense after formal deportation may be considered a felony and thus subject to more severe penalties, up to two years in prison and a fine of not more than $1,000, or both. Yet, as in the past, Mexican illegals have been caught an average of three to five times before being fingerprinted and formally deported. In fiscal 1971 only 12,163 were formally deported out of some 290,000 apprehensions. In fiscal 1974 this figure decreased to 11,678 even though 709,959 Mexican aliens were apprehended in that year.[60]

Repeaters, if they can be recognized under their many aliases, usually have not been prosecuted until the fourth time. Here again magistrates and district judges as a rule have been unusually permissive on the theory that a poor man looking for a job is not committing an overt crime. A first conviction has usually carried a sentence of six months to two years, and a fine of $100 to $1,000, but often these penalties have been suspended in whole or in part.[61] Immigration inspectors and border patrolmen frequently have expressed their bitter disappointment at judges who have given condescending lectures, instead of exemplary penalties, to inveterate violators of federal immigration statutes.

At all times aliens have the same rights as native citizens to due process protection, since they are presumed citizens until proven otherwise. In immigration hearings, the government is not obligated to pay for counsel, but this is often provided, if need be, by immigrant aid societies. Now the monumental court problem posed by hundreds of daily arrests is "solved" by having the apprehended alien "waive his or her rights" by signing a non-penalty, voluntary departure (under safeguard usually), which also saves laborious formal deportations requiring the cooperation of two governments.

Lack of detention funds and facilities, and the reluctance of material witnesses to testify, are some reasons why the apprehended illegal is usually whisked out of the country in thirty-six to fifty-two hours. After a few square meals at a detention center, the deportee may end up on a bus, train, or plane, heading for Mexico's border or interior, to a point hopefully "near the home town." All money and valuables are religiously returned, but if there is money in hand, the deportee is charged the minimum cost of transportation; "otherwise his Uncle Sam pays for it."[62] Some have been so pleased with security-travel at cut rates that after a season of good earnings, at Christmas time they have purposely surrendered to *la migra* for a safe ride, or even a free ride, across a border notorious for bushwhackers and rapacious customs agents. In any case, as critics have frequently asked in congressional hearings: Does a quick ride home to see relatives on a "voluntary return" have any deterrent effect? And do the returnees ever touch home base? It has been alleged that operators of the California plane lift, run by a Mexican contract company, take payoffs to return deportees to the border and although these allegations have been disputed, it is not uncommon, according to some immigration officers, for deportees to get off Mexican-run bus lifts not far from the border.[63] Actually, for lack of funds, most "non-penalty returns" are "dumped" into Mexican border towns, from where the legendary "Speedy González" bounces back with amazing ease.

Fraudulent use of immigration papers does not usually receive first-time leniency, but aware of this, the new-style *mojado*, once over the line, conceals or mails his border-crossing card to Mexico. Those caught using false documents or making false claims of American citizenship, or the bumbling repeater, may be tried rapidly by a magistrate system that encourages the offender "to cop a plea," that is, plead guilty and waive a court hearing on the understanding that the charge will be scaled down from a felony to a misdemeanor and that the penalty will be light, perhaps a fine that may depend on how much money one has in pocket. Mexican consuls have protested fines, arguing that the money may be from Mexico and that the deportee needs money to go home. Consequently some judges have reduced fines to a point where they seem to provide a bus ticket back to the United States.[64]

Although some district judges, particularly in flooded border cities, have been getting tougher with undocumented aliens, and although the magistrate system, inaugurated by the Federal Magistrates Act of October 17, 1968, has facilitated convictions, convictions, fines, and prisons terms have not kept pace with the tidal flow of illicit aliens.

The "Texas Proviso"

Current immigration law, that of 1952, states that an employer can be charged with law breaking only if he is caught in the act of soliciting, transporting, or harboring illegal aliens. Oddly, under this so-called Texas Proviso, providing work, and even meals and living quarters, has not been considered harboring. Because aliens are reluctant witnesses and because middlemen serve as recruiters and contractors, only the most flagrant violations by employers can be penalized, as when a Los Angeles garment manufacturer refused to admit federal officers, who had already picked up twelve "witnes-

Table 2   Convictions for Immigration and Nationality Violations for
Recent Fiscal Years

(Figures cover all alien nationalities, but principally Mexican)

	1969	1971	1973	1975
Illegal entries	1,097	5,084	13,534	11,094
Re-entries of deported aliens	1,413	1,094	603	494
Bringing in or harboring aliens	563	718	738	370
Fraud and misuse of entry permits	863	1,012	206	125
Other fraud or false statements	49	26	85	61
Alien registration or address violations	0	0	11	20
Alien crewmen overstayed	7	16	22	25
Stowaways	0	2	0	0
Perjury	1	0	2	1
Immoral purposes	0	0	2	0
False representations as U.S. citizens	497	574	64	112
Related fraud	1	1	3	3
Reproduction of papers	0	0	5	20
All other violations	132	783	183	486
Totals	4,623	9,310	15,458	12,811
Aggregate fines	$172,105	$461,231	$1,008,299	$754,746
Aggregate imprisonment— in years	3,970	5,364	5,755	5,313
Total of all aliens apprehended	283,577	420,126	655,968	766,600
Mexican aliens apprehended	201,636	348,178	576,823	680,392
Formal deportations of Mexican aliens	6,859	12,163	10,402	14,512

Source: Adapted from Tables 26A, 27B, 52, 53 and 54 of the U.S. Immigration and Naturalization Service, *Annual Report*, 1969-1975.

ses" from his plant.[65] But so long as an employer opens the gate he is beyond the law. For over fifty years southwestern employers have been exploiting this gap in congressional law, and now this exploitation has spread over the whole country.

For years immigration, labor, consular, and even Mexican officials have told

Congress that penalties for employers of illicit aliens is a *sine qua non* of "wetback control." But it was the State of California that passed the first law in American history making it illegal for an employer knowingly to hire illegal aliens, and providing fines up to $500 for each violation. This Dixon-Arnett law of November 8, 1971, was incorporated in 1972 into the California Labor Code (S. 2805, a, b, and c), and quickly denounced by Chicanos and civil rightists as prejudicial to the employment of ethnic minorities. As expected, a lower court held it unconstitutional. [66]

The question is as old as the federal republic: Can a state or a port city, like New York, Honolulu, or Miami, take the initiative from Congress on cumulative immigration problems? In the past such initiatives have sometimes served to push Congress or the high court to act. Thus on February 25, 1976, in an unprecedented decision, the Supreme Court upheld the California law, holding that congressional failure to act on a nationwide question did not invalidate the state's authority to safeguard the well-being of its workers under established police powers, so long as the state did not attempt to set conditions of admission and residence, a federal preserve. [67] The impact, if any, of this decision on future state legislation and employment patterns is not yet clear.

Meantime, influenced by state expectations of federal action, Congress started extensive hearings on illegal aliens, and finally hammered out the Rodino bills in 1971-1974. A key provision was that employers would be subject to a rather timid three-step civil penalty procedure: (1) a warning; (2) if the employer persisted in hiring illegals, an injunction; and (3) if the injunction was defied, fines and prosecution. Under a revised Rodino bill (H.R. 8713), pending since September 24, 1975, the employer, contractor, or referral agent would be liable, after ignoring a preliminary citation issued by the Attorney General, to a fine of $500 for each illegal. Further infractions could lead, after proper hearing, to a misdemeanor, higher fines, and possible imprisonment. Also, H.R. 8713 would eliminate the Texas Proviso.

After seven years of inaction, the Senate Judiciary Committee produced S. 3074, a bill introduced by Chairman James O. Eastland on March 4, 1976, that proposed penalties and modifications in immigration law similar to the Rodino and other bills, but reflecting Eastland's long-standing defense of employer interests. Thus an unsworn statement obtained from the job applicant would be deemed prima facie proof that a bona fide inquiry had been made as to the civil status of the applicant and would serve to absolve employer, contractor, or referrer from further responsibility. Also significant, S. 3074 would provide a more flexible alien-labor supply. The Attorney General would be able to admit more temporary "H-2" workers on employer requests, if the Secretary of Labor certified a need. In effect, this would provide for a modified bracero or guest-worker program. And, like the Rodino bill, the Senate version would have permitted the legalization of qualified aliens who had entered the country before July 1, 1968. [68]

False Documentation

The Immigration Service maintains a Fraudulent Document Center in Yuma, Arizona, where many false claims have been unmasked, including "mushroom cases" where over the years dozens of relatives have been brought in on what was originally a false document. [69] By all accounts the use of documentary fraud and misrepresentation of facts has been steadily increasing. [70] In fiscal 1974 Border Patrol agents detected 4,336 false claims to citizenship and 3,481 cases involving fraudulent use of border-crossing papers. [71] Most of these apprehensions involved Mexican nationals.

The forgery business, often using printing facilities in Mexico, has continued to duplicate all kinds of documents, including Chicano and Puerto Rican birth certificates to cover Spanish-speaking aliens in Chicago, New York, and other cities. The Immigrant Alien Receipt Card, I-151, issued to all legal immigrants including the so-called greencard commuter, has been so artfully forged that only a machine could detect the fact. The same is true for border-crossing cards and temporary permits to visit the interior. [72]

In recent times forgers have managed to penetrate the Immigration Service itself, acquiring seals, stamps, forms, cards, and other materials. A scandal— the first of its kind—that broke open in 1972, revealed that three or four officers on the California border were actually involved in peddling immigration documents and cooperating with marijuana smugglers. The I-151 was then being commonly sold for $500 in Tijuana and Mexicali. To prove the point a Mexican reporter bought a "valid card" with his photo on it and had it prominently displayed in a Mexico City newspaper. [73]

The Central Office of the INS responded with "Operation Cleansweep," and set up an Internal Corruption Investigation Unit as a preventive measure. Also, a new Commissioner of Immigration was named to meet the growing crisis in immigration law enforcement. Leonard F. Chapman, a former Marine commander, took over this difficult assignment in December 1973. He quickly sought funds to replace the several valid versions of the immigrant alien card (I-151) with a uniform, tamper-proof document that can be scanned electronically. He also obtained more cooperation from Mexican officials in the prosecution of forgers residing over the border. [74] Thus far, however, the forgery business has suffered little in the aggregate from binational cooperation. [75]

Bills, such as H.R. 8713 or S. 3074, would have provided broader definitions and stiffer penalties for fraudulent use of entry documents. But what about civil documents, not all fraudulent? Seasonal wetbacks living-in on farms and ranches or as domestics usually do without identification papers. The new-style illegals, however, use a union card, a driver's license, a draft registration receipt, or the like, but most commonly the social security card. [76]

Since the 1930s social security numbers could be obtained wholesale merely by filling out a post-office form. Other numbers were invented on the spot by the job applicant or his employer. Finally, the Social Security Administration, at the insistence of the Immigration Service, and beginning with the congressional revisions of 1972, has tightened up application procedures. Since 1974 the applicant must present evidence of American birth or legal entry. Also, the SSA has been trying to set up a cross-reference system for over 150 million cards so that multiple use of the same number, or a false number, might lead to an immigration check. Moreover, all incoming legal aliens are now issued a social security number at the time of entry, whether seeking employment or not. Nevertheless, hundreds of thousands of misused cards are still in circulation, and it still takes months to discover misuse or invented numbers. [77]

Increasingly, false birth certificates, in lieu of immigrant papers, are being used to cover illegal employment and settlement. Such papers are for sale in sleazy taverns throughout the country, but many aliens and their helpers have discovered that a plausible copy can be obtained simply by writing to a county court house. In some cases cemeteries are scrutinized for match-ups, like "Chinese immigration slots," and often relatives are covered in this way. With such a document an alien can frequently pass for a Mexican American from, say, south Texas, or New Mexico, and also meet the new regulations for a social security card. Meanwhile, "sham marriage," partly because it is difficult to prove "intent," has been rapidly developing into another major problem in migration control. [78]

Convictions for dealers in false papers and sham marriages require arduous efforts by INS personnel, Department of Justice attorneys, and local officials, again, with prospects of mild penalties or probation. [79] Now and then, however, an "exemplary sentence" is obtained:

As the result of liaison between Service officers and New York State officials . . . a Federal indictment was obtained charging Juan Contreras (owner of an immigration consultant company) with nine counts involving the sale of fraudulent immigration documents and birth certificates. . . . Contreras on January 18, 1973, was sentenced to 2 years' imprisonment, to begin after completion of the 4-year sentence resulting from the violation of the New York State criminal statutes. [80]

Lack of Immigration Manpower and Facilities

Without doubt the basic reason why immigration law and control have never been firmly established on American borders, or anywhere, is that Congress and the President's Office of Management and Budget have never given the low-profile Immigration and Naturalization Service sufficient funds to master the illegal-alien problem. [81] Legislators representing the so-called farm bloc and agricultural associations frequently worked, as in the 1950s, to cut the operational budget of a defenseless federal agency lacking any cabinet-level visibility . . . "in a nation of immigrants." [82] In fact, the INS was given only a paltry million dollars in 1924 to develop a border patrol for the entire republic! The possible exceptions to fiscal poverty were the 1930s, when Mexican campesinos were retreating to Mexico, and the period 1954-1960, when Attorney General Herbert S. Brownell and an outstanding reformist Commissioner of Immigration, Lt. General Joseph M. Swing, hand-picked "to defend the Mexican border," had the full support of the Eisenhower administration in a remarkable and successful effort to cut off the "wetback invasion," then mainly an agricultural phenomenon in the Southwest.

Although arrests of Mexican illegals surged dramatically from 43,844 in fiscal 1964 to 709,959 in fiscal 1974, the number of field officers in the Immigration Service rose by only a few hundred. Under the circumstances Commissioner of Immigration Raymond F. Farrell (1961-1973), an undistinguished bureaucrat in four administrations, had little choice but to concentrate most field personnel in the states facing Mexico, thus leaving the Canadian border, coastal areas, and interior cities without adequate vigilance. In 1974 the Service had approximately 1,400 immigration inspectors along the confines of the country at some 430 ports of entry for only perfunctory day and night inspection. By that year almost 90 percent of the entire Border Patrol force of nearly 1,800 unionized men was doing shift work near the Mexican border. [83]

The illegal that slipped through the "first line of defense," (averaging about one patrolman, day and night, for every ten miles of border line) then usually found the interior of the country wide open, except for occasional "special details." In 1974 the Service had scarcely 800 investigators to work the heartland, mostly in magnet cities such as Los Angeles, Detroit, and Chicago. Other meccas for illegals had only token forces. In Houston, as late as 1975, there were only eight investigators to comb through a metropolitan area containing 2.5 million people; Dallas, including Fort Worth and a vast hinterland, had but eleven investigators. The Denver district office, responsible for Colorado, Utah, and Wyoming, had but seven investigators and thirteen men in all. Moreover, like other federal agencies, much personnel was "inactivated" by piles of paper work. Little wonder that harassed officials described the alien situation as "simply out of control," and repeatedly lamented: "If we had twice as many men we could pick up twice as many illegals," or "There's no more money to pay jailing costs so we have to let some go." [84]

Congressional hearings on government appropriations have frequently concluded that the President's Office of Management and Budget and the Department of Justice have for years ignored repetitive INS pleas for funding. Concerned members of the House Judiciary Committee, like Joshua Eilberg, have worked to put the Department of Justice and its agencies under direct congressional appropriations. As a result of the Crime Control Act of October 15, 1976 (P.L. 94-503), this long-needed arrangement will go into effect, but not until fiscal 1979.

In spite of a national employment crisis in fiscal 1975, apprehensions of illegal aliens decreased for lack of funds. The Ford administration allowed only modest budgetary increases in INS funding, mainly to expand the Border Patrol to around 2,400, to increase investigators to over 1,300, and to add a hundred more inspectors. Still a token force, but apprehensions once more shot upward. Taking into account paper work, inflation, federal unionism, Third World population pressures, and lack of border fencing, some INS officers think that the Service should have at least 50,000 employees and a billion dollar budget to watch a continental spread day and night. The figures in Table 3 suggest that the immigration officer is hopelessly outnumbered.

The apprehension of 616,630 Mexican illegals by the Border Patrol alone in fiscal 1974, and 579,448 in 1975, reflected concentration on border "salmon runs" like the Chula Vista sector, "gateway to California," and in certain internal job markets. But such figures may give the uninitiated reader the erroneous impression that Mexican nationals are the only serious illegal-entry problem. Not so. Of necessity other alien infiltrations have been relatively neglected. Estimates circulated in 1975 placed the total of all illegals in the United States from 6 to 12 million or more. For instance, according to an exploratory study carried out by Lesko and Associates for the INS in the fall of

Table 3   Alien Arrests and Immigration Service Resources

Fiscal Year	*1971*	*1972*	*1973*	*1974*	*1975*	*1976*	*1977*
Total alien apprehensions	420,126	505,949	655,968	788,145	766,600	866,433	1,042,215
Total Mexican apprehensions	348,178	430,213	576,823	709,959	680,392	781,438	954,778
Total personnel of INS	7,230	6,682	6,682	7,982	8,082	8,882	9,473
Total INS budget (millions of dollars)	121.9	130.9	137.5	155.2	181.3	213.6	245.0

Note: Apprehension and budget figures may vary.

Sources: INS, *Annual Report*, Tables 23, 27B; U.S. Congress, House, *Hearings before a Subcommittee on Appropriations . . .* 92d Cong., 1st Sess., 1971, Pt. 1, 788; 2d Sess., 1972, Pt. 1, 948; 93d Cong., 1st Sess., 1973, Pt. 1; 94th Cong., 1st Sess., 1976, Pt. 4, 628-719; House Committee on Government Operations. Subcommittee on Legal and Monetary Affairs, Immigration and Naturalization Regional Office Operations, Hearings, 93d Cong., 1st and 2d Sess., 1973-1974; and correspondence with Statistics Division of Central Office, INS, Washington, D.C. With a new alien rush underway following the amnesty promises of 1977 by President Carter, INS personnel still numbered only 10,071 in fiscal 1978 and the INS budget totaled only $266 million. The proposal for fiscal 1979 was 11,000 and $300 million respectively.

The resources and responsibilities of the INS should be compared to other federal agencies. For example, the FBI in fiscal 1978 had $500 million and 19,000 employees, and the Environmental Protection Agency $849 million and 10,200 employees.

1975, a panel of specialists gave an average estimate of 8.2 million illegals, of which possibly 5 million were of Mexican origin.[85] INS officials readily admit that the sharp rise in alien arrests since 1970 does not indicate better alien control but rather the massive inflow of poverty folk from Third World countries.

The Service, which does many rescue missions and other police-type duties, including customs work, was not prepared for the present challenge, and now has found itself hopelessly hooked on a treadmill of "voluntary returns," meaningless apprehension figures, and an increasing number of insolent repeaters and smugglers, who regard the immigration officer as a nuisance. The INS has not only lacked enforcement punch, but also the technical equipment to cope with faceless numbers. Although possessing some sophisticated equipment (developed in Vietnam) and mobile units, including a fleet of motor launches and observation planes (with about forty-nine pilots in 1975), and electronic sensors on some parts of the border, incredibly the INS did not have helicopters for border patrol until 1976. The deputy sheriffs of Los Angeles County had them in 1955. Also, Border Patrol radio communications have been monitored by smuggling outfits who seem better equipped. And although proud of such Indian-type skills as sign reading and tracking, the immigration officer usually cannot finger persistent repeaters, who use assorted names and stories and nimbly shift from one control district to another, because of lack of funds to maintain fingerprint and photo files on non-criminal aliens and to develop a computer checkout system.[86]

During the cold war atmoshere of the 1940s and 1950s, employers and their Washington spokesmen badgered the INS to "take it easy on wets," and for years patrolmen, lacking enforcement means anyway, followed unwritten directives to allow illegals to finish the harvest before putting them on the merry-go-round of voluntary returns. Again, for lack of means, immigration officers stationed along the Rio Grande have customarily allowed certain ranchers, farmers, and housewives to have Mexican help.[87] And now such permissiveness, bordering on collusion, has become a "control technique of an undermanned law enforcement agency." "We know where they are. They won't try to move until the end of the work period." Or "This rancher has always had wetbacks; just so he doesn't try to shift them on us we leave him alone. We got enough to do catching the ones going inland."[88]

For similar reasons deportees held over as witnesses or on other charges have been allowed to work for nearby farmers and ranchers and thus earn their own keep (at bargain prices for the employer, of course).[89] And so allegations of "palsy-walsy" relations with employers have been made, and the Mexican government has insisted on placing consular inspectors at detention centers. Moreover, for lack of facilities, undocumented women and children have virtually free access to the interior of the United States. Often immigration investigators have avoided picking them up, much as border patrolmen avoid stopping illegals headed back to Mexico for a vacation. In the San Antonio district in 1974, for instance, perhaps as many as 15,000 "wet maids" (wetback housemaids) had practically a free run of that labor market, in part because of the problem of making house arrests and in part for lack of separate detention and transportation facilities.[90]

Elsewhere throughout the United States several hundred thousand Mexican illegals, including many women, children, and old people, are under "vigilance," to be picked up sometime when manpower increases and paper work diminishes. But, of course, nature doesn't stand still. "They intermarry; they have citizen children; they find legal aid; they put down roots; and we'll probably never get them out."[91]

From what has been said thus far, it is hardly a surprise that some people believe the chief function of the Immigration Service in the Southwest has been to serve as a pliable control valve for a cheap labor supply. As Samora's study explained, it has all seemed like an enforcement game. American immigration policies, through selective application and periodic relaxation, have served to regulate the interests of agribusiness, and "it seems that in practice the Border Patrol functioned primarily to regulate the numbers that were already in the country."[92] Chávez of the United Farm Workers continues to make this charge.

This interpretation, which some critics of the Immigration Service now believe applies to all sectors of the economy, has always been widely believed in official circles in Mexico, and has led the Mexican government to assume that Mexican *mojados* are obviously indispensable in certain sectors of the American economy, and, further, that as their numbers grow the U.S. government will sooner or later negotiate with Mexico or with ethnic leaders in regard to the full civil and economic rights of the "undocumented working class."[93]

The Concensus Problem

In January 1974 Commissioner Chapman launched an intense media campaign to bring the "invisible alien" problem before civic groups at what seemed a most opportune time, that is, when there was widespread public concern about unemployment and aliens taking "American jobs." This public relations blitz, unique in its dimensions, was aimed at Rotary, Kiwanis, the American Legion, the California Fruit Growers Association, manufacturing groups, congressional committees, and the like. It sought to win support for INS funding and for legislation to outlaw the employment and recruitment of illegal workers, as well as to counter judicial maneuvers by ethnic and civil libertarians seeking to emasculate further the enforcement capability of the immigration officer. That campaign was supported by influential and widely read newspapers and magazines, like *The New York Times, The San Francisco Chronicle, U.S. News & World Report, Time,* and *Reader's Digest,* by syndicated columnists and commentators, like James Reston and Paul Harvey, and by major TV networks, like CBS, all of which carried special reports on illegal aliens and the need for government action.

However, the federal government, which monopolizes immigration affairs, found itself so beset with civil libertarian demands and competitive claims on the welfare state (extension of unemployment benefits, for example) that consistent attention could not be given to the alien problem even by the Attorney General's office, which afterall has the ultimate responsibility for enforcing immigration statutes and standards. And, as always, countervailing forces were also at work. As vacillating legislators received more input on illegal aliens from assorted interest groups and researchers, whatever may have been the public concensus for decisive action during the job crisis of 1974-1976 seemed to have eroded away as unemployment decreased from a high of nearly 9 percent in 1975 to around 7.2 percent in early 1977.

As Chapman and the Immigration Service then saw it, the media effort was a race with time, and apparently that race failed. While tens of billions of dollars were channeled to anti-poverty programs that helped to entrench undocumented ethnic groups as a vested clientele in the welfare state, the INS budget barely kept up with inflation. When the Commissioner was pressed by a member of the House Appropriations Committee in 1976 as to why he did not plead more insistently for funding to take preventive actions, this revealing exchange took place:

General Chapman: Well, I think in the past 2 years I have made something like 45 speeches, and I forget how many press conferences, all on that very point. . . . I think I have been before congressional committees 35 or 40 times, in which I made the same speech repeatedly.

Mr. Early: You know what I think, General. No one is listening.[94]

Other Responses by the Immigration Service, 1974-1976

There are other factors favoring wetbackism that could be identified, but at this point we might ask: What responses, besides those already mentioned, did the INS make under Chapman's leadership (December 1973-January 1977) to fiscal poverty and the diminishing power of search and arrest? While seeking funds and the reversal of court decisions through carefully prepared test cases, the Central Office shifted priorities from remedial actions, such as area search patrols in interior cities which offend civil rightists and ethnic leaders and trip off more injunctions, toward preventive measures, such as concentrating more of its skeleton crews and sensor equipment on the porous Mexican border, where all kinds of aliens have always found the nation's back door open.

Immigration inspectors began screening more carefully the hordes of daily border crossers, and since checkpoints on border highways were threatened or curtailed by court decisions, investigators and patrolmen gave more attention to air and bus terminals, freight trains, trucking firms, shrimp boats, mini-buses, and private planes near the border. Also, priority was given to removing illegals from higher-paying industrial and service jobs that, supposedly, could be filled by unemployed Americans, that is, if welfare-state benefits were not so available.[95]

The Immigration Service tried to anticipate the complaints and demands of ethnic coalitions, like the Forum of National Hispanic Organizations, founded in 1974. In 1975 the Commissioner created a liason office, headed by a Mexican American, to handle such "input."[96] Then in July 1976 the Department of Justice, under Edward Levy, a strong civil rights advocate, took an unprecedented step in American immigration history, and approved a Hispanic Advisory Committee that immediately sought to monitor immigration work and to put a Chicano in charge of the nation's Immigration and Naturalization Service, much as an Indian should be in charge of the BIA under the new rules of ethnic populism.

Meanwhile, after a bureaucratic shakeup and a morale-building effort, strategic reorganization of the INS was carried out in 1976. The headquarters of the Southern Region was shifted from Richmond to Dallas so that the Regional Commissioner at Dallas, like the Western Regional Commissioner at San Pedro, could apply more resources to the southern border and coast.[97] In addition, the INS tried, and with some success, to obtain voluntary cooperation from reputable companies that have commonly employed illegals, such as Great Western Sugar, Santa Fe Railroad, Del Monte, and National Can. But, in the nature of things, little headway was made with the countless satellite plants, piece-work "sweat shops," and construction firms scattered over metro areas like Los Angeles and Houston and operating on kick-back arrangements.[98]

While the variable immigrant card, I-151, was being replaced with a single tamper-proof document, immigration officials and reformists in Congress favored issuing new social security cards containing the bearer's signature, photo, and thumb print. But this proposal has always met with loud cries of "police state" and "too costly."[99]

According to Immigration Service veterans, other basic measures were needed to achieve control and to cut down on the INS taxi service for illegal aliens, for example, the employing of several thousand more field officers, perhaps recruited from the vast ranks of unemployed youths, or the authorizing of the INS (rather than a permissive and unknowledgeable judiciary) to impose directly, like the IRS or state traffic officials, administrative fines. The illegal repeater, like a bad driver, would face escalating fines and possibly imprisonment.

Following the creation in January 1975 of the President's Domestic Council

"The alien situation is under control . . . splat!
By Ernest G. Garrison, circa 1962. Mr. Garrison was for many years a border
patrolman.

Committee on Illegal Aliens, which represented all major branches of pan-
federalism, the INS proposed research studies to HEW, Labor, and other

agencies, to determine, if possible, the number of illegals, their tax contributions, and their impact on the labor market and on public assistance programs. Moreover, in 1976 the INS obtained $1 million for a seven-part study of illegals and the immigration-control problem.[100] Such studies, presently underway, may contribute more input or more ambivalence to future government decisions.

It is expected that the flood of economic refugees from the poverty-stricken Third World will roll on, for this inflow and the search for documentation have long since become a sordid, profitable, and institutionalized business.[101] Or as an immigration official who read *The Divine Comedy* once put it, the illegal alien has become the "rock of Sisyphus."[102]

By 1976 it seemed that the nation had settled into an impasse. Some federal agencies, like the Comptroller General's Office, and some members of Congress, most notably members of the House Subcommittee on Immigration, like Joshua Eilberg, strongly urged a uniform policy of immigration standards and a commonsense budget for the Immigration Service (an "orphan child" of the Department of Justice since the 1940s). On the other hand, groups like the Domestic Council Committee task force, taking into account ethnic input, divided their concern between the social costs of the migration of surplus people and the need for a more humane immigration policy.[103] Meantime, revisionist researchers discovered unsuspected assets in the uncontrolled influx of undocumented workers. (See Chapter 10.)

The present momentum, including growing discontent in Mexico, therefore suggests that the nation has entered a new era not of strict alien control but of ombudsmanship, amnesty proposals, and perennial socioeconomic accommodations, agency by agency, community by community, and politician by politician, to spring-fed Latino groups whose political muscle in the transitional social order is "just starting to be felt."[104] This was the situation faced by the populist Carter administration that took office in January 1977 and soon after took the controversial step of naming a spokesman for the Chicano community, Leonel J. Castillo, Commissioner of Immigration.

The new race-conscious commissioner soon made it plain that he was as much interested in policing a WASP immigration service as the Mexican border:

Q   Do you get out in the field much yourself to check on how your agents are performing?

A   I travel 50 to 60 percent of the time. I've made visits to our offices, unannounced and totally unrecognized, to see how they'd treat me if they thought I was just another immigrant. Sometimes I dress poorly and speak Spanish. It's been very instructive.[105]

The ghost of Santa Anna must have grinned.

Notes

1. For a large part, the first-hand sources for this analytical report are derived from much travel and many interviews with border patrolmen, immigration officers, and administrative officials of the U.S. Immigration and Naturalization Service (INS). Also interviewed or consulted were employers, social workers, poverty fighters, Mexican migrant workers and "wetbacks," as well as some Mexican migration officials and consular officers, all during the period 1970-1975. These interviews were carried out by the principal investigator, Arthur F. Corwin, who, in the preparation of this report, collaborated with Johnny McCain, who has also researched the illegal alien problem.

2. "Ley general de población," December 11, 1973, Art. 3, par. ix-x, *Manual del extranjero*, ed. Carlos A. Echánove Trujillo (México: Editorial Porrua, 1974).

3. The dynamics of border settlement are indicated by C. Daniel Dilman, "Urban Growth Along Mexico's Northern Border and the Mexican National Border Program," *Journal of Developing Areas* 4 (1970), 487-508; and Richard L. Nostrand, "The Hispanic-American Borderlands: Delimitation of an American Cultural Region," *Annals of the Association of American Geographers* 60 (1970), 638-661.

4. Dilman, "Urban Growth along Mexico's Northern Border," pp. 501-505; and Howard L. Campbell, "Bracero Migration and the Mexican Economy, 1951-1964" (Unpublished doctoral thesis, The American University, 1972), pp. 293-335.

5. Observation by American immigration inspector-in-charge at El Paso, August 31, 1970.

6. Interviews, August 18-19, 1973, with several busloads of deported "wetbacks" at Mazatlán; and at San Luis Potosí, January 3-4 and March 8-9, 1974. Both cities are "dumping spots" in the interior of Mexico for illegal entrants returned under the voluntary departure system. See also Gary Garrison's interviews with district directors, INS, in San Antonio, Port Isabel, and Chicago, "Wetbacks Are Heading for the Cities," *Houston Post*, July 27, 1969, I-12. See also Portes, "Return of the Wetback," 40-46, wherein the author attributes the modern wetback types not so much to poverty but to growing economic mobility in Mexico; and statement by Leonard F. Chapman, Commissioner of Immigration, "'Silent Invasion' that Takes Millions of American Jobs," *U.S. News and World Report* (December 9, 1974), pp. 77-78.

7. Ibid., and House Committee on the Judiciary, *Illegal Aliens, Hearings*... (Chairman, Peter Rodino), *92d Cong., 1st and 2d Sess.* (Five parts, 1971-1972), Part 1, 114-132; Part 2, 308-309, 667-668; Part 3, 692, 758, and *passim*. Also, U.S. General Accounting Office, *Need to Reduce Public Expenditure for Newly Arrived Immigrants... Report to the Congress by the Comptroller General* (Washington, D.C., July 15, 1975).

8. Statement by American immigration inspector, Laredo, Aug. 13, 1970.

9. Julian Samora with Jorge Bustamante and Gilberto Cardenas, *Los Mojados: The Wetback Story* (Notre Dame, 1971); and Eugene Nelson, *Pablo Cruz and the American Dream. The Experience of an Undocumented Immigrant from Mexico* (Peregrine Smith, Inc., 1975).

10. Interviews with immigration officials of the Southwest (now Western) Regional Office, INS, San Pedro, Calif., March 25, 1970; and with Border Patrol agents at El Centro and Livermore, September 3 and 6, 1970.

11. Interviews with directors of employment services and migrant labor councils and with employers of Mexican and other migrant labor, including farmers, ranchers, nurserymen, food service operators, factory managers, and auto service foremen in Texas, Colorado, California, Oklahoma, Arizona, Ohio, Connecticut, Illinois, and Iowa, in period 1970-1975.

12. According to Director, County Welfare, Fresno, March 24, 1970; Senior Patrol Agent, Sacramento, Sept. 8, 1970; and officials of Office of Economic Opportunity, Urban Redevelopment, VISTA, Migrant Councils, and Employment Commissions in Laredo, San Antonio, Austin, and El Paso, April-June, 1970. See also "The Great Society Did Succeed," by S. A. Levitan and Robert Taggart, *Political Science Quarterly* 91:4 (Winter 1976-77), 601-618.

13. "The New Immigrants: Still the Promised Land," *Time* (birthday issue, July 5, 1976), pp. 16-24.

14. Interviews in Chicago, November 26-29, 1973, with spokesmen for Ethnic Relations, Mayor's Office; Register of Citizens' Complaints, Mayor's Office; Social Service Program Planner, Governor's Office; Cardinal's Commission for Spanish-Speaking; Illinois Migrant Council; Office of Minority Business; and Manpower Development and Training, State of Illinois. See also note 11, and revealing series of syndicated articles by AP writer Holgar Jensen, "Flood of Illegal Aliens," *Fort Worth Star-Telegram*, June 28-July 1, 1976.

15. Two examples of influential reports sponsored by LULACS and G.I. Forum were: George I. Sánchez and Lyle Saunders, "Wetbacks: A Preliminary Report to the Advisory Committee on the Spanish Speaking" (Austin: University of Texas, 1949); and McClellan and Idar, *What Price Wetbacks?*

16. For expression of Aztlán immigration policy see: "Infamy of the Immigration Service, Punishment by Exile," *La Raza* (Los Angeles), I: 7 (1972), 48-53; Stan Steiner, *La Raza: The Mexican Americans* (New York, 1969); *Illegal Aliens, Hearings*, Pt. 1, 269-274, ff.; and for Chicano interpretations of discriminatory policies and practices of the Immigration and Naturalization Service, special issue of *Chicano Law Review* 2 (Chicano Law Student Association, University of California, Los Angeles, Summer 1975), 129 pp.

17. Reies López Tijerina, "Tijerina Presents Another View on Mexican Entrants," *Albuquerque Journal* (May 23, 1974), p. A-7.

18. Interviews with immigration attachés, American Embassy, Mexico City, August 14, 18, 1970, and January 7, 1974.

19. According to statements made by American Consul, Nuevo Laredo, May 2, 1970; and American Vice-Consul, Visa Section, Mexico City, August 15, 1970.

20. See *Illegal Aliens, Hearings*, Part I, 224-230; Part 2, 395, 450, 472, 483-484, 592-599, and *passim*.

21. David North, *The Border Crossers, People Who Live in Mexico and Work in the United States*. Prepared for the Manpower Administration, U.S. Department of Labor (Washington: Transcentury Corp., April 1970).

22. American immigration inspector, Eagle Pass, January 4, 1975.

23. Interviews with deportees at San Luis Potosí, January 3-4, and March 8-9, 1974. See also Samora, *Los Mojados*.

24. See statements by district director, INS, San Francisco, in Denny Walsh's article, "Manpower Needs at Border Cited," *New York Times*, September 18, 1973.

25. Interviews with American consular officers, Immigrant Visa section, Mexico City, August 15, 1970, and January 9, 1974.

26. According to immigration inspectors at McAllen, April 25, 1970; El Paso, August 31, 1970; and Eagle Pass, January 4, 1975; and district directors at Port Isabel, April 25, 1970; and San Antonio, June 6, 1970, and April 10, 1974.

27. Chief, Visa section, American Embassy, Mexico City, February 25, 1974; and U.S. Congress, House, *Review of the Administration of the Immigration and Nationality Act, Hearings before the Subcommittee on Immigration, Citizenship, and International Law, 93rd. Cong., 1 Sess.* (1973), pp. 47-98; and appendices on consular service selection and training, pp. 161-296.

28. Chief, Immigration Visas, American Embassy, Mexico City, January 9, 1974; and Chief, Immigration Visas, American Consulate, Monterrey, March 12, 1974; and Vice-Consul, American Consulate, Nuevo Laredo, April 9, 1974.

29. American Consul, Visa section, Monterrey, March 13, 1974. It may be of interest to note that in fiscal 1973 the Monterrey Consulate issued 20,155 immigrant visas, and 41,648 non-immigrant visas, including 11,948 border-crossing cards, U.S. Department of State, *Report of the Visa Office 1973,* Table VI.

30. Vice-Consul, Tourist Visas, Monterrey, December 30, 1974.

31. *Review of the Administration of the Immigration and Nationality Act, Hearings,* p. 176.

32. Raul Torres Barron, "Rechazan los Consulados de Estados Unidos actas no expedidas en capitales estatales," *Excelsior,* Januarv 22, 1974.

33. Statement by Deputy Chief, Visa section, Monterrey, December 30, 1974. Information on consular agreement is from Immigration Visa section, Mexico City, September 23, 1974.

34. Immigration Inspector-in-Charge, INS, El Paso, August 31, 1970.

35. *Review of the Administration of the Immigration and Nationality Act, Ser. No. 22* (1973); U.S. General Accounting Office, *Illegal Entry at United States-Mexico Border—Multiagency Enforcement Efforts Have Not Been Effective in Stemming the Flow of Drugs and People* (Washington, D.C., December 2, 1977).

36. According to Officer-in-Charge, INS, Eagle Pass, May 30, 1970; and Deputy Chief Patrol Agent, Del Rio sector, April 2, 1970; and Wesley Stiles, retired immigration officer, Del Rio, May 2, 1970.

37. According to officials of Fraudulent Document Center, INS, Yuma, September 3, 1970.

38. According to immigration attachés, American Embassy, Mexico City, August 4, 14, 1970, and January 7, 1974.

39. Interview with Subdirector de Asunto Migratorios, Secretaría de Relaciones Exteriores, Mexico City, January 21, 1974. See also two articles by Federico Ortíz on wetback traffic in *Excelsior* (Mexico City), November 2, 3, 1974; and "Ley general de población" in Carlos A. Echanové Trujillo (ed.), *Manuel del estranjero* (1974).

40. See *Illegal Aliens, Hearings,* Parts 1, 2, and 3; and Title 20—Employee Benefits (20 CFR S416.201), Social Security Administration and Department of Health, Education and Welfare. October 16, 1974

41. Interviews with personnel of employment and welfare offices, migrant labor councils, immigrant aid services, and community development agencies in Sacramen-

to, Fresno, Phoenix, Denver, San Antonio, Chicago, Omaha, St. Paul, and other communities in the period 1970-1975; and statements by Legal Counsel, Southwest Regional Office, INS, September 4, 1970; and Acting General Counsel, INS, Central Office, December 19, 1972.

42. *Review of the Administration of the Immigration and Nationality Act, Hearings*, pp. 115-116, 136, 144; *Illegal Aliens, Hearings before the Subcommittee on Immigration... on H.R. 982, 94th Cong., 1st Sess., February-March, 1975. Ser. No. 8* (1975); David S. North and Marion F. Houstun, *The Characteristics and Role of Illegal Aliens in the U.S. Labor Market: An Exploratory Study* (Washington, D.C.: Linton Co., March 1976), pp. 173-181: policy recommendations; Domestic Council Committee on Illegal Aliens, *Preliminary Report* (Washington, D.C.: U.S. Department of Justice, December 1976), pp. 89-95.

43. For beleaguered situation of the INS. see items in note 42. For typical Chicano charges of racist brutality, see interviews with César Chávez, *Excelsior* (Mexico City), April 23, 1977, p. 1-A; and *Ovaciones* (Mexico City), April 24, 1977, p. 1.

44. *Review... Hearings*, pp. 3-9, 45, 135-137; and "MALDEF and ACLU Sue Immigration . . .," in *Agenda*, National Council of La Raza (Winter 1973), p. 21.

45. Leon Rosen, president, Association of Immigration and Nationality Lawyers, to Attorney General Richard G. Kleindienst, January 9, 1973, *Review . . . Hearings*, pp. 31-32.

46. According to Chief Patrol Agent, El Paso sector, April 1 and August 30, 1970; and Chief Patrol Agent, Laredo sector, May 20, 1970.

47. Various statements made by immigration inspectors and border patrolmen during tour of border region, April-September, 1970.

48. *Illegal Aliens, Hearings*, Part 2, 504-505, 601, 644, 657, 679.

49. Interview with former Commissioner of Immigration Joseph M. Swing (1954-1960), San Francisco, August 1, 1971.

50. Interview with Sub-Jefe de Migración, Ciudad Juárez, August 25, 1972.

51. Statement of prominent Laredo community leader, June 10, 1970.

52. *Review . . . Hearings*, pp. 131-132. See also "Sensors Watch Border," San Antonio *News*, July 18, 1973; and article by David A. Andelm, "U.S. Implanting an Electronic 'Fence' to Shut Mexican Border to Smuggling," *New York Times*, July 14, 1973. The sensor system was first tried in the Chula Vista sector of California border.

53. Senator Alan Cranston, Representative Henry B. González, and other southwestern congressmen who have a large Chicano constituency were quick to denounce the "electronic wall," which had been made possible by an additional sum in the budget of the Department of Justice, according to "Legisladores de Estados Unidos se openen a la 'pared,'" *Excelsior*, July 18, 1973. Mexican editorialists generally opposed electronic detection as "ignominious," and demanded that Mexican officials obtain all the facts from the American government. See series of articles in *Excelsior*, July 12-18, 1973.

54. James P. Sterba, "Electronic Vigil Fails to Stem Mexican Alien Influx," *New York Times*, July 22, 1973, pp. 1, 39; and "La emigración ilegal de Mexicanos . . . la barrera fiasco," *Excelsior* (July 23, 1973), pp. 1, 10.

55. *Congressional Record, House*, May 3, 1973, H3312; see also discussions in U.S. Congress, Senate, Committee on the Judiciary, *To Control Illegal Aliens, Hearings*

before the Subcommittee on Immigration and Naturalization . . . 83rd Cong., 2nd Sess. (1954), pp. 1-69.

56. According to legal counsel, Southwest Regional Office, INS, September 4, 1970.

57. According to District Director, INS, Denver, December 19, 1974; and records on file in Denver District Court: United States of America v. Juan Ortiz and Moisés Morales, No. 73-CR-286, dated August 23, 1973.

58. INS, Annual Report 1973, p. 11; and "La mayor banda descubierta," *Excelsior,* July 7, 1973. Later, it seems that the principal leaders, the "Blondes," jumped a heavy bail and escaped to Mexico.

59. 45 Stat. 1551 (1929); 8 U.S.C. 180a (1946).

60. INS, *Annual Report 1974,* Tab. 26A.

61. In a typical report on "Immigration Violators," the *Laredo Times,* August 5, 1970, noted that of 100 violators of immigration law, including repeaters and false representations, 97 were given suspended sentences.

62. Interview with Assistant District Director for Deportation at major INS detention center, Port Isabel, Texas, April 24, 1970.

63. According to immigration attachés, American Embassy, Mexico City, January 9 and February 14, 1974; and *Review . . . Hearings,* pp. 16-18.

64. In accordance with the magistrate system fines generally ranged from $10 to $500, but, according to Consul General Hector Jara, Nuevo Laredo, April 8, 1974, fines had been scaled down in Texas by Federal Judge Ben C. Connally in accordance with Mexico's request. See also Tom Green, "Mexican Officials, Connally Talk about Fines on Wetbacks," *Laredo Times,* March 17, 1974.

65. INS, *Annual Report 1970,* section on "Criminal Prosecutions."

66. The case history of Sec. 2805 and decisions by a California Superior Court and the Supreme Court are thoroughly covered by Pedro Galindo Nieto, "The Undocumented Alien Laborer and *DeCanas v. Bica,*" *Chicano Law Review* 3 (1976), 148-163.

67. *Ibid.* Still relevant are studies by Elizabeth Hadley, "A Critical Analysis of the Wetback Problem," *Law and Contemporary Problems* 21 (Spring 1956), 334-357: and "Wetbacks: Can the States Act to Curb Illegal Entry?" special issue, *Stanford Law Review* 6 (March 1954), 287-323. For resumé of recent Supreme Court decisions see *Zero Population Growth National Reporter* (March 1976), p. 1.

68. For discussion of recent immigration bills see: House Committee on the Judiciary, *Immigration and Nationality Amendments of 1973, Report No. 93-461 on H.R. 981, with Additional Views, 93d Cong., 1st Sess.* (1973), 49 pp.; *ibid., Amending the Immigration and Nationality Act . . . Report Together with Additional Views to Accompany H. R. 982, April 5, 1973, 93d Cong., 1st Sess., Report No. 39-108* (1973), 28 pp.; and *Hearings . . . on H.R. 982 (8713) . . . Illegal Aliens* (1975), 32 pp.; also see Senate Committee on the Judiciary, *Immigration 1976, Hearings . . . on S. 3074* (Eastland Bill) *to Amend the Immigration and Nationality Act . . . March-April 1976* (1976), 274 pp; also Richard Avila and James Romo, "The Undocumented Worker: The Controversy Takes a New Turn," *Chicano Law Review* 3 (1976), 164-194.

69. According to officials of Fraudulent Document Center, INS, Yuma, Sept. 3, 1970.

70. According to nearly all immigration and consular officials interviewed in period 1970-1975; see also the sordid account of false documentations in Nelson, *Pablo Cruz and the American Dream.*

71. INS, *Annual Report 1971*, p. 15; *1974*, pp. 14-15.

72. Interviews with American consular officers, Monterrey, March 13-14, 1974.

73. Manuel Mejido, "Las mafias pasan ilegalmente a Estados Unidos a 50,000 Mexicanos al mes," *Excelsior*, June 11, 1973; and "500 dólares cuesta una tarjeta auténtica," *Excelsior*, June 12, 1973; also exposé of voluntary departures that charged that Mexican operators of plane lifts accepted bribes to return deportees to border, Denny Walsh, "Ousted Mexicans Pay Off to Stay Close to U.S. Jobs," *New York Times* (April 15, 1973), pp. 1, 46.

74. According to Deputy District Director, INS, Denver, Dec. 18, 1974; and House Committee on the Judiciary, *Review . . . Hearings*, pp. 132-134, 144; also, Denny Walsh, "Immigration Inquiry Reported Stalled," *New York Times* (June 3, 1973), C-13.

75. Immigration Inspector, INS, Eagle Pass, January 4, 1975.

76. *Illegal Aliens. Hearings*, Parts 1, 2, 3.

77. Interview with deputy district director, INS, Denver, December 17, 1974. Social Security amendments of October 30, 1972, are explained by A. E. Hess, Deputy Commissioner, SSA, in House Committee on the Judiciary, *Hearings before Subcommittee No. 1 on Illegal Aliens. 93d Cong., 1st Sess., March 7-8, 1973, Serial No. 1* (1973), pp. 48-65.

78. According to officials, Fraudulent Document Center, INS, Yuma, September 3, 1970; and Associated Press report, "Mexican Illegals Resist Pressures," *Sioux City Journal*, October 4, 1974.

79. INS, *Annual Report 1971*, p. 15. See similar powder-puff sentence for Anita Mendoza, notary public in Chicago, and convicted ringleader of sham marriage racket, *1974*, p. 15.

80. *Ibid., 1973*, p. 14.

81. Testimony of high immigration officials in *Illegal Aliens. Hearings* (1971-1972), Part 1, 3-98; and *Illegal Aliens, a Review of Hearings Conducted During the 92d Congress . . . 93rd Cong., 1st Sess.* (Committee Print, February 1973), pp. 4-7 ff.

82. Craig, *The Bracero Program.*

83. According to interviews with district directors, INS, San Antonio, April 10, 1974, Houston, April 12, 1974, Omaha, May 15, 1974, and Denver, Dec. 19, 1974.

84. *Ibid.*, also Samora, *Los Mojados*, pp. 48, 88, *passim.*; and such reports as "Key Colorado Cities Ignoring Illegal Aliens . . . for Lack of Funds," *Rocky Mountain News* (Denver), February 2, 1975.

85. Nathan M. Adams, "Our Mounting Waves of Illegal Immigrants," *Reader's Digest*, 103:620 (December 1973), 115-119; and statements by Leonard F. Chapman, Commissioner of Immigration, in "Deluge of Illegal Aliens," *San Francisco Chronicle*, July 26, 1974; William B. Saxbe, Attorney General, in Ronald J. Ostrow, "Saxbe Urges Deportation of Aliens," *Los Angeles Times*, November 1, 1974; and Lesko Associates, "Final Report: Basic Data and Guidelines Required to Implement a Major Illegal Alien Study during Fiscal Year 1976" (Washington, D.C., October 15, 1975).

86. According to interview statements by border patrolmen and immigration officers in the Southwest region, INS, in period 1970-1975. See also Walsh, "Manpower Needs at Border Cited."

87. According to interviews with more than 25 Border Patrol veterans and retirees, April-June 1970. Samora and team found much the same story in researching *Los Mojados.*

88. Statements by border patrolmen, and also Texas rangers at Del Rio, Cotulla, Uvalde, Ozona, and Big Spring, April-June 1970, and December 1974.

89. Martin Waldron, "Wide Abuse Alleged in Texas Border," *New York Times*, December 19, 1972.

90. See series of articles on domestic workers and other Mexican illegals by Aziz Shihab in *San Antonio Express/News*, January 27-30, 1974.

91. Interview with criminal investigator, INS, Denver, December 19, 1974.

92. Samora, *Los Mojados*, pp. 11, 33, 48. For charges of complicity by Border Patrol and American exploitation of wetbacks see Gaston García Cantu, "La declaración sobre los braceros," *Excelsior*, October 25, 1974, pp. 6A-7A; and interview with César Chávez, "Se propicia el trafico de braceros, dice," *Excelsior*, June 19, 1973. For a refutation of Chávez' charges, which have become more shrill as his unionization problems mount, see *Review of the Immigration and Nationality Act, Hearings*, pp. 155-160.

The American Immigration Service has also been seen as subservient —along with Congress—to agricapitalism by Chicano and Mexican researchers. See, for example, Gilberto Cárdenas and Jorge A. Bustamante, "Research Memorandum and Commentary on Some Salient Issues Concerning United States Immigration Policy Towards Mexico, Mexican Migratory Movements, and Mexican Labor in the United States, With a Special Emphasis on Illegal Immigration," Prepared Testimony Before the Subcommittee of the Judiciary No. 1, of the United States Congress, Committee of the Judiciary, Chicago Hearings on Illegal Aliens, October 23, 1971, Centro de Estudios Chicanos, Department of Sociology (Unpublished paper, University of Notre Dame, 1971).

93. The bases of Mexican policy to protect emigrant workers in the United States, legal or not, were outlined by Mario Moya Palencia, Secretary of Internal Affairs (Gobernación), in Gustavo Mora, "Sienta Moya Palencia bases para un pacto sobre braceros," *Novedades*, June 13, 1973. See likewise "Defensa legal a braceros," in *Tribuna de Monterrey*, January 15, 1976.

At the Nogales meeting of President Ford and President Echeverría, held in October 1974, both agreed that a new bracero program was presently impossible. *Tiempo* (Mexico City), LXVI (October 18, 1974), 8. In subsequent statements Mexico's president emphasized that his government would do everything possible to protect undocumented workers through the consular service and diplomatic channels.

Reasons for American rejection of another bracero program, and suggested alternatives such as admitting more "H-2" temporary workers, plus more humane treatment for illegals to meet Mexico's complaints, were given by the American interagency study group, appointed by President Nixon in June 1972 and headed by Roger C. Cramton, Justice Department, with representation also from Agriculture, Immigration, Labor, and HEW, in "Final Report of the Special Study Group on Illegal Immigrants from Mexico, January 15, 1973" (Washington, D.C.: U.S. Department of Justice, 1973).

94. House Appropriations Subcommittee, *Hearings, Fiscal 1977 . . . 94th Cong., 2d Sess.* (1976), p. 704, quoted in Joyce Vialet, *Illegal Aliens: Analysis and Background* (Washington, D.C.: Congressional Research Service, Library of Congress, February 1977), p. 133.

95. INS, "Open Line" (Central Office), 2:19 (October 28, 1975). See also Manuel Vic Villalpando and others associated with San Diego County Immigration Council, *A*

Study of the Socioeconomic Impact of Illegal Aliens in the County of San Diego (County of San Diego: Human Resources Agency, January 1977).

96. INS, "Open Line," 3:1 (January 15, 1976); and National Council of La Raza, *Agenda*, 5:9 (September 1975), p. 1.

97. INS, "Open Line," 2:6 (March 26, 1975).

98. Interviews with District Director of Immigration, Denver, December 18, 1974; and with immigration attaché, American Consulate, Monterrey, January 30, 1976.

99. *Illegal Aliens, Hearings . . . on H.R. 982* (1975), pp. 32, 43, 399-400, 448-450.

100. INS, "Open Line," 2:18 (October 3, 1975).

101. See studies of Ellwyn R. Stoddard, sociologist, University of Texas, El Paso, for example, "Illegal Mexican Labor in the Borderlands: Institutionalized Support of an Unlawful Practice," *Pacific Sociological Review*, 19:2 (April 1976), 175-210; and "A Conceptual Analysis of the Alien Invasion," *International Migration Review*, 10:2 (Summer 1976), 157-188. See also Roberto Suro, "El Pan de Miedo" (7 parts), *Tribuna de Monterrey*, February 25-March 2, 1976, originally appearing in *Chicago Sun Times*; and "El Falso Paraiso," *Tiempo* (Mexico City), 69 (October 25, 1976), 6-9.

102. Interview with District Director, Immigration, St. Paul, and Regional Commissioner, Northern Region, October 26, 1973.

103. U.S. General Accounting Office, *Immigration—Need to Reassess U.S. Policy. Report to the Congress by the Comptroller General of the United States* (Washington, D.C., October 19, 1976); and Domestic Council Committee, *Preliminary Report*, pp. 77-83.

104. "Crisis Across the Borders Meaning to the United States," *U.S. News & World Report*, December 13, 1976, pp. 48-56; Orr Kelly, "Border Crisis," *U.S. News & World Report*, April 25, 1977, pp. 33-39; also statements by Mexican, Chicano, and Anglo-American delegates, including high public officials, at major symposium on "Immigration and Public Policy: The Humananistic Imperative," arranged by Chicano Training Center, at University of Houston, April 15-16, 1977.

105. Interview in "New Faces How They're Changing U.S.," *U.S. News and World Report*, February 20, 1978, pp. 28-31, 33-36.

5/ ¿QUIEN SABE? MEXICAN MIGRATION STATISTICS

Arthur F. Corwin

The Mexican-American minority is one of America's best kept
secrets.
Chicano humor

Before the general immigration act of 1917 there was virtually no immigrant supervision at land border ports. A Mexican who settled in California before that date described the "immigration experience" for himself and countless others: "I walked across the bridge and paid a penny, and then the man asked me my name and age."[1] Other migratory folk (saving the penny toll) simply by-passed Mexican and American immigration and customs officials stationed here and there along an 1,800-mile front. Such officials often observed that the native had no sense of a boundary line, and in any case, there was then, as now, a tendency, under border reciprocity, to allow the natives to cross freely to and fro, particularly where Mexican settlements were found on both sides of the line, as in the Rio Grande Valley of Texas.

Even to the present day little effort has been made to determine if casual border crossers actually return to Mexico—or Canada. It is hardly surprising that no one has yet devised a reliable method for measuring at any given time the quantity of Mexican and Mexican-descent groups in the United States.[2] Victor S. Clark, who did the first field report on Mexican labor emigration in 1908, and who noted that unskilled laborers and section hands were then working "as far east as Chicago, and as far north as Iowa, Wyoming and San Francisco," began the guessing game when he conservatively estimated that from one-fourth to one-third of the migrants, or about 20,000 per year, were then settling permanently in the United States.[3]

Immigrant registration improved little with the years because, as Paul S.

Taylor explained, registration rules and procedures followed by the Immigration Service were originally developed for seaport funnels.[4] And until 1924 and for some years thereafter, American immigration officials were primarily charged with excluding Orientals and Europeans, many of whom were attempting illegal entry from Mexico and Canada. According to old-time immigration officers, in those days hardly anyone bothered to stop Mexican migrants.[5] Moreover, most congressmen and high government officials showed little concern, for, being unfamiliar with the borderlands, they swallowed the myth propagated by southwestern employers that Mexican campesinos and their families rarely settled beyond sight of the Rio Grande. Not until the widespread public protest of the mid-1920s against the open back door and the so-called Mexican social problem did the federal government provide an immigration border patrol.[6]

Special exemptions also created data gaps. For instance, during the period 1917-1921 Mexican workers were exempted from the literacy, head tax, and public-charge restrictions of the 1917 immigration code because of the labor needs of World War I. Typically, a report of the Commissioner of Immigration in 1920 lamented that the figures for desertions of temporary workers and their whereabouts were anything but dependable. "They are compiled from reports received from employers, the majority of whom, experience has shown, are exceedingly lax in keeping their reports."[7] Thirty and forty years later the same complaint would be heard about the bracero contractors.

Without doubt the principal explanation for the failure of American immigration authorities to control or register the campesino exodus into the Southwest—once these officials were authorized to do so by the immigration acts of 1917 and after—was the lack of men and means for patrolling a primitive frontier. Before the Border Patrol was established in 1925, only sixty mounted guards were posted along the entire border. Immediately thereafter a mere 450 men constituted the Border Patrol. Much like the Keystone Cops, patrolmen were obliged to spend most of their time in model T cars or on horseback, merrily chasing liquor smugglers and "Chinese-smugglers" up and down the Mexican and Canadian borders.[8]

Since the Mexican boundary has never been tightly regulated, the fixing of Mexican migration statistics, as students of the subject soon find out, is largely a game of conjectures and calculated guesses, using wherever possible immigration and census data from both sides of the border, deficient as they may be, as points of reference. According to American figures for legal immigration, only 28,003 persons moved from Mexico to the United States in the period 1820-1900.[9] But no record of Mexican immigration was kept for the years 1886-1893, or for several thousand campesino families who drifted into the border regions of Texas at a time when there were no general immigration controls.[10]

During the decade 1901-1910 more Mexicans legally migrated over the border than during the previous eighty years. The ten-year figure of 49,642 reflected the increasing use of Mexican labor, principally in American mines, railroads, and irrigated agriculture. Probably the total number of Mexicans who settled, registered or not, in the United States in years 1901-1910 far exceeded the original Spanish-speaking population of the Southwest in 1848, which various authors place at around 75,000 to 80,000, or higher. [11]

The revolutionary violence of 1910-1920, combined with rapid economic developments in the southwestern states and elsewhere, and the shutting off of cheap alien labor from Europe and the Orient, turned a rising current of Mexican migrants, mostly from the landless peasantry, into a tidal flow. According to Mexican figures, some 218,514 persons legally emigrated to the United States in the brief period 1910-1917. [12] In each decennial census the Mexico-born population was more than doubling itself, as shown in Table 1. [13]

World War I labor needs and the economic boom of the 1920s served to maintain this exodus. From 1918 through 1928, on the eve of the Great Depression, 550,599 legal emigrants registered at Mexican border offices. During this period, excepting some religious refugees from the "Cristero Revolt," most of these emigrants were common laborers and their families brought in with the help of American employers.

Mexican emigration statistics, like American data, offer little help, as Leo Grebler recognized, in pinning down the actual number of emigrants who settled in the United States. [15] Andrés Piña, head of the Department of Migration in the 1920s, had earlier pointed out some of the strange discrepancies. For instance, Mexican migration offices on the border registered "the loss" of

Table 1   Mexican-Born Population in United States, 1900-1920

	1900	*1910*	*1920*
California	8,086	33,694	88,771
Arizona	14,172	29,987	61,580
New Mexico	6,649	11,918	20,272
Colorado	274	2,602	11,037
Texas	71,062	125,016	251,827
Illinois	156	672	4,032
Kansas	71	8,429	13,770
Other States	2,923	9,597	35,129
Total	103,393	221,915	486,418

Source: U.S. Bureau of the Census, *Twelfth Census of the United States*, 1900: Population (1901), I, clxxiv; *Thirteenth Census . . . 1910* (1913), I, 781, 875; *Fourteenth Census . . . 1920* (1922), I. Also, *Abstracts of the Census Population. Country of Origin, 1890-1910*, pp. 204-207.

769,113 nationals en route to the United States as legal emigrants during the years 1910-1928, but in the same period Mexico gained 1,103,044 "repatriates," who declared their permanent return at border migration posts.[16] Such findings prompted Manuel Gamio, who in 1927 completed an extensive field study of Mexicans in the United States, to make the cynical comment that emigration was not a disastrous labor loss; on the contrary, "the United States far from consuming our working class actually serves as a marvelous incubator that returns more immigrants than we send there."[17]

One explanation of the incubator phenomenon is that during the 1920s the Mexican government, deeply disturbed about labor and population loss (Mexico's population was then less than 16 million), was making earnest efforts to persuade Mexican workers and their families to return and to help develop the motherland. Unfortunately for statistical control, the term *repatriado* was loosely (or hopefully) applied by Mexican consuls and border officials to any returning migrant who declared Mexico to be his permanent residence and final point of destination. Many wetbacks, returning to *la madre patria* with money and goods after a season's work, sought a safe return, away from bushwack trails, through Mexican ports of entry, where they often posed as fervent repatriates, which usually meant the waiving of customs duties. They cleverly exploited Mexico's repatriation policy by using Mexican consuls in North American cities (as they used the U.S. Immigration Service) to get a free "repatriation fare" home. By the mid-1920s the Mexican government was beginning to grasp the full extent of this abuse, but meanwhile the repatriation illusion had caused havoc with statistical control. Furthermore, the migratory habits and suspicious nature of unregistered campesinos frustrated, as in 1922, any attempt by Mexican consular officials to take a census of Mexican nationals in the United States.[18]

In the meantime, federal agencies applied the general immigration requirements of 1917 and the visa control system, established in 1924, to the Mexican border. Counts of legal immigrants were made, of course, but untold numbers of peons and their families, who could not meet minimal qualifications in health, literacy, head tax, visa fees, and self-support, slipped across the border without inspection, as indeed they were accustomed to doing before 1917. The term *wetback*, or *mojado*, was soon applied to Mexican workers who crossed the Rio Grande illegally, and then was casually applied to all illegal entrants from Mexico.

According to Table 13 of the *Annual Report* of the U.S. Immigration and Naturalization Service, 727,933 immigrants arrived from Mexico in the period 1901-1930: from 1901 to 1910, 49,642; from 1911 to 1920, 219,004; and from 1921 to 1930, 459,287, totaling 727,933 people, a few of whom were from other countries originally.

During the heaviest period of Mexican migration, 1911-1930, the Immigration Service recorded 678,291 legal immigrants. This figure was considerably

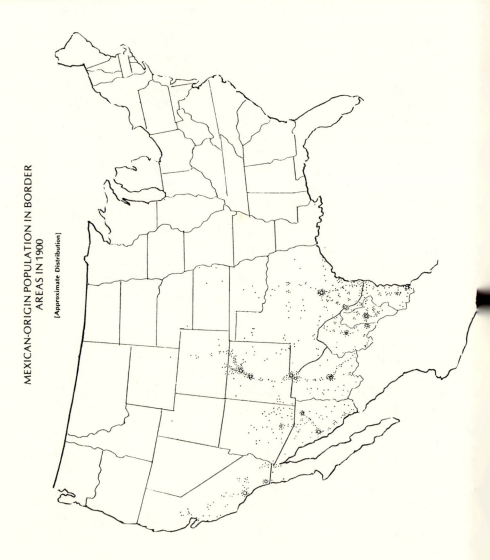

MEXICAN-ORIGIN POPULATION IN BORDER
AREAS IN 1900

[Approximate Distribution]

Population of Mexico border states according to census of 1900:

Baja California [Norte]	8,000
Sonora	222,000
Chihuahua	328,000
Coahuila	297,000
Nuevo Leon	328,000
Tamaulipas	219,000
TOTAL*	1,402,000

*Possibly 20% of total consisted of Indian tribes.

Estimated Population of Mexican origin in the United States in 1900:

	census of foreign born	plus uncounted groups+	rough totals
California	8,086	25,000?	33,000?
Arizona	14,171	15,000?	29,000?
New Mexico	6,649	115,000?	122,000?
Texas	71,062	60,000?	131,000?
Colorado	274	15,000?	15,000?
Other States	3,168	5,000?	8,000?
ROUGH TOTALS	103,410	235,000?	338,000?

+Includes native-born; unregistered immigrants; and children of immigrants, or of mixed parentage. The federal census of 1900 made no special count of such groups. In California probably half of the Mexican-origin population in 1900 was derived from the mission era, and from miners who remained after the goldrush period. In Arizona possibly 40 percent of the Mexican-origin people of that date were descended from Sonoran miners of the period 1860-1890. Also in Texas about 40 percent of these people were probably the offspring of earlier settlers. In this case, principally persons from Mexico border states who took up farm and ranch work in period 1860-1900. In New Mexico in 1900 probably 95 percent of the Mexican-origin persons were descendants of "Spanish Americans" whose ancestors settled the northern part of state before 1848; and in Colorado at that time nearly all the population of Mexican origin were "Spanish Americans" from New Mexico who went north to work in agriculture, mines and railroads.

lower than the Mexican emigration count of 769,113 for a shorter period, 1910-1928. A partial explanation is that some Mexican emigrants who had passports or visas from the interior were turned back by inspectors at American border ports, forcing a return or an illegal crossing. In other cases emigrant families who had documents simply crossed without inspection to save head tax money or to avoid inspection procedures.[19] There are probably other explanations also.

Actually there was no way, then or now, for either government to keep track of surreptitious movements to and fro. The Mexican Migration Service customarily keeps records only of those repatriates or returnees who voluntarily register their return. The American Immigration Service keeps entry records of legal immigrants, border crossers, commuters (who live in Mexico but work in the United States), non-immigrant visitors, and tourists moving through ports of entry, but does not strictly record the return of these groups, depending instead on voluntary cooperation.[20] In a word, under recording procedures, present and past, there is no way of knowing how many casual border crossers remain in the United States permanently or for extended periods of time.

Any attempt, therefore, to measure surreptitious settlement means using indirect and fragmentary measurements; for example, comparing American census data for Mexico-born residents with American immigration figures can perhaps suggest some partial evidence of illegal settlement, as shown in Table 2.

Table 2   Comparison of U.S. Census Data and Immigration Figures

U.S. census of Mexico-born (M-B)	Plus legal immigrants for decade	Expected* M-B population (approx.)	Actual census count of M-B	Illegal settlers
(1870) 42,435	5,162 (1871-80)	47,597 (1880)	68,399	20,802 (?)
(1880) 68,399	1,913 (1881-90)**	70,312 (1890)	77,853	7,541 (?)
(1890) 77,853	971 (1891-00)**	78,824 (1900)	103,393	24,569 (?)
(1900) 103,393	49,642 (1901-10)	153,035 (1910)	221,915	68,880 (?)
(1910) 221,915	219,004 (1911-20)	440,919 (1920)	486,418	45,499 (?)

*If one were to assume that all immigrants remained in the United States and that none died.
**No immigration records kept from 1886 to 1893.
N.B. Depending on sources used, census and immigration counts, and adjustments, vary slightly.
Sources: *Mexicans in California, Report of Governor C. C. Young's Fact-Finding Committee* (San Francisco, 1930), pp. 28-29, and Table 8; also, *Sixteenth Census of the United States: 1940*, Vol. II, *Characteristics of the Population*, Part 1, Tables 14 and 15 (1943); and INS, *Annual Reports*, Table 13: Immigration by Country, for Decades.

With all their deficiencies the decennial counts of 1870-1920 seem to give at least a reasonable approximation of the growth of the Mexico-born population in the United States, but this seems much less true of the 1930 findings, as suggested by the following disparities:

Census of M-B in 1920	Plus legal immigrants for 1921-30	Expected increase in M-B (approx.), in 1930	Actual census of M-B in 1930	Loss of M-B 1930
486,418	459,287	945,705	639,017	306,688 (?)

If one were to accept these rough calculations, then one might conclude that in spite of the great current of legal immigration from Mexico in the 1920s, the 1930 count showed a striking net loss in foreign-born Mexicans amounting to 300,000 or so. But then this incredulous figure seems partly explained by another: census takers suddenly found some 810,000 second-generation Mexicans of immigrant parentage and mixed immigrant and native parentage. [21] Aside from other gaps in the 1930 census, which for the first time attempted a special count of Mexican and Mexican-stock population in the United States, the apparent loss in foreign-born Mexicans seems principally due to the phenomenon of "protective coloration." The laws of 1929, providing for an alien registry and, for the first time, criminal penalties for illegal entries, had a significant influence on the 1930 census. Some Mexico-born who appeared in previous censuses were frightened back to Mexico, some avoided census takers, and many appear to have claimed second-generation or native-born status. After 1929 the actual number of native-born became an immeasurable factor in census counts. [22] The comparison of census figures shown in Table 3 throws into relief the big shift in categories that had emerged by 1930.

Table 3 Comparison of Census Figures

	1890	1900	1910	1920	1930
Mexico-born	77,853	103,393	221,915	486,418	639,017
Second generation and mixed immigrant and native parentage			162,200	274,924	810,278
Total			384,115	761,342	1,449,295

The remarkable increase in the Mexican-stock population between 1920 and 1930 was a statistic immigration restrictionists seized upon to prove that perhaps a half million Mexicans had settled illegally in the United States during a single decade and been erroneously counted as native-born. In a defensive statement, the Commissioner of Immigration, Daniel W. MacCormack, rejected such suspicions as "fantastic exaggerations," and advanced the simplistic explanation: "The increase in the Mexican population during the decade was apparently due to a high birth rate. . . . The American-born Mexican population showed an increase between 1920 and 1930 of 562,354, or 231 percent . . ."![23]

The total recorded Mexico-born population in 1930 was distributed as follows: [24]

Texas	262,672
California	191,346
Arizona	47,855
New Mexico	15,983
Colorado	12,816
Illinois	20,069
Kansas	11,012
Other states	77,264
Total	639,017

Although Mexican-descent persons could be found in most states of the union, and even in the territory of Alaska, in 1930 the Mexican-stock population was still concentrated in the southwestern states:

Texas	673,681
California	368,013
Arizona	114,173
New Mexico	59,340
Colorado	57,676
Other states	166,412
Total	1,449,295

The preceding figures do not embrace all Mexican-stock peoples, such as surreptitious settlers; nor were all the descendants of native Californios, Tejanos, and Hispanos fully counted, particularly in New Mexico. A more reasonable estimate of all Mexican-descent groups, including the descendants of the Hispanicized population of 1848, would be somewhere near 2 million. [25]

As we have seen, the number of Mexican immigrants legally admitted from 1901 to 1930, according to U.S. figures, was 727,933, but it is likely that the total number of Mexican emigrants (not counting perennial transborder migrant workers) who settled permanently, or for a number of years, on the American side would have been nearly 1.5 million.[26]

Given the custom of Mexican campesinos to migrate and work in family groups, especially in agriculture, it seems probable that better than a third of all the settlers in the years 1901-1930 consisted of females. Also, in considering rough conjectures of all long-term settlers, one should probably allow that 25 percent or so returned (not counting persons returned by the U.S. Immigration Service) to live in Mexico, especially at a time when social services and unemployment compensation for unskilled and semiskilled labor were very limited or nonexistent.[27]

During the Depression decade, there was a sharp cutoff of Mexican migration. For the ten-year period 1931-1940, according to U.S. data, only 22,319 immigrants from Mexico were legally admitted, compared to 459,287 for the decade 1921-1930. Moreover, there was a big retreat by unemployed Mexican laborers and their families. Facing fierce competition from unemployed domestic labor, including Filipinos, Negroes, poor whites, and native Spanish-speaking, and strong pressure from public relief agencies, perhaps 450,000 Mexican settlers in all, including women and children, returned to Mexico as "repatriates" in the years 1931-1940.[28]

There was, however, from the first years of massive repatriation, a return flow of disillusioned repatriados, according to American consular officers. By 1937, when the American economy had begun to revive, some repatriates were still heading south, but many more were slipping back to work for former employers or rejoin relatives in the United States.[29] No Mexican figures are available on the number of "Depression repatriates" who actually settled in Mexico. It seems likely, according to interview statements from old repatriates, that many of the repatriados were back in the American border states by 1941, and many others slipped back to help fill the labor shortage of World War II and the Cold War. Many others who had been born in the United States later returned, and continue to return, as U.S. citizens, often with families of their own.[30] As for a more realistic approximation of Mexican immigration during the 1930s, one should probably add to the 22,319 legal immigrants admitted during the decade around 150,000 repatriates who resettled in the border states and in some midwestern cities.

One version of the 1940 census of Mexican-descent groups showed 377,433 foreign-born (compared to 639,017 in 1930), 619,300 second-generation persons of foreign or mixed parentage, and 628,000 of native parentage, for a total count of 1,624,733.[31] Because of the deportation fears of the Depression years, possibly 500,000 should be added to the census figure to reach a more probable total of around 2,125,000.

The Mexican contract-labor program (1942-1964) opened a new era of statistical questions. Hundreds of thousands of temporary workers were welcomed as war-emergency labor and then as food-for-peace workers in the early

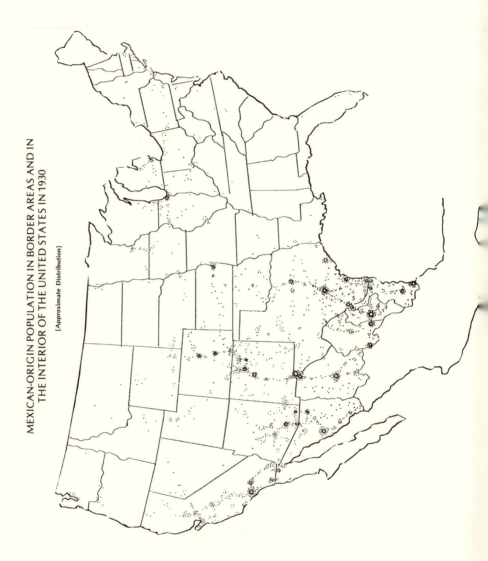

MEXICAN-ORIGIN POPULATION IN BORDER AREAS AND IN THE INTERIOR OF THE UNITED STATES IN 1930

[Approximate Distribution]

Population of Mexico border states according to census of 1930:

Baja California [Norte]	48,000
Sonora	316,000
Chihuahua	492,000
Coahuila	436,000
Nuevo Leon	414,000
Tamaulipas	334,000
Total	**2,040,000**

Population of Mexican origin in the United States in 1930:

California	368,013
Arizona	114,173
New Mexico	59,340
Colorado	57,676
Texas	683,681
Other states	226,612
Census total	1,449,295
Plus uncounted groups	550,000 ?
Rough total	1,999,295 ?

period of the Cold War. However, during the decade 1941-1950 relatively few Mexican nationals were admitted as permanent immigrants—only 60,589 were so admitted, according to U.S. figures. The high point of legal immigration was 8,730 in 1948, a figure that hardly compares with, say, the 66,766 that had come in 1927. [32] And yet by 1948 Mexican laborers, in what was described as a "wetback invasion," were settling down by the tens of thousands in the Southwest, the Midwest, and the Pacific Coast states. This "invisible migration" may be partly explained by the tighter U.S. visa controls on unskilled labor inaugurated in late 1928 as an alternative to the much debated special quota for Mexico. [33]

Nevertheless, during the 1950s legal immigration from south of the border picked up remarkably as can be seen by the U.S. data in Table 4.

One factor in the upward surge of the 1950s was the Immigration and Nationality Act of 1952, which liberalized certain provisions of immigration law so as to facilitate entry of non-Europeans and the uniting of families. Also significant, American employers, uncertain from time to time of the future of transborder contract labor and of illegal labor, especially after the "wetback sweeps" of 1953 and 1954, arranged, as in the years 1954-1957, for the immigration of a larger number of braceros and the legalization of clandestine settlers. [34] At the same time legalized immigrants with permanent jobs began bringing in their relatives under provisions favoring family unification. The effect was that Mexican immigration began to accelerate in the 1950s, the one type of immigration feeding the other, and this growing momentum has continued to the present.

In the 1960s legal immigration from Mexico averaged over 45,000 per year, accounting for 14 to 16 percent of all legal immigration to the United States. The fundamental law of 1952 was amended by the act of October 3, 1965, which, again, encouraged family migration by exempting immediate relatives

Table 4   Legal Immigration from Mexico, 1951-1960

Year	Number of Immigrants	Year	Number of Immigrants
1951	6,372	1956	65,047
1952	9,600	1957	49,154
1953	18,454	1958	26,712
1954	37,456	1959	23,061
1955	50,772	1960	32,684
		Total	319,312

Source: U.S. Immigration and Naturalization Service, *Annual Reports*, Table 14.

of American citizens and of permanent resident aliens from numerical limitations and labor certification. The system of preference categories for relatives, professional persons, skilled labor, etc., was maintained for the Eastern Hemisphere immigrants, but for Western Hemisphere countries, migrants other than immediate relatives were put on a "first come first served basis." This system has tended to favor Mexico, where there has always been a great accumulation of early visa applications. The figures for the past decade appear in Table 5. The dip in 1964 and 1965 reflects tighter labor certification, and the rise after 1965 reflects an increasing shift toward family-equity visas, which now constitute the dominant character of legal Mexican immigration.[35] The total of 443,301 for 1961-1970 nearly matched the surge of the 1920s when, according to American sources, 459,287 Mexican immigrants were legally admitted.

It appears that legal Mexican immigration for the present decade would easily surpass the total for 1921-1930:[36]

1971	50,103	1974	71,586
1972	64,040	1975	62,205
1973	70,141	1976	57,863

These figures, which nearly equaled the total immigration from West Europe, suggest an established current of kinship migration from Mexico (and other Third World countries). In recent years less than 3 percent of Mexican visa applicants have been subject to labor certification, usually because of a "citizen child" exemption.

A concerned House Judiciary Committee finally shoved H.R. 14535 through a divided Congress, and the bill was signed by President Ford on October 20,

Table 5 Legal Immigration from Mexico, 1961-1970

Year	Number of Immigrants	Year	Number of Immigrants
1961	41,632	1966	45,163
1962	55,291	1967	42,371
1963	55,253	1968	43,563
1964	32,967	1969	44,623
1965	37,969	1970	44,469
		Total	443,301

Source: Leo Grebler, *Mexican Immigration to the United States: The Record and Its Implications* (Los Angeles: University of California, 1966), Table 25; and U.S. Immigration and Naturalization Service, *Annual Reports*, Table 14. Figures are for fiscal years.

1976. This bill—an historic departure from "Pan American favoritism"—in essence extends the Eastern Hemisphere system to the Western Hemisphere, dropping the citizen child exemption and imposing the same annual limit of 20,000 immigrants, with the usual exemption of immediate relatives. It is expected that the immediate relative category will continue to expand. For as American consuls point out, the typical immigrant visa is given to an applicant who entered the United States surreptitiously, but married an American citizen or legal resident alien, or is a brother, sister, parent, or child of an American citizen or legal resident alien.

Under current law, various court orders, and the amnesty plans of the Carter administration, a vast reservoir of 5 to 10 million western hemisphere applicants with a few years of residential "equity" may be permitted to live and work as "non-deportable aliens" while awaiting adjustment of status. Such ad hoc arrangements could add anywhere from several hundred thousand to a million or more legalized Mexican immigrants by 1980. [37]

Meanwhile, how many Mexican migrants have been settling illegally in the country? For a decade after Operation Wetback of 1954, there was a semblance of tight migration control in the borderlands. Apprehensions of Mexican illegals, which had risen swiftly from 26,689 in fiscal 1944 to 1,075,168 in fiscal 1954, decreased precipitously to 29,651 in 1960. In fiscal 1965 wetback arrests were still at a comparatively low point of 55,349. By that year, however, the bracero program ceased, and Great Society programs began to reduce the mobility and job needs of various sectors of the American labor force. Once more Mexican workers and their families began moving en masse, as may be appreciated from the apprehension figures in Table 6. [38]

If one were to assume that about half of all illegal entrants elude detection—

Table 6   Deportable Aliens Located in the United States

Fiscal Year	Mexican	Other	Total
1970	277,346	57,731	335,077
1971	348,406	64,406	412,578
1972	430,211	61,978	492,189
1973	576,807	70,705	647,512
1974	709,945	71,046	780,991
1975	680,335	76,484	756,819
1976	781,438	84,995	866,433

Note: Apprehension figures may vary.
Source: U.S. Immigration and Naturalization Service, Annual Reports, for fiscal years, Tables 27B and 30.

as many immigration officials are ready to admit—then the present volume of Mexican migration over the border reaches awesome proportions indeed. [39] The foregoing speculation is subject to some qualifications. About half of the annual apprehensions seem to be repeaters or seasonal workers, under various pseudonyms, playing the voluntary departure game. Actually the pattern has not changed much since the 1880s. Most migrants, apprehended or not, return to Mexico for the winter season; yet always some settle down with better jobs or community assistance and then tend to bring in kinfolk.

When all allowances are made, it is obvious by any rule of thumb that a massive "wetback infiltration" has been underway since 1965, that it overshadows the exodus of the 1920s, when there were possibly half a million migrants surreptitiously in the United States, or the "wetback invasion" that brought perhaps a million more unregistered settlers in the contract-labor era, 1942-1964. [40] From time to time since the immigration law of 1917 many long-time illegal entrants have been allowed to legalize their status. Others have been immigrated by employers, by aid societies, or through family equities. Still others have acquired fraudulent documents, allowing them to pass as legal immigrants, visitors, or more commonly, native-born citizens from some Spanish-speaking region like south Texas or northern New Mexico, while those family members lacking documents have continued to stay hidden in the barrios of the "invisible minority." That the present infiltration will follow the same pathways of legitimation seems assured. [41]

In the meantime, the actual number of Mexican illegals who, since World War II, have settled permanently in the country may have reached 2 or 3 million by 1970, presenting a growing census problem. An overall approximation of the number of Mexican-descent persons residing, legally or illegally, in the United States for recent decennial periods would be as shown in Table 7.

The extraordinary increase, especially since 1965, in the Chicano population appears quite evident to participant observers, such as immigration or social service personnel, who have followed the migratory fan-out from high-fertility border areas and Mexico. [42] For instance, the 1970 census found 160,477 Mexican-origin people in Illinois and 65,329 in Michigan, notable increases in themselves, but rough estimates of unregistered settlers would have doubled or tripled such figures. As close observers see it, increases are underreported because of the migratory flux and because most Mexican-origin families have members who originally entered clandestinely. It is characteristic of the invisible minority that some Chicano leaders have urged residents of barrios and colonias not to cooperate with census takers, while others protest gross undercounts. As Mexican migrants settle down and obtain legitimation or plausible documentation, they may allow all or most of the family (often an extended one, in sociological terms) to be counted. But, meanwhile, there is a spreading invisibility phenomenon that has profound implications for students of ethnic acculturation and for the hapless census taker. [43]

Table 7   Estimated Spanish-Surname and Mexican-Descent Population of Five Southwestern States and the United States

	1950	*1960*	*1970*
SOUTHWEST:			
California	758,400	1,426,538	2,222,185
Texas	1,027,455	1,417,810	1,663,567
Arizona	128,580	194,356	246,390
New Mexico	248,560	269,122	324,248*
Colorado	118,715	157,173	211,585
SUB-TOTALS (Spanish-Surnamed)	2,281,710	3,464,999	4,667,975**
LESS Spanish-Surnamed of non-Mexican descent in Southwest	60,000 (?)	131,397	322,179
MEXICAN-DESCENT IN 5 SOUTHWESTERN STATES	2,221,710	3,333,602	4,345,796
PLUS Mexican-origin population in all other states	130,000 (?)	224,934 (?)	593,801
ADJUSTED CENSUS TOTAL OF MEXICAN-DESCENT POPULATION IN U.S.	2,351,710 (?)	3,558,536 (?)	4,939,597
PLUS rough approximation of legal Mexican-descent population not counted by census-takers	200,000 (?)	400,000 (?)	800,000 (?)
PLUS rough approximation of illegal settlers from Mexico not counted by census-takers	600,000 (?)	1,000,000 (?)	2,000,000 (?)
PLUS uncounted perennial transborder migrants in U.S. at any given time	400,000 (?)	200,000 (?)***	600,000 (?)
ROUGH ESTIMATE OF TOTAL MEXICAN-DESCENT POPULATION IN U.S.	3,551,710 (?)	5,158,536 (?)	8,339,597 (?)

*Reflects rapid increase of "Spanish-American" enclave numbering about 60,000 in 1848, but also incoming Mexican migration that more than replaces the outflow of native New Mexicans to other states, particularly Colorado.

**The 1970 census gives the "Mexican-origin" population of the five southwestern states as 3,938,751, and for the United States, 4,532,552. Essentially those figures represent population groups derived from Mexican migration after 1900, whereas the Spanish-surnamed figures used above represent a broader category that includes Mexican-descent population that had roots in the country before 1900.

***Reflects better immigration control on then predominantly agro-migrants.

Sources: Excepting rough approximations, *1950 U.S. Census of Population, Persons of Spanish Surname*, Table A. Pages 3b-3c; also, *Population Characteristics of Selected Ethnic Groups in the Five Southwestern States.* 1960 Supplementary Report PC(SI)-55(1968); and Bureau of Census, Population Division, *News Release*, March 9, 1972, plus correspondence with Office of Director, Bureau of the Census; and *1970 Census of Population, Persons of Spanish Ancestry.* Supplementary Report PC(SI)-30(February 1973), p. II, and Table I.

Under pressure from ethnic leaders and patronage politicians seeking a larger share of political influence and federal assistance funds, the Census Bureau tries to find more Spanish-surnamed, principally Chicanos, but also Puerto Ricans and other Latin-American groups that seem to have a high degree of invisibility. Various counts since 1970 have found sharp increases in the Hispanic tide that perhaps can be, in good part, explained by unregistered migration and its generational effects. In any case, the Bureau reported in its *Current Population Survey* of March 1975 that there were in round figures 11.2 million persons of Hispanic or Spanish origin (the current "identifier") in the United States, including over 6,690,000 of Mexican origin (compared to only 4.9 million in 1970), 1.7 million Puerto Ricans (mostly in New York state, but also in Illinois), 740,000 Cubans (mainly in Florida), and 1.4 million of other Latin-American origin. California then had a reported Spanish-origin population of 3,194,000, or 15 percent of the state population; and Texas had 2,254,000, or 19 percent of its population. In all, the five southwestern states contained 6,439,000 Spanish-origin persons, 85 percent of them reportedly of Mexican origin. Also, the reported percentage of Spanish-origin persons in the United States grew from 4.5 percent to 5.3 percent between 1970 and 1975; and from 13.9 percent to 16.8 percent in the southwestern states.[44] No data was available for Illinois, but the percentage of Spanish-origin growth there would have been much greater.

Census findings have thus far not satisfied Mexican-American congressmen, like Edward Roybal or Henry B. González, or organizations like the Cabinet Committee on Opportunities for the Spanish Speaking and the National Council of La Raza. Accordingly, some congressmen have sponsored legislation to fund a "complete census" of the Spanish-surnamed. Characteristically, the Forum of National Hispanic Organizations, meeting in Washington, D.C., in September 1975, announced that it "seeks to bring to the attention of the American public that this nation's Spanish-speaking population totals 16 million people and that, if it were considered as a separate nation, it would be the fifth largest Spanish-speaking country in the world."[45] Hispanic leaders have commonly predicted that the Spanish-surnamed will be the nation's largest minority by 1990. (By then the nation's black minority would possibly number 35 million.) On January 15, 1976, President Ford signed Public Law 94-94-311 designed to improve census data on Spanish-surnamed groups.

Since 1971 congressmen seeking a firmer statistical basis for proposed reforms in immigration law have pressed the Immigration and Naturalization Service to provide something besides data on legal immigration and apprehen-apprehensions. Under Commissioner Chapman (1974-1976), the INS began its own approximations of the number of unregistered aliens. In 1975 Congress, worried about the ultimate reach of blanket amnesty proposals, added $1 million to the INS budget for a major study of illegal aliens. In November

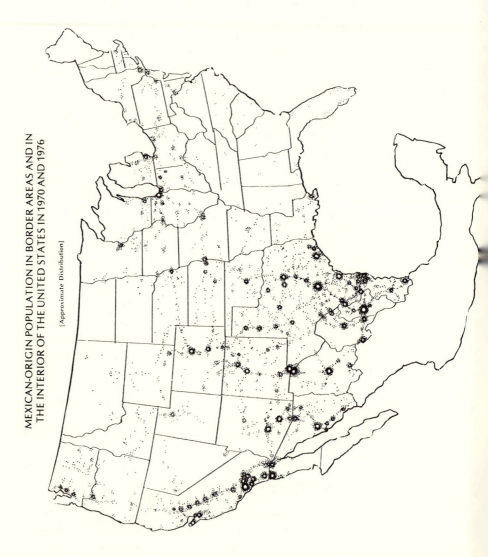

MEXICAN-ORIGIN POPULATION IN BORDER AREAS AND IN
THE INTERIOR OF THE UNITED STATES IN 1970 AND 1976

[Approximate Distribution]

Population of Mexico border states according to census of 1970:

Baja California [Norte]	870,000
Sonora	1,099,000
Chihuahua	1,613,000
Coahuila	1,115,000
Nuevo Leon	1,695,000
Tamaulipas	1,457,000
TOTAL	7,849,000

Population of Mexican origin in the United States in 1970

California	2,222,185
Arizona	246,390
New Mexico	324,248
Texas	1,663,567
Colorado	211,585
Other States	593,801
Less	-322,179+
Census Total	4,939,597
Plus Uncounted Groups	3,400,000?
Rough Total	8,340,000?

+ Spanish-surnamed of non-Mexican origin in Southwestern states.

Census update of March, 1976, showed a Mexican-origin population of 6,590,000, with uncounted groups then numbering perhaps 5 or 6 million.

1976 a one-year contract for that amount was awarded to J. A. Reyes Associates, who set a condition that the Service would have to stay away from the
barrios during that period. This condition itself was an ironic comment on the
impotence of the federal government with respect to the much denounced invisible invasion. [46]

Earlier, according to one preliminary survey, carried out by Lesko Associates under contract to the INS and reported in October 1975, a panel of persons specializing in migration studies made an average conservative estimate
of around 8.2 million illegal aliens residing in the country, of which possibly 5
or 6 million were of Mexican origin. [47]

In late 1975 immigration district officials, who usually undercount family
members, were asked to submit estimates of all illegals working or residing in
their respective districts. At least two-thirds of their total estimate were considered to be of Mexican origin, as shown in Table 8.

To continue the guessing game, it would seem probable that from 1820
through late 1976 close to 6 million Mexican emigrants settled permanently in
the United States, a probability derived from immigration data and rough estimates based on interviews in midwestern and southwestern states with immigration field officers and Mexican consuls in the period 1970-1976: (See Table
9.)

Since a lot of unregistered immigration from Mexico is recent and still dominated by young males, who later bring in family members, its full demographic and sociopolitical impact may not be fully visible for some years to come. In
any case, the conjectural figure of around 5.6 million for permanent Mexican
immigration, 1820-1976, might be compared to immigrant counts for the same
period from such countries as Germany, 6.9 million; the British Isles, 5.4 million; Italy, 5.3 million; Austria (Empire), 4.3 million; Ireland, 4.7 million; or
Canada and Newfoundland, 4 million. [48] Probably one should add something
for considerable unregistered immigration from certain countries, like
Canada and Italy.

By mid-1977 it was commonly estimated that (as in the 1920s) 10 percent of
Mexico's population, or about 6.5 million, had moved to the United States, although such estimates seem to have included a large number of seasonal transborder workers and casual visitors. [49] The amnesty rush that began early in
1977 further aggravated statistical headaches. (See Chapter 12.)

As a final conjecture, if one were to add the increase in Mexican-origin
groups since 1970 through immigration, counted and uncounted, and the
natural increase, not fully counted, then the total Mexican and Mexican-
American population in the United States by mid-1977 (again, discounting
perennial transborder migrants) might have been around 11 or 12 million, or
even more. [50] But, *¿quien sabe?*

Table 8   Estimated Total Number of Illegal Aliens by Immigration
Districts, 1975

Western Region

Honolulu	1,500 –	1,600
Los Angeles	1,350,000 –	1,500,000
Phoenix	50,000 –	55,000
San Francisco	220,000 –	240,000

Southern Region

Atlanta	75,000 –	80,000
El Paso	75,000 –	80,000
Houston	525,000 –	550,000
Miami	360,000 –	380,000
New Orleans	40,000 –	50,000
San Antonio	310,000 –	330,000

Northern Region

Anchorage	600 –	700
Chicago	375,000 –	400,000
Cleveland	75,000 –	80,000
Denver	30,000 –	35,000
Detroit	50,000 –	60,000
Helena	2,000 –	3,000
Kansas City	10,000 –	12,000
Omaha	6,000 –	7,000
Portland, Ore.	25,000 –	30,000
St. Paul	6,000 –	7,000
Seattle	10,000 –	12,000

Eastern Region

Baltimore	60,000 –	70,000
Boston	10,000 –	15,000
Buffalo	10,000 –	15,000
Hartford	7,000 –	8,000
Newark	275,000 –	300,000
New York	1,350,000 –	1,500,000
Philadelphia	80,000 –	90,000
Portland, Me.	3,000 –	3,000
San Juan	10,000 –	15,000
St. Albans	500 –	600
Washington, D.C.	50,000 –	60,000

Estimated Total	5,451,600 –	5,989,900

Source: U.S. Senate, Judiciary Committee, *Hearings before the Subcommittee on Immigration and Naturalization . . . on S. 3074 . . . March-April, 1976, 94th
Cong., 2nd Sess.* (1976), pp. 39-41.

Table 9　　Rough Estimates of Total Immigration, 1820-1976
(figures in second column rounded off)

1820-1900		
Legal immigration (no record for 1886-1893)	8,046	
Uncounted settlers (rough estimate partly based on census counts of foreign-born Mexicans in the United States)	160,000 (?)	
		168,000 (?)
1901-1930		
Legal immigration (includes many later legalized)	727,933	
Uncounted settlers (rough estimate)	750,000 (?)	
		1,478,000 (?)
1931-1940		
Legal immigration	22,319	
Repatriation to Mexico (estimate)	−450,000 (?)	
Repatriates who returned surreptitiously (estimate)	150,000 (?)	
		−277,700 (?)
1941-1976		
Legal immigration, 1941-1975 (includes many later legalized)	1,121,726	
Plus 57,863 immigrants in new fiscal 1976*	57,863	
Uncounted settlers, including perhaps 2.5 million since 1966 (rough estimate)	4,500,000 (?)	
		5,679,600 (?)
Subtotal		7,047,900 (?)
Less rough estimate of around 20 percent for long-term settlers, mostly illegals, who voluntarily return permanently to Mexico		1,410,000 (?)
Total rough approximation of permanent Mexican settlers in the United States, 1820-1976		5,637,900 (?)

Note. Rough estimates include family members, of course, but not migrant workers, legal and illegal, who cross the border seasonally, or deported persons.

Figures for legal immigration, 1820-1960, are from INS, *Annual Report*, Table 13: "Immigration by Country" (includes some non-Mexicans); and for 1961-1976, Table 14: "Immigration by Country or Region of Birth," in fiscal years. The two tables vary slightly.

In fiscal 1976 the terminal date was shifted from June 30 to September 30. Up to June 30, 1976, legal immigrants numbered 57,863, and up to September 30, 73,864.

Notes

1. Tuck, *Not with the Fist*, p. 62.

2. Statistical deficiencies in Mexican immigration have already been considered by Paul S. Taylor, *Mexican Labor in the United States: Migration Statistics*, I, University of California Publications in Economics, Vol. 6, No. 3 (Berkeley, 1929), 237-255; and *ibid.*, IV, Vol. 12, No. 3 (1934), 23-50; also, Leo Grebler, *Mexican Immigration to the United States: The Record and Its Implications*, Mexican-American Study Project, No. 2 (Los Angeles: University of California Press, 1966).

3. Clark, "Mexican Labor," p. 521.

4. Taylor, *Mexican Labor. . . Migration Statistics*, I, 6:3 (1929), 242.

5. Interviews with twelve retired immigration officers living in border cities during tour of United States-Mexico border in period April-August 1970. Most of these informants were original members of the U.S. Border Patrol founded in 1925, two of them had been mounted inspectors as early as 1916, and nearly all of them had spent a lifetime in the border region.

6. See Joe W. Neal, "The Policy of the United States toward Immigration from Mexico" (Master's thesis, University of Texas, Austin, 1941); Lipshultz, "American Attitudes."

7. *Annual Report of the Commissioner General of Immigration, 1920*, p. 427.

8. Interviews with retired immigration officers, April-August 1970. See also Mary K. Rak's *Border Patrol* (Boston: Houghton Mifflin, 1938) which said little about apprehending illegal aliens and much about the border guard's adventures with liquor smugglers; and John M. Myers, *The Border Wardens* (Englewood Cliffs, N.J.: Prentice Hall, 1971), an informal history of the border patrol that makes it quite clear that in the period before the end of prohibition in 1934 the border guards were chiefly preoccupied with the smuggling of Orientals and "bootleg liquor."

9. U.S. Immigration and Naturalization Service (INS), *Annual Reports*, Table 13.

10. See Taylor's study, *A Mexican-American Frontier*.

11. For estimates of the Spanish-speaking population in 1848 and 1850, see Richard L. Nostrand, "Mexican Americans circa 1850," *Annals of the Association of American Geographers*, 65: 3 (September 1975), 378-390; and Oscar J. Martínez, who suggests a higher range of estimates, "On the Size of the Chicano Population: New Estimates, 1850-1900," *Aztlán*, 6:1 (Spring 1975), 43-67. See also Chapter 2, Notes 20, 21.

12. Landa y Pina, *El servicio de migración*, pp. 19-23.

13. For fuller data see García y Griego, "Los Primeros Pasos al Norte," and Reisler, *By the Sweat of Their Brow*, Tables 1-3.

14. Landa y Piña, *El servicio de migración*, p. 23.

15. Letter of January 15, 1970, from Dr. Leo Grebler, Director of Mexican-American Study Project, UCLA (1964-1969). Dr. Grebler visited Mexico City in search of Mexican migration data.

16. Landa y Piña, *El servicio de migración*, pp. 19, 23. These figures also appear in Taylor, *Mexican Labor . . . Migration Statistics*, I, 6:3 (1929), p. 240; and in George N. Winters' memorandum of 1928 on "Mexican Migratory Statistics," which is partly reproduced in the *Congressional Record-Senate* (April 16, 1930), pp. 7117-7118. Winters was with the American Consulate General in Mexico City.

17. Landa y Piña, *El servicio de migración*, p. 26; see also Manuel Gamio's discussion of inconsistencies in *Mexican Immigration*, pp. 7-12.

18. *Memoria de la Secretaría de Relaciones Exteriores de agosto de 1927 a julio de 1928* (Mexico, D.F., 1928), pp. 817-824.

19. See Gamio's explanations for illegal entrance, *Mexican Immigration*, pp. 10-11; also Taylor's account of procedural variations, *Mexican Labor . . . Migration Statistics*, I, 6:3 (1929), 248-251.

20. Interviews with U.S. and Mexican border officals, Laredo, El Paso, Ciudad Juárez, Tijuana, and Mexico City, May-August 1970 and August 1972. Also Taylor, *Mexican Labor . . . Migration Statistics*, I, 248-251. Notably, U.S. border officials seek seriously only to record legal immigrants returning to Mexico or Canada for a long period, for this could endanger future resident-alien status.

21. The 1930 census gives a figure of 616,998 for foreign-born Mexicans, but the 1940 census gives a revised figure of 639,017. The latter is used in this study. See *Fifteenth Census . . . 1930. Population. Special Report on Foreign-Born White Families* (1933), p. 6; and *Sixteenth Census, II, Characteristics . . .* part 1, Table 15.

22. See also Robert N. McLean, "Tightening the Mexican Border," *Survey Graphic*, LXIV: 1 (April 1, 1930). McLean, a missionary and social worker, discussed some of the panic effects on the Mexican colonies in the United States caused by the law of March 4, 1929, which made it a felony for an alien to enter the country illegally after once being deported. Excerpts of the McLean article appeared in *Congressional Record - Senate* (April 16, 1930), p. 7129. Moreover, according to interviews with Mexican settlers in south Texas (May-June 1970), in Laredo, Brownsville and San Antonio before the 1929 law, which also made a first illegal entry a misdemeanor, surreptitious settlers had little fear of penalties and felt more at ease with census-takers. But after 1929 many unregistered settlers sought birth certificates from county court houses, or legal visas, or they "disappeared" in the Mexican *colonias* and *barrios*.

23. "Immigration and Naturalization Service," in *Annual Report of the Secretary of Labor, 1935*, pp. 78-79.

24. The figures for Mexico-born population by states is from *Fifteenth Census, 1930: Population*, II, 446. The total figure for the United States is from *Sixteenth Census, 1940: Population*, II, Part 1, 42, 88, which gave a higher total figure than the 1930 census count. This means that 1930 figures for each state would be slightly higher than indicated in table.

25. Figures for distribution of Mexican-stock population are from: Taylor, *Mexican Labor . . . Migration Statistics*, IV, 30; U.S. Bureau of Labor Statistics, *Monthly Labor Review*, XXXVII (July 1933), 46-47; and E.S. Bogardus, *Mexicans in the United States* (University of Southern California Press, 1934), pp. 13-14.

A rough estimate of over 2 million in 1930 is based, in part, on the fact that U.S. census counted only foreign-born Mexicans and second-generation Mexicans as people of Mexican origin. Not fully counted were the decendants of native Mexican-American groups whose ancestors were in the country in 1848; nor uncounted Mexican migrants who settled in the border areas in the period 1848-1900; nor unregistered Mexican settlers after 1900; and apparently some second-generation settlers in the period 1910-1930 were overlooked, or counted in the general white population.

Unlike the Chinese, Filipinos, Indians, and Negroes, who have been consistently identified as groups in the U.S. census, the 1930 census and previous (and subsequent) censuses counted third-generation, or older Mexican-descent, groups as part of the general white population. That large groups of Spanish-speaking were not included in the 1930 Mexican-stock population is indicated by the estimate that there were 200,000 or more persons of Hispano or Hispano-Mexican descent in New Mexico, yet the 1930 census figure was only 59,340 for Mexican-stock population there. See Taylor, *Migration Statistics*, IV, 28-30. McWilliams (*North from Mexico*, p. 56) estimated 2,100,000 for all Mexican-descent groups in the United States in 1930: about 500,000 in California; 1 million in Texas; 120,000 in Arizona; 250,000 in New Mexico; and 90,000 in Colorado; the remainder were scattered over several states. Other estimates of Mexican population around 1930, ranging from 1.4 million to 2.5 million, are indicated in the *Congressional Record-Senate* (April 16, 1930), p. 7133.

26. One source for this rough calculation is based on interviews with retired immigration officers in border states, April-August 1970. There seems little doubt that illegal immigration increased greatly through the 1920s in spite of the establishment of a civil service border patrol in 1925. Also taken into account were the calculations of the probable number of illegals given in *Mexicans in California* (1930), pp. 18-21, 27-39; and in Louis Bloch, "Facts about Mexican Immigration Before and Since Quota Restriction Laws," *Journal of the American Statistical Association* (March 1929), p. 51. Bloch compared Mexican immigration figures with U.S. census data on Mexican population in 1900, 1910, and 1920, and reached an estimate of 200,000 illegal immigrants for the period 1900-1920. See, also, Taylor, *Migration Statistics*, I, 252-253; and Santibañez, *Ensayo acerca*.

27. Data on the number of long-time Mexican settlers in the United States who return to live in Mexico has always been fragmentary. For recent years some Mexican officials estimate that around 3-5 percent of legal emigrants return as repatriates to Mexico, but some of these become border commuters; and that the percentage of illegal emigrants who voluntarily return would be much higher, according to interviews with Mexican consular officers in Mexico City, San Antonio, Dallas, and Kansas City, February-April 1974.

28. A thorough account of massive deportation from southern California is given by Hoffman, *Unwanted Mexican Americans*. The Mexican side is told by Carreras de Velasco, *Los mexicanos que devolvió*. Aside from Hoffman and Carreras de Velasco, statistics on repatriation during the peak years 1930-1934 can be found in Taylor, *Migration Statistics*, IV, 23-25, 48; Bogardus, *Mexicans in the United States*, pp. 90-97; and in U.S. National Archives, Record Group 59, file 811.111 Mexico.

29. U.S. consular correspondence in R.G. 59, file 811.504 Mexico, 417-423; and 811.111 Mexico/1188/1236/1238.

30. Statements based on interviews with U.S. immigration officers in Laredo, San Antonio, El Paso, and Yuma, June-August 1970; and on consular correspondence during the 1930s in R.G. 59; also, on interviews with Mexican repatriates established in the agrarian colonies of Valle Hermoso, Colonia "18 de Marzo" and other agrarian settlements in the state of Tamaulipas; and in Colonia Anahuac, Nuevo Leon, August 23 and December 20-21, 1970, and July 1-2, 1971.

31. Figures on foreign-born Mexicans and Mexican-descent groups vary somewhat. Those used here were taken from *Sixteenth Census: 1940. Population*. Vol. II: *Characteristics*, 12, 42; and *U.S. Census of Population: 1950. Special Reports on Persons of Spanish Surname*, Report of Vol. IV, Part 3, Chap. C (1953), 3C6.

32. INS, *Annual Reports*, Tables 13, 14: Immigrants admitted by country, or region of birth; and Grebler, *Mexican Immigration*, p. 106.

33. Interviews with U.S. consular and immigration officers in Mexico City, August 14-15, 18, 1970; Nuevo Laredo, May 2, 1970; and Ciudad Juárez, August 25, 1972.

34. Grebler, *Mexican Immigration*, pp. 34, 89.

35. According to several interviews with U.S. consular officers in Mexico City, January 9 and February 28, 1974; and Monterrey, March 12-13, 18, 20, 1970.

36. INS, *Annual Reports*, Table 14. In 1976 the ending date of the fiscal year was changed from June 30 to September 30.

37. Chicano and other Latino groups had strongly protested discrimination in the immigration reforms of 1965 which permitted Eastern Hemisphere residents only to adjust status without having to return to an American consular office in the home country. See House Judiciary Committee, *Illegal Aliens, Hearings before the Subcommittee on Immigration, Citizenship, and International Law, 94th Cong., 1st Sess., on H.R. 982 . . . February-March, 1975, Serial No. 8* (1975); and Senate Judiciary Committee, *Immigration 1976, Hearings before the Subcommittee on Immigration and Naturalization, 94th Cong., 2d Sess., on S. 3074 to Amend the Immigration and Nationality Act . . . March-April, 1976* (1976). For court-ordered stays of deportation and legitimation proposals of the Carter administration, see William Cooney, "Illegal Aliens Who May Get to Stay," *San Francisco Chronicle*, June 13, 1977, p. 9; and Austin Scott, "A U.S. Plan for a New Class of Aliens," *Washington Post*, June 11, 1977, reprinted in *Excelsior* (Mexico City), June 12, 1977, p. 2A.

38. See also Samora, (et al.,) *Los Mojados*. According to this study, apprehensions of Mexican illegals numbered 5,628,712 in the period 1924-1969; of course, many of these were repeaters.

39. A rough rule-of-thumb was derived from interviews with immigration and border patrol officer, April-August 1970, August 1972, and April 1974.

40. Rough conjecture is, in part, derived from interviews with employers, Mexican laborers, social workers, Mexican-American residents, and immigration officials during tours of southwestern states in summers of 1970 and 1972, and during visits to midwestern cities such as St. Paul, Omaha, and Chicago in the fall of 1973.

41. U.S. Congress, House Committee on the Judiciary, *Illegal Aliens, Hearings . . . 92d Cong., 1st and 2d Sess.* (five parts, 1971-1972).

42. In general the Mexican-origin population, receiving a constant and unmeasured infusion of folk customs from Mexico, has one of the highest rates of natural increase among America's minorities, probably about 2.7 percent in the 1960s and early 1970s. Not surprisingly the Census Bureau in its current population report of March 1973 found that this group had jumped to 6.29 million, or an increase of 27 percent in three years! Obviously uncounted groups were also a big factor. See *The News*, Mexico City, January 17, 1974. And for the demographic characteristics of the south Texas subculture see Browning and McLemore, *A Statistical Profile*.

43. According to Ralph Guzman, a participant in the UCLA Mexican-American Study Project (1966-1970), a census-taker, or any official visitor, "triggers nervousness" among poor Chicanos who seem to have "invisible antennae that warn them about the enemy." See *Availability and Usefulness of Federal Programs and Services to Elderly Mexican-Americans. Hearings before the Special Committee on Aging*, Senate, 90th Cong., 2d Sess., Part 1 (1969), 80-81. For profiles of rapid Mexican population growth and resultant migratory displacement toward Mexican cities and the American border, see Weaver and Downing (eds.), *Mexican Migration*.

44. U.S. Department of Commerce, Bureau of the Census, "New Release," March 22, 1976; and *Current Population Reports: Population Characteristics, Persons of Spanish Origin in the United States, March, 1975,* Series P-20, No. 290 (Washington, D.C., 1976), pp. 4, 20.

45. National Council of La Raza, Washington, D.C., *Agenda* (newsletter), 5:9 (September 1975), 1.

46. Dick Seelmeyer, Newhouse News Service, "$1 Million, One year, Alloted for Study of Illegal Aliens," *Fort Worth Star Telegram*, November 14, 1976.

47. Lesko Associates, "Final Report." Also, for rough estimates of all illegal aliens in the United States by INS, AFL, and others, ranging from 5 to 12 million and higher, see Harvey Ardman, "Our Illegal Alien Problem," *The American Legion Magazine*, 97:6 (December 1964), 6-9, 37-40; and estimates of then-Attorney General William B. Saxbe, in Ronald J. Ostrow, "Saxbe Urges Deportation of Aliens," *Los Angeles Times*, November 1, 1974.

48. INS, *Annual Report*, Table 13.

49. "10 % of Mexico's Population," *The New York Times*, May 16, 1977, as reported in *Excelsior* (Mexico City), May 17, 1977; "Cada noche 1,000 Mexicanos," *Excelsior*, May 25, 1977; "5 y medio millones de indocumentados trabajan," *Excelsior*, June 6, 1977.

50. Mexican-American leaders, who have been interviewed, commonly have placed the present Mexican-origin population at between 9 and 13 million.

6/ A STORY OF AD HOC EXEMPTIONS: AMERICAN IMMIGRATION POLICY TOWARD MEXICO

Arthur F. Corwin

She: My ancestors came over on the *Mayflower*.

He: It's lucky they did. The immigration laws are a little bit stricter now.

Americana

Patterns of Restrictions and Exemptions

In the popular mind American immigration policy is symbolized by the Statute of Liberty and by the poetic words of Emma Lazarus dedicated to the "Mother of Exiles" and the "poor . . . huddled masses."

Yet even before the monument was completed in 1886 the national government was beginning to close the front door, if not the back door, on a historic policy of unrestricted immigration. From 1875 to 1929 Congress passed a number of immigration laws which established qualitative and quantitative restrictions.[1] The exclusionist principles contained in this legislation may be briefly summed up as (1) the non-admission of (a) persons of criminal character, (b) persons of defective mental or physical health, (c) paupers or persons likely to become a public charge, (d) aliens recruited or contracted to work as cheap labor, (e) anarchists or others who advocate the violent overthrow of government, and (f) illiterate adult immigrants, after 1917, (2) the non-admission of Orientals of the coolie-labor class and the ineligibility for naturalization of Orientals who had immigrated, and (3) quota restrictions on most countries, according to the acts of 1921 and 1924.

Cumulative immigration controls reflected two principal concerns of Congress. First and foremost, North American cultural traditions and the proper functioning of its civil institutions seemed threatened by the avalanche of immigrants coming from radically different cultural backgrounds. In the period 1850-1917 most of some 30 million immigrants were from central,

136

eastern, and Mediterranean Europe, and it seemed that Uncle Sam's complaint of alien indigestion could only be relieved by restricting the intake of aliens. Second, many of these immigrants were illiterate, poverty-stricken peasants recruited and transported to urban slums and company camps as helpless, low-cost labor for the benefit of American manufacturers and industrialists. Civic leaders naturally became concerned about protecting American living and working standards, particularly for wage earners, from the undermining effects of foreign labor competition.[2]

Oddly, none of this restrictionist concern was aimed specifically at transborder migration. Up until World War I, except for some efforts to check clandestine European and Oriental immigration by way of Mexico and Canada, the federal government manifested no serious concern about the contracting of unskilled labor from contiguous countries. In fact, peon labor from Mexico had been crossing the border without inspection since the 1880s, when a network of railways linked the two countries. And yet not until Victor S. Clark's field study of 1908 did the federal government take note of the increasing use of low-cost Mexican labor in the mines, railroads and agriculture of the Southwest and beyond.[3]

The Dillingham Report, the outcome of an exhaustive inquiry by the Joint Commission on Immigration of the American Congress, 1907-1911, published in forty-two volumes in 1911, had relatively little policy interest in the many Mexican aliens discovered working in the southwestern states. It noted laconically that Mexicans made better workers than citizens but assumed, conveniently, that few would remain permanently in the United States.[4] In retrospect, it seems that the Dillingham Commission, which provided the rationale for the general immigration act of February 5, 1917, was exclusively preoccupied with developing a case against "unqualified immigration" from Europe and the Orient.[5]

Furthermore, there is little or no published evidence that the Mexican Revolution, which erupted in 1910 and drove tens of thousands of refugees over the border, had any influence on the qualitative restrictions codified in the law of 1917, or on the quota system first established, in principle, by the law of May 19, 1921. On the contrary, it was during the Mexican upheaval that the federal government first applied to transborder migration its ad hoc policy of exemptions, as panic-driven refugees crowded against the gateways to border cities. Following the advice of the State Department and with the approval of the Secretary of Labor, who was then responsible for immigration affairs at the cabinet level, immigration officials quietly had qualitative restrictions suspended, as when thousands of refugees were paroled—temporarily, it was believed—into the border states. A border immigration official in the *Annual Report* of 1912 explained the "border asylum policy," which has been in effect from time to time, as a humanitarian response to a drama taking place on the doorstep of the United States:

No inconsiderable number of aliens, resident of Mexico have sought refuge in this country, some of whom, practically destitute, have been as a measure of humanity, given asylum. . . . It was felt that the unusual and oftentimes harrowing circumstances influencing their applications justified a more than liberal interpretation of the law.[6]

Border immigration authorities were more inclined to be permissive because American missionaries and social workers, who saw forced Mexican migration as a God-given evangelical opportunity, were more than willing to give temporary aid to indigent refugees, thus obviating to some extent the need to apply the "likely to become a public charge" restriction.[7] Also, American consular and immigration officials along the Mexican border were under the impression that refugee migration was temporary. The immigration chief at El Paso noted in 1912 that "there is every reason to believe that when the affairs of our sister republic have become settled, a large majority of these aliens will return."[8] Would not the same border proximity that had facilitated refugee access to American border cities likewise facilitate refugee return?

However, like subsequent developments in Mexican migration history, a temporary phenomenon soon acquired a more permanent character. Only a year later the El Paso office had revised its assessment, predicting that "unless conditions in Mexico become settled in the near future, a satisfactory disposition of the refugees may become a serious problem," and, noting further, that even the "better classes" who had arrived in border cities with some material means of support soon ran out of funds and were seeking employment.[9] Some of the refugees who possessed special skills or a high degree of literacy soon made a successful and even prosperous adjustment to southwestern cities like El Paso, San Antonio, and Los Angeles. Most of the refugees, however, were of the illiterate campesino class, lacking in industrial, agricultural, commercial, or professional skills, and thus, by circumstance, they joined the pre-revolutionary wave of migrant labor described by Clark.

Before the end of the 1920s another odd facet of American exemptions for border peoples had taken root—the border commuter, who has been defined as an alien who resides (or sleeps) in a contiguous country and crosses daily, several times a week, or seasonally to employment, supposedly stable, on the American side. Years before the general immigration act of February 5, 1917, several thousand Mexican and Canadian nationals were commuting as a "customary right" across the border to work without a passport or immigration document. They were free to do so if they did not infringe on health, national security, and contract-labor restrictions. General immigration acts made no change in the commuter status.[10] True, the act of 1924 required an immigrant visa and a $10 fee from each immigrant seeking to reside in the United States, but since residence and not employment was the criterion, the Immigration Service characteristically made an administrative decision to classify border residents commuting to American jobs as "temporary visitors for business purposes," thus exempting them from visa requirements.

The American Federation of Labor protested the "businessman fiction," especially since Canadian "visitors" were being used as strike breakers in the 1920s. The Department of Labor responded on April 1, 1927, with General Order 86, which classified the commuter as an immigrant and stated that future applications for commuter-immigrant status would have to follow standard immigration procedures. Also, the commuter was not to be absent from the job for more than six months, but for many years this rule was not consistently enforced, particularly on the Mexican border. Critics considered the commuter-immigrant an administrative invention without a footing in immigration laws, but the Supreme Court upheld the commuter-immigrant status in 1929. [11] The federal government tended to see this arrangement as harmonious with non-quota exemptions for Pan American countries, the give-and-take nature of border relations, and a humane concern about job dislocations and personal hardships. [12]

Since a new visa for each commuter entry would be an administrative burden, the Immigration Service devised a multiple-entry "immigrant border-crossing card" with a photo of the holder. By 1940 it was known as a "resident-alien border-crossing card," or "green card." By the time of the Immigration and Nationality Act of 1952, it had evolved into the "Alien Registration Receipt Card" (Form I-151), a blue card now held by all immigrants. In the meantime, "green-carder" status received further sanction or countenance by Congress in the Alien Registration Act of 1940 and in subsequent court hearings. [13]

Presently most commuters are domiciled in Mexican border towns (and some are American citizens of Mexican origins who prefer to live there). At a given time, probably half of all Mexican commuters cross the line to work at permanent, part-time, or seasonal jobs. Since the 1940s Mexicans holding legal "green cards" have numbered around 100,000; by comparison, Canadian commuters have numbered between 10,000 and 20,000. Green carders are, by the way, eligible to move to the United States as permanent resident aliens. [14]

Since the Depression of the 1930s, the commuter flux has been denounced for its adverse effects on jobs, wages, and unionizing efforts of American natives in border areas, particularly where Mexican commuters have often been used as strike breakers in agriwork. But larger considerations have overridden such complaints. A 1954 decision of the Board of Immigration Appeals described the special character of commuter labor policy as a form of Good Neighbor favoritism: "The commuter situation manifestly does not fit into any precise category found in immigrant statutes. The status is an artificial one, predicted upon international relations maintained and cherished between friendly neighbors." [15]

Actually the commuter green card or blue card is a license to hunt for a permanent job on the American side. Once secured, it can give the commuter and his immediate relatives the incentive and the means to immigrate permanently. Over the years, thousands of commuter-immigrants have moved to the United States from Mexico, their place immediately filled by new commuters. Perhaps the final word on border commuting should be given to an American consul of Irish extraction: "He would not exist if the border area involved was the Atlantic Ocean which effectively prevented my own ancestors from becoming commuters."[16]

Another facet of border reciprocity has quite innocently facilitated labor migration from contiguous countries. After the general act of 1917 imposed closer inspection at all borders, the Immigration Service, following a policy of reciprocity, began issuing in good faith, permanent nonresident border-crossing cards to presumed residents of Mexican and Canadian border towns for shopping, visiting, and business purposes. For many years these cards were not subject to a time or space limit. Because of frequent abuses, however, the act of 1952 limited each visit to seventy-two hours and to a 150-mile limit. No limit was placed on the number of seventy-two-hour visits, and no effective control system, then or now, has been devised, computerized or not, for determining the misuse of visitor cards.

Since 1969 the use of the border-crossing card, held by over a million Mexican nationals, has been further limited to the immediate border area (twenty-five miles), unless the holder obtains a pass from the Immigration Service for a temporary visit to interior points. Through the years visitor cards, now issued as Form I-186 (I-185 for Canadians), have served to admit countless thousands of Mexican workers and settlers to the United States, under the guise of shoppers and visitors, where they simply disappear into Mexican-American communities. [17] Many obtain false birth certificates, and if undetected they have, in fact, immigrated. For a small fee Mexican border officials have always been ready to vouch for the long-time residence of the applicant, and to issue the needed identity document for obtaining the border-crossing card. [18]

Form I-186, like the green card, can be used by an alien as a license to hunt for a job or as a settlement opportunity. Where else would one find thousands of aliens using "shopping cards" to work part-time in border cities as domestics or in other low-paying jobs? Because of poverty and lack of economic opportunities in Mexico, the misuse of Form I-186 is much more common on the Mexican border than on the border to Canada, where standards of living equal those of the United States.[19]

Another instance of the relaxation of immigration standards for border peoples is the admission of emergency labor. An early but instructive example of this policy is the period of "departmental exceptions." As a reaction to the labor shortage of World War I, the Secretary of Labor authorized immigration officials to exempt illiterate temporary laborers of the Mexican campesino class from the immigrant qualifications and head tax provisions of the general act of 1917. [20] These exceptions, which ran from May 23, 1917, to March 2, 1921, are especially significant because, for the first time, the federal government practiced its ad hoc policy that regards neighboring non-quota countries, like Canada and especially Mexico, and overpopulated islands like Jamaica, the Bahamas, Haiti, and Puerto Rico to be handy pools of emergency labor to be turned on and off from time to time according to national needs, as in the war-time bracero program that started in 1942.

One might have thought that the Alien Contract Labor Act of 1885, which prohibited the importation of unskilled alien workers, and which was incorporated into the general act of February 3, 1917, had prohibited this practice once and for all. But the 1917 act contained an emergency clause known as the Ninth Proviso, which authorized the Commissioner of Immigration to admit temporary contract labor upon approval from the Secretary of Labor. [21] This proviso was not intended to favor the use of Mexican labor. It simply happened that Mexican labor was the most available.

Unfortunately for immigration control, tapping a surplus labor pool in a poverty-stricken border country has always proved much easier than shutting off the flow. During the four-year period of departmental exceptions, more than 72,000 Mexican peons were legally admitted to work primarily as unskilled contract labor on railroads and in agriculture. No one knows how many thousands of workers crossed illegally during this period, many of them excited by the reports of high wartime wages and encouraged by the example of temporary exemptions. [22]

The depression of 1921 was a signal for a cutoff of emergency Mexican labor. The Secretary of Labor ordered the Immigration Service to return contract workers together with illegal wetback entries and those who had skipped contracts. Thus, in 1921 the federal government inaugurated the first of its "wetback drives," which have become a unique facet of American immigration control of the Mexican labor pool. In the period 1921-1924 some 24,000 temporary workers who had left their original employers were tracked down and returned to Mexico. At the same time it was estimated that this drive, which centered on the western and midwestern states, frightened more than 100,000 wetbacks across the border. But in the same time period it is probable that two or three times as many wetbacks filtered into the United States. [23]

The "Mexican Problem" of the 1920s and the Response

In the 1920s we have other examples of exceptions. On May 19, 1921, Congress passed the first quota law seeking to limit certain ethnic groups and favor the admission of others. The immigration act of May 26, 1924, provided for a permanent quota system. From July 1, 1924, to June 30, 1929, the quota was set at 2 percent of the foreign-born residents in the United States as of 1890. After

1929, quotas were based not on the number of foreign-born at a given date, but on the early origins of the U.S. population according to studies of the census of 1790 and 1920. This arrangement, which set the total number of quota immigrants at 150,000 per annum, was designed to reinforce the Anglo-American heritage by favoring immigration from the British Isles. From 1929 until the quota system was abolished in 1965, the allotment for the British Isles was set at 65,721; that for Germany, 25,957; Ireland, 17,853; Poland, 6,524; and Italy, 5,677. Thereafter, the size of the quotas diminished rapidly, many countries having a standard quota of 100, and most Oriental countries, except the Philippines, no quota allowance at all. [24]

Mexico and other western hemisphere countries were in no way subject to the quota system. But by 1921 Congress was fully aware of the proportions of legal and illegal immigrants from Mexico and the rising protests against a growing social problem in many southwestern communities. During the period 1921-1931, several amendments and bills were introduced in Congress that would have included western hemisphere countries in the quota system. These hotly debated proposals were aimed principally at Mexican campesino migration, which rose remarkably after the immigration acts of 1917, 1921, and 1924. [25] In 1910 only 17,700 Mexicans had legally immigrated to the United States, but in 1920 some 51,000 did so, and in 1924 more than 87,000. This latter figure was larger than the entire quota for the British Isles.

It was common knowledge that many Mexican immigrants were being sponsored by southwestern employers seeking to import low-cost labor. Of greater concern to certain congressional leaders was the rising current of Mexican settlers coming in illegally as wetbacks without meeting any of the inspection standards embodied in immigration law. [26] Senator Frank B. Willis of Ohio, one of the sponsors of a Mexican quota and an outspoken opponent of special exemptions for transborder laborers, pointed out in the quota debate of 1924 that unrestricted back-door migration was a ridiculous contradiction:

The Senate yesterday very definitely adopted the policy of restricted selected immigration. . . . Now what does it amount to if we shut and padlock the front door . . . yet leave the back door open? . . .

Mr. President, upon what theory shall it be said that applied to Englishmen, for example, only two per cent on the basis of the census of 1890 can come in, and yet as to Mexicans . . . practically without education and largely without experience in self-government, and, in most cases, not at all qualified for present citizenship or for assimilation . . . say in effect, "As many as you please. . . ?"[27]

For different motives State Department officials and congressional liberals joined with legislators representing railroad, mining, and agricultural employers in southwestern and midwestern states to defeat easily the proposed western hemisphere quotas. [28] A decisive factor was the administration's concern with safeguarding special relations with Pan American governments, particu-

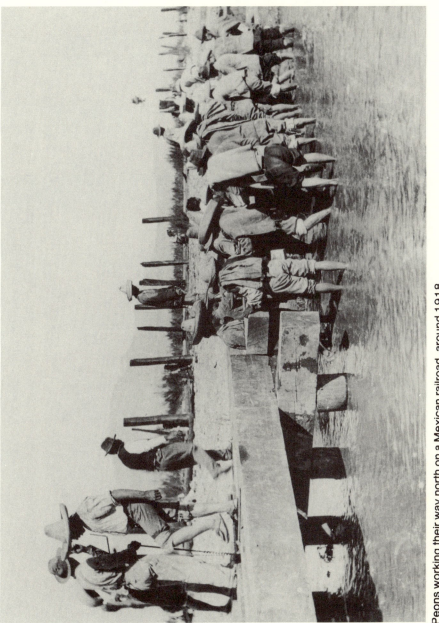

Peons working their way north on a Mexican railroad, around 1918
Courtesy Archivo Casasola (Mexico City)

The United States Border Patrol versus the wetback—a posed photo from the 1920s
Courtesy of Judge Fletcher L. Rawls, former Chief Patrol Agent, McAllen, Texas

Imperial Valley carrot pickers, 1939

Photo by Dorothea Lange, Library of Congress

Typical plantation-type migrant housing, Ed Couch, Texas, 1939
Photo by Russell Lee, Library of Congress

Cheaper than machines—Mexican pecan shellers in San Antonio during the Depression, 1939
Photo by Russell Lee, Library of Congress

Welcome for Mexican beet workers who arrived by bracero train,
Stockton, California, May 1943
Office of War Information Photo, Library of Congress

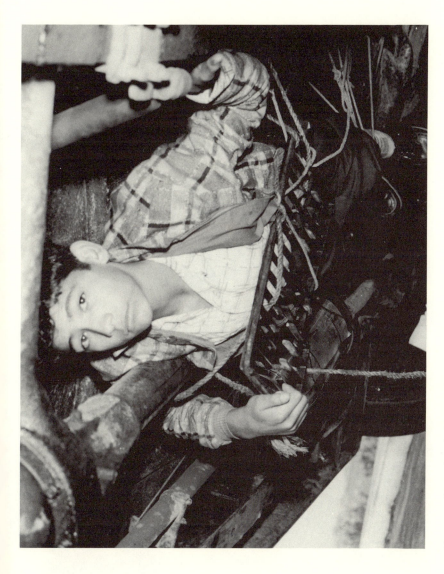

Young emigrant headed for the Promised Land, 1973

U.S. Immigration Service Photo

Guadalupe Salas Villarreal, who arrived in 1907 from Parral, Chihuahua,
today a community leader, president of the Comisión Honorífica,
and retired steelworker, Pueblo, Colorado, 1973
Courtesy of Pueblo Chieftain and Pueblo Star-Journal

From Silao, Guanajuato, Manuel D. Carmona, skilled machinist, Topeka, 1976
Courtesy of *The Atchison, Topeka and Santa Fe Railway Company*

Accommodation politics: the mayor coming to terms with the
Mexican colony in Chicago, 1975
Copyright, Wide World Photos, Inc., New York

Population dynamics as seen by noted Mexican cartoonist Carreño, March 26, 1975.
Courtesy of Siempre! Presencia de México, *Mexico City*

larly Mexico and Canada. At the time the federal government was deeply concerned about the sensitive state of American relations with revolutionary Mexico, where North American investments in oil, mining, and ranching were
threatened with expropriation. In the 1920s nearly all U.S. foreign investments
were concentrated in Mexico, Canada, and Cuba.[29]

Pan American considerations were exemplified by Senator David A. Reed of
Pennsylvania, who spoke in the quota debate of 1924 as one deeply concerned
about excluding the illiterate and unskilled, and yet as one who would not offend Mexico or any part of Latin America, chiefly because this might adversely
affect American commercial expansion under the aegis of the Pan American
Union:

So far as Central and South America go, the policy indicated by this amendment is obviously unwise if we intend to attach any importance to the Pan American ideal. We are
alien to our neighbors in South and Central America by language. Their natural resort
is to Paris and Madrid. For everything they buy and almost every thought they think
they naturally refer to those two centers. If we want to hold them to us—and I think we
do so long as we maintain the Monroe Doctrine—we have to treat them differently from
the rest of the world, and we ought to treat them differently in the measure now
pending, because there is no occasion for singling them out and slapping a quota down
upon them.[30]

Such sentiments, no matter how naive, far-fetched, or misinformed, had the
effect of placing Mexican transborder migration (less so, Canadian) under the
protective umbrella of Pan American rhetoric, where it still remains.

Also, legislators not familiar with the Southwest were impressed by spokesmen for employer interests, like John Nance Garner, who swore that Mexican
laborers were not immigrants at all, but merely migrant workers, who, like so
many homing pigeons, conveniently returned to the mother country at the end
of the harvest season.[31] This simplistic explanation was partly true for seasonal farm and ranch labor along the Rio Grande frontier, but elsewhere the homing pigeon myth could have been exploded—as it later was in California—by a
simple analysis of census data.[32]

Congressional reluctance to slap a quota on Mexico was also shaped by the
reflection that, after all, a quota would be a useless act. As Representative John
E. Raker of California explained in 1924, if the many qualifications of existing
laws were faithfully applied, legal immigration from Mexico would virtually
dry up, "for 75 to 90 percent of all Mexicans are illiterate." Not only were Mexican campesinos unable to pay the $8 head tax, but if the law against contract
labor were enforced, "none of these men could come in." Raker then went to
the heart of the matter, when he raised the perennial question of an unguarded
frontier: "The Secretary of Labor has said that if he had enough men on the
border . . . there would not be a thousand Mexicans (a year) entering the United
States."[33]

The Quota Act of 1924 temporarily slowed campesino migration. A new system of consular visas and a new $10 visa fee were imposed on all would-be immigrants. More significant in the long run was the decision of Congress to establish the land-border patrol on a professional basis. Previously there had been only a handful of mounted inspectors on the Mexican border (not more than sixty in 1923), and they were so exclusively concerned with stopping illegal Chinese and European immigration "through the back door" that they were commonly known as "Chinese inspectors." These early officers were tough "Texas Ranger types" recruited from the border frontier. They usually took Mexican migrants for granted and rarely bothered to stop them, unless they were bandits or contrabandists.34 Now, however, anticipating a rise in illegal migration due to visa requirements, Representative Albert Johnson of Washington state, one of the sponsors of the 1924 act, introduced an amendment to provide that the Department of Labor use $1 million of its appropriation for no other purpose but to expand the land-border patrol.35 Then followed the act of February 27, 1925 (43 Stat. 1049), which established the statutory basis for the new immigration Border Patrol. Consequently, some 450 men were selected by civil service for the new rank of patrol inspector; motor vehicles were provided, and patrol activities were extended to the Canadian border and to the nation's coastline.

The administration generally believed that fees, visas, and the Border Patrol would sharply curtail Mexican migration, both legal and illegal. In 1925 legal immigration decreased to 32,378, compared to 87,600 in 1924. Optimism, however, was cut short when Mexican visa immigration bounced up to 42,638 in 1926, and 66,766 in 1927.36 Apparently, many American employers of Mexican immigrants were willing to pay the visa fee, and American consuls did not seem to be consistently enforcing literacy and public-charge requirements. Wetback migration, meanwhile, was greater than ever.

In 1926 Representative John R. Box of east Texas, who thought the heritage of black slavery was problem enough, introduced a bill, not merely an amendment, to place Mexico and other western hemisphere countries under a quota. Box, who believed that wide-open recruiting of Mexican campesinos made a farce of a half-quota system, provided the rationale for the measure when he attacked the employers of migrant labor:

The more intelligent, dependable natives . . . who own or desire to own homes, who have employment and business of their own, and possess stability, social, and business standing, are not the kind sought. These gentlemen have their eyes on the floating Mexican peons . . . sometimes stolen and carried away by the carloads in the night. They are to be imported in trainloads and delivered to farmers who have contracted to grow beets for the sugar companies . . . and to do menial work.

People of that type, whatever their nationality, are not desirable as immigrants. They are objectionable as citizens and as residents. The interests proposing these labor importing measures say frankly that they want them because they are of that class, and do not desire to own homes or even rent land. [37]

From 1926 until the full onset of the Depression in 1931, Congress debated the Box bill and compromise proposals such as the Johnson and Harris bills, presented in 1930, which would have placed low quotas on Mexico and other Latin-American countries, but would have allowed a higher quota for Canada. [38] The supporters of a Mexican quota had now enlisted in their ranks the Secretary of Labor, the Commissioner of Immigration, labor leaders, churchmen, social workers, educators, journalists, and outspoken members of the academic profession such as economist Roy L. Garis of Vanderbilt University and Robert Foerster of Princeton University. [39] A growing number of senators and congressmen rallied to the restrictionist cause, impressed by public feeling in many communities about the "Mexican social problem," and the complaints that Mexican migrant labor, consisting of men, women and children, was depressing wages and displacing American labor. To the "Mexican race," both sides applied the same pseudo-scientific arguments that had characterized the debates on the literacy test of 1917 and the quota restrictions of the 1920s against non-Nordics and Orientals. [40]

The State Department, acutely aware of official Mexican resentment at the quota movement and the alleged social inferiority of Mexican migrant peoples, and fearful of possible retaliations against American investments, sought desperately to devise an alternative method of immigration control less offensive to Mexican nationalists. Again, the expediency was a special administrative control policy, in this case, tighter visa controls. The State Department's view, shared by a number of knowledgeable men in Congress, was the one Representative Raker expressed in 1924: if the immigration standards of 1917 were enforced, legal immigration, at least, could be, *ipso facto*, radically reduced without a special quota law. After all, it was not the responsibility of the Immigration Service, according to the immigration act of 1924, but that of the State Department, to enforce visa standards in its consular offices abroad. Now a department memorandum of 1928 entitled "Enforcement of the Existing Immigration Laws" revealed the embarrassing fact that visa standards were decidedly lower in United States' consular offices in Mexico than in Europe. This memorandum, comparative in nature, exonerated consular officers in Mexico from any "deliberate failures." Rather, it explained that "a certain laxity" had arisen in visa standards there because Mexican labor had been urgently needed during World War I and after, and that various liberalization precedents had been established, which led to relaxation of standards, including an *ad hoc* arrangement of 1926 between immigration officials and California employers by which Mexican settlers who entered during the temporary labor exemptions of 1917-1921 could legalize their status merely by paying a head tax of $8. [41]

As early as April 1928, Secretary of State Frank B. Kellogg, who opposed the quota in congressional hearings, advised consuls in Mexico to tighten up visa standards. In a consular conference held in Mexico City in February 1929, strict guidelines for "administrative control" were spelled out. [42] Aside from more rigid tests of literacy and health, the visa applicant now had to prove that he had visible means of support for himself and, if married, for his family. If the applicant stated that support consisted of an American job offer, a visa could be denied on grounds that the applicant was being recruited, or assisted, in violation of the Alien Contract Labor Law of 1885, embodied in the general act of 1917. On the other hand, if the applicant could not present a job offer, visa denial was usually based on the "likely to become a public charge" clause of the 1882 act also incorporated in the restrictive code of 1917. [43] Mexican visas fell from 40,154 in 1929 to 12,703 in 1930, and to a mere trickle of 3,333 in 1931. But in evaluating these statistics, one must bear in mind that the Depression was then paralyzing the national economy. In any case, quota proposals were "apparently no longer necessary." [44]

The policy of visa controls sought to close off recruitment of common labor through legal channels. Thereafter, employers found, with some exceptions, as in certain moments of visa relaxation during World War II and the bracero program (1942-1964), that it was no longer such a simple matter to immigrate unskilled laborers and their families merely by paying fees and presenting an offer of employment.

Meanwhile, during the quota debate, Congress passed two laws which promised to establish better immigration control. The Registry Act of March 2, 1929 (45 Stat. 1512), provided for the legalization of unrecorded long-time resident aliens who were otherwise admissible as immigrants, but it also provided for the formal deportation of all aliens found to be illegally in the country. More important, the act of March 4, 1929, for the first time made illegal entry by an individual a misdemeanor, punishable by imprisonment for not more than one year, a fine of not more than $1,000, or both. [45] Previously, the 1917 act, which had not contemplated overland migration, had made illegal entry a misdemeanor, but only for carriers or smugglers who brought in illegal aliens. The penalties did not apply to individuals who entered the country through their own efforts.

The act of March 4, 1929, also struck at repeaters by providing that any alien arrested and deported in pursuance of law "shall be excluded from admission to the United States," and that if such a deportee enters or tries to enter the United States "he shall be guilty of a felony." If convicted of a reentry attempt, deportees faced up to two years in prison, a fine up to $1,000, or both. [46]

In passing this law, Congress was only partly influenced by reports of an uncontrollable wetback problem on the Mexican border. Since it was still generally believed that most Mexican illegals were not permanent settlers, but "homers," this measure was aimed as much at illegal entries of Orientals and Europeans. Nevertheless, the thought of criminal penalties for illegal entry

"El cuento de nunca acabar" (The story that never ends)
Originally done by Bismarck Mier and redrawn by an anonymous immigration officer in 1953. From private file of John W. Holland, former District Director of Immigration, San Antonio.

sent tremors through Mexican barrios and colonias in the United States. Like the military conscription fear of World War I, and the roundup of "skips" and wetbacks in 1921-1924, the illegal entry act of 1929 frightened an undetermined number of Mexican nationals back over the border.[47]

The concern of the Mexican government and American employers was partly allayed by the fact that the registry act of 1929, like the ad hoc legalizations of 1926, permitted certain groups to acquire immigration papers *ex post facto*, that is, if they had entered the United States prior to 1929 and could show at least five years continuous residence, paid visa fees, and were otherwise admissible. Only two "reliable witnesses" were needed to prove continuous residence. [48] Many Mexican nationals, aided by employers, Mexican consuls, and immigrant aid societies, took advantage of this opportunity to obtain a bona fide resident-alien status. Present immigration law provides that any illegal alien who entered the country prior to June 30, 1948, and has been, more or less, a continuous resident can be admitted as a lawful immigrant, provided he is of the admissible type. [49] As for the penalties of the 1929 act for illegal entry by individuals, they have never been applied to the majority of illegal aliens. By that date an administrative expedient called voluntary departures was commonly in use.

The significance of the voluntary departure policy, more frequently applied after 1917, can hardly be overemphasized, for it is one of the more remarkable examples of ad hoc exemptions from the regular deportation procedures and penalties established by immigration laws. Actually, the privilege of voluntary departure was not designed to favor Mexican illegals, but has always been available to any non-criminal alien, provided he or she (or the contractor) agrees to pay transportation back to the country of origin. Thus, formal deportation is avoided, and the deportee can still be, theoretically, eligible to return as a legal immigrant, whereas if the federal government had paid the return, the alien could fall under the public-charge restrictions of immigration law. [50]

Some reasons underlying this permissive policy are: Until the act of March 4, 1929, the penalties for illegal entry by an individual (or a guide or an alien smuggler working overland) were not clearly established in law, and illegal aliens seeking work or to join relatives have never been considered guilty of criminal intent by American judges or immigration officials. [51] Moreover, aliens from contiguous countries were hardly considered a deportation problem, since even the poorest Mexican (or Canadian) could walk back home and was encouraged to do so. [52] Later, during the bracero period, 1942-1964 and after, this non-penalty departure practice was considered the only way to handle wetback invasion. The basic reason, however, is simply that Congress has failed to provide the Immigration Service with sufficient funds, personnel, and detention facilities to carry out complicated penalty and deportation procedures. In many cases the illegal entrant has been released on his or her recognizance to go back, hopefully, to the mother country. In other cases, it has been a common custom since 1917 to "shoo wetbacks" across the border. [53]

The Depression Era

During the economic collapse of 1930-1940, there was such a desperate competition for jobs that Mexican migration rolled backwards. In the depths of unemployment, 1930-1935, most Mexicans were "repatriated" under voluntary departure. About 150,000 repatriados, mostly from southern California, had their way paid to Mexico by city and county welfare agencies, by Mexican consuls, and by the American Immigration Service. Perhaps another 250,000 made their own way back, moved by fear of formal deportation, by increasing hostility in the job market, or by a promise of a job or a parcel of land in Mexico.[54] Essentially, this repatriation drive, like that of 1921-1924, had the same purpose of shutting off the Mexican labor pool until the next cycle of American labor needs.

After the repatriation sweep of the early 1930s, American immigration policy toward Mexico consisted of watchful vigilance against the perennial return of the repatriados. Here it might be noted that since 1929 the legal resident alien leaving the United States for a visit to Mexico was encouraged to register with American immigration officials.[55] At least after this date immigrations inspectors had some registration data with which to judge the thousands of claims of repatriates who wished, almost immediately, to return to the United States under a claim of legal residence. Repatriates who had been on relief, or who had their passage to Mexico paid by a public agency, were considered public charges and were not to be readmitted, a policy that included some who had originally had a legal resident-alien status. Others claimed readmission on the grounds that they had a citizen child born in the United States. Later, the citizen child claimed readmission. This problem of sorting out claims, which went on for two generations after the repatriation movement and still goes on, was characterized, in part, by Commissioner of Immigration MacCormack in 1935:

On the southern border the utmost vigilance is now demanded to prevent the illegal entry of those Mexicans who, during the depression, either returned to Mexico on their own initiative or were repatriated at the expense of American communities. In applying for readmissions they commonly represent themselves as returning after a temporary visit. . . . The most careful examination by experienced inspectors is required to elicit the real facts.[56]

During the Depression years, the policy of "utmost vigilance" could depend on the Border Patrol, since Mexican migrants were no longer filtering through the border in overwhelming numbers, and since, after Prohibition ended in 1933, the border guards could at least bear down on alien smuggling rather than liquor smuggling.[57] As for limiting legal immigration, the Depression experience served to reinforce the State Department's conviction that tight visa controls, rather than a quota, were the final answer. During the Depression decade, 1931-1940, fewer than 23,000 legal immigrants were admitted from Mexico. Indeed, it seemed that no further control measures were called for.

Later legislative acts of the 1940s and 1950s, designed to insure alien registration and control, were not directly concerned with Mexican migration, legal or illegal. For example, the Alien Registration Act of 1940, which required all immigrant aliens to register with the Immigration Service, and the Internal Security Act of September 23, 1950, which required all immigrant aliens to report their current addresses to the Immigration Service in January of each year, were mostly aimed at controlling fascist and communist infiltration from Europe.[58] Aliens entering the United States without immigrant documents naturally ignore compliance with such laws.

By late 1942 bracero contract laborers were being welcomed back by the War Manpower Commission and American employers as worker-soldiers and allies in the cause of defending democracy against the Axis powers.[59] The fact that Mexico joined the Allies in 1942 helped support this rationale. Also, Mexican labor was considered an ally in the struggle to contain the red menace that followed World War II.

Braceros and Wetbacks Since 1942

The contract-labor era, 1942-1964, is another illustration of ad hoc decisions. The federal government would again tap the Mexican surplus labor reservoir, but this time, or so it was believed, there would be adequate supervisory controls over the recruiting and return of temporary agrilabor. Both the American and the Mexican governments thought that they had learned a lesson from the exemption period of 1917-1921. This time not employers but Mexican and American officials would supervise the program, aided by a mechanized Border Patrol.[60]

When, in 1940, the Immigration Service was transferred from the Department of Labor to the Department of Justice, the emergency authority contained in the Ninth Proviso was vested in the Attorney General, who employed this power to admit the first braceros in 1942. Later, special acts of Congress (for example, Public Law 45, in force from early 1943 to December 1947, and Public Law 78, in force from July 1951 to December 1964) served to supplement the executive authority to admit and supervise alien contract labor.[61] Significantly, the current Immigration and Nationality Act of 1952, which replaced the general act of 1917, retained an authorization similar to the Ninth Proviso in Section 212 (d) (3), which enables the Attorney General to admit alien workers when there is a certified shortage of domestic labor according to the Department of Labor. Furthermore, the 1952 law established for the first time the H-2 non-immigrant category in Section 101 (a) (15) (H), which authorizes the temporary admission of unskilled alien workers on a small scale without special approval from Congress. It also gives some legal cover to commuter workers along the border.[62] When the bracero program, under Public Law 78, ended in 1964, several thousand Mexican workers were admitted under the H-2 provision so that California and Arizona agribusiness could more easily adjust to the bracero cutoff.[63]

As it turned out, the bracero program became, like the revolutionary violence in Mexico, 1910-1920, or the special exemptions of 1917-1921, a catalyst for Mexican immigration, only a much greater one. As a spokesman for the · National Agricultural Workers Union so ably expressed it in 1952:

Agreements with the Republic of Mexico for the legal entry of 45,000 to 200,000 contract workers each year since 1942 . . . acted as a magnet drawing hundreds of thousands to the border from deep in the interior of Mexico. When the Mexican worker arrives at the border and finds that he cannot be accepted as a legal contract worker . . . it is a relatively easy matter to cross the 1,600 miles of practically unguarded boundary. Once in the United States there are always employers who will hire them at wages so low that few native Americans will accept. Thus, legal importation of Mexicans has created the vicious situation now prevailing.[64]

Here Mexico's insistence that braceros be protected by labor standards that were superior to those in the United States or Mexico had an unfortunate backfire effect. Disgusted with red-tape requirements and supervisory controls, the employer preferred free-lance wetbacks; besides, they were cheaper.[65] Soon incredible administrative exemptions made a parody of immigration laws and solemn international agreements.

During the period 1947-1952 there was really no need for employers to wait for legal braceros to be processed in Mexico. At Mexico's request, thousands of wetbacks already at work in the United States were "dried out," or legalized, as contract labor. During the years 1947-1949, when this practice was most prevalent, only 74,600 braceros were contracted in Mexico, whereas 142,200 wetbacks already in the United States were put under legal contract.[66] The Immigration Service opposed this practice because, obviously, it undermined immigration law enforcement. But Mexico insisted that recruiting was pointless if thousands of Mexican nationals were already in the United States. To save appearances, a charade was worked out whereby wetbacks were brought to the border and "deported" as they momentarily stepped over the boundary line. The dried-out wetback was then "paroled" to an employer as a legal bracero.[67]

In other cases braceros and wetbacks were "immigrated" by their employers. The 1952 immigration act required the Department of Labor to certify to the Secretary of State and the Attorney General that, if qualified domestic laborers were not available, the type and place of employment sought by the visa applicant would not adversely affect the condition of American workers [Sec. 212(a)(4)]. But Department of Labor agencies in the various states followed no standard procedures and were dominated by insistent demands from agribusiness employers. It was not until the amendments of the 1965 act that each visa applicant seeking employment was required on his own responsibility to obtain a specific job certification from a Labor Department office prior to visa consideration by U.S. consuls.

Another example of relaxation during the early bracero era was the allowing of "wet labor" by certain Border Patrol units to finish the harvest, particularly in the Rio Grande Valley of Texas. [68] This was done, in part, because the Mexican government had prohibited the use of legal braceros in Texas on grounds of alleged discrimination against Mexican-origin groups, and because during the Cold War crisis and the Korean War, 1950-1953, even illegal Mexican labor was still thought of as wartime emergency help by the federal government. [69]

During the bracero program American immigration laws were simply subordinated to diplomatic and employer interests. As the President's Commission on Migratory Labor lamented: "Actually, we have done worse than that. We have used the institutions of government to procure alien labor willing to work under obsolete and backward conditions and thus, to perpetuate those very conditions." [70] This same commission also pointed to the curious fact that citizen workers from Puerto Rico were passed over in favor of non-citizen labor from Mexico and from Jamaica and the Bahamas. Puerto Rican labor was rejected by midwestern and western employers, apparently because they feared that Puerto Ricans, being citizen labor, could not be sent home during the off-season, and that if they didn't work out, they might drift around the countryside. [71] Yet this was precisely what several hundred thousand Mexican "homing pigeons" were doing in western and midwestern states.

By 1952 private citizens and interest groups were again protesting a wetback invasion and new forms of wage peonage, vagrancy, child labor, and displacement of native labor. Congress was forced to take special action. Public Law No. 283, signed by President Truman on March 20, 1952, made it not a mere misdemeanor, but a felonious offense to recruit, transport, conceal, or harbor illegal aliens. [72] This law was apparently the first one designed expressly for the purpose of controlling illegal Mexican migration. It also strengthened border control by authorizing immigration officers to enter suspected premises within twenty-five miles of the border without a search warrant.

The foregoing law, actually passed at Mexico's insistence, ended a remarkable period of postwar laxity. But although it closed some loopholes, it left others open. No penalty was provided for the employer of illegal aliens, and it was understood that providing illegal laborers and their families with living quarters and other such practices incident to employment were not to be considered "harboring illegal aliens." An employer could be subject to prosecution only if he was caught "wet-handed" in the act of assisting or soliciting illegal aliens to enter the country. Since the majority of illegals made their own way to places of employment, or were brought in by Spanish-speaking contractors and crew leaders, the employer was virtually exempted from any responsibility for upholding immigration laws. This exemption was appropriately called the Texas proviso, for it was a concession to powerful agribusiness interests in the southwestern states, especially those in Texas, who had influential farm bloc spokesmen in Congress, like Sam Rayburn, Lyndon Johnson, Carl Hayden, James O. Eastland, and William R. Poague. Only occasionally has the Justice Department been able to prosecute an employer under the 1952 law. [73]

The wetback invasion also influenced the penalty provisions of Public Law 414 of June 27, 1952, still the basic Immigration and Nationality Act, as amended. Section 275, incorporating the law of March 4, 1929, makes illegal entry a criminal offense, and the second and subsequent offenses felonies, rather than misdemeanors. A person found guilty of a felony would be subject to imprisonment up to two years, a fine of not more than $1,000, or both. [74] However, U.S. District Court judges proved remarkably lenient, repeaters usually receiving a moderate penalty or a suspended sentence only, after the fourth offense, and rarely would alien smugglers be prosecuted for a first offense. [75] Nevertheless, such legislation marked a step forward in congressional concern about wetbackism.

In 1954 a new Commissioner of Immigration, Joseph M. Swing, with the full support of the Eisenhower administration and American labor groups, launched a massive deportation drive against contract skips and wetbacks. By the end of the year more than a million men, women, and children had been given voluntary departures and, literally, herded back to Mexico, under Operation Wetback. [76] This roundup, and Swing's stern and efficient policy of enforcement along the border, ended an era of easy access by employers to illegal agrilabor, and forced most large employers to use legal braceros. Thereafter, the program functioned properly. By 1964, the year the bracero program ended, the number of wetback apprehensions had dropped to fewer than 45,000.

However, since the close of the bracero program the number of Mexican illegals apprehended each year has steadily risen to a point where immigration officials now speak of a new wetback invasion. In fiscal 1971 apprehensions of Mexican nationals reached 348,000, or 83 percent of all illegals apprehended in that year; and in fiscal 1976 out of a total of 866,433 alien apprehensions, 781,438 were Mexicans, including, of course, many repeaters. In fiscal 1977 arrests of Mexican aliens constituted 954,778 out of a total of 1,042,215. Obviously the voluntary departure policy, described by border patrolmen as an "exercise in futility," has not discouraged the return of illegal aliens, nor has judicial leniency. Over the years since the illegal entry act of March 4, 1929, only about 1 or 2 percent of illegal entrants have been formally deported or prosecuted for violations of immigration laws, and only after repeated offenses. In fiscal 1975, for example, only 12,811 aliens from all countries, but principally Mexico, were actually penalized, out of 766,600 apprehensions.[7] Given enough chances to go back to "Start" under the non-penalty voluntary return, it seems that the chronic repeaters, like "Pablo Cruz," finally learn how to win out in the strange game of "Wetback versus Border Guard." [78]

Family Unification and the Third World Phenomenon Since 1952

Legal immigration from Mexico has meanwhile been favored by new immigration law. Congress believed that Uncle Sam, as a free world leader, should liberalize immigration policy to make it more favorable to non-Europeans and refugees. During World War II and after, Congress passed refugee assistance acts that admitted immigrants from devasted Europe and communist-controlled countries like Poland, Hungary, China, and Cuba. More significant was the basic Immigration and Nationality Act of June 27, 1952, which replaced that of 1917. Restrictionist principles and a modified quota system were retained, but three important policy changes were made that have served to favor immigration from Third World countries. First, Congress sought to allow a greater representation of non-Nordic immigration and to eliminate Oriental exclusions. Second, Latin America was again exempted from quotas because of a "traditional Pan American policy," and because it was believed that non-quota status, like foreign aid, would help keep Latin-American governments aligned on the American side against communist powers. Third, and most important, higher priorities were given to family unification. [79] Mexican laborers who immigrated to the United States during the bracero program found it easier to bring in family members.

The remarkable rise in legal immigration from Mexico since the act of 1952 may be seen in the following figures: [80]

1952	9,600
1953	18,454
1954	37,456
1955	50,772
1956	65,047

Once more Mexican immigration reached the high levels of the 1920s.

National immigration policy was further liberalized by the amendments of October 3, 1965. This law, reflecting the leveling trend of social democracy and ethnic egalitarianism, abolished the historic quota system in favor of hemispheric ceilings, the admission of any qualified immigrant, and above all, the uniting of families. After July 1, 1968, the eastern hemisphere had a ceiling of 170,000, with a country-by-country limit of 20,000. The western hemisphere was limited to 120,000. But, oddly, new world nations were not put on a preference-category system like eastern hemisphere countries; instead they were on a first-come, first-served basis, and there was no maximum per country. Even more astonishing, the western hemisphere applicant with an immediate relative in the United States, such as a citizen child born in an American border town, was exempted from labor certification—an exemption described by a State Department official "as a major inducement to fraudulent entry." [81] Furthermore, no limit was placed on the admission of immediate relatives.

The consequences of the 1965 amendments were simply not foreseen by federal legislators. [82] Putting no limits on immediate relatives unintentionally favored poverty-stricken countries where kinship migration is common, like Jamaica, Haiti, the Philippines, Portugal, or Taiwan, but most of all Mexico simply because Chicano and Mexican populations live in border proximity. These groups have strong cultural and extended obligations to send for relatives. Moreover, all along the border it is common for Mexican Americans and resident aliens to marry Mexican nationals and bring them in as no-wait immediate relatives. Furthermore, the huge backlog of prior visa applications from Mexico gave immigration from that country an ahead-of-the-line advantage on a first-come, first-served basis over all other new world countries. [83]

From 1956 to 1966 legal immigration from Mexico averaged around 40,000 per year. An upward trend was accelerated after the 1965 act went into effect on July 1, 1968. In fiscal 1971 immigrants born in Mexico totaled 50,103; in 1972, 64,040; in 1973, 70,141; in 1974, 71,586; and in 1975, 62,205. [84] Such figures constitute between 18 and 20 percent of all immigration, and around 40 percent of western hemisphere immigration. In addition, it appeared that in the period 1970-1975, perhaps 2 to 3 million Mexican illegals, not counting transients, have taken up residence in the United States. [85]

The radical shift in the national origins of immigrants to the United States in recent years, not counting illegals, may be illustrated by the comparisons in Table 1.

Seen in global perspective for a ten-year period, in this case 1966-1975, a total of 1,289,067 immigrants entered from all Europe and the British Empire combined, while in the same decade 2,461,732 entered from Asia, Latin America, and the West Indies. Leaving aside the huge currents of illegal immigration from the latter area, this turnabout in migration currents is mostly the consequence of kinship priorities not always subject to the full standards of immigration law, for example, literacy tests or labor certifications. Insofar as Mexico is concerned, such figures suggest the dormant nature of the State Department's policy of administrative restrictions first inaugurated in 1928 as an alternative to a Mexican quota. [86] Once again, however, public concern about an economic recession and a flood of aliens, legal and illegal, in the American job market has prodded the State Department to limit, as far as possible, the issuance of resident-alien visas in consular offices in Mexico. As a result Mexican immigration dropped to 62,205 in fiscal 1975, and to 57,862 in fiscal 1976 (up to June 30), but then a new upward trend began as court decisions and amnesty pressures led to more permissive legalization procedures.

Before 1965 Canadian immigration (including Newfoundland) had been

Table 1   Legal Immigration from Selected Countries
(according to country of birth for fiscal years)

	1961-1970	1972	1973	1974	1975
Mexico	443,301	64,040	70,141	71,586	62,205
Canada	286,667	10,776	8,951	7,654	7,308
West Indies (less Cuba)	262,730	41,327	29,571	40,011	37,887
British Isles	230,452	10,078	10,070	10,710	10,807
Italy	206,650	21,427	22,151	15,884	11,552
Germany	199,980	6,848	6,600	6,320	5,154
China-Taiwan and Hong Kong (1962-1971)	136,065	21,730	21,656	22,695	23,427
Philippines (1962-1971)	127,298	29,376	30,799	32,857	31,751
Poland	73,286	4,784	4,914	4,033	3,941
France	34,300	1,966	1,845	1,732	1,364
Ireland	42,395	1,780	2,000	1,572	1,285
Cuba (less parolees)	256,769	20,045	24,147	18,929	25,955

Source: Figures adapted from U.S. Immigration and Naturalization Service, *Annual Report*, 1961-1975, Table 8.

greater than Mexican. But after 1965 it gradually dropped, and more so after 1968, when the hemispheric ceiling of 120,000 went into effect. By fiscal 1975 it was reduced to 7,308, compared to 62,205 from Mexico.[87] The difference is mainly the result of kinship priorities. A much higher percentage of Canadians, many originally from Europe, seek to immigrate as individuals, and so are subject to the rigid labor certifications imposed after 1965. In 1972, for example, 22,395 immediate relatives, not subject to certification, immigrated from Mexico; the comparable figure for Canada was 6,318.[88]

The rapid rise of extended family migration from the Third World, and the historic decline in European migration, have become matters of deep official concern, and likewise the related fact that federal and local agencies spend billions of dollars annually trying to make anti-poverty and bilingual programs work, especially in the inner cities, where the "new immigrants" tend to settle, often in familiar "cultures of poverty." The 1975 amplifications of the Voting Rights Act of 1965 have also provoked a groundswell of concern, for hundreds of counties with 5 percent of more foreign-language population, particularly Spanish-speaking, Oriental, and American Indian, must now provide costly voting information in two or more languages. It is feared that this, and lack of immigration control, could lead to institutionalized bilingual politics and confrontment in the border states and elsewhere.

Illegal Aliens—Recent Legislative Efforts

The recession of 1972-1976 fixed federal attention even more on the Mexican border sieve, the chief source of illegal entrants from many countries besides Mexico. Since the appointment of reformist Commissioner Chapman in December 1973, the Immigration Service has tried harder to screen border crossers, tourists, students, and anyone seeking to enter from Mexico, and by allocating some of its thin resources to industrial cities, to open up jobs for jobless Americans.

Earlier, in September 1972, Mexico and the United States appointed their own high-level study groups to explore binational cooperation in migratory control, and to consider a new bracero program as a control measure. The Nixon administration (1968-1974) had to reject the contract-labor proposal due to protest from American labor unions and bureaucratic groups committed to anti-poverty and job-training experiments. But the two governments did agree to cooperate in the pursuit of alien smugglers and fabricators of false documents on both sides of the line, and to assure more humane treatment for apprehended aliens. [89]

During the Ford administration (1974-1976), there were many more top-level meetings between diplomats of both countries, and among officials representing inter-secretarial advisory groups, such as the President's Domestic Council Committee on Illegal Aliens, appointed in January 1975, and Mexico's Commission for the Study of Surreptitious Labor Migration, functioning since 1972. Moreover, in the annual meetings of the United States-Mexico Interparliamentary Conference, legislative leaders continuously explored amnesty, cooperative border control, racial discrimination, drug traffic, immigration bills that might adversely affect Raza groups, and more contract-labor proposals to prevent exploitation of undocumented workers.

The fact is, however, that in the period 1965-1975, the American government took no decisive legislative action to deter slick smuggler organizations, vendors of fraudulent documents, and kinship migration that blended easily into America's ethnic colonies. In the absence of federal action, California, which, from time to time over the past century has sought to protect its Garden of Eden against a flood of cheap alien labor and the social consequences, took a unique step in 1972. The so-called Dixon Arnett Law, which imposed fines ranging from $200 to $500 on an employer who knowingly hired illegal aliens, was incorporated into the State Labor Code, Sec. 2805. Civil libertarians and ethnic leaders cried out that the law discriminated against minorities; yet it was jobless farm-working Chicanos who, in late 1972, provided grounds for a test case by charging that contractors were using illegals. The State Supreme

Court held that Sec. 2805 was unconstitutional, but as the authors of the law had intended, the question of hiring illegal aliens was then pushed squarely before Congress and the Supreme Court.

The foregoing discussion does not mean that Congress was idle. Actually, modifications in immigration law and enforcement were proposed in dozens of extensive congressional hearings after 1970 and in numerous immigration reform bills. These modifications, from major to minor, were suggested in order to control illegal entries, equalize admission rules for both hemispheres, give more preference to political and religious refugees or to skilled labor, and so on. Of these proposals the Rodino bills, the outcome of exhaustive hearings on illegal aliens in 1971-1975, received by far the most attention from Congress, from Mexico, and from an amazing assortment of conflicting interest groups. First introduced in 1971 as H.R. 981 and H.R. 182, they were passed in 1973 by the House, after substantial amendments, but were not acted on by the Senate. Some provisions of these original bills were reintroduced in January 1975, by Peter W. Rodino Jr. and Joshua Eilberg of the House Judiciary Committee and were combined into one bill, H.R. 982, which became H.R. 8713 in July 1975.

Like its predecessors, H.R. 8713, a prototype of employer-penalty bills, sought to revive Senator Paul Douglas's proposal of 1951-1952, the recommendations of the President's Commission on Migratory Labor of 1951, and the intent of the California labor law,—that is, "cut off the source" and castigate the employer, contractor, or referral agent who, knowingly, hires or places illegal aliens. Such legislation would avoid a first-time criminal sanction as originally conceived, and follow a compromise civil penalty procedure: first, an administrative citation, or warning, would be issued by the United States Attorney General; second, if this injunction to cease and desist were violated, the Attorney General, after a hearing, could assess a civil fine of $500 for each illegal alien hired; and, third, if the employer or his agent, after being assessed such a penalty, again violates the law, he could face a $1,000 fine for each alien, imprisonment not exceeding one year, or both, for each illegal alien involved, all in accordance with due process. [90]

At the same time, to meet the objections of ethnic lobbyists, such a bill as H. R. 8713 would authorize the Attorney General, like the Equal Opportunity Employment Commission, to bring civil action suits, if possible, against an employer or agent who refuses to hire or refer a person because of racial discrimination. Also, to meet rising complaints about aliens on public assistance and social security programs, the proposed bill would obligate the Department of Health, Education and Welfare to disclose to the Attorney General the name and most recent address of any alien not lawfully admitted for residence. Furthermore, to meet Immigration Service control needs, it would authorize the confiscation of vehicles used by alien smugglers.

After a delay of several years, Senator James O. Eastland, Chairman of the Senate Judiciary Committee, submitted a bill, S.3074, on March 4, 1976, the principal purpose of which was also to equalize the two hemispheres and provide civil penalties to curtail employment of illicit aliens, much like the Rodino bill, but with more safeguards for employer interests. An unsworn statement from a job applicant as to his or her legal status would suffice to relieve employer, contractor, or referrer from any further responsibility. Eastland, a big-scale planter and long-time advocate of imported labor and other farm subsidies, would also have his bill authorize the importation of needed agrilabor on H-2 temporary work permits.

Other bills in the congressional mill competed for attention, for instance, S. 3826, introduced by Senator Edward Kennedy in 1974, and again in February 1975, would have provided stiffer penalties for the employers of illegal aliens, $1,000 for a second offense and $2,000 for a third. Or another example, in the spring of 1975, Congressman Burt Talcott of California introduced a series of bills—the first such—that would have attacked the illegal alien problem on a broad, seamless front by providing for increased penalties for alien smugglers, more Border Patrol agents, the conversion of the social security card into a reliable identity document with photo and vital data (also supported by Senator Robert Packwood of Oregon and others), criminal penalties for any American citizen who marries an illegal alien solely to create an immediate-relative status, and so on. [91] All such bills faced a watering down by amendments and numerous due process safeguards that would limit their effectiveness.

It seemed that decisive congressional action was in conflict with traditions of civil liberties and the Statue of Liberty symbolism of "send me your teeming masses." Such traditions and sentiments, firmly planted in the school books, had always been easily manipulated by political interest groups such as the agricultural associations and immigrant-aid lobbyists. Thus, an examination of the last few years of immigration hearings reveals a sterile dialectic such as the following:

1. Amendments that would authorize the Immigration Service to confiscate vehicles used by alien smugglers, a *sine qua non* of effective wetback control, according to field officers, have been opposed as a threat to the citizen's constitutional right to private property. (Yet the Customs Service has for years been authorized to confiscate vehicles of contraband smugglers.)

2. Proposals that all adult residents of the United States present a foolproof social security card or a national identity card (as in some parts of the world) when seeking employment, or a share of the welfare state, have been consistently rejected as an infringement of civil liberties, or as a fascist-like measure that could be used to discriminate against Third World minorities.

3. Attempts to reduce visa preferences for immediate relatives and increase preferences for skilled technicians, scientists, and professional persons have collided with the established family priorities and humanitarian sentiments.

4. Efforts to raise visa standards and have a rigorous application of the "likely to become a public charge" clause conflict with the social fact that sev-

eral million low-skilled illegal aliens have already settled in the United States, many of them with the citizen child in hand, and under the patronage of immigrant-aid societies. So such efforts have been deplored as "inhumane," "retroactive," and even a "violation" of the equal rights provisions of the Fourteenth Amendment.

5. Legislation to penalize the employer who knowingly hires illegals has been contested as contrary to the Bill of Rights, and on the grounds that it is not the business of the employer to determine immigrant status.

6. Ethnic-rights leaders have vehemently objected to a job seeker's having to sign a statement as to civil or immigrant status, or present a special identification card, on grounds that this could be "self-incrimination" or cause employers to avoid hiring "suspicious-looking Latinos." [92]

Legal Admissions—the Search for Equity

Reducing legal immigration from Mexico to more equitable proportions has been, of course, a problem related to the wetback phenomenon. The Department of Labor has, since 1965, clamped down on labor certifications, but this has little effect on kinship migration. American consuls, always shorthanded, have tried, mostly on their own initiative, to tighten visa controls for "suspected immigrants," including tourists, students, shoppers, and commuter applicants. But the consuls could do little about the "first come, first served" arrangements that have favored Mexico, or the fact that millions of Mexicans and other Third World nationals have been building up "equity" and "skilled job" claims as family residents and workers surreptitiously in the United States. [93] And equity claims have been increasingly aided by private and federally funded anti-poverty agencies. [94] Furthermore, Chicano bishops and clergy have been promoting the vocation of immigrant counselor among priests and laymen in the United States and Mexico, with a view toward creating a grand network of services for all undocumented aliens. [95]

Since 1970 proposals to limit or promote legal migration from Mexico have come thick and fast. For example, organizations of Chicano activists (some of them seeking "colonial liberation" through a political alliance with Mexico) have presented demands that range from the return of the Southwest, or an open border, to blanket legalization, or special exemptions, for Mexican nationals already in the United States. [96] On the other hand, some legislators have sought a compromise. For one, Senator Edward Kennedy, concerned about the relative neglect of political and religious refugees compared to poverty refugees, introduced S. 1373 on March 24, 1971, a bill that would have fixed a limit of 20,000 immigrants on western hemisphere countries, but would have favored Mexico and Canada with special allotments of 35,000, including immediate relatives. House Resolution 2328, the so-called Administration

Bill, introduced in January 1971 contained a similar concession to contiguous neighbors.[97]

That most congressmen still objected to instituting a special relationship for Mexico and Canada in immigration law, such as the British Isles—the "mother country"—once enjoyed under the quota system, 1921-1965, seemed quite evident in the amendments a large House majority added to the original western hemisphere bill, H.R. 981. A 20,000 limit was to be placed on all countries, yet immediate relatives were excepted. Had the amended H.R. 981, or the later H.R. 8713, been in force in fiscal 1973, Mexican immigration would have included 26,650 immediate relatives plus 20,000 others, for a total nearly twice as high as the next largest immigrant group.[98]

Congressional reformers were unable to push through any important alien-control bills in the period 1971-1975, with one or two exceptions, such as the amendments of 1974 to the Farm Labor Contractor Registration Act of 1963, according to which all contractors would be subject to criminal penalties for failure to register and knowingly engaging the services of illegal aliens.[99] How well the Department of Labor can enforce this act is thus far a matter of guesswork.

The bicentennial year contained one notable legislative success. The House Judiciary Committee, feeling that half a loaf was better than none, had doggedly stuck by H.R. 981. Just before the end of the 94th Congress, that bill, amended and retitled as H.R. 14535, slipped through both houses of Congress in a surprise move, and President Ford signed it on October 20, 1976, reluctantly, to be sure, for 1976 was an election year and Chicano leaders had roundly condemned it. Known as Public Law 94-571, and also as the Immigration and Nationality Amendments of 1976, this was the most important immigration act since the amendments of 1965. For the first time Congress had abandoned, at least temporarily, its Pan American preference system, and Mexico and all other new world countries were placed on a quota much as certain congressmen in the 1920s had wanted.

Beginning on January 1, 1977, the eastern hemisphere limit of 20,000 resident visas per country was to be imposed on western hemisphere countries as well, but, of course, with no limit on immediate relatives, namely parents, spouses, and children of American citizens. Furthermore, the same preference categories, with but minor modifications, would apply to the western hemisphere (Sec. 202; Sec. 203). Thus, quota visas would be allotted as follows: 20 percent reserved for unmarried sons or daughters of American citizens who were born abroad and became foreign nationals; 20 percent for spouses and unmarried sons and daughters of an alien lawfully admitted for permanent residence; 10 percent for professional persons who have exceptional ability in the sciences or arts and would "substantially benefit the United States"; 10 percent for the married sons and daughters of American citizens; 24 percent for brothers and sisters of adult American citizens; 10 percent for literate immigrants capable of performing skilled or unskilled labor for which there is a certified need; and in spite of the Statue of Liberty, only 6 percent for political and religious refugees.

The annual ceilings of 120,000 for the western hemisphere and 170,000 for the eastern were retained, with immediate relatives excepted. In this respect most immigration and consular authorities strongly favored a fixed ceiling on immediate relatives, particularly brothers and sisters, and heavy penalties for the increasing fraud in marriage, birth certificates, and naturalization papers. Significantly, the new act eliminated the citizen-child privilege whereby western hemisphere parents were exempted (since the law of 1965) from labor certification and given special visa consideration; not until the age of twenty-one could the child seek immigrant status for the parents. However, amnesty proposals based on residential equities would restore, in a *de facto* manner, the citizen-child privilege.

The backlog of western hemisphere persons, mainly Mexicans, who would apply for resident visas under the new measure was probably close to half a million. Importantly, if they were already in the United States, they would be allowed to adjust their status at the nearest immigration office rather than at the consulate in their home country. Immigration officers commonly regarded such an arrangement, already in effect for the eastern hemisphere, as a special encouragement for illegal residents from neighboring countries.

Immigration and consular personnel felt that P.L. 94-571 (90 Stat. 2703) rectified some inequities, such as those faced by broken families and highly skilled persons lacking family connections, and that it constituted an important step toward placing eastern and western visa applicants on an equal footing. Yet they did not expect a reduction in Mexican immigration. On the contrary, they anticipated a steady rise fed by immediate-relative claims springing from the vast number of illegal settlements, the buildup of adult citizen children over the years, and a newfound interest in American citizenship by immigration consultants and their clients. And, since over the years some 150,000 Cuban refugees had been incorrectly charged against the western hemisphere allotment, a court order, given early in 1977, would make admission retroactive for an equal number of non-preference applicants, principally Mexicans. Since many such applicants have meanwhile been raising a family in the United States, the so-called Chicago stays could mean anywhere from 150,000 to 300,000, or more, Mexican admissions not subject to P.L. 94-571.[100]

The Emergence of an Illegal Alien Dilemma

All the while untold numbers of Third World aliens had been steadily incorporated as deserving clients into federal caretaker agencies, the anti-poverty bureaucracy, the civil rights movement, and the new-style populist politics and patronage. In fact, undocumented aliens had become a vested interest group, like dozens of others in the welfare state.[101]

During the Ford administration pressures mounted to legalize long-term residents who entered the country before a certain cutoff date. H.R. 8713 and the Eastland bill S. 3074, for instance, would have shifted the cutoff from 1948 to July 1, 1968. President Ford's Domestic Council Committee, engaged in interagency studies of illegals, favored that date or a closer date, for "massive deportation is both inhumane and impractical."[102] But Ford's advisers generally opposed blanket amnesty for an estimated 8 to 11 million uninvited aliens, unless tied to an annual ceiling per country, for they were afraid of stimulating a bigger influx of surplus population from Mexico, Central America, the Caribbean, the Philippines, and other Third World countries. After all, a legalized alien, *ipso facto*, would have an implied right to bring in immediate relatives in the no-limit category.

Outside a foot-dragging Congress, proposals to resolve the heaping problem of illegals began to acquire a more desperate character. Some officers of the Border Patrol, which numbered about 1,800 in 1975, thought the United States should follow the example of Mexico and set up a border "free zone," where shoppers, tourists, and visitors would be admitted without documents, and, like Mexico, pull back the effective frontier twenty-five miles inland, and on that inner line fix inspectional checkpoints for immigration, tourism, customs, health, and agriculture. The abandoned area would become *de jure*, what it already was *de facto*, a free-trade zone maintained by the federal government for the benefit of border mercantile groups, forwarding agents, labor contractors, contrabandists, and substandard employers, who rarely have shown concern about the inward flow of drugs and illegal aliens. Had not border communities and chambers of commerce always been tenacious defenders of the open port and the Good Neighbor Policy, leaving it to a handful of immigration officers to sift out wetbacks? A hopeless task.[103] In fiscal 1976, for example, Mexican shoppers and visitors crossed the border more than 100 million times, and over 1.6 million Mexican non-immigrants were admitted as tourists, students, and businessmen.[104] How many of these visitors overstayed?

Impossible qualifications follow free-zone proposals. Federal and state subsidies for welfare, education, and food stamps would be suspended in the zone, also federal minimum wage laws, closed-shop unionism, and standard antipoverty programs, so that socioeconomic conditions would be equalized, more or less, on both sides of the line. With cheap labor flowing in, "like water seeking its natural level," presumably American companies would move subsidiary plants into the area, just as in Mexico's free zone or in Puerto Rico, and generate employment. And, as on the Mexican side, there would be tax customs exemptions for local residents.[105] Others, who believe in the moral right of

Third World poverty folk to emigrate, would have abolished the border altogether except for customs, drug, and health controls.[106]

Some state officials and legislators, disgusted with the federal government's failure to protect each state from invasion (Art. IV, Sec. 4, U.S. Constitution) and to uphold the socioeconomic standards of the local community, believed that state initiatives were more than justified under the residual powers guaranteed by the Tenth Amendment. Thus in 1975, David Finney, a Texas state legislator, proposed a Federal Interstate Border Compact and Border Development Program, whereby California, Arizona, New Mexico, and Texas would establish control over the "invasion" of the borderlands by poverty folk, with or without the cooperation of Mexico and its border states. Also state governments would try to gain more control over the labyrinth of federal anti-poverty programs manipulated by dog-in-the-manger bureaucrats and ethnic politicians.[107]

A growing number of state laws sought to prohibit employment of illegals through civil penalties. As we have seen, the forerunner was a 1972 California statute embodied in the State Labor Code (Sec. 2805), whereby the employer who knowingly hired illegals would be subject to fines. That law and a similar law in Connecticut (1972, P.A. 275, Sec. 1-3, effective May 24, 1972) were upheld by the Supreme Court on February 25, 1976, in an unprecedented decision. The Court found that federal inaction on a matter of national concern did not invalidate the state's right under the "police powers" to protect local workers and working conditions against illegal aliens, and that such laws did not actually conflict with federal control over admission, residence, and naturalization of aliens.[108] Since then other states and governmental units, including New Mexico, Colorado, Arizona, Massachusetts, Kansas, Florida, New Jersey, New Hampshire, Vermont, Virginia, Puerto Rico, and Las Vegas County, Nevada, have passed similar bills, some even providing for prison terms.[109]

As always, Texas labor agencies and the State Employment Commission pumped in an endless stream of Mexican migrant families, who, moving on, frequently passed as "deserving Tex-Mex Americans" in the interior of the United States. But by 1977 the Texas legislature had still failed to agree on a penalty bill because vested interest groups could not agree on exclusions for agrilabor, domestic servants, and other groups that subsidized the Texas life style and marginal economic sectors.[110] The hundred-year open-door policy in Texas seemed especially to beg for federal action.

During 1976 a new cycle of bills to penalize the employment of illegals was churning in the congressional hopper. However, the key phrase "knowingly hires" appeared to be a major due process obstacle to the acceptance or enforcement of a functional employer-penalty law, state or federal. A thicket of court tests lay ahead.[111] And Chicano and Latino organizers, who protested that undocumented aliens were being made the scapegoats of high unemployment rates and welfare costs, were moving rapidly to the side of the "exploitative employer" in a common effort to keep the back door open and to sponsor counter bills.[112]

Meantime migrant labor specialists, like North and Houstoun or Marshall, maintained that, even without employer penalties, federal and state agencies could achieve alien-labor control if they would cooperate in enforcing laws and regulations on fair labor practices, minimum wages, safety and health, and tax deductions.[113]

Virtually all persons and agencies researching the alien invasion proposed a substantial increase in the manpower, budget, and technical efficiency of the Immigration Service and the visa service of the State Department. Some urged the creation of an interagency "strike force" to protect aliens from border predators and extortionists and to uproot the alien-smuggling and fraudulent document business, now interlaced with the drug traffic. And as in some European countries the local police would also be authorized to cooperate.[114]

Other researchers, like economist Briggs or Mexican sociologist Bustamante, and Mexico watchers, like Carey McWilliams, commonly urged that more American developmental loans—even a Marshall plan—be used to expand labor-intensive industries in rural Mexico in order to absorb surplus labor. Such aid would be channeled through international lending institutions, like the World Bank, so as not to offend sensitive Mexican nationalists.[115] President Ford's Domestic Council Committee on Illegal Aliens, and various members of Congress who met with Mexican counterparts in the annual interparliamentary conferences, endorsed such recommendations.

Naturally proposals for a border-control treaty and for an international labor program continued to pop up. Senator Montoya of New Mexico, for one, introduced a bill in 1974 to supply, under joint control, needed labor for American agriculture.[116] And the Eastland bill would have expanded the H-2 proviso to something like a European "guest worker" program. North and Houstoun, as well as political scientist Cornelius and economist Piore, both from M.I.T., made similar recommendations involving international labor permits as a control measure. Their suggestions were made on grounds that certain classes of alien workers did not compete with domestic labor. Piore even held that unskilled aliens served to push up local labor, especially if job-training programs were available to the latter![117]

It seemed that the more researchers and research groups, such as Villalpando and associates, looked into the economic impact of illegal labor, the more they questioned that illegals contributed to America's unemployment problem. On the other hand, by 1976 there was general public alarm over the rising social, educational, and welfare costs generated by Third World poverty folk, who perhaps were settling in at a rate of 800,000 or more per year.[118]

Alarm or not, many federal and state legislators hesitated to speak out on what had meanwhile become a major populist issue in American politics, and so slid from one accommodation to another. Typically, California's Alan Cranston, Senate majority whip and master of the "new coalition" politics, sponsored, as a counter to P.L. 94-571, his bill, S. 68, which would give Mexican and Canadian immigration a higher quota with all unused visas going to Mexican applicants.[119] And as ethnic politicians moved more into power in "accommodation politics," ambivalent attitudes increased. How, for example, could black leaders, disturbed at the prospect of the Latinos becoming the number one recipient minority and Spanish becoming a required language (rather than Swahili-Bantu), publicly favor closing the door on their brown brothers? Realistically politicians started to learn Chicano Spanish and dust off the Treaty of Guadalupe Hidalgo.

On the other hand, even those who sympathized with unregistered aliens, most of them unskilled, functionally illiterate in English, and prone to fall on public assistance, expressed frustration about the treadmill of uncontrolled migration. "All our successes in dealing with poverty and other problems," said a Chicano official destined to be an ambivalent Commissioner of Immigration, "are wiped out by new arrivals. The bottom of the barrel is always filling up."[120] Yet it seemed a futile gesture that S. 3074, and similar bills, would have provided for deportation of public charges—an historic proviso hardly ever applied. Things were moving the other way. Armed with court injunctions, open-door militants amplified claims on tax money for biculturalism and challenged every effort by the federal gatekeepers to hold off the huddled masses of poverty folk from the heaving bosom of Mother America.[121] Here one could always rally around the Statue of Liberty, possibly by circumstance, the leading symbol of national purpose.

Those who would stabilize American population growth, like Zero Population Growth, began to campaign against an apparently endless influx of economic refugees from the Third World.[122] Others feared the Mexicanization or Latin Americanization of large sectors of the country. However, every such concern was more than matched by countervailing sentiments:

The character of the Hispanic people, and the culture from which that character derives, is the clear antithesis of the neuter, necrophiliac culture a-building in the United States. For the Hispanics, a man is a man, a woman is a woman, and a child a treasure. They delight in life. . . .

Yes, they are pouring into this country in a flood, bearing their poverty, their pride, their children, their religion, bearing also their high aquiline nose, the nose of the aboriginal Indian. In them, the hounded and vanquished American Indian may be taking his revenge upon us. It may be the sweetest revenge of all, that of saving us from ourselves.[123]

The Ford administration, politically weak, avoided any direct confrontation with Chicanos or enforcement needs, and so did little more than promote study and discussion through the Domestic Council Committee on Illegal Aliens.[124]

The Committee task force, in a fretful and hand-wringing evaluation of America's immigration dilemma, wavered between the obvious need for effective migration control and liberal concern for individual liberties. It could only plead for more studies of illegal aliens, while confessing that "the paradox we face rests with the realization that as time brings more knowledge about the illegal, time may also entrench illegal immigration so as to render it an increasingly irreversible trend.[125]

Studies begat more studies. A new presidential administration would find a bewildering pileup of research findings and proposals, done during the Ford administration, all of which pointed out the glaring inconsistencies in American immigration policy and practice, and the rapid spread of invisible alien ghettos furtively avoiding civic participation.[126]

One cannot comment here on all the vexations and ironies implicit in America's alien dilemma. Suffice it to say that years of ad hoc exemptions, and spotty support for immigration control, seem to have had the cumulative effect of turning the furrowed brow of the Statue of Liberty toward the Third World and, more specifically, toward Mexico, which, in *de facto* fashion, had become entrenched as a most-favored nation in American immigration policy and practice.

Notes

1. For restrictive legislation see Charles Gordon and Harry N. Rosenfield, *Immigration Law and Procedure* (Albany: Banks and Co., 1959, and Supplement); Frank L. Auerbach, *Immigration Laws of the United States* (Indianapolis: Bobbs-Merrill, 1961, and Supplement); and for restrictive sentiments, John Higham, *Strangers in the Land: Patterns of American Nativism, 1860-1925* (New Jersey: Rutgers University Press, 1963).

2. Varden Fuller, Executive Secretary, *Report of the President's Commission on Migratory Labor in American Agriculture* (Washington, D.C., 1951), p. 64.

3. Clark, "Mexican Labor in the United States," U.S. Bureau of Labor *Bulletin*, 78 (September 1908), 466-522.

4. Dillingham Commission. *Report of the United States Immigration Commission*, 61st Cong. (42 vols., Washington, D.C., 1911), including *Abstracts of Reports of the Immigration Commission*, Vol. 1. For data and brief comments on Mexican laborers in mining, agriculture and transportation industries in the southwestern states see, particularly, Vol. 24: *Immigrants in Industries. Part 25. Japanese and other Immigrant Races in the Pacific Coast and Rocky Mountain States . . . Agriculture;* and Vol. 25: . . . *Diversified Industries.*

5. See "Memorandum by Oscar Handlin" in *Hearings Before the President's Commission on Immigration and Naturalization* (Washington, D.C., 1952), pp. 1839-1863.

6. *Annual Report of the Commissioner General of Immigration to the Secretary of Labor 1912*, pp. 224-225.

7. For the evangelical viewpoint see McCombs, *From Over the Border*; Lipshultz, "American Attitudes."

8. *Annual Report of the Commissioner General . . . 1912*, p. 225.

9. *Annual Report of the Commissioner General . . . 1913*, pp. 336-337.

10. U.S. Congress, Senate. *Migrant and Seasonal Labor Powerlessness. Hearings . . . Committee on Labor and Public Welfare, 91st Cong., 1st and 2nd Sess.* (Washington, D.C., 1970), pp. 2016-2017.

11. Karnuth v. Albro, 279 U.S. 231, 1929, cited in *ibid.*, p. 2017. See also "The Impact of Commuter Aliens along the Mexican and Canadian Border," *Hearings Before the Select Commission on Western Hemisphere Immigration* (Washington, D.C., 1968), Part II, 5-6.

12. U.S. Congress, Senate. *Migrant and Seasonal Labor Powerlessness*, p. 2018.

13. *Ibid.*, p. 2018.

14. The results of a 1967 commuter count are given in *Hearings Before the Select Commission*, II, 6-12. Other statistical information can be found in North, *The Border Crossers*, pp. 176-177; and in *Migrant and Seasonal Labor Powerlessness*, pp. 2194-2527. Commuter estimates are also based on interviews with immigration officials, Central Office, INS, Washington, D.C., December 10, 1970, and December 18, 1972.

15. Matter of H.D. 5, I & N, Dec. 716, 1954, cited in *Migrant and Seasonal Labor Powerlessness*, p. 2020. It should be noted that the U.S. Court of Appeals for the District of Columbia in a recent opinion, April 16, 1973 (in No. 72-1178, Robert Bustos et al., United Farm Workers Organizing Committee, appellant v. John Mitchell, Attorney General of the United States et al.) has again maintained the legal precedents for daily commuters, but denied the legality of seasonal commuters, a post-1964 phenomenon that followed the demise of the bracero program.

16. Statement of John Killea, U.S. Consul General, Tijuana, February 9, 1968, in *Illegal Aliens, Hearings Before the Select Commission*, II, 16.

17. Before 1969 one could travel 150 miles inland with a border-crossing card, which, in effect, permitted many holders to live and work in such cities as Los Angeles and San Antonio. After 1969 the white card was limited to 25 miles. See North, *The Border Crossers*, pp. 134-135; Lamar B. Jones, "Alien Commuters in the United States Labor Markets," *International Migration Review* 4 (Spring 1970), 65-86; and testimony of George K. Rosenberg, District Director, INS, Los Angeles, in *Hearings Before the Select Commission*, II, 13.

18. Interviews with U.S. immigration officials along the Mexican border, June-August 1970, and August 1972.

19. Ruth Z. Murphy, executive vice-president, American Immigration and Citizenship Conference, "Current Concern of the Private Sector," *International Migration Review* 4 (Spring 1970), 62.

20. "Text of Secretary W.B. Wilson's Order Suspending Sections of the Immigration Act to Permit Laborers to Enter U.S.," *The Official Bulletin* (Committee on Public Information), Vol. 2, No. 343 (June 24, 1918), 10-12.

21. See statement of John C. Box questioning the legality of "Admission of Mexican and Other Alien Laborers into Texas and Other States," *Hearings Before the Committee on Immigration and Naturalization, House . . . 66th Cong., 2nd Sess., May 13, 1920* (Washington, D.C., 1920), pp. 3-7. Authority under the Ninth Proviso is explained by Grebler, *Mexican Immigration to the United States,* D-13, D-14.

22. Otey M. Scruggs, "The First Mexican Farm Labor Program, 1917-1921,"

Arizona and the West, 2 (Winter 1960), 319-326; and *Congressional Record*, Vol. 72 (April 16, 1930), 7115.

23. See also statement by James J. Davis, Secretary of Labor, made on April 15, 1924, and quoted in *Mexicans in California. Report*, p. 18.

24. Auerbach, *Immigration Laws of the United States*; and Gordon and Rosenfield, *Immigration Laws and Procedures.*

25. Robert A. Divine, *American Immigration Policy, 1924-1952* (New Haven, Ct., 1957); Lipshultz, "American Attitudes toward Mexican Immigration"; Martínez, "Mexican Emigration to the United States"; and Reisler, *By the Sweat of Their Brow.*

26. House Immigration and Naturalization Committee, *Temporary Admission of Illiterate Mexican Laborers. Hearings . . . on H.J. Res. 271, Jan. 26-Feb. 2, 1920* (Washington, D.C., 1920).

27. *Cong. Record*, 68th Cong., 1st Sess., Vol. 65 (April 18, 1924), 6621.

28. Joe W. Neal's pioneer study presents a full coverage of the arguments pro and con and the reasons for the defeat of the Mexican quota movement in "The Policy of the United States," pp. 108-121.

29. Mira Wilkins, *The Emergence of Multinational Enterprise: American Business Abroad from the Colonial Era to 1914* (Cambridge, Mass.: Harvard University Press, 1970); and Max Winkler, *Investments of United States Capital in Latin America* (Boston, 1928). It is not clear how many anti-quota congressmen were spokesmen for U.S. investment interests in Mexico.

30. *Cong. Record*, Vol. 65 (April 18, 1924), 6623.

31. *Temporary Admission of Illiterate Mexican Laborers* (1920), pp. 3-19.

32. *Mexicans in California. Report* (1930), pp. 17-39.

33. *Cong. Record*, Vol. 65 (April 8, 1924), 5841. In this discussion Raker also made the point that the immigration officials did not have enough money to deport Mexican and Chinese illegals known to be in the country illegally.

34. Interviews with retired border patrolmen in California, Arizona and Texas, April-August 1970.

35. *Cong. Record*, Vol. 65 (April 18, 1924), 6627-6628; also *Annual Report of the Commissioner General of Immigration . . . 1924*, p. 23; and *1925*, pp. 14-15.

36. *Annual Report of the Commissioner General . . . 1927*, p. 42.

37. House Committee on Immigration, *Seasonal Agricultural Laborers from Mexico. Hearings . . .* 69th Cong., 1st Sess. (Washington, D.C., 1926), p. 325. See also Neal, "The Policy of the United States," p. 146.

38. Divine, *American Immigration Policy*, Ch. 3.

39. Robert F. Foerster, *The Racial Problems*; and Roy L. Garis, *Immigration Restriction: A Study of the Opposition to and Regulation of Immigration to the United States* (New York, 1927).

40. Lipshultz, "American Attitudes toward Mexican Immigration," pp. 6-29; and Neal, "The Policy of the United States," pp. 147-188. See also Reisler, *By the Sweat of Their Brow*, Ch. 6: "The Anglo Perception of the Mexican Worker."

41. Memorandum is reprinted in *Cong. Record*, Vol. 72 (April 16, 1930), 7114-7116. See also "Confidential Memorandum. Immigration Work in Mexico," by Consul Thomas McEnelly, November 9, 1928, 811.111 Mexico/113 1/2, Records of the Department of State, R.G. 59, National Archives, Washington, D.C. See also Robert N.

McLean's account of legalization of "bootleg" laborers in the Imperial Valley in 1926, in *That Mexican!*, pp. 118-123.

42. Correspondence between the Secretary of State and Ambassador Dwight W. Morrow, April 10, 1928, to January 1929, concerning excessive leniency in visa issuance, the need for restriction and a possible "Gentleman's Agreement" with Mexico, like that with Japan, is contained in file 811.111 Mexico/36/43/113/120, R.G. 59.

43. "Immigration Work—Annual Report," by Richard F. Boyce, American Consul, Nuevo Laredo, to Secretary of State, July 1, 1929, 811.111 Mexico/248, R.G. 59, N.A., pp. 12-13; also Abraham Hoffman's study of administrative restrictions, "El cierre de la puerta trasera norteamericana: Restricción de la inmigración mexicana," *Historia Mexicana*, XXV:3 (1976), 403-422.

44. *Annual Report . . . Immigration . . . 1931*, pp. 15-16.

45. Act of March 2, 1929, in *Naturalization, Citizenship and Expatriation Laws, July 1, 1929* (U.S. Department of Labor, Bureau of Naturalization, Washington, D.C., 1929), pp. 35-39; and act of March 4, 1929, in *The Statutes at Large of the United States of America*, from December 1927 to March 1929, Vol. 45 (Washington, D.C., 1929), 1551-1552.

46. "Wetbacks: Can the States Act?" in *Stanford Law Review* (March 1954), 287-322.

47. See, for example, *Cong. Record*, Vol. 72 (April 16, 1930), 7129; and correspondence, with newspaper clippings, sent by Richard F. Boyce, American Consul, Nuevo Laredo, to Secretary of State, January 14, 1929-May 7, 1929, in 8111.111 Mexico/150/214/248, R.G. 59.

48. *Ibid.*, and General Order No. 129, "Regarding Registry of Aliens Act," from Harry Hull, Commissioner of Immigration, to all personnel, April 6, 1929, in Immigration and Naturalization Service Subject Correspondence 1906-1932, 55598/496, R.G. 85.

49. The act of October 3, 1965, amended the organic act of 1952 so that in Sec. 249 the former cutoff date of June 28, 1940 was moved to "June 30, 1948." See *Immigration and Nationality Act with Amendments*, 5th ed. Revised through December 31, 1965 (Washington, D.C., 1966), p. 87.

50. Interviews with U.S. immigration officials, Central Office, INS, December 10, 1970, and December 8, 1971.

51. *Ibid.*, interviews.

52. Interviews with Border Patrol officers, active and retired, in California, Arizona, and Texas, April-August 1970; and *The Immigration and Naturalization Systems of the United States, Report of the Committee on the Judiciary Pursuant to S. Res. 137, 80th Cong., 1st Sess.* (Washington, D.C., 1950), p. 634.

53. *Ibid.*, interviews.

54. Abraham Hoffman, "The Repatriation of Mexican Nationals from the United States During the Great Depression" (Doctoral dissertation, University of California, Los Angeles, 1970).

55. *Annual Report of the Secretary of Labor 1935*, pp. 78-79.

56. *Ibid.*, p. 79.

57. Interviews with border patrolmen, active and retired.

58. Auerbach, *Immigration Laws*, pp. 10-12.

59. McCain, "Contract Labor." Also, "Conversations with the President of

Mexico," in George Messersmith, U.S. Ambassador, Mexico City, to Secretary of State, Sept. 29, 1943, in 811.504 Mexico/129 1/2; and March 18, 1946, 811.504/3-1846, R.G. 59.

60. *Ibid.*, file 811.504 Mexico/6-146/7-146. And copy of correspondence of Department of State and War Manpower Commission on formulation of binational agreements for contract labor in Agricultural History Files, III B 1 b(2)(a), Agricultural History Branch, U.S. Department of Agriculture, covering period July 1942 to August 5, 1942.

61. *President's Commission on Migratory Labor* (1951), pp. 41-42.

62. Sec. 101(a) and 214(c) of *Immigration and Nationality Act* (1952); and *Migrant and Seasonal Labor Powerlessness*, p. 2020.

63. Grebler, *Mexican Immigration*, D-14. Presently because of the Huelga movement and other union protests only a few hundred H-2 workers are being admitted from Mexico; most now come from the West Indies. See INS, *Annual Report 1972*, tables 16A and 18.

64. *Hearings Before the President's Commission on Immigration* (1952), pp. 1630-1632.

65. See Ernesto Galarza, *Merchants of Labor*; and Samora, *Los Mojados*.

66. *President's Commission on Migratory Labor* (1951), pp. 40, 52-53.

67. *Ibid.*; see also Samora, *Los Mojados*, pp. 46-48; and Galarza, *Merchants of Labor*, pp. 63-64.

68. *President's Commission* (1951), p. 75.

69. Interviews with immigration officials and border patrolmen in border region, April-August 1970.

70. *President's Commission* (1951), p. 23.

71. *Ibid.*, pp. 39, 49-50; and statement by Varden Fuller in *President's Commission on Immigration* (1952), p. 1063.

72. *United States Statutes at Large 1952*, Vol. 66 (1953), 26.

73. According to Lee Cremer, president of the National Council of Immigration and Naturalization Service Unions, there are at least 2 million illegal aliens working in the United States. UPI news release, Washington, D.C., March 6, 1972.

74. 66 Stat. 229 (1952), 8 U.S.C.A. 1325 (1953), text in *United States Statutes at Large 1952*, Vol. 66 (1953), 229-230.

75. Interviews with immigration officers and apprehended aliens in border region, April-August 1970, and August 1972.

76. INS, *Annual Report 1954* and *1955*; and *Report of the American Section of Joint Commission on Mexican Migrant Labor*, submitted by Joseph M. Swing, Commissioner, INS, September 3, 1954 (mimeographed).

77. Statistics from INS, *Annual Report*, Tables 27-B and 54.

78. See Nelson's biographical account of *Pablo Cruz and the American Dream*. Probably the highest percentage of formal deportations of apprehended illegals took place immediately after the act of March 4, 1929, and during the depths of the Depression when there was strong public pressure to remove illegal aliens from the job market and the relief rolls, and when the Immigration Service had much less "wetback pressure" on the border.

79. Divine, *American Immigration Policy*, pp. 175-176; and Auerbach, *Immigration Laws*, pp. 14-17. Immigration policy precedents and reformist thought that helped

shape the law of 1952 may be found in the 925-page report: *The Immigration and Naturalization Systems* (1950).

80. INS, *Annual Report 1952* and *1956*.

81. U.S. Congress, Senate Committee on the Judiciary, *Immigration 1976, Hearings Before the Subcommittee on Immigration and Naturalization on S. 3074 to Amend the Immigration and Nationality Act, March-April, 1976, 94th Cong., 2d Sess.* (1976), p. 7.

82. *Ibid.*; and House Committee on the Judiciary, *Illegal Aliens, Hearings Before the Subcommittee on Immigration, Citizenship, and International Law on H.R. 982 and Related Bills, 94th Cong., 1st Sess., February-March, 1975, Serial No. 8* (1975). See also "U.S. Immigration 1970: Policies, Procedures, Problems," Special Issue of *International Migration Review*, IV (Spring 1970).

83. Interviews with American consular officers in Mexico City, July 19, 1970; Nuevo Laredo, May 5, 1970; and Ciudad Juárez, August 25, 1972.

84. INS, *Annual Report*, Table 14: Immigration by Region or Country of Birth.

85. For estimates of illegal aliens by immigration service see: Senate Committee on the Judiciary, *Immigration 1976*, table on pp. 39-40; Lesko Associates, "Final Report"; and Ardman, "Our Illegal Alien Problem"; also House Committee on the Judiciary, *Hearings Before Subcommittee No. 1, March 7-8, 1973, 93d Cong., 1st Sess. Serial No. 1* (1973), pp. 27-28, 36, 66.

86. Interviews with immigration officers in California, Arizona, and Texas border areas, April-August 1970, and August 1972; as well as March 1975. See also note 85.

87. INS, *Annual Report*, Table 8.

88. William G. Hartley, "United States Immigration Policy: The Case of the Western Hemisphere," *World Affairs*, 135:1 (Summer 1972), 67.

89. U.S. Department of Justice, "A Program for Effective and Humane Action on Illegal Mexican Immigrants. Final Report of the Special Study Group on Illegal Immigrants from Mexico," (Washington, D.C., January 15, 1973); and interviews with members of Mexico's interagency commission for the study of surreptitious emigration, Mexico City, December 27-28, 1972, and January 21 and February 12, 1974.

90. House Committee on the Judiciary, *Illegal Aliens, Hearings* (Five parts, 1971-1972); and U.S. Congress, House, *Hearings . . . on H.R. 982 and Related Bills, Illegal Aliens, 94th Cong., 1st Sess., February-March 1975. Serial No. 8* (1975). For detailed discussions of "due process" problems raised by the Supreme Court decision of 1976 to uphold California Labor Code Sec. 2805, and the Rodino, Eastland and other important penalty bills in Congress, see Galindo Nieto, "The Undocumented Alien Laborer"; and Richard Avila and James Romo, "The Undocumented Worker: The Controversy Takes a New Turn," *Chicano Law Review*, 3 (1976), 148-194.

91. "Controversy over Proposals to Reduce the Number of Illegal Aliens . . . Pro and Con," *Congressional Digest*, 54:1 (June 1975), 1-32.

92. Ibid., and House Committee on the Judiciary, *Amending the Immigration and Nationality Act . . . Report Together with Additional . . . Views, 94th Cong., 1st Sess., Report No. 94-506*, submitted by Mr. Eilberg (September 1975), pp. 37-41; also commentaries in *Chicano Law Review*, see note 90.

93. Interviews with American consuls, Mexico City, August 15, 1970, and January

9, 1974; Nuevo Laredo, May 2, 1970; Ciudad Juárez, August 25, 1972; and Monterrey, March 12-13, 1974, and February 17, 1976.

94. House Committee on the Judiciary, *Illegal Aliens, Hearings*, pp. 1-85. See also note 90.

95. Seminars and workshops sponsored principally by Patricio Flores, Auxiliary Bishop, San Antonio Archdiocese, and Immigration Department of the United Catholic Conference promote the new ministry of immigration counseling, as in El Paso, June 30-July 3, 1974; or Mexico City, April 21-24, 1975. Moreover, the Catholic Bishops' Campaign for Human Development has sought to influence federal immigration policy and practice. Sources: interviews with Bishop Flores, April 1, 1974, and Raúl García, Coordinator, Immigration Service, Denver Catholic Community Service, December 18, 1974; *The Witness* (archdiocesan paper-Dubuque), LIX (November 28, 1974); and *Excelsior* (Mexico City), April 22-24, 1975.

96. *Illegal Aliens, Hearings* (1971-1972); also militant literature such as "Infamy of the Immigration Service, Punishment by Exile," *La Raza* (Los Angeles), 1:7 (January 1972), 48-53; "Ley Dixon Arnett," *ibid.* (April 1972), 8-9; and "Bert Corona Speaks on La Raza Unida Party and the Illegal Alien Scare," January 22, 1971 (pamphlet, New York: Pathfinder Press, 1972). A more balanced view of immigration policies and practices by Gilbert Cárdenas and others is found in a special issue of *Chicano Law Review*, II (Summer 1975), 129 pp., published by Chicano Law Student Association, University of California, Los Angeles.

97. Donald G. Hohl and Michael G. Wenk, "Current U.S. Immigration Legislation: Analysis and Comment," *International Migration*, 10-3 (1972), 91-94.

98. *Ibid.*, pp. 94-103; also, House Committee on the Judiciary, *Western Hemisphere Immigration, Hearings . . . 93d Cong., 1st Sess., on H.R. 981, March 28-29, April 12, June 6-7, 13-14, 1973* (1973). For account of immigration reform efforts see *Immigration and Nationality Amendments of 1973, with Additional Views, 93d Cong., 1st Sess., September 11, 1973. Report No. 93-461* (1973); David S. North, "Pulling in the Welcome Mat," *Agenda* (National Council of La Raza, Washington, D.C.), II (Winter 1973), 12-14; see also note 90.

99. Senate Committee on Labor and Public Welfare, *Hearings Before the Subcommittee on Employment, Poverty, and Migratory Labor, on S. 2070 . . . S. 3202 . . . to amend Farm Labor Contractor Registration Act, 93d Cong., 2d Sess., February 8, April 8-9, 1974* (1974); and Senate, Committee on Labor and Public Welfare, *Farm Labor Contractor Registration Act Amendments of 1974 . . . October 1, 1974. Report No. 93-1206* (1974).

100. Information provided by District Director, Immigration, Omaha, January 10, 1977; District Director, Los Angeles, March 22, 1977; and District Director, Chicago, September 8, 1977.

101. "Latest Wave of Immigrants Brings New Problems," *U.S. News and World Report* (April 5, 1976), pp. 25-29; Chapman, "Deluge of Illegal Aliens," *San Francisco Chronicle*, July 26, 1974; L. H. Wittemore, "Can We Stop the Invasion of Illegal Aliens?" *Parade* magazine, February 29, 1976, pp. 10-12; Chapman, Commissioner of Immigration, "Illegal Aliens," 188-192.

102. Domestic Council Committee on Illegal Aliens, *Preliminary Report* (Washing-

ton, D.C.: U.S. Department of Justice, December 1976), p. 243.

103. Interviews with immigration officers in border states, April-August 1970, and August 1972; and, additionally, at Laredo, April 8-9, 1974; Dallas, March 17, 1974; McAllen, March 21, 1975; Eagle Pass, January 4, 1975; and Phoenix, September 1-3, 1975.

104. INS, *Annual Report*, Tab. 3, and Tab. 15A.

105. Interviews with immigration officers, and proposals by Dr. Wendy Gamm, economist, Texas A & M University, and others, in Regional Meeting of National Conference of Catholic Bishops Bicentennial Subcommittee, San Antonio, April 7-10, 1975.

106. "Ethnicity and Race," and "The Spanish Speaking," in *Liberty and Justice for All*, Committee for the Bicentennial, National Catholic Conference of Catholic Bishops (Washington, D.C.), pp. 31-44.

107. David Finney, "The Federal Interstate Border Compact: An International Economic Solution to the Border Problem" (unpublished paper, Ft. Worth, Texas, January 1975).

108. See Chicano reaction and legal analysis in Galindo Nieto, "The Undocumented Alien Laborer," 148-163.

109. Howard Goldberg, "Turning Off the Job Incentives for Illegal Aliens," *Zero Population Growth National Reporter* (July 1977), 6,8.

110. Information provided by District Director, Immigration, San Antonio, April 5, 1977. See also James Flanagan, "North of the Border: Who Needs Whom? *Forbes*, 119: 8 (April 15, 1977), 37-41.

111. Galindo Nieto, "The Undocumented Alien Laborer."

112. Fausto Fernandez P., "Campaña civica . . . por la Raza Unida," *Excelsior* (Mexico City), July 6, 1977, pp. 1, 17. For Raza immigration proposals, see special issue "Hispanics in the Carter administration," particularly bills introduced by Edward Roybal and others, *Agenda*, The National Council of La Raza, Washington, D.C., 7:4 (July/August 1977), 43-44.

113. David North and Marion Houstoun, *The Characteristics and Role of Illegal Aliens in the U.S. Labor Market: An Exploratory Study* (Washington: Linton and Company, March 1976), pp. 173-178; and F. Ray Marshall, "Employment Implications of the International Migration of Workers," in National Council on Employment Policy, *Illegal Aliens: An Assessment of the Issues* (Washington, 1976), pp. 52-65.

114. See note 113; and Domestic Council Committee, *Preliminary Report*, pp. 214-216.

115. Vernon M. Briggs, Jr., *The Mexico-United States Border: Public Policy and Chicano Economic Welfare* (Austin: Center for the Study of Human Resources, University of Texas, 1974), pp. 21-28; Briggs, "Mexican Workers in the United States Labor Market: A Contemporary Dilemma," *International Labour Review*, 112 (November 1975), 351-368; Jorge A. Bustamante, "The Impact of the Undocumented Immigration from Mexico on the U.S.-Mexican Economies: Preliminary Findings and Suggestions for Bilateral Cooperation," paper presented at annual meeting of the Southern Economics Association, Atlanta, November 1976; also statements by Bustamante in *Excelsior*, August 6, 1976, pp. 4A-5A; and in *El Porvenir* (Monterrey), December 30, 1976, p. 1A; and Carey McWilliams, "No Trespassing: What Became of the Land of Opportunity," *Skeptic*, 20 (July/August 1977), 49-53.

116. "S.3412, a Bill to Establish a Temporary National Commission on Alien Labor . . .," introduced by Senator Joseph Montoya, 93d Cong. 2d Sess., May 4, 1974.

117. North and Houstoun, *The Character and Role of Illegal Aliens*, pp. 178-179; Wayne A. Cornelius, "Illegal Mexican Migration to the United States: A Summary of Recent Research Findings and Policy Recommendations," (briefing paper, Cambridge, Mass.: Department of Political Science, M.I.T., April 1977), pp. 17-23; Michael J. Piore, "Illegal Immigration to the United States: Some Observations and Policy Suggestions," in National Council on Employment Policy, *Illegal Aliens*, pp. 86-88; also Piore statements in "What Illegal Aliens Cost the Economy," *Business Week*, 2487 (June 13, 1977), 86-88.

118. Controversial research findings on social costs are summarized by Joyce Vialet, *Illegal Aliens: Analysis and Background* (Washington: Congressional Research Service, Library of Congress, February 1977); and questions raised by M. Vic Villalpando, and others associated with the San Diego County Immigration Council, *Illegal Aliens: A Study of the Socioeconomic Impact of Illegal Aliens on the County of San Diego* (County of San Diego Human Resources Agency, January 1977).

119. "Cranston Proposal," *Zero Population Growth National Reporter* (January-February 1977), 3.

120. Attributed to Houston Controller, Leonel Castillo, in "Latest Wave of Immigrants . . . ," *U.S. News and World Report* (April 5, 1976), 28.

121. Senate Committee on the Judicary, *Immigration 1976*, pp. 181-190; and House Committee on the Judiciary, *Review of the Administration of the Immigration and Nationality Act, Hearings before the Subcommittee on Immigration . . . on Legislative Oversight of the Immigration and Nationality Act, July 26; September 13, 18, and 20, 1973, 93d Cong., 1st Sess., Serial No. 22* (1973), pp. 3-9, 11-19, 27-32, 45, and ff. See also note 90.

122. See various issues of *Zero Population Growth National Reporter* in the period 1974-1977; and "Recommendations for a New Immigration Policy for the United States," adopted by the Executive Committee, ZPG, Inc., January 19, 1975, Washington, D.C.

123. Patrick Riley, Editor, NCR, "Illegal Aliens Opposed by Anti-People Forces," *National Catholic Register*, Los Angeles (August 15, 1976), p. 5.

124. Campaigning for reelection, Ford, on October 20, 1976, signed P.L. 94-571, which placed a 20,000 limit on all non-preference immigrants by country. But, if reelected, he promised to work for a special immigration status for Mexico, since the United States "has a very special and historical relationship with our neighbor to the South." See Pilar Saavedra's balanced account of Latin-American expectations and "The New Immigration Law: A Plus for Some, a Minus for Others," *Agenda* 7:1 (January/February 1977), 17-20.

125. Domestic Council Committee on Illegal Aliens, *Preliminary Report*, p. 223.

126. For instance, U.S. General Accounting Office reports, such as *Immigration—Need to Reassess U.S. Policy. Report to the Congress by the Comptroller General of the United States* (Washington, D.C., October 19, 1976); also, the Domestic Council Committee's *Preliminary Report* serves to summarize reform proposals made during the Ford administration.

7/ MEXICAN POLICY AND AMBIVALENCE TOWARD LABOR EMIGRATION TO THE UNITED STATES

Arthur F. Corwin

> These people (illegal immigrants) are not coming here with any sense of shame. They feel they have a moral right to migrate to the United States for work. If the Southwest still belonged to Mexico, it would have been a major economic power in the world today.
>
> Alberto Juárez, legal-aid attorney,
> One-Stop Immigration, Los Angeles
> (1976)[1]

The Shaping of a National Dilemma

In 1848—a date fixed in the minds of Mexican school boys—peace commissioners had to sign away one-third of the national territory before General Scott would go home. The onerous terms of the Treaty of Guadalupe Hidalgo provoked one of the first expressions of official policy and feelings toward Mexicans under United States sovereignty: national leaders grieving for some 80,000 brothers of La Raza swallowed by Anglo imperialism in California, Texas, and New Mexico, tried helplessly to repatriate them, or at least to leave them with certain treaty rights to property and culture. Following the "amputation of 1848," as Mexican historians commonly describe it, the mother land suffered further humiliation when France imposed the puppet emperor Maximillian (1861-1867) upon her. After such traumatic facts, it is hardly surprising that fostering defensive nationalism and multiplication of the race became for nearly every Mexican government not only a policy of national development, but of frontier defense.[2] Later, how could any government look on with indifference when members of La Raza were sucked over the border to serve the *yanqui* colossus?

Even before the Revolution of 1910 released a new wave of xenophobia, voices were raised to protest the drain of labor to American railroad, mining, and agricultural employers in the border states. The dictatorship of Porfirio Díaz (1876-1910), striving to secure the northern frontier, to increase the population, to colonize rural Mexico with European farmers, to import an Oriental labor force, to encourage foreign entrepreneurs, industrialism, and modernism, and, in general, to overcome the national debility that had led to territorial dismemberment, could only look on with growing consternation as laborers and their families (some of them fleeing peonage) began moving by the thousands into Anglo-American borderlands and beyond to offer their muscle and sweat to the gringo employers. Some of their countrymen were tempted to cry out after them: ¡*vendepatrias*! ¡*malinchistas*! ¡*pochos*! ¡*agringados*! ¡*ingratos*! and other terms of reproach that one might hurl at a prodigal son who abandons his struggling kinfolk. On the other hand certain nationalists and revolutionary reformers, like the Flores Magón brothers and Francisco Madero had lived as exiles in the United States, cried out not against the migrating peons but against the government; only a feudal dictatorship serving foreign interests would force deserving Mexicans over the border into the hands of Anglo exploiters! Apparently the Díaz regime, disturbed by editorial opinion and consular reports, was at the point of undertaking a full-scale investigation of the causes of this out-migration when it was torpedoed by the Madero revolution of 1910-1912.[3]

The revolutionary fervor touched off by Madero and carried through the administration of Lázaro Cárdenas (1934-1940) not only served to accelerate for two decades the exodus of campesinos and, less so, political refugees, but it accentuated that nationalist sentiment that has colored so much of Mexican policy and attitudes toward emigration to Anglo-America. The report that thousands of workers and refugees, together with their families, and even servants, were on their way to the United States was, by 1920, regarded as "a fatal bleeding," in the words of one excited editorialist—that not checked would only serve to exhaust Mexico's growth potential and leave her submissive to Anglo-Saxon economic power.[4]

Furthermore, the ideologists of the Revolution were convinced, like national leaders before them, that Mexico was underpopulated and because of that fact she lost the northern provinces. At the inception of independence in 1821, Mexico's population was less than 7 million. Nearly a century later, in 1910, it was scarcely 15 million. Due to revolutionary anarchy and out-migration, the population dropped to 14.3 million by 1920. By 1930 it was hardly 17 million, although one should here take into account perhaps a million and a half emigrants who, since 1910, had moved permanently or temporarily across the American border.

Mexican intellectual leaders responded to "population anemia" with what could be called "demographic nationalism." Perhaps this thinking is best ex-

emplified by the late Gilberto Loyo, an outstanding demographer and economist, who for many years, beginning in the late 1920s, sought to educate the
National Revolutionary Party on the need for a more vigorous pro-natalist
policy that would not only foster the increase of population through public
health and education facilities, but also serve to keep the laboring class at
home through industrial development, irrigation, and agrarian colonies for
landless peasants.[5] Some of the land reform proposals of Loyo and other
writers, such as Manuel Gamio and Narciso Bassols, were taken up by President Calles in the late 1920s, and more important, by President Cárdenas in his
revolutionary Six-Year Plan of 1934, a plan that called for a massive land distribution in favor of the peon class, and proposed to bring all Mexicans under
the protective wings of the social revolution, even those in the "lost territories."[6]

However, during the depths of political anarchy, 1912-1920, the diaspora of
La Raza continued. The labor demands of World War I in the United States,
the cutoff of labor immigration from other countries by congressional legislation, and the continuing political uncertainties in Mexico all served to stimulate the outflow of poverty-stricken workers and refugees, some of whom were
skilled workers, artisans, shopkeepers, and professional persons. Aside from a
general alarm about a labor shortage, government officials worried about a
growing national obligation to protect hordes of illiterate, undocumented
campesinos, children in tow, following seasonal work, camp-style, in the
United States. Emerging labor unions, dominated by the Confederación Regional de Obreros Mexicanos (CROM), joined in the cry of Mexican consular
officers abroad to stop mass emigration because migrant workers—and, indeed, Mexican self-respect—were subject to segregation, ridicule, and exploitation.[7]

Why not a blockade on the border? Mexican officials might have defended
such action on the grounds that an imperialist power should not have access to
Mexican labor. After all, the American government had intervened on several
occasions in the period 1912-1917 in a vain attempt to influence the course of
the revolution and to protect American investors and property holders. But,
aside from bankruptcy conditions, there were other reasons for not attempting
a costly migration block along a 2,000-mile desert frontier. The early revolutionary regimes of Carranza, De la Huerta, Obregón, and Calles, covering the
period 1915-1934, regarded an open border as an "escape valve" for revolutionary unrest and political enemies. Moreover, they were painfully aware that
prostrate Mexico had little to offer miserable peons and underpaid industrial
and mine workers, except unfulfilled revolutionary promises. The alternative
for expatriate workers, in the words of a border official, was to return to "absolute misery."[8] In addition, under the new order of civil rights spelled out in the
Constitution of 1917, the right of Mexican citizens to travel and migrate any-

where, subject only to administrative procedures in cases of transborder travel, was clearly established.[9]

Another consideration that worked against the nationalist outcry for strict emigration control was the need of shaky revolutionary governments for diplomatic recognition and support from Washington. Thus, in spite of a widespread anti-American sentiment, President Wilson's meddling in revolutionary affairs, American occupation of Vera Cruz in 1915, Pershing's "invasion" of north Mexico in 1916, and a German promise to help restore the lost territories, Presidents Carranza, De la Huerta, and Obregón permitted North American employers, under no Mexican supervision, to recruit labor at the border during World War I and after, under special American exemptions for contract labor in force during the years 1917-1921.

No and Yes, Dissuasion and Protectionism, 1915-1940

The foregoing does not mean that Mexican leaders were taking a passive attitude toward transborder migration. On the contrary, as soon as the semblance of a stable constitutional government was reestablished under President Venustiano Carranza, Mexican officials turned to the problem of outmigration. The Carranza government (1915-1920) formulated and applied, as far as possible, the main outlines of nationalist emigration policies that successive governments have more or less consistently maintained to the present day. These policies might be summarized as: dissuasion, contract protection, and, if possible, the Mexicanization of émigrés, but not prohibition. Such policies were, in fact, the alternative to the demands of nationalists and employers, especially hacienda owners, that the government must forcibly stop migration to *el otro lado*.

Actually Mexican officials, as early as 1915 and before, did what they could to discourage emigration, on the one hand, and to protect Mexican workers in the United States on the other; but it was during the period of mass recruitment of wartime labor by American agents under contract-labor exemptions that the Mexican government felt forced to elaborate control policies and measures. In the years 1917-1921 the government prohibited the recruitment of labor within Mexican borders by representatives of American employers and labor agencies, established check points on railways leading north (in a vain attempt to detain migrants without bona fide contracts or passports), ordered all would-be emigrants to register at border migration offices, and instructed officials there to refuse passports to emigrants without proper documents.[10] The governors of the northern states were urged to cooperate in all these efforts. During the war Carranza officials sought to prevent the military conscription of Mexican workers in the United States, and the government sought for the first time to make full use of the press in an effort to dissuade workers from leaving the country without contracts. In 1920 a short-lived Workers' Protective Office was established in Ciudad Juárez and El Paso to regulate labor contracts; elsewhere in the border towns and in the interior of the United States a handful of consuls tried to supervise contracting and cut out the exploitative middlemen, or *coyotes*.[11]

As for some 72,000 contract workers legally admitted to the United States under war emergency exemptions to work on railroads and in sugar beet fields mostly, the Mexican government insisted, with little success, that contract obligations be met by American employers under the supervision of federal agencies, namely the Department of Labor and the Immigration Service; and that contract work be of a temporary nature with the employer obligated to pay the return passage of the worker. But this labor-import program was unilateral in nature, and Mexican officials and consuls had no direct authority in its administration, although the Carranza administration did resort frequently to diplomatic channels to protest reported abuses and to propose stronger contract guarantees.[12] More important, Mexican officials learned valuable lessons from the frustrations of 1917-1921; so that in 1942, when the United States would again propose an emergency labor program, Mexico would be prepared to insist, *sine qua non*, on joint governmental control.

Meanwhile, the Mexican government was under mounting pressure to stop the outflow of La Raza, for Mexican consuls continued to report that American employers and labor contractors (*enganchistas*) were exploiting workers, and that streams of *mojados*, or wetbacks, totally without contract protection, were pouring pell-mell over the border. But, in July 1920, the dictator General Adolfo de la Huerta, seeing no alternative, reaffirmed the Carranza emigration policy. The alarming loss of labor and population was, he said, certainly regrettable, but, unfortunately, the government could not directly intervene because that would be restraining the individual liberties incorporated in the Constitution of 1917.[13]

Through the years, critics, including American immigration officials, have accused the Mexican government of using "constitutional liberties" as a perennial excuse for inaction on emigration problems. However this may be, the question of border control has always been enmeshed in a complex of ambivalent policies and feelings. On the one hand, successive Mexican governments have passed migration and population laws which have prohibited leaving the country without a passport or a labor contract. On the other hand, these laws and regulations, then as now, have never carried any specific penalties for failure to comply. Why this reluctance to penalize? For one thing, after the cession of 1848, successive governments encouraged Mexicans to settle and hold the border zones, offering as one incentive easy access to cheaper American goods. Then, considerations of reciprocity came into play. Until the American law of 1917 it was an open border, and increasingly, Mexican border residents were accustomed to visiting kinfolk on the American side and to taking up work there, bringing money and goods back to Mexico. Even after 1917 (to the present) the immediate border zone was wide open to tourists and shoppers, neither government requiring official permission other than border resident cards. How could anyone tell just what might be the real intention of a casual border visitor or shopper? There seemed to be no juridical way in which the Mexican government could allow some of its citizens to visit the border and not others.[14] To complicate the situation, families that swarmed around border towns lacked such elementary documents as birth certificates and marriage licenses, and many of them were illiterate or ignorant of national laws, or pretended to be. Were they seeking to reside on the Mexican side or to sneak across?

Furthermore, since the Revolution the government has been inclined to regard *mojados* as innocent victims of unfortunate circumstances. In most cases Mexican border officials have treated the job-seeking emigrant with compassion. Others feel a sense of grim satisfaction when a humble campesino fools the gringo border guards and sneaks through to former Mexican territory. In other cases the rhetoric of dissuasion never meant anything, with some border officials engaging in the deep-rooted business of accepting *mordidas* for arranging registration papers and border-crossing cards, and for permitting labor recruiters to operate in border towns along with professional alien smugglers.[15]

As the exodus continued unabated in the 1920s, Mexican consuls were swamped with protective obligations, and the government, with the patriotic collaboration of leading newspapers, stepped up its campaign of dissuasion for whatever it was worth. Here the government was moved to some extent by the possibility of an unwanted quota on Mexican immigration, seriously proposed in the U.S. Congress, and by the pressure of American friends of the Mexican Revolution and of the Mexican labor movement, such as first Samuel Gompers and then William Green of the American Federation of Labor (AFL), who wanted Mexico to adopt the principle of "voluntary self-restriction," especially in the period 1923-1929. Also, a concerned Department of State, in view of national sensibilities in Mexico, hoped that a Gentleman's Agreement on voluntary restriction (such as that worked out with Japan in 1907) could be substituted for a quota. But dissuasion, not restriction, was as far as proud Mexican officials or labor leaders, like Luis Morones, would go.[16]

Restrictionist proposals were consistently opposed by Mexican leaders not only for reasons of national pride, but because they felt that Mexican citizens, registered or not, had indeed a moral right to migrate to the "lost territories." On the other hand, reports that members of La Raza were being victimized by predatory labor agents and Anglo exploiters were also a matter of national pride. Therefore, the governments of Obregón and Calles, in the 1920s, undertook a more intensive propaganda campaign, using the Mexican press to warn job seekers and their families not to pursue the illusion of El Dorado on the far side of the Rio Grande. Stories of stranded families, discrimination, mistreatment, and the enserfing of *mojado* labor were widely circulated, true or not; and Mexican labor leaders, border officials, and state and municipal authorities were urged to warn aspiring emigrants of the dangers and uncertainties that lay in wait across the boundary line. Editorialists and government officials called for patriotic and cooperative efforts to keep migratory families at home. Works of semiofficial propaganda were circulated like that of Alfonso Fabila, who, writing in 1928, pictured the fate that awaited Mexican settlers and their children in the land of the gringos—not the least of the dangers would be the forced Americanization by public schools and the inevitable erosion of La Raza.[17]

The government, seeking to defend the new revolutionary order, also used the press and the semiofficial labor leadership of the CROM to educate political critics toward a more realistic understanding of the causes of the exodus and the efforts of government officials to control it. Supplied with circulars, memoranda, and interview statements from the Ministry of Foreign Relations, the Mexican Consulates, the Department of Labor, and other government agencies, the Mexican press suggested that the revolutionary government was doing all in its power to promote the welfare of the laboring classes, but that many simple people were being seduced by American wages and Mexican go-betweens. *Enganchistas* and *coyotes*, who had infested many parts of Mexico, and who were paid so much a head for delivering unskilled workers to labor agents on the other side, or who sold false promises, were often characterized by editorialists as scavengers and *malos Mexicanos* living off the foolish hopes of their fellow countrymen. Hand-in-hand with this propaganda campaign, government officials increased the consular force, subsidized Manuel Gamio's field survey of Mexicans in the United States (1926-1927), appealed to Mexican industries to raise wages, sponsored the Migration Law of 1926 providing for labor contracts and outlawing free-lance recruiting, renewed threats to cut off all consular aid to illegal emigrants, and, in general, sought to calm excited nationalists.[18]

During the 1920s, however, the Mexican government had little objection to legal emigration to the United States, even though the numbers rose to disturbing proportions. In 1900 legal emigration was less than 300; in 1910, according to U.S. figures, it had risen to near 19,000; and in 1920 it reached over 52,000. From 1920 to 1929 the annual average was near 50,000, touching high points of 89,336 in 1924, and 67,721 in 1927. Legal emigration at least satisfied Mexico's protectionist criteria. The legal emigrant carried a passport, and he complied with Mexican and American laws. He not only would have certain civil rights in the United States, but he could register with the Mexican consulate and seek protection there, and so long as he did not become "lost" as a naturalized American citizen, there was always the hope that he would come home to *la madre patria* at a propitious time.

As Mexican officials saw it, an immigrant visa was like a permanent work permit, providing a form of contract protection, for most immigrant workers were sponsored by employers who presumably offered permanent, high-paying jobs. And a legal immigrant was also free to accept any other job, and, theoretically, to join labor unions. He posed no serious protectionist problem for the Mexican consul, and it was assumed that he sent home money.[19] So it was no inconsistency that Mexican diplomats exerted pressure on the American State Department to intervene and cut short "unfriendly proposals" by American congressmen that would have placed western hemisphere countries on the quota system and limited Mexican legal immigration to less than 3,000 a year. After all, could not Mexico retaliate against American investment interests in Mexico? The State Department, already disturbed about Japanese resentment against Oriental exclusions, got the message and through its consular service in Mexico, began quietly in 1928 to limit the issuance of visas to "unqualified applicants" without giving offense to the Mexican government; by 1930 the State Department and President Hoover had prevailed upon Congress to drop the quota movement and abide by the policy of administrative restrictions.[20]

Insofar as possible, the principle departments of the Mexican government, namely the Ministry of Foreign Relations, which controlled the consular service, and the Ministry of Internal Affairs (Gobernación), which controlled the migration service, worked with American restrictionist efforts, not merely to avoid a special quota, but to avoid a growing protectionist and repatriation problem. By 1929 both Mexican and American consuls in the borderlands were reporting that many Mexican migrants were unable to find work, and were becoming stranded as the American economy began showing the first signs of a recession. Also, in March of that year the American Congress passed an alien registry act, accompanied by a new enforcement law that for the first time established criminal penalties for persons who, on their own, illegally enter the United States. The American Immigration Service promptly began a deportation drive, while many other Mexican nationals on their own fled across the border. Mexican officials cooperated with American requests by giving wide circulation to reports of rising unemployment in the United States, and the threat of deportation penalties resulting from new immigration laws. Mexican campesinos—if they would listen—were advised to meet all requirements of a bona fide immigrant before moving northward. In March 1930, the Mexican Migration Service established offices in four major transportation centers, including Guadalajara and Monterrey, in an effort to intercept laborers heading north without visas.[21]

Mexican diplomacy was successful in preventing a quota, but at no time did the government establish any form of effective dissuasion over the labor exodus of the 1920s. Judging by the number of legal emigrants who sought to settle over the border from 1917 to 1930 (more than 600,000), and the number of wetbacks who sought to settle there (probably a million or more), the grapevine of the unlettered campesinos which spread word of high wages, charity help, adventure, and better living conditions on the other side was more persuasive than official propaganda on labor exploitation. "By word-of-mouth is how most came over," said Paul S. Taylor. During the Great Depression of the 1930s, the same grapevine magic, not official discouragement, served to cut off mass emigration. Wetback crossings dropped precipitiously, and a mere 22,319 legal Mexican immigrants were admitted in the decade 1931 to 1940, according to American figures. 22

Bracero Problem, 1942-1964

After the Depression, a second exodus was triggered by World War II and the emergency labor program initiated in August 1942. The history of bracero contracting (1942-1964) shows that, as in the period 1917-1921 and after, the Mexican government again made frequent efforts to obstruct, discourage, or control migratory labor. The difference is that the government tried to use the bracero program to channel surplus labor to the United States. Government officials and planners, but not the general public, were aware of a growing farm-labor surplus as on the Central Plateau studded with small peasant villages. From such areas Mexican officials sought to select braceros, with some success during World War II. Also, the government, except for track labor on American railroads during the war, insisted that braceros be used in farm work only, and this partly to conserve industrial labor in Mexico, and partly to avoid public opposition in both countries, particularly from labor leaders. Hoping to avoid another *mojado* exodus, and to cut out *enganchistas*, *coyotes*, *polleros* (border guides), and other go-betweens, contracting centers were at first set up in the interior of the country under binational supervision. President Camacho, (1941-1946) and President Alemán (1947-1952) agreed to extend farm-labor contracting to help the United States meet world food needs after the war, for, after all, this wartime program cooperative had served to improve relations between the two countries. Yet by 1947 an uncontrollable rush to the border was underway, and not merely by campesinos and their families, but by a wide variety of workers and adventurers. By then both governments were again speaking of a "wetback crisis" and seeking desperately to "dry out" or legalize "wet labor." 23

The number of braceros rose from 4,203 in 1942 to an average of about 55,000 for the years 1943-1945. Yet in 1947 only 19,632 braceros were contracted in the interior of Mexico. What was the point of contracting when Mexican consuls conservatively estimated the number of wetback workers at around 119,000? At that time most *mojados* were, ironically, in Texas, which had been "blacklisted" by Mexico for discriminatory practices. Beginning in 1947 Mexican officials insisted on a number of special accords and revisions in order to sponge up the wetbacks.[24] By that date Mexico plainly had lost control of the migratory labor program, and many a Texas employer was grinning with satisfaction. After 1947 Congress (feeling that the war emergency was over) no longer authorized the federal government to serve as principal employer and contractor, and with the wetbacks available at the snap of a finger, American employer associations and independent farmers had things pretty much their own way, especially in the Texas borderlands, where Mexican population tended to spill over. As a Border Patrol veteran described it:

Farmers and ranchers there were living in a wetback paradise. You have no idea. Wetbacks were like "smoos." You remember that comic strip, *Lil' Abner*, where Al Capp painted a funny picture of utopia. Those happy, adorable little smoos, shaped like blimps, and fat and savory, came whenever you wanted them. Nobody ever wanted for a thing for smoos were good for everything. Slice 'em this way you had ham, and that way chicken, and they made good pets. Those lovable creatures never complained.[25]

Mexican officials and public opinion were again incensed at the reported exploitation of undocumented workers. The government fitfully threatened to cancel the bracero program, but could not do so, for it was the one narrow bridge of contract protection, other than legal immigration, for an otherwise uncontrollable stream of out-migration. During the war bracero wages were fixed at Mexico's insistence on the American minimum of $.35 per hour, then in the postwar period, raised to $.50 per hour, and later, $.75. Yet, *mojados*, or wetbacks, were receiving as low as $.10 an hour in 1948, and some of their families were living in holes and caves. All those elaborate provisions for housing, sanitation, medical care, insurance, employee complaints, paid transportation, minimum wage, etc. seemed ridiculous! An intolerable situation!

Mexican officials saw little choice but to cover as many *mojados* as possible with contract protection. Again, the bracero quota was sharply raised. By 1951 contract workers numbered 190,745, and eventually reached a high of 447,535 in 1959. Significantly, the Mexican government seized on the Korean War emergency to reassert diplomatic power and to reestablish an intergovernmental program of control, with more amendments approved by the American Congress under Public Law 78 on July 12, 1951.[26]

In spite of an established policy not to oppose forcibly the emigration of "surplus labor," Mexican officials were sorely tempted to blockade the border on several occasions, for wetbacks were placing in jeopardy not only national self-esteem, but other high policy objectives of the contracting program: for example, prevention of unilateral recruiting by American employers, denial to Texas employers of the use of Mexican labor so long as discriminatory practices in that state continued against the Mexican population, and, above all, placing all emigrant workers under contracts supervised by both Mexican and American officials. In the late 1940s, in pursuit of such objectives, the government actually stationed troops on the frontier in reluctant and fruitless attempts to halt wetbacks. Also, on several occasions, frustrated Mexican officials closed border recruiting ports, which had been opened temporarily at American insistence. For instance, this was done at Ciudad Juárez in October 1948, and again at several points on the California border in January 1954, to prevent employers from recruiting braceros without meeting Mexican conditions spelled out in the bracero convention of August 2, 1951. In the melee at Calexico, aspiring braceros fought like caged animals against Mexican police and border guards in an effort to cross over and sign up with waiting contractors. Such confrontations led to a serious diplomatic impasse. Mexico, unable to control wetbackism, could only back off from attempts to gain more supervision over the program.[27]

The spectacle of brother against brother, photographed by the national press, was enough to convince Mexican officials that a constitutional government could not forcibly detain the migration of surplus workers. Likewise, the Mexican public was shocked and sobered to see photographs of La Raza struggling to reach the outstretched arms of Anglo immigration officers, as if one were reaching for the promised land! Nationalist sentiment had always pictured emigration as humble campesinos driven involuntarily from the bosom of the mother country into the jaws of Anglo capitalists. But increasingly after 1954 the Mexican public shrugged its shoulders as if to say: "Let 'em go, it's no longer a national tragedy."[28] Since then the government has made no further show of force and, in effect, has left the matter of border migration control—not without mixed feelings—to the American Immigration Service, which carried out a massive cleanup of wetbacks in 1954-1955. Afterward the program functioned well. When, in 1964, the United States—not Mexico—terminated importation of bracero labor, Mexican officials were not certain what to say, except to prophesy the return of the wetback.[29]

At no time, however, has the Mexican government abandoned its policy of discouragement. During the bracero era the Mexican press and labor leaders, principally from the Confederación de Trabajadores Mexicanos (CTM), continued to sponsor a country-wide campaign to warn would-be *mojados* and *alambristas* (fence jumpers) against the certain exploitation that awaited workers without valid contracts or immigration papers, and often pleaded for national cooperation and a unified front, for Mexico was in a policy struggle with the United States over bracero control. Again, to judge by the huge number of wetback apprehensions, running into the millions during the period 1947-1955, the policy of discouragement had no appreciable effects on deterring illegal migration, nor on legal emigration.[30]

Legal emigration was moderate enough in the decade 1941-1950, amounting in all to 60,589. But employers had meanwhile rediscovered how to bring in permanent braceros. In the next decade, 1951-1960, emigration of legal Mexicans and their families jumped up to 299,811; and in the next five years, 1961-

1965, to 228,401.[31] By 1964, when the bracero program ended, the government passively accepted a rising level of legal emigration for the reasons previously given and because, by then, it was obvious that the population problem had inverted itself. More and more, the United States was regarded as an outlet for surplus people—no matter how much political critics and social reformers shouted down the concept of surplus population.[32]

Discouraging emigration has hardly been a successful policy, if measured statistically, but it is important to note that during the past fifty or sixty years other purposes have been served by the rhetoric of dissuasion. The National Revolutionary Party (PRI) that rules Mexico has expressed proper political and compassionate concern about an unsolved national problem, and this in turn has become a powerful rationale for pushing agrarian reform, industrial development, and social security programs—with limited means, to be sure— as the only long-range solutions to rural poverty and underdevelopment, and an explosive population that touched 25 million in 1950 and 35 million in 1960.[33]

The Consular Role

If through the years the government could do little to keep La Raza at home, then at least it could do all in its power to protect expatriate groups. This policy, also traced to the Carranza administration, was succinctly expressed by the Secretary of Foreign Relations in 1917: "Since it is not possible for the government to prevent emigration, it must take every measure to reduce the hardships of our fellow citizens while they reside abroad."[34]

In defending displaced nationals, the Mexican consuls since Carranza's time have displayed, all in all, an unmatched dedication. Besides serving emigrants, foreign-service protection was designed to convince political critics that the established party was assiduously protecting the Mexican colonies in the United States from labor abuse, discrimination, social abandonment, and other indignities. Explaining protectionist achievements and needs gave rise to a small body of revealing literature written by migration and consular officers. One example is an apologetic work by Andrés Landa y Piña, then head of the Department of Migration, entitled *La migración y protección de Mexicanos en el extranjero* (1928).[35] A similar account by Enrique Santibañez, then Mexican consul in San Antonio, carried the title: *Ensayo acerca de la inmigración mexicana en los Estados Unidos* (1930).[36]

Perhaps the most remarkable expression of consular protectionism has been Mexico's undeviating concern for the rights of laborers abroad. During World War I recruitment, the Mexican consuls were instructed to apply the ultramodern labor code contained in Article 123 of the *Carrancista* Constitution of 1917.[37] Among stated worker rights were contract guarantees, unemployment compensation, disability benefits, minimum wage, and the right to unionize and strike. Labor protection abroad was promoted not merely for doctrinaire reasons and to meet the complaints of spokesmen for the then-powerful CROM, but because Mexican workers, often illiterate, illegal, and job-hungry, were, in fact, men, women, and children easily exploited by crew leaders, contractors, and employers, and shunned by American labor unions.[38] In some cases Mexican consuls intervened directly in farm labor strikes, most notably in the El Monte berry strike of 1933.[39] Often the consuls found themselves insisting on rights that were generally more advanced than anything enjoyed by American labor before the New Deal era of the 1930s, or even the War on Poverty era dating from 1965. In fact, certain labor guarantees, amplified in the Mexican labor code of 1931, are still not clearly conceded to American farm labor.[40]

During the bracero program, 1942-1964, labor protectionism was carried to the level of a binational accord whereby both governments agreed to uphold an elaborate listing of guarantees. Students of these accords, and of U.S. Public Law 71, putting power behind bracero contracts, have made ironic—even bitter—comments that alien workers were better protected than natives, or, for that matter, than labor in Mexico, where many constitutional guarantees were simply *letra muerta*; and that, in general, American farm labor derived greater indirect benefits from Mexico's protectionism than from the indifference of the American Congress! To point out another irony, bracero protection was a major factor in encouraging American employers to prefer wetbacks.[41]

Another remarkable dimension of consular activities has always been the tenacious defense of nationals and Mexican-Americans from discrimination and segregation in schooling, housing, and social services, and from military conscription as during World War I and World War II, and, of course, from arbitrary arrest, incarceration, or deportation.[42] All this has been in accord with the official view that under Mexican law emigrants, including children born abroad, were still Mexican citizens (unless they expressly renounced this status), and thus entitled to foreign service protection.[43] Also, protectionist ardor was, and is, an expression of a pervasive national folk consciousness that regards all Mexican-origin peoples over an arbitrary border as members of La Raza, or the national family.

This deep emotional commitment was influenced by writers and advisers who doubted that émigrés of the Indo-Meztizo laboring class would ever be accepted as equals by North American society due to cultural disparities and racial prejudice. Among these influential *pensadores* were Mexican consuls like Enrique Santibañez; distinguished social scientists like anthropologist Manuel Gamio, who carried out a field study of Mexican emigrants in the United States in 1926-1927; and economists like Gilberto Loyo, who pioneered the study of population movements in Mexico. Gamio, in particular, personified the feeling that emigration was, all in all, beneficial to Mexico and the emigrants, but that this migration should be placed under strict intergovernmental control, so that Mexicans could work abroad on a contract basis, and not try to live there permanently with their families in an alien culture and on an inferior social plane. In such thinking one finds the genesis of the future bracero program. [44]

In the 1920s the Ministry of Foreign Relations created a special "protection" division in the Foreign Service that was principally concerned with Mexicans in the United States. The frustrating task of registering and protecting the rights of a floating population—often likened to migratory birds—was the responsibility of understaffed Mexican consulates, here and there, in the principal cities of the United States, aided by ingenious organizations such as the Comisiones Honórificas and the Brigadas de la Cruz Azul which flourished in the 1920s and early 1930s. The Brigades, consisting of emigrant women, were functioning in Texas by 1920, and were actually self-help beneficent societies similar to those founded by other immigrant groups in the United States before the age of the welfare state. Placed under consular guidance and expanded in 1921, the uniformed brigadiers played an important role in emigrant assistance and repatriation efforts. The Honorific Commissions were something more uniquely Mexican. Originally established at the first general consular convention held in San Antonio in 1921, to meet the growing protectionist crisis, these quasi-official organizations consisted of the more prominent or permanent male emigrants. Their principal function was to serve as a "third arm" by assisting the consular service to carry out protective duties in localities lacking consular offices. Within his own district the consul served as the honorary president of these commissions. [45]

Other extensions of consular authority employed to meet the needs of a labor exodus, for the most part undocumented, were honorary consuls named in far-flung towns and cities. Also, American and Mexican-American lawyers were employed to defend Mexican emigrants, more so since the 1930s when President Cárdenas insisted on providing legal counsel for expatriate groups threatened with loss of jobs or deportation during the Depression. [46]

The Camacho administration (1941-1946) struck a telling blow for protectionist authority during World War II, when Anglo-Americans were again imploring Mexico's cooperation in meeting labor needs. Mexico, which joined the allied cause in June 1942, fixed as its price the "Consular Convention Between the United States of America and the United Mexican States," signed August 12, 1942, and ratified on June 1, 1943. This instrument was, for Mexico's Ministry of Foreign Relations, headed by the able Ezequiel Padilla, more than a supplementary authority to watch over bracero contracts. It was a reciprocal confirmation of broad consular powers to intervene in a gamut of matters concerning the welfare and rights of nationals residing abroad, temporarily or permanently. Earlier the Foreign Service Law of 1934 had spelled out in detail the protectionist obligations of the Mexican consular service. [47]

After World War II the Mexican consuls continued as zealous defenders of

Mexican colonies in the United States, but on a smaller scale. Beginning in the 1920s Mexican and Mexican-American organizations began emerging, such as LULACS, then the American G.I. Forum after World War II, and more recently, PASO and La Raza Unida, to name only a few. All of these organizations seek to defend the Mexican colonies through political action. Furthermore, since the Depression the American federal government has taken over the responsibility of providing welfare benefits, public housing, food commodities, school desegration, legal protection, minimum wage, unemployment compensation, old age pensions, and the like, for the benefit of both native and alien residents. Moreover, the Mexican government since the 1930s has been much more selective in its protection of prodigal sons. Since then consuls have given first attention to those Mexican emigrants and visitors with legal authorization to be in the United States, and in this respect, the consular zeal has not diminished. [48]

Mexicanidad

Protection of La Raza in the United States has always gone hand-in-hand with an intensive Mexicanization program that has no exact counterpart in American immigration history. Simply stated, *Mexicanidad* has sought to prevent emigrant groups from being assimilated by Anglo-America. From the Carranza administration, 1915-1920, up until World War II, the Mexican consuls, assisted by the previously mentioned citizen committees carried out this mission with a devotion little short of religious. [49] This dedication reflected a widespread popular belief that the Revolution must do all possible to restore *la patria* and the Indo-mestizo culture to the *hermanos de la raza* who had been driven into exile by conditions of political anarchy and economic want.

Until the restoration, the consuls and patriotic committees were charged with guarding against insidious forms of *pochismo* or de-Mexicanization, for it was felt that *pochos*, that is, Mexicans who had adopted Anglo-Saxon customs or standards of materialism, would not easily fit again into Mexican society. [50] On *fiestas patrias*, such as independence day, celebrated on September 16, and other feast days, such as "5 de Mayo," the consuls, particularly in the border states, rarely missed an opportunity to harangue assemblies of emigrants and their families on the virtues of Raza loyalty and patriotism, the glorious figures of Indo-revolutionary history like Juárez and Zapata, and the disgrace of *pochismo* in a land that once belonged to Mexico.

Robert N. McLean, a Protestant missionary noted for social rescue work among Mexican emigrants, and a man who struggled to understand the Mexican resistance to Americanization, reported a typical consular speech to La Raza brotherhood: "When I say 'Mexican' I do not mean that nameless hybrid creature who proves false to the mother who bore him by taking out American citizenship." And, noted McLean, "the chorus of '¡Viva Mexico!'

drowned the speaker's voice." Then the Anglo-American bystander added in wonder: "These strangers have not really crossed the boundary line; they have pushed it ahead of them."[51]

That the migratory experience itself—a constant flux back and forth over the border— also played a major role in the development of a Raza consciousness or subculture that resisted Americanization or naturalization can hardly be doubted. As Gamio observed, the emigrant experience, together with feelings of social discrimination, transformed what was formerly a tribal sense of village identity—*la pequeña patria*—to a larger and deeper sense of nationality.[52] This new sense of identity was reinforced by the Mexicanization mission of the consuls. In this respect, it is probably no exaggeration to say that up until World War II, and even after, in many cases, Mexican migratory groups of the campesino class were, all in all, more in contact with the Mexican Revolution's message of nationalization, political indoctrination, and modernization than the isolated rural population of Mexico that still clings to ancient folkways in many regions.

Another element in official thinking was that *Mexicanidad* could serve to hold and develop emigrant groups as a possible political lever. During the 1920s, for example, certain Mexican officials considered that the rapidly growing Mexican population in the United States could be organized as pressure groups to influence American policy toward revolutionary reforms in Mexico. During this period the Mexican government was concerned about possible North American reactions to nationalist plans for restricting or expropriating foreign investments in mines and oil lands.[53]

Mexicanidad also appreciated Mexican workers abroad as a source of national income. In December 1917 the Carranza government decided to lift the ban on postal money orders from the United States (a ban that had been in force since August 1914).[54] The first full taste of the dollar flow occurred during World War I and after, when many Mexican workers averaged around $1,500 per year in U.S. employment, and some over $5 a day, a fabulous sum compared to Mexican wages at that time.[55] The Mexican government was advised to follow the example of Italy and Poland, and through the consular service, to teach emigrant workers how to organize saving accounts and credit unions, and how to send money back to relatives. A branch system of Mexican banks in the United States was also proposed.[56] That the consuls succeeded in teaching some of these lessons seems substantiated by Gamio's study of postal money orders sent to Mexico in the 1920s.[57]

The Depression decade cut down emigrant income, but soon after the bracero program (1942-1964) was regarded as an opportunity to promote a money flow to Mexico, and, at the same time, to avoid consular outlays for repatriating unemployed braceros. A percentage of the bracero's earnings was sent to the National Bank of Agricultural Credit to be held for the returning worker, and, relatedly, the employer was to pay round-trip transportation. Also, under consular eyes, braceros were to receive the highest minimum wage possible under American standards.[58] If a binational labor program were to be revived, there seems little doubt that Mexico would insist on such basic conditions.[59]

In the meantime, labor program or not, the most frequent protectionist activity of the consuls since the 1920s has been, undoubtedly, the collection of unpaid wages and insurance for countless undocumented workers. In this effort the American Immigration Service has cooperated, in part to deter wetback employers. For Mexican officials, however, collecting from exploitative Anglo employers money that rightly belongs to Mexican workers has also been a matter of national pride, the sums being totaled up and duly reported in such annual reports as the *Memorias de la Secretaría de Relaciones Exteriorer.*

Repatriation

Although Mexican officials have sought to utilize a labor emigration that could not be checked, they have never ceased to encourage repatriation, since 1848 one of the most sacred obligations of defensive nationalism. Since Madero and Carranza, Mexican leaders have believed that when the promise of revolutionary reform had been fulfilled, especially agrarian reform, many members of La Raza—preserved by a *Mexicanidad* mission—would reembrace the motherland, and that every Mexican government should facilitate *el retorno.*

Actually, after 1848 various unstable Mexican governments considered repatriating at least some of the *hermanos* in the lost provinces. However, not until the strongman Porfirio Díaz was the government firm enough to offer colonization aid, and with few exceptions Porfirian attempts to attract *repatriados* failed, for the same reasons that attempts to attract foreign colonization failed.[60] The new spirit of mestizo nationalism— ¡ *Mexico para los mexicanos*! —aroused by the Revolution of 1910 denounced foreign colonization and embraced the historic repatriation policy with new fervor.[61] Why not turn to Mexican groups in the United States as a source of easily assimilable immigrants who, more than foreigners, have a right to the land? The great exodus of campesinos and political refugees during the years of political anarchy, 1912-1917, gave a new sense of urgency to repatriation thought. By 1920, not counting Mexican-origin groups who were in the border states before 1900, there were at least 500,000 Mexican settlers in the United States. By 1930 the number of first- and second-generation Mexican settlers had reached 1.5 million or more, or nearly a tenth of Mexico's population.[62]

Beginning in 1917 the Carranza government, concerned about conscription of Mexicans in the United States, and the return of emergency labor recruited during World War I, began to encourage repatriation. Mexican officials, although desperately short of pesos, made heroic efforts to subsidize the return of Mexican nationals and their families. 63 During the recession of 1921-1922 in the American economy, when a great return flow of contract workers and wetbacks was expected, the Obregón government set up a Department of Repatriation in the Ministry of Foreign Relations and in five months spent 3 million pesos. 64 Also, plans were laid to colonize the deserted northern frontier with Mexican families left jobless by the recession. 65 However, according to Mexican consuls, repatriation aid was frequently exploited by migrants seeking a free ride home during the off-season, only to return again in the spring. 66 After 1922, the government, out of patience and pesos, inaugurated a tougher policy of repatriation aid only for verified hardship cases. 67 After all, the government had duly warned workers and their families (who often helped in the fields) not to emigrate.

Still, Mexican leaders have always left the border door open to the *repatriado*, defined in Mexican migration law as a national who has resided abroad for six months or more, but understood in a broader sense to mean any Mexican-origin person, even the deportee who seeks to return to the bosom of the mother country. From time to time, the government, without direct monetary aid, has encouraged a return flow through free transportation on Mexican national railroads, exemptions of customs duties on non-luxury goods, trade tools, farm implements and animals, and occasional offers of land, and through consular sponsorship of immigrant-aid societies, as well as consular contacts with American social help agencies and responsible employers. Repatriation efforts reflected a belief, commonly professed by Mexican leaders, that emigrant families were learning useful agricultural and industrial skills and much more, while residing over the border. This thinking, which conceived of the United States as a kind of technical training school for temporarily displaced Mexicans, was described by Manuel Gamio:

During the last thirty years the United States has played the part of a giant university in which more than a million Mexicans, for the most part, poor and unschooled, have gained a free practical education of great importance; consisting not of reading and writing but of learning to live on a higher scale. In food standards, they eat meat and milk; they have better furniture and clothing. They have learned to operate machinery and use modern tools. They have become acquainted with sports and hygienic practices. Returning to their homeland many of them have contributed a great deal to the progress the country has made in recent times. 68

How much the transborder flux, to and fro, has actually influenced the "Americanization of Mexico," consumer habits, balance of payments, capital investments, individual gains, broken families, cultural erosion, etc., has long been an emotional question in Mexico. Gamio's own studies and those of Taylor, Menefee, and others show that many Mexican families remained in "little Mexicos" on the American side, barely in contact with social agencies.

When they returned to conformist folk villages in *la madre patria*, much of their acquired knowledge of mannerisms proved useless.[69] However, Mexican officials and writers would later justify the binational bracero accords, 1942-1964, as an educational opportunity for the rural peasantry. By then Mexico was committed to industrialization and agricultural planning, and could better utilize any knowledge or funds acquired by migrant workers. More recent surveys by Leal Carrillo, Campbell, Bustamante, and Cornelius have examined the slippery question of socioeconomic impact.[70]

Actually not until the Calles era, 1924-1934, did the government make a serious effort to settle repatriates in planned agrarian colonies, along with other native groups. Such efforts were carried out with some ambivalence on the part of Mexican officials and customs officers. Why, after all, should those who abandoned the mother country for gringo dollars receive special treatment as repatriates? The Mexican consuls often felt the same about their protectionist duties in the United States.[71] Ambivalence or not, the Great Depression was at first regarded as a providential opportunity to reincorporate Raza people. The Mexican government readily cooperated via its consuls with American welfare agencies and the American Immigration Service in transporting unemployed Mexicans and their families to Mexico. But Mexico, still struggling with economic underdevelopment and a regressive agrarian structure, soon found that it could not begin to meet the expectations of some 400,000 repatriates in the period 1930-1935. Many of these disillusioned prodigal sons soon drifted back to gringo land.[72]

Under Cárdenas, 1934-1940, the Mexican government, which had its own sense of disillusionment with *ingratos*, initiated a more cautious policy of "selective repatriation" which was tied in with a major agrarian reform.[73] Only those who had actually acquired useful skills, or who had not been spoiled by relief agencies—as a consul in San Antonio put it—were to receive transportation aid and an opportunity to settle in a planned agrarian community.[74] Old repatriates described it as "bringing the good ones home."[75] During the Cárdenas years possibly 40,000 or more repatriates were successfully settled in Mexico, mostly on small irrigated land grants of ten to twenty hectares in the lower Rio Grande in the years 1939-1940. This project, directed by Eduardo Chávez, was apparently the most successful of all large-scale repatriation efforts.[76]

After Cárdenas, repatriates were no longer recruited. Nevertheless, on an individual basis Mexican population laws still encourage repatriation. Any Mexican residing abroad with a useful skill, trade, or business is given consular encouragement to apply for repatriate status and customs exemptions.[77]

Binational Cooperation

American cooperation in emigration matters has naturally been of fundamental importance to Mexico. Although the deportation efforts of gringo immigration officers have run against the grain of public feeling, the Mexican government has, hesitation or not, always recognized the necessity of American cooperation in patrolling the border, collecting *mojado* wages, and returning unwanted or undocumented nationals to Mexican territory. Aside from seeking binational labor supervision, Mexican officials have more or less consistently urged Mexican nationals to abide by American immigration laws and civil ordinances under the "Carranza Doctrine" of mutual respect for the laws of nations. In fact, since the late 1920s Mexican officials have circulated notices from the American State Department concerning visa requirements, penalties for illegals, employment problems, and other information that might deter or regulate emigration. [78]

At the high diplomatic and consular levels, Mexican-American migratory relations have often been cool but formally correct, but at the level of enforcement or protective agencies, there have been many erratic policies, points of friction, and contradictory actions, particularly at the border ports. For instance, American immigration officials for years complained that Mexican consular authorities offered improper protection to nationals who wished to remain in the United States by issuing papers of doubtful authenticity, such as a certificate of marriage to a Mexican-American. [79]

Likewise, public officials in Mexico border towns have been accused of selling certificates of residence and border-crossing privileges to *mojados*. Friction resulted also over the refusal of Mexican officials to accept formal deportations unless American authorities could prove all the facts of Mexican nationality, illegal entry, or criminal behavior—for example, alien smuggling, a most difficult task given the shrewd custom of Mexican illegals to migrate without documents. [80] For their part Mexican authorities since the 1920s have often suspected collusion between employers and American officials. Again and again they have protested arbitrary deportations and arrests by the American Immigration and Naturalization Service, commonly denounced as *la migra*, and have opposed "the dumping anywhere over the border" of *mojados* or criminal types (sometimes mixed in with Guatemalans and other Latin Americans). [81]

Identification problems and the vast number of undocumented deportees has led both governments to support a system of non-penalty "voluntary departures" whenever possible. Since the general immigration restrictions of 1917, this system has had no proven deterrent effect, and actually seems to encourage "repeaters," but at least it avoids paperwork, costly hearings, and bitter disputes. For many years "voluntary returns" were turned loose at the border, from where, it is commonly said, they beat the escorting officer back to the starting point. Since 1948, however, some returnees have been lifted to interior pionts like Mazatlán, León, or San Luís Potosí by American-run train, plane, bus, and, at one time, boat lifts. These lifts, operating at Mexican sufferance, were originally intended to protect the legal bracero from wetback competition. [82]

Mexico's continued collaboration with the voluntary departure is dictated by humanitarian considerations, by the hope that some returnees will stay home, particularly those taken to the country's interior, and by the fact that Mexican law provides no specific sanctions for unregistered exits (although theoretically, there could be administrative sanctions). Mexican authorities, like American judges, generally feel that job-seeking migrants have committed no crime. In any case, "to prosecute migrants who only seek a better way to support large families would raise a storm of public criticism, if not a revolution."[83] Under the circumstances, Mexican officials prefer to look on the expulsion of Mexican nationals by *la migra* as a form of "forced repatriation."[84]

Since official cooperation with the voluntary departure program and the "wetback lifts" could be interpreted by Mexican critics as an infringement of the Mexican citizen's right to travel and to earn a living such cooperation rests not on a firm international accord, but on shaky ad hoc agreements between Mexican and American officials.[85] It may be noted that, except for a brief effort in the 1950s to enforce the bracero program, aided by the American Border Patrol, the Mexican Migration Service has never dared to maintain a special agency charged with preventing unauthorized emigration. Now more than ever such an agency would seem inconsistent with present efforts to protect "surplus workers" in the United States.

According to Mexican officials, the problems of wetbackism and improvised voluntary departures are enmeshed in a border-crossing situation and a border reciprocity program that, year by year, becomes more complicated. In the 1920s the Mexican government found that it was impossible to distinguish between the real and the alleged intentions of Mexican shoppers, visitors, businessmen, students, and other commuters, all of whom crossed the border daily by the tens of thousands with various documents issued by officials on both sides, or with no documents at all on certain "border fiesta days." Today the crossings are on the scale of several hundred thousands a day, counting repeaters and return trips.[87] The two governments have agreed to a reciprocity arrangement whereby American visitors without visas or tourist permits are restricted to a thirty-kilometer border fringe, and Mexican visitors without special permits are, theoretically, limited to a zone twenty-five miles deep on the American side.

Mexican officials readily admit that border reciprocity is often abused by Mexican "visitors" and "shoppers" seeking work on the American side or joining relatives. But as one migration officer observed: "When the bracero program was in operation we had some interest in stopping wetbacks, but the American government, not the Mexican, stopped the program. ¿No es cierto?"[88]

In recent years both governments again have become "prisoners" of a delicate question: how to limit a disproportionately large current of Mexican emigration. By late 1970, many Mexican and American officials were beginning to perceive this as the most urgent question between the two countries. Since then the American Congress, taking into account Mexico's longstanding opposition on principle to any special limit on Mexican immigration, has been wrestling with restrictionist formulas that would be fair to all countries and ethnic groups.[89]

Echeverría and Third Worldism, 1970-1976

During the fiscal period 1965-1974, the United States admitted 514,028 Mexican immigrants, or close to 14 percent of all legal immigration. But this was merely the proverbial tip of the iceberg. By the mid-1970s Mexican illegals working over the border were probably five or six times more numerous than bracero contract labor at its height in 1959, when 447,000 were legally admitted. In addition, there were probably 3 million or so Mexican family members of recent origin living surreptitiously on the American side.[90] How to shelter all those who lacked valid documents? This was the exploding question President Luís Echeverría faced when he began his six-year term in the fall of 1970.

Echeverría, an ardent nationalist and restless left-wing social reformer, seemed ideologically predisposed to defend La Raza against capitalist exploitation at home and abroad; yet, like previous chief executives, he began ritualistically by repeating that there was no need to leave the country, since remunerative employment was more available than ever before in Mexico's industrializing economy and agrarian reform programs. However, his administration could not long ignore rising left-wing criticism about the insensitivity of the fat ruling party (PRI) to "forced emigration" and common reports of wetback humiliations always widely circulated, true or not, in the Mexican and the American press. (Here the old journalistic cliché seemed to apply: Never let the truth stand in the way of a good story.) Apprehension statistics seemed alarming enough; arrests of Mexican nationals by *la migra* surged upward from 55,349 in fiscal 1965 to 430,200 in fiscal 1972, with no sign of a letup.[91]

The chief executive was also influenced by a tour of the Chicano colonies in the United States in the summer of 1972, where he found himself besieged by *mojados* asking *el Jefe* for a contract-labor program, or some form of legalization. Thereafter the Echeverría government began to take the most active interest in expatriate colonies since Cárdenas. In the fall of 1972, through Echeverría's initiative, both governments set up high-level inter-secretarial study groups to examine, unilaterally, the migratory problem, and to exchange proposals on what could be done by way of international cooperation and internal measures.[92] Top Mexican officials then had in mind a new bracero accord, with more influence on American deportation procedures.

Among other things, American officials promised, early in 1973, the most humane treatment possible for apprehended aliens, and to assist even more in the collection of unpaid wages and other claims. For their part, Mexican officials offered more cooperation in the prosecution of smuggling and immigration fraud cases, and in reducing abuses of border-crossing reciprocity agreements. Aside from this, the Echeverría administration promised a campaign to apprehend and punish with severe fines and prison sentences all unauthorized labor contractors on the Mexican side, as well as persons engaged in smuggling Mexicans, and increasingly Latin Americans and other groups, into the United States or across Mexico. A related step was taken in January 1973, when the Mexican government inaugurated a national effort to promote and implement fertility control for the proletarian classes through the public health service.[93] Provisions for national population planning and for control of labor recruiting and smuggling appeared in the Population Law of January 7, 1974.[94]

During the period 1973-1974 Echeverría promised the country a new contract-labor program as a protective measure for Mexicans abroad, and pressed hard, through Foreign Minister Emilio Rabasa, for a binational accord. Privately many American State Department, diplomatic, and immigration officials agreed with the Mexican initiative as the only way to control a new wetback invasion.[95] It was a lost opportunity. The American Secretary of State, Henry Kissinger, replied that the Watergate scandals, 1973-1974, had discredited the Nixon administration (1968-1974), and that the War on Poverty bureaucracy, American labor unions, particularly the United Farm Workers of César Chávez, and a serious recession in the American economy, all worked against official American involvement.[96]

The American position, then, was essentially this: a farm-labor program on top of the *mojados* already in the country would be simply impossible. The most that could be offered was to admit 10,000 or 20,000 Mexican workers under the H-2 category of American immigration law. Under this clause, about 10,000 to 15,000 British West Indians, Canadians, and some Orientals have been admitted each year as temporary harvest labor, as in Florida, for example.[97] In fact, after the bracero accord lapsed in 1964, several thousand Mexicans were admitted as H-2's under a temporary "Basic Accord," 1965-1967, to help California and Arizona growers adjust to the cutoff of braceros.[98] Echeverría rejected the H-2 offer as a totally inadequate outlet for surplus labor and as no mechanism for binational labor control.

The Nogales meeting in late October 1974 marked a turning point. There the President of Mexico personally informed President Gerald R. Ford that Mexico was no longer seeking a bracero agreement. By then Echeverría, the author of a sweeping "Charter of the Economic Rights and Obligations of Nations," had become a prominent spokesman for Third World countries. His new advisers, like sociologist Jorge Bustamante, insisted that Mexico should not subsidize American economic imperialism, whether in Mexico or the United States, through another cheap-labor program, or endanger the Chicano working-class movement over the border.[99] Instead, Mexico would protect, by every means possible, "undocumented workers" and their families already in the United States as a *de facto* labor arrangement economically more beneficial to Mexico and La Raza than a low-quota agrilabor program. Also, Mexico would step up socioeconomic development, vocational education, and even patriotic instruction, under a plan of national priorities, in order to absorb labor in relatively overpopulated areas.

Echeverría said bluntly that Mexico must accept its share of responsibility for the surplus labor problem, but for its solution, and this he emphasized, Mexico "must look to its own resources."100 Repeatedly raising minimum wages for labor in the period 1973-1976 (more than 100 percent in all), expanding the infrastructure of economic development, such as a rural electrification and roads, and boldly promoting family planning, were some of the actions resulting from the search for internal solutions.

Actually, the Echeverría administration had gone as far as national pride would permit in repeatedly promising a bracero program. High Mexican officials had believed that, because of the massive presence of *mojados* over the line, the Americans would sensibly negotiate an accord such as that of 1947 or 1949 for legalizing "wet labor" already in the United States.101 Following American refusal, played up in the Mexican press, editorial themes became more nationalistic and more Third World in sentiment.102 Yet it was not unlike the bracero debates of the 1940s and 1950s, when Mexico considered whether or not to keep migrant workers at home—somehow, for the wetback problem then was beyond Mexican control.103

As in the past, the least rumor of a new bracero accord led to an undignified rush of campesinos to the border. The spectacle of rustics selling their cow for fictitious "bracero permits" and "guaranteed transportation to American jobs" from the same seedy class of border parasites and *coyotes* grated on official pride. Echeverría realized that these developments (perhaps predictable to students of Mexican bracero history) gave some weight to the American argument that a new labor program would only set off a pell-mell exodus over the border.104

Echeverría's policy modifications were also influenced by empirical studies. The interagency commission, Comisión Intersecretarial para Estudio del Problema de la Emigración Subrepticia de Trabajadores Mexicanos a Estados Unidos de América, created in the fall of 1972, began to carry out, for the first time ever, extensive official research on the causes and consequences of surrepetitious emigration, and to approximate how much money emigrants were contributing to Mexico's economy. After interviewing more than 3,000 deportees in the period 1972-1974, and after examining many consular reports, interagency officials concluded that the dimensions and character of the problem were not quite as previously imagined.

Among the study commission's findings were the following:105 an estimated 1 to 2 million undocumented Mexican workers were in the United

Paso del Norte
POR MARINO

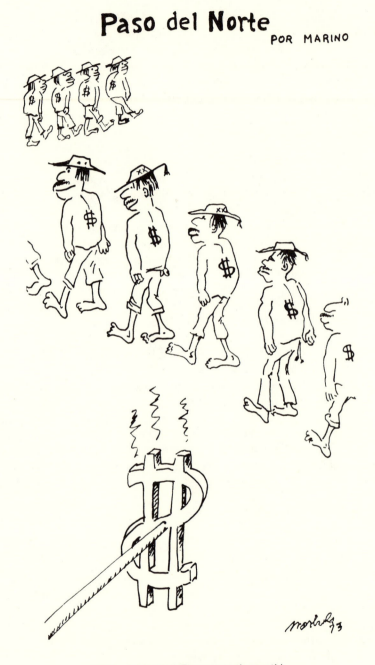

"Paso del Norte" (The way to the north)
By Marino, Excelsior (*Mexico City*), 1973.

States, most of them on a quasi-permanent basis; the majority were originally rural campesinos, whose villages had come to depend on dollar earnings, but most were no longer content with farm labor and were seeking, whenever possible, higher pay in service and industries usually far from the low-paying American border area; it, therefore, seemed desirable economically for the industrial and service workers to be in the United States, since most of them learned their trades there and probably could not be absorbed by the Mexican economy in any case; around 1973, Mexicans in the United States were sending home somewhere near $1 billion a year, in addition to whatever came to Mexico in the pockets of returnees or as goods and gifts purchased in the United States;[106] and as apprehensions of Mexican emigrants increased, from 277,377 in fiscal 1970 to 709,959 in fiscal 1974, according to American figures, there was no point in insisting on a bracero program as originally conceived with a modest quota of 200,000 or 300,000, for such an arrangement would obviously not cover *mojados* already in industrial and service work, or more than a fraction of campesinos seeking agriwork.

Administration officials further learned that apprehension data disguised the fact that hundreds of thousands of better-paid Mexican industrial and service workers were going undetected in the American economy (an exhilarating find in many respects); and that many deportees, typically in the age group from sixteen to thirty, had never tried to work in rural Mexico, allegedly because of low wages (from $1 to $5 a day in U.S. currency), and had sought their first job on the American side, as if the United States were a natural dimension of Mexican life! Wage averages of deportees, mainly in agriwork, were nearly $1.50 an hour (often with room and board besides), being lower in the immediate border area and higher in the interior. Most deportees were determined to return to the United States, hoping for better luck.[107]

The findings of the Intersecretarial Commission have since been updated and expanded by revisionist research on illegal immigration by Bustamante, Weaver and Downing, North and Houstoun, Cornelius, Villalpando, and others. Some of these studies were sponsored by President Ford's Domestic Council Committee on Illegal Aliens, founded in January 1975, the U.S. Department of Labor, and the Immigration Service, while others have been collaborative efforts by Mexican and North American social scientists associated with research centers at El Colegio de México, the Instituto Nacional de Antropología, and Anglo-American and Chicano study centers at universities in California, Arizona, and Texas, as well as at Notre Dame, Harvard, M.I.T., and elsewhere.[108]

While still regarding surreptitious emigration as a lamentable "exportation of a social problem," as President Echeverría described it in a 1972 address, Mexican planners, ambivalence or not, had come to regard "expatriate labor," along with tourism, mining, American-bound fruits and vegetables, and the "twin plants" of the Border Development Program, as one of the pillars of Mexico's export economy, and as a national resource to be harbored and marketed at the highest possible price, for reasons also of national dignity.[109] The official position had become explicit: there are no illegals abroad, only undocumented workers subsidizing the American economy and therefore deserving of a full wage and humane treatment.

Without abandoning dissuasion, the Echeverría government sought to protect a vested interest in the American economy and welfare state, including any immigrant equity, civil rights, social security, pensions, old age or insurance claims, and wages—especially wages—claimed by Mexican workers and their families, documented or not. Understandably any announcement by an immigration official, attorney general, congressman, federal judge, or state governor, that the American government planned a "crackdown on illegal aliens" was met with a flurry of concern by Mexican officials. Typically, in 1973, the Ministry of Foreign Relations and Mexican editorialists, along with Chicano militants, protested the extension of the electronic sensor on the American border as an inhumane device and contrary to the spirit of the Good Neighbor. Behind this public stance was official concern that Mexico's border population might be cut off from long-established seasonal jobs.[110] Similarly, in the period 1965-1974, official concern mounted over proposals by American labor spokesmen, including Huelga leader César Chávez, that would cut off Mexicans holding immigration cards from "commuter work" on the American side. In November 1974, the American Supreme Court decided in favor of the daily but not the long-ranging seasonal commuter.[111]

Echeverría also opposed American initiatives to penalize employers of illegal aliens, such as the Rodino bills under consideration by Congress since 1973. During the farm-labor program of 1942-1964, Mexico called for such legislation, but later, having no contract workers to defend against intruding *mojados*, reversed positions. After all employer penalty bills could mean a serious economic loss to Mexico and possibly a repatriation crisis like that of the 1930s.[112] With guerrilla warfare a threat in rural Mexico, and public outrage over an inflation rate of 15 to 25 percent in 1973-1976, these concerns seemed well-founded. In September 1976 the administration, trapped in an inflationary spiral devalued the peso from 12.5 to around 22 per dollar, and immediately had to meet strikers demands by again raising wages.

Mexican officials have never questioned the legislative right of the American government to control immigration and the labor market. However, they have made use of diplomatic channels, and the Mexico-United States Interparliamentary Conference, which meets annually under binational sponsorship of legislative leaders, to voice dissent and recommendations concerning protection for *obreros sin documentos*, and other touchy matters like drug control and prisoner exchange.[113] Likewise, periodic meetings of labor leaders from the semiofficial Confederación de Trabajadores Mexicanos (CTM) and the

AFL-CIO have often served Mexico's purpose of extraofficial communication.[114]

Under Echeverría Mexican consuls stepped up assistance for the legalization of Mexican families abroad, making increasing use of federal anti-poverty programs, such as legal aid, and private agencies like the immigration and refugee service of the United States Catholic Conference. As always unionization of Mexican labor was encouraged; and, in accord with the recommendations of the two interagency commissions created in 1972, consular attachés were stationed at immigration detention centers, as at El Centro, El Paso, and Brownsville, to oversee collection of unpaid wages and humane treatment. [115] Relatedly, consuls have sought to reduce fines imposed by American magistrates on illegal "repeaters," Mexico insisting that the money rightly belongs to the worker.[116]

Concurrently Mexican "bracero diplomacy" has urged some form of "guest worker" status for undocumented nationals abroad such as that given alien workers in western Europe. Moral support has been found in the accords of the International Labor Office, Geneva, which propose that all the basic socioeconomic rights of the native be guaranteed to the transnational worker and his family, excepting citizenship.[117] This position reflects the recommendations of the United Nations Social and Economic Council, and the situation of some 8 or 9 million aliens and family members in Common Market countries, many such persons lacking documentation. Moral support also is found in papal sponsorship of the migrant ministry in Europe and the United States. Such apostolic letters as "Pastoralis Migrantium Cura," August 15, 1969, advocate the moral right of the worker and his family to cross international boundaries in search of economic security and to retain their language, culture, and religion. Thus far Washington has pointedly ignored such *carte blanche* proposals partly because AFL-CIO "labor statesmen" have always feared an alien-labor threat to their policy of achieving total closed-shop domination of American industry.

More realistically, Mexico increasingly favored some form of blanket amnesty, as in talks with members of President Ford's Domestic Council Committee on Illegal Aliens (1975-1976). American immigration law then permitted legalization only for long-term qualified residents in the country since 1948 or before. Reform bills would have moved the date to 1968 or 1970, or, if Mexico had its way, to a more recent date.[118]

Related to protectionism were steps the Echeverría government took to enforce to the letter laws pertaining to aliens, principally Americans, who invest, work, reside, retire, or recreate in Mexico. After the nationalistic population law of January 7, 1974, migration officials began to reexamine every request for an immigrant visa, tourist, or visitor card. Fees were raised sharply, as when the Ministry of Internal Affairs began charging $80 for the annual renewal of "immigrant status" during the five-year trial period, for, unlike Tío Sam, Mexico does not concede full immigrant status at entry. These measures were taken to raise revenues and remove aliens working or residing on tourist cards as well as for other reasons.[119]

Perhaps a hundred thousand American pensioners, Bohemian types, business executives, as well as "hippies" (who, some believe, harm tourism, spend little, and often engage in drug activities) were affected. Stiffer regulations may also have reflected Echeverría's dissatisfaction with the Rodino bills and the American refusal to negotiate a new bracero accord. However, the overriding purpose of such measures was to establish firmer "Third World control" over foreign corporations operating in Mexico, and to protect jobs for citizens much in the traditional revolutionary spirit of "Mexico for the Mexicans."[120]

Perhaps the greatest achievement of Echeverría (the father of eight children) was to establish population planning as a national goal. Despite this goal, however, during his administration, 1970-1976, Mexico added about 15 million people, equal to the total population in 1910, when land-hungry peasants started a revolution. The population, near 35 million in 1960, rose to 48 million in 1970, and in 1976 ballooned to over 63 million (not counting expatriates), with a prospect of 90 million by 1990.

Since land distribution had run its course and industrialization could not fully absorb population growth, the Echeverría government came to regard emigration not only as income compensation for the closing of the bracero programs, but as an outlet for unemployed millions otherwise open to demagoguery.[121] To build a "Berlin Wall" would have been a foolish confession of national failure on Echeverría's part, and the PRI would have shut off an economic and psychological safety valve.[122] Moreover, halting out-migration would only have shifted responsibility for full employment squarely onto the shoulders of a government whose border industrial program (started in 1965), public works projects, and regional development efforts could not fully sponge up migratory folk.[123]

In its protectionist stance the government had to take into account increasing public ferment, for concern about Mexicans and Chicanos in the United States since the late 1960s had been spreading beyond the usual small circle of Mexican officials, editorialists, and social reformers, stimulated by a new wave of reported "barbarities," such as juvenile gangs ambushing wetbacks on border trails or Texas farmers shooting at Mexican labor organizers. A new generation of outspoken and critical Mexican social scientists, particularly sociologists, demographers, economists, and political scientists, often trained abroad, and in contact with the Chicano studies and liberation movement in the United States, were inclined to tie in the historic dilemma of out-migration and the "exploited *mojado*" (a fixture in the Mexican press) with overwhelming problems of internal migration and social marginality, as well as shocking disparities in the distribution of national income. Most visibly in recent years such cities as Guadalajara and Monterrey, and also border cities like Tijuana and Ciudad Juárez, have been inundated with peasants moving into miserable shanty towns. Mexico City alone, counting slum spread, reached an estimated 14 million people by 1976. As the new reformers saw it, the solution to appalling migratory problems had to involve radical reforms—even revolutionary ones—in Mexico's half-capitalist, half-socialist, half pre-Columbian economic structure. [124]

In brief, the Mexican Revolution, originally an agrarian one, seemed to face an alarming rural and urban crisis. Consequently Echeverría felt pressed to move leftward—at least rhetorically—in his efforts to assist the migratory lumpen proletariat in Mexico, and display more aggressiveness in his efforts to assure "humane treatment" and the "right to work" for La Raza in the United States. This was the same pressure situation the Party faced in its choice for president of Mexico during the term 1976-1982.

López Portillo and the Long-Range Solution

First off, the new chief executive, José López Portillo, taking office in November 1976, faced the embarrassing fact that in spite of the effort of the Echeverría administration (in which López Portillo served as finance minister) to reduce out-migration, *mojado* arrests rose to 781,438 in fiscal 1976. Following the peso devaluation of September 1976, the Mexican economy was in shambles; real wages were rapidly eroding; land-hungry peasants were threatening revolt; and some Mexican and American officials feared that a new revolutionary situation could set off another pell-mell refugee exodus as in 1912-1916. In any case, it seemed that *mojado* arrests would go over 1 million in 1977. [125]

Another blow was an American law (P.L. 94-571), effective January 1, 1977, designed mainly to limit Mexican immigration to 20,000 per year, excepting, of course, countless immediate relatives. On principle, at least, it ended a Pan American preference that dated back to 1921, when new world countries were exempted from quotas. Raza leaders everywhere deeply resented this insulting attempt to limit access to the lost territories, and predicted a rise in surreptitious migration.

Moreover, the new president was overwhelmed by urgent petitions from delegations of consular personnel, undocumented emigrants, Chicano students on pilgrimmage, and Raza Unida activists seeking official intervention, or a diplomatic alliance for ethnic rights, amnesty measures, a contract-labor program for industrial workers also, and the political reconquest of the Southwest, or at least the overthrow of a culturally oppressive Anglo-Texan establishment. Shades of the Alamo! [126] Nor could the President dodge Chicano militants like Reies López Tijerina, who demanded billions of dollars from the Mexican government as compensation for land-grant losses resulting from Mexico's humiliating territorial cession of 1848. [127]

A distinguished scholar and public official, the new president believed that, like the Indian civilizer Quetzalcoatl (one of López Portillo's favorite subjects), the governing elite had a special civilizing and developmental mission in Indo-Mexico. He lost no time in turning the ship of state onto what he considered a more conciliatory course. Even before the ritualistic elections, he began to dissociate the new administration from Echeverría's bombastic Third Worldism, which had alienated Mexico's industrial and commercial leaders, frightened off foreign investors, and done little to detain peasant flight to Mexican cities and the United States.[128] He also felt that, curse or not, Mexico's "special good neighbor relationship" with the *Yanquí Coloso* should not be ignored, but rather used to mutual advantage.[129]

Since the Carter administration fervently supported a number of Third World demands in Africa, Latin America, and elsewhere, and since López Portillo had toned down Mexico's demand for a new Third World economic order, the two chief executives established a friendly dialogue during López Portillo's visit to Washington in February 1977. Both agreed on more cooperation in solving common border problems, such as the prosecuting of the drug traffic, prisoner exchange, common use of irrigation waters, land claims on the shifting Rio Grande, tariff discrimination, but above all uncontrolled transborder migration and related problems of protecting migrants from assault and robbery by border predators, including Mexican police, and from exploitation by sweat-shop employers and extortionists. They agreed further to establish a bilateral commission to work on mutual problems.[130]

As López Portillo and his advisers saw it, the emigration problem called for policy initiatives on both sides of the border. On Mexico's side the first step was to restore confidence in the national economy and the shattered peso, and thus to halt the inflationary threat to political stability. Consequently in the spring of 1977, a national emergency program called "Alianza para la Producción" was launched. This carrot-and-stick program, half-voluntary, half-regulatory, included price controls on consumer goods, a limit on annual wage increases (the 10 percent limit was abandoned by August 1977), and some government financing and incentives for the private sector. Domestic and foreign investments were to be channeled toward the expansion of labor-intensive industries, which, it was hoped, would absorb surplus labor and export foods and fibers to American markets under American tariff reductions, as advocated by Bustamante and others concerned about out-migration.[131] Furthermore, capital and technology would be directed toward strategic developmental needs, such as the petrochemical industry. Relatedly, Mexico would exploit and export newly discovered oil and gas resources to a fuel-hungry United States, as a major counter to serious trade deficits. For the same reason tourists would receive red carpet treatment and protection from guerrilla bands.[132]

The Alliance, loudly trumpeted, pleaded for national unity and patriotic sacrifice reminiscent of the 1920s, when the American Congress threatened to impose a tight quota on Mexican labor immigration. Again the theme was that Mexico can, in time, solve its own problems, that is, if all groups, meaning also emigrants and Chicano descendants over the line, would cooperate by investing wage savings in Mexico, consuming products labeled"*hecho en México*," and lobbying for transborder migration rights.[133] "No matter where we are found, Señior Presidente, we are still Mexicans to the core," responded enthusiastic Raza leaders.[134]

Also, a policy of *"asentamientos humanos"* was initiated. If possible, Mexico's surplus labor would be resettled around labor-intensive development projects. Yet at the same time the government reaffirmed the citizen's constitutional right to settle anywhere in the republic and to travel anywhere, including across the border. Relatedly, in March 1977 Mexico suspended the American-sponsored bus, train and air lifts that carried a good percentage of apprehended *mojados* to Mexico's interior. This was done because touchy nationalists denounced the "voluntary departure" lifts as a violation of the constitutional right to travel, and because interior dumping points, like Mazatlán, were already overloaded with surplus workers.

Since the border strip was more than ever overloaded with deportees, more emphasis on labor-absorbing border development programs and continued access to the American labor market were essential corollaries to such policies. In defending transborder access, the Mexican president repeatedly stressed that most emigrants took only jobs that Americans did not want, like "hard work in agriculture or as domestics," and that Mexican labor subsidized both the American economy and the American standard of living while many Americans remained on welfare.[135]

Government planners still hoped for a contract-labor program to cover "seasonals" while industrial workers and families would stay put "over there."[136] President Carter had promised to import migrant labor unilaterally when needed. Thus in June 1977, when some 800 temporary workers were admitted to harvest onions near Presidio, Texas, it was taken as a sign that, sooner or later, the Americans would have to confess their nearly total dependence on Mexican harvest labor and set up a binational labor exchange with official Mexican participation.[137]

More so than previous national leaders, López Portillo, Foreign Minister Santiago Roel, Secretary of Labor Pedro Ojeda Paullada, and others fingered Mexico's major problem as surplus people. Inefficient bureaucracy and lagging industry simply could not create half enough jobs for the 800,000 or more young people who entered the job market each year (70 percent of the population was then under thirty years of age). But people forced to emigrate should never be treated as law breakers or criminals, these leaders contended, for they were only seeking economic security like other immigrants to the United States. Now, as before, said López Portillo, Mexico could do nothing to arrest the outflow: "They would go anyway." The only solution had to be long range:

the improvement of the Mexican economy and the reduction of population growth.[138]

López Portillo, even more than Echeverría, pushed the "Responsible Parenthood" program. It seemed that his government was willing to accept international loans for this purpose. Some thought the birth rate had decreased since 1970 from 3.6 percent to 3.2 percent, but massive emigration complicated such estimates. (Was 10 percent of Mexico's population actually in the United States?) In any case, a decrease in the migratory population hung on the response, or non-response, of the tradition-bound Indo-Mestizo peasantry.[139]

Although some leaders of editorial opinion, like the national daily *Excelsior*, could still sputter pro-natalist sentiments, most Mexican leaders in economic planning, public health, and social security programs (the latter do not cover the poor) had come around to support the surplus-people interpretation, and the need to defuse the population bomb in Mexican cities. This was perhaps the most positive element in a new ara of Mexico-United States relations.

As for the American side of the solution, López Portillo's government advocated the following:

First, the Americans should feel obliged, as border neighbors and out of their own self-interest, to assist Mexican economic development, but not by paternalistic "Marshall aid" plans, or free-market investment, as commonly proposed by American sympathizers and task force advisers. Rather the balance of trade between an industrial power and a developing nation must first be equalized in Third World terms. If the Americans want Mexican oil, they should lower tariffs and encourage tourists and businessmen to buy more from Mexico at a fair price in order to offset the balance-of-payment drain to the United States amounting to around $2 or 3 billion a year. Through his Third World spokesman, Andrew Young, President Carter reaffirmed support for the Mexican position.[140]

Second, American investments in Mexico must be in accord with priorities set by the Production Alliance, and any American developmental loans should be routed, with no strings attached, through international agencies such as the Inter-American Development Bank and should be linked to export-import needs.[141]

Third, while long-range programs are underway, the American government must not insist on strict border control or mass deportations. If such actions should be taken, Mexico could not meet the balance-of-payment deficit, and more ominously, the pileup of millions of jobless Indo-Mestizo squatters and *mojados* in Mexican cities, particularly border cities, could lead to political anarchy and possibly a military takeover. López Portillo explained that such considerations were not to be taken as a threat but simply as a statement of a precarious economic situation. For better or worse, the two countries are back-

yard neighbors.[142] Or put another way, Mexico's surplus population has become America's surplus population problem.[143]

Fourth, American federal and state agencies should do more to protect migrant workers and their families from wage exploitation and the denial of social, educational, and health services. Mexican officials were troubled by
American federal and state measures that sought to exclude "illegal aliens,"
who also paid taxes, from such services. Mexican leaders were pleased by the
appointment of a new American ambassador, former Governor of Wisconsin,
Patrick J. Lucey, a long-time Irish-Catholic defender of migrant workers from
Texas and Mexico. Before leaving for Mexico City in May 1977, Lucey pushed
through the Wisconsin legislature a unique law that protected migrant labor,
legal or illegal, from any form of exploitation or denial of social services, and
provided penalties for offending employers. Mexican officials and editorialists saw such a model law as a possible counter to other states, such as California and Connecticut, which had passed legislation, still to be enforced, that
would prohibit employment of illegals and restrict social services.[144]

More important, Lucey's appointment was taken as another signal that the
Carter administration had accepted Mexico's view of the illegal alien problem,
that is, the view that the problem is not one of preventing unregistered immigration but a problem in protecting Mexico's workers from social injustice—
not in Mexico, but in the United States. Getting this policy position accepted in
Washington, for whatever reasons, represented a major diplomatic victory for
the López Portillo administration.

Fifth, the American government should meanwhile promote legalization for
Mexican and other "undocumented aliens" suffering exploitation and discrimination. Naturally, Raza leaders on both sides of the border, still upset
with P.L. 94-571, immediately seized on Carter's evangelical promise to protect human rights everywhere as a most handy rationale for legalization. Protectionist hopes were further encouraged by court findings in the so-called
Chicago stays. It seems that prior to January 1, 1977, when P.L. 94-571 went
into effect, 150,000 Cuban refugees had been erroneously (or intentionally?)
charged against the western hemisphere allotment of 120,000 non-preference
immigrants. As a result of a court order, perhaps a hundred thousand Mexican visa applicants, plus family members, could immediately be eligible for
immigrant status whether legally in the United States or not.[145]

Much more important to Raza expectations was the Carter task force proposal to create an unprecedented double amnesty plan. As delivered to Congress in early August 1977, this plan would offer permanent immigrant status
to all non-criminal aliens who had resided in the United States before January 1, 1970. For those who had taken up residence between that date and December 31. 1976, a vaguely defined non-deportable alien status would be available during a five-year probation period. A "non-deportable"—if he or she

came forth to register—would receive a work permit transferable to any job and full legal protection, but would not be able to bring in (more?) relatives or legally use tax-supported services. The arrangement, similar to the guest worker program in Europe, presumed that most illegal aliens had left family members behind. Moreover, as an added incentive to legalization, Carter favored giving Mexico a special limit of 50,000 non-preference immigrants annually.[146]

In the interim, just as the "old immigration hands" had predicted, more Mexican emigrants than ever before were rushing a half-guarded border, hoping to come under various *planos de amnistia*, while the smuggling and fraudulent document business, dealing flexibly as always with "commodity immigrants," promptly offered at skyrocketing prices special "amnesty packages" containing birth certificates, social security cards, rent receipts, and instructions for false witnesses.[147]

Innocent American officials, congressmen, visitors, and reporters were hoping for some gesture of border control from the Mexican government in return for Carter's concessions, but they were soon informed by López Portillo that Mexico remained absolutely opposed to any "police solutions." "Forget about police measures," he said bluntly, "these people aren't criminals. They are ordinary people looking for jobs."[148] Except for continued cooperation in control of drug traffic and border banditry, the Mexican government definitely would not use military or police forces to detain emigration. The government, he repeated, must guarantee freedom of movement and settlement anywhere. "Mexico is not a prison for its population."[149]

This stance, based as always on the constitutional guarantees of 1917, meant that López Portillo's policy was essentially that of his predecessors since World War II: to maintain the status quo of a half-open border—the safety valve—until such time as economic planning could absorb surplus people and, in the meantime, to secure for Mexican workers abroad, documented or not, all the rights guaranteed by the Mexican Constitution (Article 123), and by subsequent United Nations resolutions. When a mob of over 200,000 transients rushed the border at Tijuana, after the announcement of the Carter double-amnesty plan, Mexican officials could only stand by, *con brazos cruzados*, although they did try to sort out and detain non-Mexican migrants from Guatemala, Costa Rica, Colombia, and points south.[150]

In his stand that the only acceptable solution had to be long-range, López Portillo found, astonishingly, a kindred soul in Leonel Castillo, Raza Commissioner of the United States Immigration and Naturalization Service, whom Carter appointed in March 1977 mainly to acknowledge a political debt to Chicano voters. Castillo, a third-generation Mexican-American politician and civil rights activist from Houston, took over his new post in May 1977, and he immediately made it clear that he sympathized with Raza feelings about the open border and the hated *migra*, and that he opposed criminal penalties for employers of illegal aliens as a discriminatory threat to Raza job holders. Rather than paramilitary or "police solutions," he favored long-term developmental assistance for Mexico:

You could put 10 divisions of Marines along the border and not seal it. . . . Of course . . . we can improve and streamline border enforcement efforts but we must do much more than that. In cooperation with Mexico, we must begin to address Mexico's economic and social problems, because they are our problems too.[151]

To some, such statements may have seemed like a Peace Corps version of the white man's burden or a Chicano version of the Quetzalcoatl mission, but perhaps it was as good an illustration as any of the Raza or civil rights fatalism that surrounded a population dilemma increasingly shared by two countries.[152]

Naturally Mexican officials were jubilant that the Carter administration had committed itself wholeheartedly to Mexican and United Nations resolutions on human rights for international migrant workers, and had agreed to view the migration problem not as one of immigration standards but of economic justice: No illegal aliens in the world, only displaced people deserving of protection. The White House had even stopped using the term *illegal alien*, using instead *undocumented alien*, the term recommended by Castillo and the Mexican government, even though most unregistered aliens were documented in one way or another. Therefore Mexican officials could afford to sit back and savor an astounding turnabout, not only in American foreign policy but in American immigration policy. They had only to suffer a parade of ethnic spokesmen, Leonel Castillo, Annie Gutíerrez, César Chávez, Andrew Young, and others, and an assortment of Washington officials and messengers, who descended on Mexico City to announce rather than negotiate Carter blanket amnesty proposals. It was indeed a strange new "open diplomacy" phase in Mexican-American relations.

The prospect of a non-deportable status for several million aliens who had entered the United States in the period 1970-1976 was more than Mexican leaders had ever dared ask for. They could only hope that Congress shared Carter's and Young's sense of Third World migration rights and the Mexican view that certain sectors of the American economy were dependent on Raza labor.[153]

Editorial reaction in Mexico to Carter's sweeping offers were not uniformly favorable. Said one editorialist:

An excellent opportunity to demonstrate that the policy of President Carter is really friendly not only to Mexico but to all Latin American countries. No more abuses, nor persecutions against workers, but rather legal protection.[154]

As reformers saw it, however, the ruling oligarchy would not face up to internal reform needs so long as the United States absorbed Mexico's responsibilities. Said one critic, no matter how sincere Carter's amnesty proposals for possibly 10 percent of Mexico's population, they would do nothing to remove realities:

What forced and forces millions of compatriots to violate United States immigration laws is a high rate of unemployment . . . enormous differences in the distribution of wealth and . . . grasping politicians of the ruling Revolutionary Party.[155]

The main concern of a still ambivalent Mexican government about double-amnesty proposals offering access to any American job was that they could serve, unintentionally on Carter's part, to force or induce certain groups, like hundreds of thousands of perennial migrant workers, as well as countless family members already surreptitiously over the line since 1970, to settle permanently on the American side, thus eventually cutting down on income flow to Mexico and accentuating a problem in Mexican identity. Mexican negotiators therefore sought to make any non-deportable alien plan more flexible, more permanent, and "more humane," so that all members of La Raza could move freely back and forth. On this point of negotiations many observers, including spokesmen for the PRI and the outspoken Bustamante, believe that both López Portillo and Carter—especially Carter—were letting slip a statesmanlike opportunity to formulate a new bracero program, or even a treaty by which both governments could establish a rational control system and accept mutual obligations to detain workers and relatives lacking proper permits or documentation.[156]

Curiously, as one reporter found out, the Mexican government itself, with millions of unemployed at home, was continuing to operate an exemplary bracero program of sorts on its southern border for 25,000 Guatemalan coffee pickers (including illegal child labor). The Mexican government guaranteed the full protection of its laws, but imposed an entry fee and a licensing system that required the exit of the alien worker by the end of the year.[157]

Controls such as those applied to Guatemalan coffee pickers (some of whom end up in the United States) seemed conspicuously absent in the American proposal for a non-deportable alien status. But the Carter administration was apparently so eager to display its commitment to civil rights and avoid American labor opposition to another bracero program that Mexican officials were not pressed to consider any important cooperative solution of a binational nature, nor did American civil rights negotiators seek any significant *quid pro quo* tradeoffs. Under the circumstances, therefore, López Portillo made no important commitments for cooperation beyond those already made by his predecessor Echeverría. It seemed that Mexico's severe legal restrictions on businessmen, investors, and aliens illegally in the country would not be modified, although severe penalties against drug use involving American visitors would be lessened. And although López Portillo offered more cooperation in eliminating drug and alien smugglers and sent more police and migration officials to the northern boundary, the main objective was clearly to protect the constitutional right of undocumented workers to cross and recross the border freely without fear of extortion or physical abuse. In a word, Mexico was sticking by historic emigration policies and attitudes toward Raza migration to the lost territories.

Meantime, a new "amnesty exodus" was underway. And since the Carter administration had already compromised itself on universal rights, while seemingly incapable of taking tough unilateral or "police" measures against a rampant "wetback business," the prospect by late 1977 was that the protection of Mexican emigrant groups would continue to be, in López Portillo's words, "the most important problem in the relations between Mexico and the United States."158

That in the future the Mexican government will surely not neglect its protectionist mission for the children of Guadalupe over the line was indicated by President Echeverría's visit of "renewal" in June 1972 to Mexican colonies, as in Chicago, where La Raza by tens of thousands under the fluttering banners of the Virgin and the Aztec eagle, shouted a crescendo of ¡Viva! ¡Viva!, and joyously waved sombreros, serapes, and other badges of national folk identity, while the Immigration Service made a point of standing aside.159 López Portillo planned similar visits.

Like the Cárdenas government of the 1930s, the present and future governments of Mexico will naturally seek ways to use Raza groups abroad as a diplomatic lever against a powerful neighbor, and, *sin duda*, the government will continue to sponsor the open border, selective repatriation, *Mexicanidad*, and cultural missions among heavy concentrations of La Raza in the United States, and through "La Hora Nacional," a radio program that for years has been sponsored by the Ministry of Foreign Relations, to remind Mexicans on both sides of the arbitrary border that not for one moment have they been forgotten by Mother Mexico.

Notes*

1. Quoted in a syndicated series of reports on "Flood of Illegal Aliens," by Associated Press writer Holgar Jensen, *Fort Worth Star-Telegram* (June 28, 1976), p. 1.

2. See González Navarro, *Población y sociedad,* II; and Joseph B. Fichandler, "The Porfirian Response to the Mexican Migrant Phenomenon and the Problems of the Mexican Community in the United States, 1876-1911" (Unpublished manuscript, Storrs: University of Connecticut Department of History, 1976).

3. The 1906 reform plan of the Liberal Party accused a tyrannical dictatorship of depopulating Mexico; likewise, the Anti-Election Party, headed by Francisco Madero, blamed the government for expatriation, according to González Navarro, *La colonización en México*, pp. 123-139. Another precursor of the revolution, Ricardo Flores Magón, in a border newspaper, *Regeneración*, charged that the Díaz regime failed to protect Mexican workers in the United States, one of the first instances of a perennial

denunciation; see file: "Asunto Varios," 12-7-2/241 (73-1)/1911, in Archivo Histórico de la Secretaría de Relaciones Exteriores (AHSRE).

4. *El Universal* (Mexico City, August 9, 1920), p. 9; also, *Excelsior* (Mexico City, March 2 [?], 1928, as reported by Dwight Morrow, American Embassy, Mexico City, to Secretary of State, March 3, 1928, U.S. National Archives (NA), Record Group 59, 811.111/14.

5. Gilberto Loyo, *Las deficiencias cuantitativas de la población de México y una política demográfica nacional* (Roma, 1932); and *La política demográfica de México* (Mexico, 1935). See also, Gustavo Durán González, *Problemas migratorios de México. Apuntamientos para su resolución* (México, 1925): and Arthur F. Corwin, *Contemporary Mexican Attitudes toward Population, Poverty and Public Opinion* (Gainesville: University of Florida Press, 1963).

6. Loyo, *La política demográfica*; and Lazaro Cárdenas, *El problema de los territorios federales. Un llamamiento al patriotismo y al sentido del pueblo mexicano. Mensaje de 28 de septiembre de 1936* (México, 1936); and Partido Nacional Revolucionario, *Plan Sexenal del P.N.R.* (México, 1934).

7. *El Universal*, March 30, 1920, p. 4; March 4, p. 15; March 10, p. 1; March 16, p. 11; March 17, p. 3; April 6, p. 5. See also Harvey A. Levenstein, *Labor Organizations in the United States and Mexico: A History of Their Relations* (Westport, Connecticut: Greenwood Press, 1971).

8. *El Universal* (March 17, 1920), p. 3; and statement by Plutarco Elías Calles, then Secretary of the Interior, ibid. (December 19, 1920), p. 9.

9. Article 11 of the Constitution of 1917 provides that: "everyone has the right to enter and to leave the Republic, to travel through its territory and to change his residence without need of a letter of security, passport, safe conduct or other similar requirements. The exercise of this right shall be subordinated to the powers of the judicial authority in cases of criminal or civil responsibility, and to those of the administrative authority with respect to the limitations which may be imposed by the laws in regard to emigration, immigration, and the general health, or in regard to undesirable foreigners resident in this country." John T. Vance and Helen T. Clagett, *A Guide to the Law and Legal Literature of Mexico* (Washington, 1945), p. 194. It might be noted that earlier, by a law of December 22, 1908, the Porfirian government established an immigration service.

10. Some of the restraining decrees are summarized in *Diario Oficial*, March 17, 1920, pp. 1225-1226. Throughout the 1920s other restraining measures were taken. See Martínez, "Mexican Emigration to the United States." Lawrence Cardoso, "Socio-Economic Causes of Mexican Migration to the United States" (Doctoral dissertation, University of Connecticut, 1974); and González Navarro, *Población y sociedad*, II, 34-47, 207-214.

11. *El Universal*, June 22, 1920, p. 9; June 23, 1920, p. 1.

12. See file on temporary labor importations in AHSRE, 12-64-84/242(72:73), 1918. Under "Departmental Exceptions" for temporary illiterate laborers some 72,000 Mexican contract-workers were legally admitted by the U.S. Immigration Service, but during this same period, 1917-1921, probably four or five times as many "wetbacks" found employment on the American side. See Congressional Record, April 16, 1930, Vol. 72, 7115; and *Mexicans in California. Report of Governor C.C. Young's Fact-Finding Committee*, p. 18.

13. *El Universal*, July 14, 1920, p. 1.

14. Interview with Acadio Ojeda García, Departamento de Población, Secretaría de Gobernación, August 20, 1970; and Rubén Maldonado, Sub-jefe, Oficina de Población, Nuevo Laredo, April 8, 1974.

15. *El Universal*, June 19, 1920, p. 2; March 19, 1923, p. 1. Also, Secretaría de Gobernación, *Memoria 1929-1930*, p. 277; and ibid., *1928-1929*, p. 147.

16. Harvey A. Levenstein, "The AFL and Mexican Immigration in the 1920s: An Experiment in Labor Diplomacy," *Hispanic American Historical Review* Vol. XLVIII (May 1968), 206-219.

17. Fabila, *El problema.* This thirty-eight page pamphlet was printed by the government and distributed to the consuls and to Mexican newspapers. United States consular communiqués occasionally summarize Mexico's official propaganda efforts and note their lack of practical effect, for example, American Consul in Charge, American Embassy, Mexico City, to Secretary of State, November 11, 1920, NA R.G. 59, 811.504/203; and David Myers, American Consul, Durango, to Department of State, March 7, 1924, ibid., 150.126/141. See also Martínez, "Mexican Emigration to the United States," and Cardoso, "Socio-Economic Causes of Mexican Migration."

18. *El Universal*, March 11, 1920, p. 11; March 19, 1920, p. 1; and March 28, 1920, p. 2. The migration law of 1926 made written contracts for recruited laborers mandatory. These contracts, which guaranteed hours, wages, and transportation costs, in accordance with Article 123 of the Constitution, were to be visaed by American consuls as if they were emigration documents! American employers, or their recruiters, were required to deposit money in the Mexican Labor Bank to guarantee payment of return passage of the worker. According to Martínez, illegals simply ignored the law which, perhaps, was designed more to pacify public criticism, and he suggested that probably the government threat of no consular aid to surreptitious workers was a more effective deterrent, "Mexican Emigration to the United States," 140-141.

19. Interview with veteran migration official Ojeda García, Departamento de Población, August 20, 1970.

20. U.S. Congress, Senate, *Restriction of Immigration from Republic of Mexico. Report No. 1594, 71st Congress, 2nd Session, 1930*, pp. 1-8; and *Report of the Commissioner General of Immigration to the Secretary of Labor 1931*, pp. 15-16; also Abraham Hoffman, "El cierre de la puerta," pp. 403-422.

21. D. G. Dwyre, American Consul, Mexico City, to Secretary of State, May 12, 1930, National Archives, Record Group 59, 8111.111/373. Also file: "Informe sobre Comite Pro Inmigrante," AREM. IV/523(73-11)/1, (1929), IV-99-34, in AHSRE.

22. Comments by Dr. Paul S. Taylor during session on Mexican labor in the Southwest up to 1940 at meeting of the Southwest Social Science Association, San Antonio, Texas, March 29-April 1, 1972. Immigration data is from U.S. Immigration and Naturalization Service (INS), *Annual Report*, Table 14.

23. Craig, *The Bracero Program*; and Scruggs, "The United States, Mexico, and the Wetbacks," 149-164.

24. For example, "Mexican Agricultural Workers, Legal Employment of Certain Workers who Entered the State of Texas Illegally. Supplementary Agreement Between the United States and Mexico" (Washington, 1947). This and other such agreements to "dry out" wetbacks are considered by Nelson G. Copp, "Agreements Between the United States and Mexico Concerning Migrant Labor, 1942-1951" (Master's thesis,

Trinity University, San Antonio, 1952).

25. Interview with veteran border guard W. T. Toney, Deputy Chief Patrol Agent, Border Patrol sector headquarters, Del Rio, Texas, May 3, 1970.

26. Craig, *The Bracero Program*.

27. Ibid., pp. 103-113; and Galarza, *Merchants of Labor*, pp. 56, 66-67.

28. According to Arcadio Ojeda García, long-time Chief of the Departamento de Población, August 20, 1970.

29. Interview with long-time Mexican consuls, José Inez Cano, San Antonio, Texas, May 21, 1970; and Hector Jara, Laredo, Texas, April 8, 1974. Also, resumés of annual Mexico-United States Interparliamentary Conferences in AHSRE.

30. For data on apprehensions see the *Annual Reports* of the U.S. Immigration and Naturalization Service, Table 30: Principal activities and accomplishments of the Immigration Border Patrol. See also Samora, *Los Mojados*.

31. U.S. Immigration and Naturalization Service, *Annual Reports*, Table 14.

32. Interviews with United States immigration officials attached to the American Embassy, Mexico City, August 14, 1970, and February 23, 1974.

33. Manuel Germán Parra, *La industrialización de México* (Mexico, 1954); and Frank Brandenburg, *The Making of Modern Mexico* (Englewood Cliffs, N.J.: Prentice-Hall, Inc., 1964), chap. 8-10.

34. *El Universal*, September 21, 1917, p. 5. See similar statement of the Secretary of Interior (Gobernación), ibid., March 20, 1920, p. 1.

35. Landa y Piña, *La migración*.

36. This work, which originally appeared as a series of articles in a Mexico City newspaper, *Excelsior*, was published as a book in San Antonio, Texas, in 1930 by Clegg and Co.

37. H. P. Blocker, Vice Consul, Piedras Negras, to Department of State, August 10, 1917, R.G. 59, 511.504/45.

38. *El Universal*, December 22, 1919, p. 1. See also Levenstein, *Labor Organizations*.

39. Charles Wollenberg, "Race and Class in Rural California: El Monte Berry Strike of 1922," *California Historical Quarterly*, LI (Summer 1972), 155-164; and Ronald W. López, "The El Monte Berry Strike of 1933," *Aztlán*, I (1970), 101-114.

40. Vance and Clagett, *A Guide to the Law*, pp. 227-235.

41. *President's Commission on Migratory Labor* (Washington, D.C., 1951), pp. 52-53; and *Hearings Before the President's Commission on Immigration*, pp. 1630-1632.

42. Many examples of this protectionist activity can be found in National Archives, R.G. 59, file 311.12/ (1910-1929), and in correspondence of Mexican consuls, "Labor Consular," under various file numbers, in AHSRE.

43. For the concept of Mexican nationality at home and abroad, see S. A. Bayitch and José L. Siqueiros, *Conflict of Laws: Mexico and the United States* (Coral Gables, 1968), pp. 30-34.

44. Gamio, *Mexican Immigration*, pp. 181-186.

45. "Informe - situación general de los Mexicanos en los Estados Unidos, Comisiones Honoríficas, Brigadas de la Cruz Azul," by Enrique A. González, Consul General Visitador de Consulados, January 21, 1930, in AHSRE, IV/524(73) "30"/18-22-7. A list of 100 *Comisiones* and twenty-six *Brigadas* is given in *Memoria de la Secretaria de*

Relaciones Exteriores de agosto de 1930 a julio de 1931, Tomo II, 1777-1783. Also, "Acuerdos tomados en la primera convención consular en San Antonio, April 9-15, 1921, AREM. 27-12-71, IV/362(73-46) "921"/2, in AHSRE.

46. Ernesto Hidalgo, *La protección de los Mexicanos en los Estados Unidos, Defensorías de oficios anexos a los consulados—un proyecto* (Mexico, 1940).

47. Interviews with personnel of Mexican Consulate General, San Antonio, Texas, May 21, 1970, and January 4, 1973.

48. Interviews with veteran consular officials Rafael de la Colina and Rafael Reyes Spindola, May 10 and May 13, 1974, Washington, D.C.

49. According to Gamio, "There is hardly an immigrant home in the United States where the Mexican flag is not found in a place of honor, often altars are made for saints and flags . . . giving patriotism thus an almost religious quality," *Mexican Immigration*, p. 128.

50. See, for example, Fabila, *El problema*; and a theatrical work that portrays the anguish of Mexican emigrant parents who look on helplessly as their children reject their Mexican heritage, *Los Desarraigados* (México, 1962), by Humberto Robles.

51. McLean, *That Mexican!*, p. 163. See also the patriotic songs of the immigrants, in Gamio, *Mexican Immigration*, pp. 84-107.

52. Gamio, *Mexican Immigration*, pp. 74-75, 128-130.

53. See, for example, Memorandum, June 10, 1922, Archivo General de la Nación (AGN), Ramo Obregon-Calles (Presidential Papers), exped. 711-M-30.

54. *El Universal*, December 15, 1917, p. 1; April 9, 1918, p. 1; March 4, 1920, p. 4.

55. See note 53.

56. Ibid.

57. Gamio, *Mexican Immigration*, pp. 13-30. Apparently emigrants were also encouraged to send money orders by private agencies, which made a business of handling money affairs for Mexican workers, as in Los Angeles and San Antonio. See Laird's study of workers on the Santa Fe Railway, "Argentine, Kansas."

58. See Craig, *The Bracero Program*.

59. Interviews with personnel of Departamento de Población, Secretaría de Gobernación, August 20, 1970; with immigration officials attached to U.S. Embassy, Mexico City, August 14, 1970; and with Under-Secretary of Migrant Affairs, Secretaría de Relaciones Exteriores, January 21, 1974.

60. See González Navarro, *La colonización en México*; and Moíses T. de la Peña, "Problemas demográficos y agrarios," in *Problemas Agricolas é Industriales de México*, II:3-4 (julio-diciembre, 1950), 9-327.

61. de la Peña, "Problemas demográficos."

62. The U.S. census figure for Mexico-born and second-generation Mexican population was 1,449,295. But the Secretary of Foreign Relations estimated that by 1928 there were approximately 2 million Mexicans in the United States requiring 58 consulates; see Martínez, "Mexican Emigration," p. 136. For similar estimates, see "Informe—situación general," previously indicated in note 45.

63. Cardoso, "Socio-Economic Causes."

64. *El Universal*, May 11, 1921, p. 1; September 2, 1921, p. 3. See also Martínez, "Mexican Emigration," pp. 131-132.

65. A typical plan to colonize Baja California with *repatriados* was described in *El Universal* (Mexico City), January 29, 1921, p. 6. As in the time of Porfirio Díaz the gov-

ernment was also attempting to solidify a desert frontier against possible *yanquí* expansion.

66. Frequent complaints of abuse of repatriation aid are found in consular correspondence of 1920s, e.g., files IV/350 to IV/560, AHSRE. For repatriation in the early 1930s, see Carreras de Velasco, *Los mexicanos que devolvió la crisis.*

67. *El Universal*, April 5, 1922; and Circular from Consul General Enrique Santibañez, San Antonio, to all Consuls, Comisiones Honoríficas, February 15, 1929, IV/524.5 (015) (73-46)/1; IV, 107-94, AHSRE.

68. Gamio, Migration and Planning, *"Survey,"* 66:3 (May 1, 1933), 1.

69. Gamio, *Mexican Immigration*, and *The Mexican Immigrant: His Life Story* (Chicago, 1931); Paul S. Taylor, *Mexican Labor in the United States* (ten parts, University of California, Berkeley, 1928-1934); and Selden C. Menefee and Owen Cassmore, "The Problem of Underpaid and Unemployed Mexicans"(Washington: Works Project Administration, 1940). Likewise relevant: Taylor, *A Spanish-Mexican Peasant Community*; James Gilbert, "A Field Study in Mexico of the Mexican Repatriation Movement" (master's thesis, Los Angeles: University of Southern California, 1934); and Carreras de Velasco, *Los mexicanos que devolvió la crisis.*

70. Stella Leal Carrillo, "Importancia económica y social de la población mexicana en los Estados Unidos de Norteamérica" (thesis in economics, Universidad Nacional Autónoma de México, 1963); Howard L. Campbell, "Bracero Migration and the Mexican Economy, 1951-1964" (Ph.D. thesis, Washington, D.C.: The American University, 1972); Jorge Bustamante, "Mexican Immigration to the United States in the Context of the Social Relations of Capitalism" (Ph.D. thesis, University of Notre Dame, 1974); and Wayne A. Cornelius, with Juan Diez-Cañedo, *Mexican Migration to the United States: The View from Rural Sending Communities* (Cambridge, Mass.: Center of International Studies, M.I.T., 1976).

71. Consular files of the AHSRE contain many references to the concern of government officials about the political activities of expatriates, abuses of repatriation and consular aid, problems of protecting elusive migrants, and ambivalent attitudes toward repatriates seeking land and subsidies when the government already had commitments to citizens at home.

72. See U.S. consular correspondence from Mexico for 1930s in NA, R.G., 59, 811.504/440 and 811.111/1188-1236.

73. On mission of Ramón Beteta in 1939 to select agricultural repatriates, see AHSRE files IV/524.5(72:73)/1; IV-744-49; and AGN, Ramo Cárdenas, Expediente 503.11/3-1, Leg. 2, #05827, April 10-11, 1930; and Exped. 503.11/3, Leg. 1, August 11, 1939.

74. Memorandum sobre repatriación, by Rafael de la Colina, Consul General, San Antonio, September 7, 1935, B/525.5(73)/91, AHSRE.

75. Interviews with repatriate families established in the colony "18 de Marzo," and Valle Hermoso, in State of Tamaulipas. These settlers of the 1939-1941 period were interviewed on December 18, 1969, and August 12, 1970.

76. Interview with Eduardo Chávez, director of irrigation and colonization development in the lower Rio Grande valley in period 1936-1940, in Mexico City, July 15, 1971.

77. Interviews with Mexican Migration Office personnel, Ciudad Juárez, August 25, 1972, and Jorge Aguilar Saldaña, Director General del Servicio Consular, Mexico City, February 26, 1974.

78. The "Carranza Doctrine" is mentioned in *El Universal*, October 14, 1919, p. 1; and in U.S. consular correspondence, R.G. 59, file 811.504/135 and subsequent items. In the late 1920s the Mexican government began giving wide circulation to American information on immigration law in order to cooperate with the State Department's effort to restrict Mexican immigration without resorting to a quota, and because this cooperation fitted in with Mexico's policy of discouragement. According to *Excelsior*, April 22, 1929, the Secretary of Internal Affairs (Gobernación) gave nationwide circulation to the news that the American Congress had passed a law in 1929 providing for criminal sanctions for illegal entrants, and had 50,000 copies of American requirements for legal immigration printed for distribution. Mexican migration officials say this same policy is followed today.

79. See the section on "Protección" in the *Memorias de la Secretaría de Relaciones Exteriores*—for example, that of 1929-1930, pp. 828-831. An example of American complaints is given in Richard Boyer, American Consul, Nuevo Laredo, to Department of State, November 1, 1929, NA R.G. 59, 811.111/285. Another source concerning the complaints of American officials through the years is based on interviews with American immigration officers and border patrolmen, active and retired, in California, Arizona, and Texas in the period April-August 1970.

80. An example would be correspondence regarding a meeting of American and Mexican migration officials on deportation questions, notice of October 1938, NA R.G. 59, 150.126/398a.

81. Frequent references to Mexican concern about dumping deportees on border and arbitrary procedures are found in Mexican consular correspondence, AHSRE, for the period 1920-1945; and American diplomatic correspondence, NA R.G. 59 and R.G. 85, for the period 1920-1947. For the period of the bracero program, 1942-1964, see *Memorias de la Secretaria de Relaciones Exteriores*.

82. Interviews with American immigration personnel in border states, April-August 1970; and at American Embassy, Mexico City, August 14 and 18, 1970; January 9 and 14, 1974; May 27, 1975.

83. Interviews with Mexican border officials, Ciudad Juárez, August 25, 1972; and Piedras Negras, January 3, 1975.

84. Questionnaire replies from Mexican officials, Oficina de Población y Departamento de Migración, Secretaría de Gobernación, prepared by Professor Romeo Flores, El Colegio de México, November 14, 1972. The Regulations of the General Population Law of Mexico (1962) state that a national leaving the country must "meet all the requisites needed to enter the country of their destination" (Art. 84,I); and "The necessary vigilance shall be established along the borders and sea coast to prevent clandestine emigration, for which purpose the federal and local authorities shall cooperate." (Art. 79,II). But Mexican migration officials say that *mojados* easily avoid any emigration requirements, and that since the suspension of the bracero-contract labor program there is no serious effort to enforce vigilance against illegal emigration.

85. See exposé in *New York Times*, April 15, 1973, describing corrupt handling of the plane lift used (rather than the usual busing system) to remove apprehended illegals to Mexico's interior from the California border. This article, entitled "Ousted Mexican Aliens Pay Off to Stay Close to Jobs," suggests the fragility of this removal system which depends on a kind of Gentleman's Agreement between U.S. immigration officials and Mexican officials of Secretariat of Gobernación. This same story, circulated in Mexico, caused considerable turmoil in official circles and in the press.

86. According to interviews with John W. Holland, District Director of Immigration, June 6 and 18, 1970. Mr. Holland entered the Immigration Service in the early 1930s.

87. The volume of two-way border traffic is frequently cited as a major factor in the alien-control problem on land borders, as in House Committee on the Judiciary, *Illegal Aliens, Hearings* . . . .

88. Interviews with Mexican migration officials and private citizens, as well as consular officers in Mexico City, August 16-20, 1970; Guadalajara, August 22, 1972; Ciudad Juárez, August 25, 1972; and San Antonio, Texas, January 4, 1973.

89. Beginning in 1971 a number of American immigration bills proposed to establish uniformity in policy for both hemispheres, new preference categories, penalties for those who knowingly hire or contract illegal aliens, and new enforcement procedures and penalties against alien smuggling and immigration fraud. For discussion of so-called Rodino bill, H.R. 8713, and similar Eastland bill, S. 3074, see House Committee on the Judiciary, *Hearings Before the Subcommittee* . . . and Senate Committee on the Judiciary, *Immigration 1976, Hearings Before the Subcommittee on Immigration and Naturalization*.

90. Interview with personnel of Dirección General del Servicio Consular, Mexico City, April 8, 1975.

91. U.S. Immigration and Naturalization Service (INS), *Annual Report*, Table 27B.

92. U.S. Department of Justice, "Program for Effective and Humane Action." This interagency group, appointed by President Nixon, ceased to exist after delivering its report; but a similar group, The President's Domestic Concil on Illegal Aliens, was established by President Ford in January 1975, with a view toward maintaining some contact with the ongoing interagency commission in Mexico City. See also Comisión Intersecretarial para Estudio del Problema de la Emigración Subrepticia de Trabajadores Mexicanos a Estados Unidos de América, "Informe de Actividades y Recomendaciones" (Mexico City, December 14, 1972).

93. *Tiempo* (Semanario, Mexico City), February 12, 1973, pp. 19-23.

94. Ley General de Población, *Diario Oficial* (Mexico City), January 7, 1974, pp. 1-13. Later regulations require that couples seeking a marriage license, or to report a birth, be informed of public birth-control services, Reglamento de la ley general de población, *Diario Oficial*, November 16, 1976.

95. Interviews with immigration officials, American Embassy, Mexico City, February 25 and 28, 1974; with two members of the American interagency study group on illegal aliens (appointed by President Nixon) in Washington, D.C., January 5-7, 1973; and with Director of Migratory Affairs, Secretaría de Relaciones Exteriores, Mexico City, January 21, 1974, and April 3, 1975.

96. Ibid.

97. Ibid. See also INS, *Annual Report*, Tab. 18: Foreign Laborers Admitted.

98. See *Memorias de la Secretaría de Relaciones Exteriores*, 1965-1968.

99. Interviews with members of Mexico's Intersecretarial Commission, Mexico City, April 3 and 10, 1975.

100. Declarations of President Echeverría as reported in *Tiempo* (Mexico City), 66:1695 (October 28, 1974), p. 9.

101. See note 95.

102. According to articles in leading Mexican dailies, *Excelsior*, for example, June 14, 17, and 19, July 9, August 6, September 4, 28, and October 8, 1973; and January 29, February 4, June 28, October 11 and 25, November 4, 10, 17, 25, 28, 1974; *El Universal*, February 2, 1974; or *El Porvenir* (Monterrey), June 13, 1973, and October 24, 1974.

103. Craig, *The Bracero Program*, pp. 57, 61, 68, 126, 186, and *passim*.

104. According to discussions of January 21 and 31, 1974, and April 3, 1975, with Director of Migratory Affairs, Relaciones Exteriores.

105. Ibid., and Comisión Intersecretarial, "Informe de Actividades." See note 92.

106. According to studies on surreptitious emigration made for Mexico's Intersecretarial Commission by Victor Ramírez Izquierdo, Subdirector de Estudios del Desarrollo de Recursos Humanos, Instituto de Estudios Políticos, Económicos y Sociales (PRI), interview, Mexico City, February 12, 1974.

107. See notes 102 and 103.

108. Examples: The border studies program, supported by the Ford Foundation, and headed by Jorge Bustamante, a sociologist with El Colegio de México and an influential member of the Intersecretarial Commission, in collaboration with Julian Samora, director, Chicano studies, Notre Dame University; or, a profile study of Mexican migratory flows, involving also Mexican social anthropologists and demographers, in Thomas Weaver and Theodore E. Downing, eds., *Mexican Migration*. See also Cornelius' study, note 70. Among other influential studies has been a report by David S. North and Marion F. Houstun, *The Characteristics . . . Illegal Aliens*.

109. See note 97.

110. See note 95.

111. File: "Commuters," ACTM, XIII/662(73-85), AHSRE; and Informes sobre la reunión interparlamentaria México-Estados Unidos, ACTM, XIII/341.1 "70"/1, AHSRE.

112. See note 97.

113. For example, declarations against the Rodino bills and in favor of an international agreement on humane treatment for emigrant labor were expressed by Mexican deputies and senators at the fourteenth Mexico-United States Interparliamentary Conference, Washington, D.C., May 13-16, 1974.

114. Harvey A. Levenstein, *Labor Organizations in the United States and Mexico*.

115. Interview with deputy commissioner, U.S. Immigration and Naturalization Service, May 6, 1974, Washington, D.C.

116. Interviews with Federal Magistrate Tom N. Goodwin, Laredo, Texas, April 9, 1974; and with Hector Jara, Mexican Consul, Laredo, April 9, 1974; also, "Mexican Officials . . . Talk about Fines on Wetbacks," *Laredo Times*, April 17, 1974.

117. Bertha Martínez Garza, Conselor, Secretaría de Reforma Agraria, in "8.5 milliones de 'espaldas mojadas' deportó Estados Unidos en medio siglo," *Excelsior*, November 18, 1976, p. 19-A. See also note 104.

118. The current Rodino bill, H.R. 8713, and the Eastland bill, S. 3074, introduced in March 1976, proposed a cut-off date of June 30, 1968.

119. "Ley General de Población," December 11, 1973, and January 7, 1974, and "Reglamento," in Echánove Trujillo, *Manual del Extranjero*, pp. 5-110; and according to interviews with American consular officers, Monterrey, December 31, 1974, and Mexico City, January 3, and April 2, 1975; also with Director of Dirección General del Servicio Consular, Mexico City, April 8, 1975. See also Oswaldo Schön, *Americans*

Under Mexican Law (México: Turmex, 1974).

120. Interviews with American consular officers, March 13, 1974, Monterrey.

121. Manuel Mejido, *México amargo* (México: Siglo Venintiuno, 1973); and Aguilar M. and Carmona, *México*. See also Alan Riding's assessment of "Mexican Government's Family Planning," *The New York Times*, January 9, 1977, p.11.

122. Questionnaire replies from Mexican officials; see note 83.

123. Ibid. Also, for fixed facts of poverty, subemployment, maldistribution of national income, see Hansen, *Politics*; González Casanova, *La democracia*; and Stavenhagen et al., *Neolatifundismo y explotación*.

124. Some of Mexico's social scientists, who have studied and written influentially about Mexico's migratory and population problems, sometimes in collaboration with Anglo-American and Chicano scholars, are: Luís Unikel, Rodolfo Stavenhagen, Jorge Bustamente, Raúl Benítez, Víctor Urquidi, Fernando Camara, Gustavo Cabrera Acevedo, Pablo González Casanova, Margarita Nolasco, and others, usually associated with autonomous organizations such as El Colegio de México, Universidad Nacional Autónoma de México, and occasionally with the semi-autonomous Instituto de Estudios Políticos, Económicos y Sociales (PRI). For an account of recommendations made by Mexican social scientists to the ruling party's pick for the next president, José López Portillo, see "Reunión nacional sobre población y desarrollo," as reported in *Excelsior* and *La Tribuna de Mexico*, February 17-20, 1976.

125. Information from District Director, Immigration, San Antonio, April 5, 1977; and Public Information Office, Western Region, Immigration Service, San Pedro, March 18, 1977.

126. *Tribuna de Monterrey*, April 3, 4, 19, 1976; also proposals for an ethnic alliance by professors of Chicano studies in American universities and by Raza Unida leaders, like José Angel Gutíerrez, in Roberto Vizcaino and Federico Gómez Pombo, "En 20 años seremos duenos del sureste de Estados Unidos," *Excelsior*, May 22, 1976, p. 12A; and Francisco Juaristi, "Genocidio cultural contra 20 millones de Chicanos," *Excelsior*, February 12, 1977, p. 14A.

127. "Demandarán a México," *El Porvenir*, June 17, 1977; see also James Flanigan, "South of the Border—A Legacy of Bitterness," *Forbes*, 118:8 (April 15, 1977), 43-48.

128. "López Portillo: El Mexico que encuentra," *Visión*, Mexico City, 47:12 (December 1, 1976), i-vi, 6-10.

129. "Address to the U.S. Congress by José López Portillo," *The Wall Street Journal*, February 18, 1977, p. 9.

130. *Excelsior*, February 17, 18, April 22, 26, May 26, June 1, 9, 1977.

131. Jorge Bustamante, a specialist in surreptitious labor emigration, associated with El Colegio de Mexico, Mexico City, has been consultant to Mexican and American officials. His "Plan" would also include a new bracero program, *Excelsior*, August 6, 1976, pp. 4A, 5A. See also statements of Foreign Minister Santiago Roel, *Excelsior*, May 25, 1977, p. 3A; and proposals to solve the "illegal alien dilemma," made by Mexican, Chicano, and Anglo-American delegates, including high officials and advisers, in Symposium on Immigration and Public Policy: The Humanistic Imperative," sponsored by the Chicano Training Center, and held at the University of Houston, April 15-16, 1977.

132. Address by Hugo B. Margaín, Mexican Ambassador to the United States, *Journal of Commerce*, New York, reprinted by *Excelsior*, June 9, 1977, p. 11A.

133. Salvador Flores Llamas, "El Presidente instó a los Mexicano-Norte-Americanos," *Ovaciones* (Mexico City), April 23, 1977, p. 1.

134. Statement by leader of Mexican American Political Association (MAPA), and other statements at Tijuana meeting, in "Pide JLP apoyo a los Mexico-Norteamericanos," *El Porvenir*, April 23, 1977, pp. 1, 8.

135. Carl J. Migdail, "Time Bomb in Mexico—Interview with José López Portillo," *U.S. News and World Report*, 83:1 (July 4, 1977), 28-30; and "Imposible frenar el bracerismo," *Excelsior*, July 4, 1977, pp. 1, 14. For presidential policies, see also state of the nation address: "Texto integro del primer informe," *El Porvenir*, September 2, 1977, pp. 1, 8-14.

136. "La amnistía alentaría el bracerismo," *Excelsior*, May 26, 1977, p. 1; and Alan Riding, "Mexican [Bustamente] Says U.S. Alien Program a Myoptic Policy," *The New York Times*, reprinted in *The Des Moines Tribune*, May 26, 1977.

137. *Excelsior*, June 22, 1977, pp. 1, 16; June 24, 1977, pp. 1, 19; and statements by Raúl Roel Martínez, Director, Mexican Consular Service, in Carlos Ravelo, "No se elimina la posibilidad de un nuevo convenio," *Excelsior*, June 23, 1977, p. 1.

138. Migdail, "Time Bomb in Mexico—Interview," pp. 28-30; Frank Del Olmo, interview with López Portillo, reprinted in "Los braceros no son criminales," *Excelsior*, April 26, 1977, pp. 1, 16; and in *Ft. Worth Star Telegram*, April 25, 1976, p. 1.

139. Migdail, "Time Bomb in Mexico—Interview," pp. 28-29; and statements by economist Victor L. Urquidi, "Indicios de menor natalidad," *Excelsior*, June 11, 1976, pp. 1A, 11A. For dimensions of the migratory problem, see Thomas Weaver and Theodore E. Downing, eds., *Mexican Migration* (Tucson: Bureau of Ethnic Research, University of Arizona, 1976). For probability of population aid, see "Mexico Considering Loan," *The New York Times*, September 29, 1977, p. 59.

140. For Mexico-United States trade proposals, see interview statements in: Flanigan, "North of the Rio Grande—Who Needs Whom?" *Forbes*, 119-18 (April 15, 1977), 40-41; "Pretender solucionarlo por via policiaca es eligir el peor camino," *Excelsior*, June 1, 1977, p. 4A; "Urgen a Carter crear condiciones," *El Porvenir*, April 24, 1977, p. 1; Migdail, "Time Bomb in Mexico—Interview," pp. 28-30; statements by Mexican delegates to XVII Interparliamentary Conference, in "Corregir políticas," *Excelsior*, May 27, 1977, p. 14A; and for Carter approval, see Carlos Ravelo and Jaime Duran, "Igualdad, pidió el Presidente: Young," *Excelsior*, August 9, 1977, pp. 1, 10.

141. Speech in Dallas by Ambassador Patrick J. Lucey, reported in *The Des Moines Register*, May 23, 1970. See also note 131.

142. "Address to the U.S. Congress by José López Portillo," *The Wall Street Journal*, February 18, 1977, p. 9; Migdail, "Time Bomb in Mexico—Interview," pp. 28-30; and John Huey, "Danger Signals, Mexico's Economic Ills Could Topple Coalition," *The Wall Street Journal*, August 8, 1977, pp. 1, 4.

143. Melanie Wirken, Director, Immigration Program, Zero Population Growth, Washington, D.C., "Border Hoppers: Check the Traffic in Illegal Aliens," *Skeptic, The Magazine of Great Debates*, 20 (July/August 1977), 43-47, 59-60.

144. "Benefica ley," editorial in *Excelsior*, June 7, 1977; "No más explotación," *Excelsior*, June 7, 1977, pp. 1, 9; and Joe Nash, "Lucey Supports Migrant Workers," *The News* (Mexico City), April 28, 1977, p. 1.

145. William Cooney, "Illegal Aliens Who May Get to Stay," *San Francisco Chronicle*, June 13, 1977, p. 9; and information from District Director, Immigration, San An-

tonio, April 5, 1977.

146. "Undocumented Aliens Fact Sheet, and Message to Congress by President Jimmy Carter, August 4, 1977," Office of the White House, Press Secretary; "A U.S. Plan for a New Class of Aliens," *San Francisco Chronicle*, June 13, 1977, p. 9; "Una nueva clase," *Excelsior*, June 12, 1977, p. 2A.

147. Information from District Director, Immigration, San Antonio, April 5, 1977; and "200,000 Migrants . . . Mass at Tijuana," *The New York Times*, reprinted in *The Des Moines Register*, August 8, 1977, pp. 1A, 7A.

148. Migdail, "Time Bomb in Mexico—Interview." See also note 138.

149. Aurora Berdejo Arvizu, "Braceros," *Excelsior*, August 9, 1977, pp. 1, 10-11.

150. "200,000 Migrants . . . Mass at Tijuana."

151. James P. Sterba, "Illegal Aliens Pose a Growing Problem," *The New York Times*, April 24, 1977, p. 21L. See also Castillo's ambiguous enforcement statements in Richard E. Kipling, ed., "Illegal Aliens: The Permeable Line," *Skeptic, The Magazine of Great Debates* 20 (July/August 1977), p. 46.

152. Migdail, "Time Bomb in Mexico—Interview," pp. 27-34; Declarations by Foreign Minister Santiago Roel, in "Cada noche 1,000 Mexicanos tratan de ingresar ilegalment," *Excelsior*, May 25, 1977, p. 3A; and Kipling, ed., "Illegal Aliens: The Permeable Line."

153. "Braceros, el principal problema con E.U.," *Excelsior*, August 9, 1977, pp. 1, 10.

154. "Destino de Mexicanos," editorial in *Excelsior*, July 13, 1977.

155. Luís Díaz Flores, "Sobre los ilegales," *El Porvenir*, August 9, 1977.

156. "El problema de los braceros 'bomba de tiempo' dice el PRI . . . y Bustamante," *Excelsior*, July 30, 1977, pp. 1, 12.

157. M. Ruíz Redondo, "25,000 braceros guatemaltecos," *Excelsior*, August 9, 1977, pp. 10-11.

158. "Braceros, el principal problema," pp. 1, 10.

159. Official reportorial account of Echeverría's visit to the United States by Gullermo Ochoa, *En la sal y el cesped: Echeverría en Norteamérica* (Mexico: Editorial Novara, 1972).

*Interviews indicated in these notes were carried out by Arthur F. Corwin.

8/ MEXICAN REPATRIATION DURING THE GREAT DEPRESSION: A REAPPRAISAL

Abraham Hoffman

For some two decades prior to the economic crisis that began in the fall of 1929, Mexican workers had been steadily taking over jobs that Anglo-Americans or other immigrant groups apparently did not want, such as picking cotton and fruit, construction and maintenance jobs, and pick and shovel work. By 1930 Mexican migratory laborers and their families, numbering perhaps a million in all, were found mostly in the border states, but especially in south Texas and in southern California. By then they were beginning to face vicious competition from jobless Americans, including Mexican Americans.

The reasons are not hard to find. Unemployment in the national economy rose from 4 million in October 1930 to over 13 million by March 1933. Many who still had jobs were then working part-time or for half salaries. Even in 1939 unemployment was still fluctuating near 10 million. Meanwhile, average industrial wages fell 60 percent by 1932, and the income of agriculturists, many of whom employed migrant workers, fell by more than 55 percent.[1] The Southwest, where most Mexican laborers were concentrated, was no exception to this general picture of economic misery. Nor was it an exception to a growing "nativist sentiment" that looked with increasing hostility at employers who kept foreigners on the payroll, particularly if they were non-naturalized or lacked immigration documents.

Furthermore, as the Depression abolished jobs, particularly unskilled jobs, the unemployed, including many Mexican nationals, turned in desperation to relief services offered by public and private agencies. Here again bitter nativist resentment focused on aliens whose presence on relief rolls apparently reduced the amount of aid available for American citizens. And since public relief services, according to the poor-law system inherited from sixteenth-century England, were then intended for natives of the local community and funded by local taxpayers and donors, the administrators of this parochial system were under an obligation to eliminate from the public case load all nonresidents or part-time residents, including, of course, migrant workers and their families. At that time the federal government, under the prevailing laissez-faire philosophy of federalism, contributed nothing toward the relief needs of the local communities. In effect, this left each community to fend for itself.

Since local funds, public and private, could not meet such a nationwide industrial crisis, there were increasing cries for federal action. At first President Herbert Hoover (1928-1932), a Republican and a sincere defender of the traditional system of free-enterprise capitalism and individual self-reliance, vetoed congressional proposals for emergency federal aid. In 1930 he said:

This is not a question as to whether people shall go hungry or cold in the United States. . . . It is a question as to whether the American people on the one hand will maintain the spirit of charity and mutual self help through voluntary giving and the responsibility of local government as distinguished on the other hand from appropriations out of the Federal Treasury. . . . My own conviction is strongly that if we break down this sense of responsibility of individual generosity . . . and mutual self help . . . if we start appropriations of this character we have not only impaired something infinitely valuable in the life of the American people but have struck at the roots of self-government.[2]

Finally in 1932 Hoover approved a law establishing the Reconstruction Finance Corporation and providing $3 million for public works and employment subsidies. To say the least, the measure was inadequate; nevertheless, it marked the beginning of a radical change in the American political system. This change soon became institutionalized as the "welfare state," or New Deal, during the prolonged administration of Franklin D. Roosevelt (1932-1945), a Democrat, who assumed presidential powers in January 1933. Congress, controlled by New Deal Democrats, quickly passed emergency economic laws, one of which created the Federal Emergency Relief Administration in 1933. This agency channeled funds to public relief agencies in each state. Soon after, massive public-works programs were put into operation with federal funds and federal supervision. By April 1933 over 4 million persons were receiving work relief or direct relief. Also, federal food commodities were given to hard-pressed families. By 1934 federal programs had removed much of the financial burden from local charities. Federal work relief was continued, but under local administration when the Works Progress Administration (W.P.A.) was inaugurated in January 1935. By then there was a notable decline in the aggressive efforts of welfare officials to send migrant families back to their own local communities. Also, by then public officials were discovering the possibilities of political patronage in federal programs for the "deserving poor." An era had ended and a new one had begun.

Nevertheless, during the critical years of the Depression, 1930-1933, there was as yet little federal help for unemployed workers, and employers and relief agencies were still under increasing public pressure to exclude foreign-born applicants and other outsiders. For example, California in 1933 raised its residency requirements to three years. In California and elsewhere the general immigration act of 1917 (the so-called Burnett Law) was used to frighten unemployed aliens out of the country, or to keep them away from relief services. The 1917 law provided that even a legal immigrant who solicited relief within five years after his arrival could be subject to deportation as a public charge. The federal government itself, as an emergency gesture, offered to pay the repatriation of indigent immigrants who had legally entered during the previous three years. Moreover, migrant families, native and foreign, often found that charity agencies enforced the traditional rule that the solicitor of aid must prove his legal residence in the local community or county, otherwise all that could be provided was travel aid back to the previous place of residence. Under such rigid attitudes millions of poor whites and blacks returned to the southern states. Facing the same rule, plus deportation fears, many jobless Mexican nationals, especially those lacking entry papers, had little choice but to consider a return to the native village, and when the Mexican government responded with a warm *bienvenido*! a massive repatriation movement was soon underway.[3]

Now that exodus has since given rise to oversimplified impressions, as found in the early writing of Carey McWilliams, and echoed by other writers, for instance, that Mexican repatriation during the Depression was primarily the work of penny-pinching relief agencies that often employed methods of doubtful legality in "getting rid of the Mexican." And as Chicano authors would later tend to see it, aliens and citizen children were simply made the scapegoat of a capitalist depression, and subjected to arbitrary deportation pressures as a temporary solution to an unemployment crisis.[4]

Actually *el retorno* consisted of two major currents, or phases. The first began in late 1929 and reached a high point in late 1931. It was mostly self-aided and self-propelled. Families made their way back to the border usually in their own autos and trucks, rather than trains, and most carried some money or household goods. Here writers critical of "forced repatriation" tend to overlook the fact that the greatest number of *repatriados* returned to their homeland under this form of self-help migration. In a brief period between November 1929 and December 1931, over 200,000 did so.[5] Of this number probably 75 percent or more made their own way, although in many cases help was given by Mexican consuls and Mexican mutual-aid societies.

The early phase of mass repatriation lacked sensational headlines in American papers. Since reporters hardly covered these self-organized movements and since migrant families hardly kept diaries (at least none have yet come to light), we must depend on United States and Mexican consular reports or on the observations of sympathetic social workers. In particular, U.S. consular officers stationed in Mexican border towns often described in detail the southward flow of returning migrants: "In crossing the international bridge," reported the consul at Nuevo Laredo in late 1930, "one can always see a line of cars with licenses from nearly half the United States filled with household effects of Mexicans returning and waiting to make the necessary arrangements with the Mexican authorities."[6]

Another consul likened the *repatriados* to gypsies, "as they usually return by either wagon or broken down motor car in which children, household furniture, and domestic animals are loaded."[7] In early March 1930 the Nogales consul stated that forty families entered Mexico "with all their household goods and possessions packed in automobiles and wagons, the Government allowing them free entry." This group intended to colonize land in Sonora that had been made available by the Mexican government.[8] The consul in Ciudad Juárez relayed a report from the Mexican government in January 1931 that over 2,000 automobiles had been brought in by repatriates.[9] From Piedras Negras came the estimate that 25 percent of the *repatriados* brought in money, farm implements, trucks or automobiles, farm animals, and household furnishings.[10]

While many Mexicans could thus show some material gain from their residency north of the border, the picture on the whole was a dismal one. Vehicles broke down on the trip south, money and food ran out, and many Mexican families were destitute upon reaching the border and were unable to move on. In the winter of 1930-1931 stranded families in Ciudad Juárez, a principal port of entry, taxed the town's ability to provide donations of food. As a noted Protestant social worker described it: "Women swarmed about the warehouses picking up one by one the beans which spilled through holes in the sacks."[11] The Mexican government reacted by providing special trains that shipped without charge some 2,700 repatriates to the interior. Thereafter, several cars were attached to southbound trains to relieve the congestion in Ciudad Juárez. Other border towns experienced similar difficulties.[12]

The other major current or phase of repatriation did not begin until mid-1931, when relief agencies decided it was more economical to send home an indigent alien family than to continue relief payments perhaps indefinitely, for there was apparently no end to the economic paralysis in sight. This phase of repatriation was characterized by organized inducements, subsidies, and persuasive techniques applied by social-welfare agencies often in cooperation with the U.S. Immigration Service, the Mexican consulates, and railway management in the United States and Mexico.

The type of subsidy and the degree of persuasion used by public relief agencies varied. In southern California, for example, county relief officials offered small cash inducements, food parcels, medical aid while en route, and a train ticket all the way to the native community in Mexico, not just to the border. On the other hand, some welfare personnel threatened to deny relief payments unless the travel subsidies were accepted. Also, some Mexican nationals were advised by relief agencies to leave on their own, unaided, since being illegally in the country, they might be subject to formal deportation proceedings or penalties. They were further informed that if deported as a public charge one could not legally reenter the United States. In effect, this meant that if the U.S. government, or a public welfare agency, paid the repatriate's fare to Mexico, the recipient could be denied a reentry visa under that clause of immigration law, first established in 1885, that prohibits the admission of immigrants "likely to become a public charge."[13]

In the meantime, a deportation drive that the federal government launched early in 1931 against illegal aliens, using the rationale that aliens were holding jobs rightfully belonging to American citizens, persuaded many Mexican nationals of the possible advantages of voluntary repatriation, with or without aid.[14] Although the campaign was aimed at all aliens regardless of nationality, it set more Mexican nationals in motion than any other group. The campaign as it was carried out in southern California was designed not so much to deport Mexicans illegally in the country but to frighten them across the border, a technique periodically employed by the U.S. Immigration Service with Mexican and Canadian illegal entrants "who can walk home." This campaign, together with deportation scares that the Los Angeles Chamber of Commerce placed in local newspapers, caused thousands of migratory families to leave California.[15]

Thus far few cities or counties—with the exception of the southern California locale—have been thoroughly studied to determine the nature and extent of organized repatriation.[16] But from available published accounts and consular reports, it appears that organized repatriation covered a broad range of efforts by local relief agencies, church charities, the Red Cross, the International Institute, and immigrant aid societies in several states. It also seems evident that Los Angeles County's Department of Charities became the principal sponsor of organized and subsidized repatriation.[17]

Los Angeles County officials naturally hoped to remove as many aliens as possible from the relief rolls, but by careful planning. Repatriate families were not shipped out like so many trainloads of cattle and dumped over the Mexican border, as some persons were inclined to believe. Train trips were crowded with economy fares, but relief officials carefully supervised health and sanitary conditions, and made provisions for food and medical care, at least as far as the border port of exit. Mexican consular officers frequently accompanied the trains, and Los Angeles relief agents actually met with Mexican officials to propose and promote agricultural colonies in Mexico for displaced migrant families.[18]

These special organizational efforts on the part of Los Angeles County officials may be explained in part by the peculiar migratory labor problem of southern California. There, because of the seasonal nature of agribusiness employment, many migrant families had become accustomed to following the crops along the Pacific Coast and wintering in Los Angeles and San Bernardino Counties, often with the aid of charitable organizations, public and private. The Great Depression had simply overloaded this unplanned system of subsidizing the migrant-labor cycle, and now, because of the vast desert areas separating southern California from central Mexico, where most migrant families had originated, special efforts and subsidies were required to achieve repatriation. On the other hand, in south Texas, where Mexican migrant families tended to winter, such systematic efforts at repatriation were not attempted. For generations migratory families had been taken for granted; they were much less dependent on the relief agencies of Texas communities, which generally could not match California cities in benevolent care; and they were much closer to central Mexico and to highways and railroads leading into Mexico; moreover, many of the migratory families had originally come from the border states of Tamaulipas, Nuevo Leon, and Coahuila. In any case, many thousands of migrants moved from south Texas over the Rio Grande with little or no help from Texas relief agencies, although emergency committees in Texas border towns helped feed repatriate families.[19]

Elsewhere in the distant interior of the United States, there were organized repatriation efforts similar to those of Los Angeles County. The Detroit Department of Public Welfare, for example, set up a Mexican Bureau that urged repatriation as a solution to the problems of indigents, while at the same time the Mexican consulate sought to repatriate the most recent arrivals.[20] Scattered reports from other areas, such as the Chicago-Gary industrial zone, suggest that state, county, and city funding was used to transport unemployed migrant families to the Mexican border at reduced fares arranged with U.S. railroads. In Ohio, for example, 300 persons from Lucas County were repatriated early in 1934 at a cost of $15 per person, with the money coming from the state. From Chicago came a report that several carloads had been sent out by January 1933 and "more are contemplated," and St. Paul repatriated at least 400 indigents between 1932 and 1934.[21]

Various motives moved repatriates. Probably most of them had originally walked over the American border as wetbacks seeking employment with no intention of remaining permanently in the United States or of becoming naturalized citizens. Many of them were accustomed to making a seasonal return to Mexico over a half-open border, and repatriation usually meant only another visit to the home village, where they could await the return of prosperity in the United States. Others—as we shall see—returned with high expectations of receiving a good job or a parcel of land from the Mexican government. Still, there were other Mexican nationals and their families who, after several years in the United States, found they preferred to live there, and they hoped someday to legalize their status by applying for an immigrant visa, especially if they had one or more children born in the United States. To avoid formal deportation or the classification of public charge—either one would have disqualified an alien for a permanent immigrant visa—this type of Mexican national was inclined to follow the advice of immigration officials and social workers and accept self-repatriation as the best way of obtaining his long-range goals. In weighing the repatriates' various motivations, one could not overlook patriotic sentiments, but, obviously, it would be difficult to draw lines between "advice," "persuasion," "self-interest," and "patriotism." In this respect, it should be pointed out that many repatriates were not told, or did not understand, that the federal government would apply strict visa standards for any unskilled or unemployed repatriate seeking to reenter the United States.[22]

Tracing the pathways of repatriation suggests the geographical spread of Mexican migratory labor before the crisis of 1929. Paul S. Taylor, in one of his monographs under the general title *Mexican Labor in the United States*, charted the stream of southward migration in the early 1930s.[23] He found the most significant movements came from Texas, California, Arizona, and Colorado, plus a large number from the "Calumet" region that touches on Illinois, Indiana, and Michigan. Existing railroads and highways served to funnel the travelers through the border towns of El Paso, Brownsville, Laredo, and Nogales, and some lesser points of exit.[24] Border towns along the Baja California boundary, like Calexico, Mexicali, and Tijuana, received relatively few repatriates, since geographical isolation inhibited passage from there to central Mexico.

Taylor's statistics, based on figures gathered by the Mexican government, revealed that for a three-year period, 1930-1932, over 130,000 *repatriados* left Texas, almost 53,000 departed from California, and over 18,000 left Arizona. From Colorado came some 8,000, and over 6,000 were from New Mexico. In view of the common impression that Mexican migrant groups were found almost exclusively in the Southwest, we should note that in this same period over 14,000 departed from Illinois, almost 7,500 from Michigan, 6,600 from Indiana, 1,600 from Ohio, 1,500 from Nebraska, and over 3,300 from New York. Other states contributed close to 11,000 returnees.[25]

The repatriation exodus declined sharply after 1932, even though many thousands of indigent migrant families were still in the United States. Reports coming back from unhappy repatriates already in Mexico deterred many would-be repatriates. Also, word spread rapidly through the Mexican barrios in the United States that the American consular and immigration services would not readmit indigent repatriates once they had left the country. Another significant factor was the emergency relief program launched by the New Deal after January 1933. Local taxpayers and relief officials were pacified by federal funding of a large share of the aid for jobless migrant families. Moreover, New Deal employment and relief programs, although technically restricted to citizens and legal aliens, were made available, through flexible interpretation, to many aliens lacking immigration documents. Increasing availability of federal aid was thus a factor in the decision of many Mexicans to remain where they were. A related story is that of migrant workers on relief, as in southern California, and growers' efforts to force them off.[26]

The decline of mass repatriation after 1932 can be seen in the following figures:[27]

1929	79,419
1930	70,129
1931	138,519
1932	77,453
1933	33,574
1934	23,943
1935	15,368
1936	11,599
1937	8,037
Total	457,023

Besides the total indicated above, probably another 50,000 repatriates, or more, did not bother to report their return to Mexico but crossed the border at some isolated spot. In all, it is likely that at least 500,000 *repatriados* sought to return permanently or temporarily to Mexico during the years 1929-1937. However, in considering such an estimate, the reader should bear in mind that perhaps 30 to 50 percent of the annual totals were part of a preestablished seasonal backflow of migrant workers who divided their time between Mexico and the U.S. border states, particularly in south Texas, where for many years past a "little Mexico" had been transplanted. Many such migrants were loosely counted as "repatriates" by Mexican border officials. As they were accustomed to doing, with deportation rides that the U.S. Immigration Service offered or repatriation fares that the Mexican consuls provided for destitute migrants in the 1920s, these "professional repatriates," who often moved under an assumed name, accepted a free train ticket and food basket from welfare agencies with no other purpose than to enjoy a royal visit with relatives and friends in Mexico and then return again as a wetback. On one occasion the Mexican press called these transborder migrants *"turistas con pase."*[28]

General public ignorance concerning the casual flow of migratory "repatriates" back and forth over the border, at least since the 1880s, has led, and continues to lead, critics to exaggerate the extent of the "repatriation crime" of the Depression era. It is worthy of note, said Paul S. Taylor, that during four years of prosperity and high labor demands, 1926-1929, the Mexican Migration Service reported 218,000 repatriates. This number was more than two-thirds of the Mexican figure of 306,268 repatriates for the Depression years, 1930-1933. The principal difference between the repatriation in the 1920s and that of the Depression years, continued Taylor, is that because of a depressed economy and the tighter immigration restrictions inaugurated in 1929 (as an alternative to a special "Mexican quota"), the Depression repatriates found it difficult, if not impossible, to return by legal means. 29

One can assume that a certain percentage of the perennial "repatriates" had, as usual, slipped back into the borderlands and that some were probably counted as repatriates more than once during the Depression by Mexican migration authorities. As McWilliams observed, "They have been shunted back and forth across the border for so many years by war, revolution, and the law of supply and demand, that it would seem that neither expatriation nor repatriation held any more terror for them." 30 In short, the term *repatriate*, as applied to the migratory subculture in the borderlands, was rather meaningless. In any event, it is quite likely that about a third of the Depression repatriates were back in the United States by 1940. 31

From what has been said thus far, it is evident that there were several categories of repatriates. 32 *Formal deportation* was a small category. Since illegal entry by an individual did not carry a criminal penalty until the law of March 4, 1929, most repatriates were not subject to fines and imprisonment, although they could be formally deported. In practice, however, the Immigration Service usually reserved this procedure for inveterate violators of civil and criminal laws. The number of formal deportations was therefore small. During the height of repatriation, from July 1, 1931, to June 30, 1932, only 7,116 Mexican nationals were formally expelled. 33

Voluntary departure, as always, applied to most apprehended aliens. Voluntary returns spared the government the costs of detentions, court hearings, and transportation, while the alien, once returned to the homeland, could, theoretically, apply for a reentry visa.

Voluntary repatriation, understood as a category, included all those who returned on their own to Mexico with little or no aid. As previously indicated, this was the most numerous group.

Repatriation of destitute aliens by the federal government accounted for only a fraction of returnees. The government was reluctant to pay for the transportation of Mexican immigrants legally admitted to the country. To do so would have opened the way for legal aliens of all nationalities to request similar aid. 34

Organized repatriation by relief agencies, public and private, included efforts by the Red Cross, the International Institute, immigrant-aid societies, religious groups, and, most important, county and city welfare agencies. Perhaps over 90,000 Mexican nationals received some kind of assistance from such sources during the years 1930-1937, and of this number probably two-thirds were from southern California, where destitute families needed special help to cover several hundred miles of desert land between California and central Mexico. The Los Angeles County Department of Charities alone shipped out 13,332 repatriates from March 23, 1931, to April 15, 1934, at an average total cost of about $72 for a family of five persons. [35] The percentage of these returnees that were persuaded to leave "against their will" is a matter of conjecture.

Assisted repatriation by the Mexican consuls and Mexican community organizations in various states was undoubtedly an important dimension of repatriation, but given the lack of firm statistical information, one can only guess at the number of *repatriados* who received full or partial assistance from such sources during the Depression. According to the Mexican government, the number of repatriates who registered their return to Mexico in 1931 was 126,204, divided into the following categories:

1. Repatriated at Mexican government expense	597
2. At the expense of Mexican beneficent societies in the United States	3,519
3. At repatriate's own expense	6,166
4. At expense of U.S. agencies (e.g., U.S. Immigration Service and welfare agencies)	13,462
5. Not specified	102,460
Total	126,204 [36]

It should be noted, however, that a large proportion of the "Not specified" received some form of subsidy for transportation to the border from American companies, and from there to the interior the National Railroads of Mexico gave many returnees free transit or reduced rates. In addition, according to Mexican figures, the Mexican consuls, mostly in southern California, gave special assistance to 19,840 repatriates in 1931, 32,225 in 1932, and 8,891 in 1933.

Rough estimates of repatriation groups by percentages for the period 1929-1937 would be as follows:

Formal deportation	4 percent
Voluntary departure under escort	15 percent
Voluntary repatriation by aliens themselves (Some of this group received transportation subsidies from Mexican and U.S. sources.)	40 percent
Repatriation of destitute aliens by the federal government	1 percent
Organized repatriation by local U.S. relief agencies	20 percent
Assisted repatriation by Mexican consul and Mexican community groups	20 percent
Total	100 percent

Perhaps more should be said about the Mexican side of repatriation, especially since some American critics of national behavior during the Depression have tended to see Mexican repatriation as principally a unilateral effort by American agencies to push unwanted proletarians across the border now that their labor was no longer needed by a depressed capitalist system.[37] There seems to be much truth in this interpretation; yet it distracts attention from the important contribution the Mexican government, its consuls, and Mexican mutual-aid societies in the United States made to the repatriation movement.

From the very inception of the economic crisis, Mexican consular officers in cities from Los Angeles to New York raised funds—as they were accustomed to doing—for the relief of indigent laborers and their families, and like American welfare agencies, they sought to return Mexican nationals at the lowest possible cost. The consuls obtained cut-rate train fares, provided gasoline and tires for trucks and cars, raised money by sponsoring stage shows, dances, and patriotic events, and sought cooperative aid from local welfare officials and the U.S. Immigration Service, and often acted as *padrinos* to needy families. Also, the consuls shielded Mexican nationals, and Mexican Americans, from the zeal of certain immigration agents bent on deporting any suspicious-looking alien. In Los Angeles alone in 1931 the Mexican consul intervened in over 1,200 deportation cases.[38] Moreover, mutual-aid societies in Mexican barrios, like the Comité Mexicano de Beneficencia, or the Brigada de la Cruz Azul, provided food and clothing, and transportation aid, for departing compatriots.[39] Evangelical church groups formed ad hoc committees to assist in repatriation, and so did Mexican-American border communities in El Paso, Laredo, and elsewhere. The Mexican consuls did most of the coordinating work.[40]

Repatriation efforts were not new to Mexican officials, for successive Mexican governments had always wanted and expected the return of Mexican laborers and their families with whatever useful knowledge they may have absorbed in the United States. Various administrations, beginning with Carranza (1915-1920), frequently made transportation subsidies and customs privileges available to avowed repatriates or destitute migrants. Abuse of this generosity by perennial repatriates led to an emphasis on repatriating the "dedicated farmer." Since the mid-1920s the government had occasionally announced the availability of land for serious agricultural colonists. Consuls posted notices and publicized news of these projects, which included lands confiscated from insurgent generals and politicians as well as wealthy *hacendados*. Furthermore, by 1928 nine dams had been constructed, or were under construction, making available over 750,000 acres of irrigated land for agrarian colonies. Several hundred families who returned to Mexico in the late 1920s, most with sharecropping or tenant farming experience in south Texas, had already taken advantage of these offers.[41] But, in general, Mexico's agricultural economy and landholding system was not prepared to receive the sudden and massive repatriation that followed the crash of 1929.

As we have seen, the swarms of repatriate families camped in Mexican border towns, waiting for transportation or government help, soon strained the limits of fraternal hospitality. An American consul made the typical observation about a Mexican community, in this case, Saltillo, near the Texas border, that there was "a very noticeable desire on the part of the municipal authorities . . . to hasten their departure."[42] Yet national pride and humanitarian sentiment demanded that the mother country open her heart, and her purse, to these prodigal children of La Raza. After all, *yanqui* materialism and *yanqui* capitalism had failed them, and now Mexico and its social revolution would have an opportunity to demonstrate that perhaps *la madre patria* could at least do as much for its people as the rich and powerful Colossus of the North.[43] Mexican newspapers literally leaped forward to welcome the repatriates, seeing in their return a vindication of the editorial criticism so often directed at the ingratitude and egocentrism of Anglo-American society.[44] In this atmosphere of fervent feeling and *dignidad nacional*, the Mexican government and its consuls were pressed to promise too much assistance.

While it is beyond the scope of this study to discuss government-sponsored emergency programs for Depression repatriates, suffice it to say that some notable efforts were made by Mexican officials, federal and state, including the beginnings of a coordinated national program of employment and land opportunities for the returnees.[45] These efforts were made even though the government had some misgivings about giving preferential treatment to certain repatriate groups which, experience had shown, would again depart for the border at the first good opportunity. After all, Mexico had her own land-hungry campesinos to care for. As it turned out, repatriation fervor soon fell off and the crush of repatriates subsided as disillusion spread. Many Mexican nationals still in the United States thereupon dropped any sentimental plans for self-aided repatriation, or they began to resist subsidized repatriation by social welfare agencies.[46] But meanwhile many repatriate families had been set in motion.

In the United States removal of Mexican indigents had been frequently justified on the grounds that the Mexican government, through such special agencies as the National Committee for Repatriation, founded in November 1932, was actively undertaking a number of agrarian colonies and public works programs that would not fail to benefit the repatriate and his family. Along with some Mexican consuls, U.S. welfare officials were inclined to exaggerate job and land opportunities in Mexico. A. C. Price, assistant superintendent of the Los Angeles Department of Charities, for one, stated that "with the cooperation of the Mexican government and Mexican charitable agencies, we are sending these needy non-citizens back to Mexico as rapidly as jobs can be provided for them there."[47] In Detroit the claim was made that "Mexico offered to welcome back expatriates with open arms. A house, a plot of farm land, implements, food, and other assistance until they are rehabilitated...."[48]

In Ciudad Juárez, in early 1931, Reverend McLean spoke with a repatriate on the road to Chihauhau City, his car loaded down with family and belongings. "No more Mexicans in the United States!" the man said. "We're all going home." McLean asked the man, who had lived in the United States for thirteen years, what he would do when he got there. "The government will give me a farm, and tools and seed, and loan me money." Asked how he knew this, he replied with an air of finality: "I read it in the paper." [49]

A flurry of colonization efforts and announcements by federal, state, and private groups in Mexico had, in fact, created a confused situation. For example, the invitation of some northern governors to settle on state lands were mistaken for federal projects, and as always there were the Mexican *coyotes* feeding on the hopes of rustic campesinos. The Mexican Ministry of Agriculture and Mexican consular officers soon found it necessary to issue warnings about "unscrupulous persons" who formed land companies for the purpose of defrauding naive investors. [50] All this mix of propaganda and actual planning gave the impression that the Mexican government was doing far more for the expatriates than was actually the case.

True, the Mexican government continued to provide transportation from congested border towns, to waive customs duties, and, within its means, to develop employment opportunities, as in highway construction. [51] Nevertheless, as the Depression wore on, negative reports from Mexico (after all, the Depression was suffered by the Mexican economy as well) probably influenced some relief officials, as Humphrey's study of Detroit suggests, to employ more persuasive methods to achieve "voluntary repatriation." [52] Also, in this respect, one might take note of Los Angeles County, where repatriation trains were at first crowded with eager volunteers. [53] Later, as potential repatriates hesitated, county welfare officials began to exert pressure, but, to their credit, they at least attempted, as already indicated, to ascertain whether colonization projects could accommodate returnees. This apparently was not the case in Gary, Indiana. [54]

It seems that most repatriates gravitated back to their native villages on Mexico's central plateau. Given economic conditions in Mexico and the United States, where else could they go? Welfare agencies, labor unions, and immigration officials in the United States had made it quite clear that in times of depression they were not welcome, and they met similar treatment in Mexican border towns. Moreover, the native village followed the traditional mode of life, and it was home after all. Sociologist Emory S. Bogardus, who observed the repatriation movement, estimated that around 5 percent were involved in colonization projects, another 15 percent went to the large cities, and fully 80 percent returned to their original villages. [55]

One of the few pieces of field research to emerge from this period, a master's thesis by James C. Gilbert, a University of Southern California student, contained the general observation that the more successful repatriates were usually colonists who had returned to Mexico before the Depression, carrying with them some practical farming experience and some equipment to pioneer agrarian colonies, such as the Don Martín Dam, an irrigation project located near the tenant-farming region of south Texas. Gilbert's impressions were obtained through personal interviews in 1934 with over a hundred *repatriados* living in Mexican cities, villages and irrigation projects.[56]

Another common misconception about Depression repatriates is that large numbers of them were American citizens, either naturalized or by birth, and that such persons were often induced to accept repatriation in violation of their constitutional rights.[57] No thorough study of Mexican naturalization has yet been done, but from time to time the data presented in the *Annual Reports* of the U.S. Immigration and Naturalization Service, and the comments by various writers on the resistance or indifference of Mexican resident aliens to American citizenship, compared to other immigrant groups, suggests that few repatriates were naturalized citizens.[58] Yet various writers have accused welfare agencies of ignoring the legal rights of citizen repatriates. According to Norman D. Humphrey, writing in 1941, the Detroit Department of Public Welfare, in its zeal to cut case load costs, strongly urged repatriation even in cases involving naturalized citizens. Another charge was that "the rights of American-born children to citizenship in their native land were explicitly denied or not taken into account." Humphrey concluded, much like Carey McWilliams' accounts of Los Angeles repatriation, that relief officials may have saved money, but they failed to rehabilitate "a rightful segment of the American population."[59]

That a number of citizen children were sent back to Mexico on repatriation trains is not disputed. But how many? And under what circumstances? Since migratory families often did not keep birth records, and usually crossed the border without inspection, there was no way of knowing precisely how many repatriate children were born in the United States. Moreover, if relief agencies prepared passenger manifests giving the birthplace of repatriates, they have not yet come to light. Normally the Immigration Service did not require vital facts from Mexicans returning voluntarily to their homeland, and apparently Mexican migration authorities recorded no facts beyond those that established the parents' nationality.

Quite by accident we do have manifests for several hundred Mexicans stranded in Mexicali in late 1931. These indicated that 77 out of 865 persons were American citizens by birth, but only five of this number were over the age of fifteen.[60] Moreover, the Mexican government considered the child of an emigrant couple to be a Mexican citizen no matter where that child may have been born. And according to Mexican family custom, if the father decided to return to Mexico, the children were expected to go along. American immigration officers did not attempt to detain repatriate families with American-born children, for Mexico's policy of dual citizenship was well understood.[61] In any case, for immigration personnel and welfare workers, questions of nationality were made rather meaningless by migratory habits and the practical need to keep the family together.

Whether repatriate children were American citizens or not, American consuls soon had to consider the adjustment problems of repatriate families. Having grown accustomed in many cases to running water, motion pictures, radios, and electricity, as well as neighborhood schools, *repatriados* who returned to peasant villages missed these conveniences and amusements. An American consul reported on the problem:

This office continues to receive applications daily for immigration visas from repatriated Mexican citizens, who give as their reason for wanting to return to the United States, that their children cannot become accustomed to the mode of living in Mexico... that their children cannot have such educational opportunities . . . that they cannot find employment or earn wages that will support their families. . . .62

One consul's analysis of these visa applicants indicated that the maladjustment of repatriate children was often a pretext for gaining reentry as migrant workers:

Many of these Mexican repatriates have moved from place to place in Mexico, and end by claiming that they cannot accustom themselves to living in Mexico after having lived for a long period in the United States. Especially is this true of those families which include grown children born and reared in the United States. These motives, however, are rarely the true ones, as almost invariably it appears, on examination, that the children have never gone to school in the United States.63

U.S. consuls advised Mexican repatriates that if an American-born child maintained continuous residence in Mexico, the child would risk in time loss of American citizenship; yet the parents could not meet visa requirements to return to the United States. American consuls, following the visa control policy inaugurated in late 1928 as an alternative to a quota on Mexican immigration, enforced immigration standards to the letter, rejecting nearly all visa petitions from migrant or unskilled workers.

Some American-born Mexicans, usually older children, remained north of the border with relatives or friends. Others in Mexico, upon reaching a majority of age, were admitted as American citizens. Once gainfully employed in the United States, these young adults, through a provision of immigration law encouraging family reunification, were usually able to bring their parents and siblings back to the United States. 64 This process went on long after the Depression ended. During the Depression decade, however, only 22,319 Mexican immigrants were legally admitted. 65

Aside from the efforts of U.S. consular authorities and the U.S. Border Patrol, the Mexican government itself sought to discourage the return of the repatriates. Having waived customs duties and registration fees, and having provided transportation and, in some cases, employment and land grants, the government had no desire to see the repatriates resume their migratory habits, or to permit the recurrence of a problem in national protection—namely, unemployed and indigent Mexican nationals in a neighboring country. Mexican officials cooperated with official American requests to discourage illegal crossings and the unscrupulous recruiting activities of Mexican *enganchistas*.66 Mexican news media warned *repatriados* and other migrant workers about the dismal economic and social situation of unskilled workers in the United States.67 Also, Mexican state governors were informed that repatriates who had already received government aid should be prevented from recrossing the border.68 But, undoubtedly, many repatriates recrossed a half-guarded frontier and returned to farm or ranch work with former employers, or returned to the barrios of the cities, especially once the economy began to improve after 1934.69

In the meantime, repatriation had declined to a point where by 1937 it no longer attracted the interest of American observers. By that date John Steinbeck was writing *The Grapes of Wrath* and caravans of poverty-stricken Anglo-American families were being driven from small farms in Oklahoma, Texas, Arkansas, Colorado, and elsewhere by the Depression and a prolonged drought. These refugees from the Dust Bowl sought any kind of field work in the western states, where they took the place of Mexican labor crews lost through repatriation or federal relief programs. The problems of native-born migrants and the efforts of some states, like California, Arizona, and Colorado, to close their borders to such interstate refugees then captured the attention of American writers.70

One might have thought that by 1937 repatriation concern would likewise have faded out in Mexico. On the contrary, the administration of President Lázaro Cárdenas (1934-1940) decided to take the initiative and sponsor a unique effort to recruit repatriates for agrarian colonies. One reason was a fear, communicated by Mexican consuls, that members of La Raza who had not become American citizens would be forced off federal relief programs by legislative proposals.71 This was a real possibility during the "recession" of 1937-1938, when WPA rolls again surged to over 3 million. But perhaps more important, the spirit of national socialism initiated by Cárdenas looked upon repatriation as a national duty. His government launched a radical program of agrarian reform and nationalization of natural resources, and this included expropriation of great estates, the development of communal agriculture (*ejidos*), the expansion of irrigation colonies, and Mexican control of oil and mineral wealth. All of this was undertaken in a spirit frequently summarized as "Mexico for the Mexicans," meaning, in particular, the landless peons, including the migrant families *en el otro lado*. All loyal members of La Raza were to share in the reconquest of the national patrimony.72 Moreover, since Cárdenas had opened Mexico to Spanish refugees, he could hardly do less for Mexicans suffering exile in the United States, or so it was believed. And, after all, Mexico seemed more prepared to receive repatriates now that agrarian reform was making land available for small farmers.

In November 1938 Minister of the Interior Ignacio García Tellez toured Texas and other border states, inviting Mexicans to return to their homeland. [73] But repatriates were still suspicious of government promises. At a conference on population in Mexico City in late 1938, the question of why the government should recruit repatriates, when the country could hardly absorb the present small flow of returnees, arose. [74] Others pointed out that many repatriates did not want to settle in communal *ejidos* but wanted private property preferably in irrigation districts. The consuls warned that many repatriates were unsuitable for agrarian experiments, that they should be carefully selected. Otherwise why should they receive preference over other Mexicans seeking agrarian opportunities? [75]

Recruitment was suspended while the Cárdenas government more carefully prepared irrigation colonies and worked out a selective program that would include subsidies and a choice of proprietory or communal land parcels. A huge irrigation development, calculated to take care of most selected repatriates, was being prepared on the lower Rio Grande between Reynosa and Matamoros. The water would come from a series of locks and dams on the river. The colony itself was named "18 de Marzo" in honor of the date in 1938 when Cárdenas nationalized foreign oil properties in Mexico; and now he was taking a fair share of the waters of the Rio Grande, which previously had been monopolized by Texas farmers. Eduardo Chavez, an innovative engineer, was placed in charge of the project. [76]

In the spring of 1939 the Ministry of Foreign Relations sent Undersecretary Ramón Beteta on a recruiting tour of the United States. His mission was to sign up persons with agriculture experience and to provide transportation assistance for family, furniture, farm tools and farm animals. Beteta presented repatriation as an opportunity to help develop *la madre patria*, but, keeping in mind past repatriation failures, he also stressed hard work, sacrifice, and the need for farming experience. [77]

In south Texas, where Mexican sharecroppers, tenant farmers, and migratory farm labor were concentrated, the response was overwhelming. The Cárdenas administration soon feared that the colonies, especially the nearby "18 de Marzo," would be swamped with recruits, and Beteta was advised to be even more cautious in his promises. [78] Elsewhere, as in the cities of Chicago, New York, and Los Angeles, the response was enthusiastic, with many cries of ¡*Viva Mexico!*, but few persons actually signed up, in part because Beteta was reluctant to encourage persons who had little farming knowledge. He doubted that casual laborers, unskilled industrial workers, the unemployed, or persons accustomed to relief payments, would stick out a hard life in agrarian colonies on untried land. He found that Mexicans outside Texas were, in any case, living much better. Jobs were more available in states like Illinois, New York, and California, and relief standards were notably higher. [79]

Work relief on WPA gangs usually provided around $55 a month for a family man. But family aid from county welfare agencies, such as food, clothing, medical care, and rent subsidies, varied greatly by regions, ranging from as low as $5 or $6 a month in some Texas counties to as much as $46 a month in Los Angeles County. In San Antonio, a winter camp for migrant labor, Mexican workers—men, women, and children—received only pennies a day for such menial jobs as shelling pecans (although they could eat all they wanted). If a man was not fortunate enough to get WPA work, his family was forced to seek small dabs of relief and food commodities. Mexican families in California were much better off. The State Relief Agency gave cash payments to qualified households, up to $51 a month, according to need. And growers were paying around $.22 an hour, partly to attract people from relief or WPA. A 1935 study by the WPA found some 55,000 Mexicans on relief rolls. Many of them had become American citizens meanwhile. Naturally many of them were reluctant to leave relief for an uncertain short-term job. [80]

Beteta, a graduate of the University of Texas, understood conditions in the United States. He knew that Mexico, however earnest her patriotic intentions, could do little to improve the situation of Mexican groups over the border, particularly in California. After conferring with Governor Olson and getting his word that publicly funded employment programs would not be closed to Mexican nationals, Beteta departed without attempting a recruiting tour. By then he had been warned that repatriation funds were limited (approached on the question of sharing transportation costs, the American government meanwhile had refused), and he was reminded that there were more than enough eager agriculturists in poverty-stricken south Texas alone to overrun Mexico's few irrigation colonies. [81]

During the Cárdenas years over 40,000 Mexican nationals returned to the homeland as repatriates, most of them attracted by Cárdenas' recruitment policy. The "18 de Marzo" colony on the Rio Grande delta, where each head of family received fifty acres of land with irrigation rights, was by far the largest and most successful of all repatriation colonies. [82]

The Beteta mission was the last major effort of the Mexican government to promote massive repatriation through agrarian reform. The mission also served to modify popular beliefs concerning unfortunate expatriates "suffering exile" in the neighboring republic. When the Minister of Internal Affairs (Gobernación) stated that discrimination against Mexicans in the United States, and actual living conditions, were not so terrible that they would want to leave, Mexican newspapers, which had presented that viewpoint to the general public, were somewhat surprised, especially after the administration's buildup for recruitment. One newspaper reacted thus: "While the statement surprises us, we accept it, because it must be assumed . . . that the Government possesses recent and reliable data regarding this matter."[83]

By the end of Cárdenas' term, repatriation policy had evolved from one of intermittent and sentiment efforts to recover La Raza in the United States to a more realistic and selective policy encouraging individuals with useful farming and industrial skills to return to *la madre patria*. This is Mexico's current repatriation policy.

Notes

1. John M. Blum et al., *The National Experience* (2nd ed., New York: Harcourt Brace and World, 1968), p. 664; and Dwight L. Dummond, *America in Our Time, 1896-1946* (New York: Henry Holt Co., 1947), pp. 448-449, 464. The Anglo-American systems of local relief and immigrant aid, which have some roots in the "poor laws" of sixteenth-century England, are indicated by Edith Abbott (ed.), *Historical Aspects of the Immigration Problem* (University of Chicago Press, 1926); and also in another work edited by the same author, *Immigration: Select Documents and Case Records* (University of Chicago, 1924). The influence of the Great Depression on the evolution from a system of local and private relief to a system sponsored by the federal government is also described by Grace Abbott, *From Relief to Social Security* (University of Chicago, 1941).

2. Quoted by Dummond, *America in Our Time*, p. 448.

3. An account of U.S. immigration law and repatriation questions is given by Carreras de Velasco, *Los mexicanos que devolvió la crisis*, pp. 32-33, 62-66, 147-148.

4. See, for example, McWilliams' account of repatriation pressures in Los Angeles County, "Getting Rid of the Mexican," *American Mercury* 28 (March 1933, 322-324. This and other works by McWilliams have been critically evaluated by Abraham Hoffman, "Mexican Repatriation Statistics: Some Suggested Alternatives to Carey McWilliams," *Western Historical Quarterly* 4 (October 1972), 391-404. Typical of Chicano interpretations of repatriation would be Vilma S. Martínez, "Illegal Immigration and the Labor Force: An Historical and Legal View," *American Behavioral Scientist* 19 (January-February 1976), 335-350.

5. Consul General T. D. Bowman, Mexico City, to State Department, August 28, 1933, National Archives, RG 59, file 811.111 Mexico/1069. Bowman used data supplied by the Mexican Ministry of National Economy.

6. R. F. Boyce, American Consul, Nuevo Laredo, to State Department, November 26, 1930, RG 59, 311.1215/17.

7. J. E. Holler, American Consul, Monterrey (?) to State Department, October 17, 1931, RG 59, 311.1215/25.

8. M. W. Altaffer, American Consul, Nogales, to State Department, March 7, 1930, RG 59, 812.5511/93.

9. W. P. Blocker, American Consul, Ciudad Juárez, to State Department, January 3, 1931, RG 59, 812.5511/102.

10. P. H. Foster, American Consul, Piedras Negras, to State Department, January 27, 1931, RG 59, 812.5511/105.

11. Robert N. McLean, "Goodbye, Vicente!" *Survey*, 66:3 (May 1, 1931), 182.

12. *La Opinión* (Los Angeles), January 12, 1931.

13. Gordon and Rosenfield, *Immigration Law*, pp. 244, 501-505, 664.

14. *New York Times*, January 6, 1931.

15. Abraham Hoffman, "Stimulus to Repatriation: The 1931 Federal Deportation Drive and the Los Angeles Mexican Community," *Pacific Historical Review* 42 (May 1973), 205-219.

16. The most complete study thus far of repatriation from southern California is Abraham Hoffman's "The Repatriation of Mexican Nationals." This work in revised form has been published by the University of Arizona Press, Tucson, in 1974 under the title *Unwanted Mexican Americans in the Great Depression: Repatriation Pressures, 1929-1939*. One of the few community studies is Neil Betten and Raymond A. Mohl, "From Discrimination to Repatriation: Mexican Life in Gary, Indiana, During the Great Depression," *Pacific Historical Review* 42 (August 1973), 370-388.

17. Hoffman, *Unwanted Mexican Americans*, chap. 6.

18. The facts of repatriation planning by U.S. agencies and Mexican consuls seem to contradict McWilliams' indignant account of repatriation from southern California, where, according to him, trains were hurriedly packed with hapless families to save relief funds—"Getting Rid of the Mexicans," pp. 322-324.

19. According to field interviews of August 23 and December 20-21, 1970, and July 1-2, 1971, by Arthur F. Corwin, Department of History, University of Connecticut, with several repatriate families settled permanently in agrarian colonies in Colonia Anahuac, state of Nuevo Leon, and in the colonies of Valle Hermoso and "18 de Marzo" in the state of Tamaulipas.

20. Norman D. Humphrey, "Mexican Repatriation from Michigan: Public Assistance in Historical Perspective," *Social Service Review* 15 (September 1941), 502 ff.

21. *New York Times*, March 20, 1934; "Back to the Homeland," *Survey* 69 (January 1933), 39; and *The Mexican in Minnesota, A Report to Governor Elmer Anderson* (St. Paul: Governor's Interracial Commission, 1953), pp. 44-47. The Minnesota report originally appeared in 1947. See also Betten and Mohl, "From Discrimination to Repatriation . . . Gary, Indiana."

22. See, for example, I. F. Wixon, Deputy Commissioner of Immigration, to Secretary of State, October 5, 1937, RG 59, 150.126/370; R. Wormuth, American Consul, Nuevo Laredo, to Secretary of State, February 21, 1938, RG 59, 150.126/273; and *Annual Report of the Secretary of Labor 1936*, p. 97.

23. Taylor, *Mexican Labor . . . Migration Statistics* IV, 23-49.

24. A report of August 15, 1932, RG 59 811.111/57, Enclosure 1, gives a town-by-town listing of arrivals and departures for February 1932.

25. Taylor, *Migration Statistics* IV, 45.

26. See Donald L. Zelman's informative "Mexican Migrants and Relief in Depression California: Grower Reaction to Public Relief Policies as They Affected Mexican Migration," *The Journal of Mexican American History* 5 (1975), 1-23; and Hoffman, *Unwanted Mexican Americans*, pp. 156-164.

27. Based on RG 59, 811.111, Mexico Reports 59, 80, 99, 122, 141, 142; and Hoffman, "Mexican Repatriation Statistics," p. 399. For slightly varying Mexican figures, see Carreras de Velasco, *Los mexicanos que devolvió la crisis*, pp. 173-176.

28. Harry Pangburn, American Vice Consul, Ciudad Juárez, to State Department, January 17, 1935, RG 59, 811.111/1188.

29. Taylor, *Mexican Labor . . . Migration Statistics* IV, 24-25.

30. McWilliams, "Getting Rid of the Mexicans," pp. 322-323.

31. Estimate based on U.S. consular correspondence during the 1930s in RG 59, e.g., S. E. McMillin, American Consul, Piedras Negras, to State Department, October 11, 1933, 811.111/1090(?); R. Wormuth, American Consul, Nuevo Laredo, to Secretary of State, February 21, 1938, RG 59, 150.126/79-150-26/273; and on field interviews during 1969 and 1970 by Arthur F. Corwin with repatriate families in states of Nuevo Leon and Tamaulipas.

32. See articles by Robert N. McLean: "Goodbye, Vicente!" p. 183; "Hard Times Oust the Mexican," *Mexican Life* 7 (September 1931), 31; and "The Mexican Return," *Nation*, 135 (August 24, 1932, 166.

33. *Annual Report of the Secretary of Labor*, 1932, p. 72.

34. National Archives, RG 85, 55091/6 contains examples of requests for federally supported repatriations.

35. See tables in Hoffman, "Mexican Repatriation Statistics," pp. 402-403.

36. For official Mexican statistics see: *Memoria de la Secretaría de Relaciones Exteriores, 1931-1932*, p. 314; and *1933-1934*, pp. 437-438; and Carreras de Velasco, *Los mexicanos que devolvio la crisis*, pp. 173-176.

37. For example, McWilliams' oversimplified impressions have been repeated by Grebler, *Mexican Immigrants to teh United States*, p. 26; and Betten and Mohl provide an interpretation similar to that of McWilliams, see "From Discrimination to Repatriation. . . , Gary, Indiana."

38. Hoffman, *Unwanted Mexican Americans*, p. 72.

39. For the role of the mexican consuls and the Secretaría de Gobernación and other government departments in subsidizing repatriation, see Carreras de Velasco, *Los mexicanos que devolvió la crisis*, pp. 73-86, *passim*.

40. Ibid.

41. See F. Suastegui, "Irrigation Projects in Mexico," *Pan Pacific Progress* 9 (July 1928), 4; and a field survey of repatriates in irrigation colonies and elsewhere by Gilbert, "A Field Study in Mexico."

42. S. Sokobin, American Consul, Saltillo, to State Department, November 5, 1931, RG 59, 311.1215/26.

43. For Mexican attitudes toward repatriates and the Yanqui Colossus, see Carreras de Velasco, *Los mexicanos que devolvio la crisis*.

44. *Excelsior* (Mexico City), June 2, 1932.

45. Hoffman, *Unwanted Mexican Americans*, Chap. 8; and Carreras de Velasco, *Los mexicanos que devolvió la crisis*, Chap. 2.

46. See, for example, Norman D. Humphrey, "Mexican Repatriation from Michigan"; and Betten and Mohl, "From Discrimination to Repatriation . . . Gary, Indiana."

47. *Los Angeles Express*, April 24, 1931.

48. *Detroit Free Press*, October 8, 1932.

49. Quoted in McLean, "Goodbye, Vicente!" p. 182.

50. National Archives, RG 59, 811.111, contains various reports by American consuls of actual and proposed projects.

51. Examples of decrees concerning customs exemptions and eligibility are given in Carreras de Velasco, *Los mexicanos que devolvió la crisis*, pp. 153-156, 171-172.

52. Humphrey, "Mexican Repatriation from Michigan," pp. 504 ff.

53. W. F. Watkins to R. C. White, State Department (?), February 21, 1931, RG 85, 55739/674.

54. Betten and Mohl, "From Discrimination to Repatriation ... Gary, Indiana," pp. 380-388.

55. Bogardus, *The Mexican in the United States*, p. 9.

56. Gilbert, "A Field Study in Mexico." Taylor also interviewed repatriates in his study of *A Spanish-Mexican Peasant Community: Arandas*.

57. For instance, Wayne Moquin and Charles Van Doren (eds.), with Feliciano Rivera, *A Documentary History of the Mexican Americans* (New York: Praeger, 1971), p. 294; and Humphrey, "Mexican Repatriation from Michigan," pp. 512-513.

58. Leo Grebler, "The Naturalization of Mexican Immigrants in the United States," *International Migration Review*, I (Fall 1966), 17-32.

59. Humphrey, "Mexican Repatriation from Michigan," pp. 512-513.

60. Correspondence and manifests are found in RG 85, 55739/674.

61. Ibid.

62. S. E. McMillin, American Consul, Piedras Negras, to State Department, January 16, 1935, RG 59, 812.5511/16.

63. S. E. McMillin to State Department, June 1, 1934, RG 59, 311.1215/59.

64. R. D. Wormuth, American Consul, Nuevo Laredo, to State Department, May 12, 1932, RG 59, 150.062 Public Charge/414.

65. INS, *Annual Reports*, Table 13.

66. A. F. Tower, American Consul General, Mexico City, to all consul officers in Mexico, Circular No. 421, July 14, 1933, RG, 811.111/1056.

67. Joseph Daniels, U.S. Ambassador, Mexico City, to Secretary of State, July 18, 1933, No. 368, RG 59, 811.504/423.

68. J. S. Littell, American Consul (place unknown) to State Department, April 6, 1932, RG 59, 311.1215/32.

69. R. Wormuth, American Consul, Nuevo Laredo, to Secretary of State, February 21, 1938, RG 59, 150.126/273.

70. Paul S. Taylor, for one, turned his attention from a receding Mexican labor migration to poverty-stricken Anglo-American migrants; see, for example, Taylor (with photographer Dorothea Lange), *An American Exodus; a Record of Human Erosion in the Thirties* (1939), revised and republished by Yale University Press for the Oakland Museum, 1969); and his "Migratory Agricultural Workers on the Pacific Coast," *American Sociological Review* 3 (April 1938), 225-232.

71. Memorandum from Chargé d' Affaires ad interim, U.S. Embassy, Mexico City, for Lawrence Duggan, Chief of the Division of American Republics, State Department, July 22, 1937, RG, 311.12/503.

72. A survey of Mexican repatriation policy and colonization efforts in the 1930s is given by González Navarro, "Efectos sociales," 536-558. See also Cárdenas, *El problema de los territorios federales* ... ; Loyo, *La política demográfica*; and *Memoria de la Secretaria de Relaciones Exteriores, 1938-1939*, II, p. 187.

73. R. Wormuth, American Consul, Nuevo Laredo, to Secretary of State, December 23, 1938, RG 59, 311.1215/106.

74. J. B. Stewart, Consul General(?), Mexico City, to State Department, December 23, 1938, RG 59, 311.1215/108.

75. See report on repatriation policy sent by José Angel Ceniceros, Subsecretario,

Relaciones Exteriores, to Francisco J. Mugica, Secretario de Comunicaciones, September 11, 1935; and "Memorandum sobre repatriación" by Rafael de la Colina, Consul General in San Antonio, September 7, 1935, in Archivo de Relaciones Exteriores (ARE), B/524.5(73)19, B-8-10, 1935 and B. 1524.5(73)/91. See also article on Beteta mission and Mexican objectives in *Los Angeles Herald*, July 17, 1939.

76. Mexico City, Department of Publicity and Propaganda (DAPP) press release, April 5, 1939; *La Prensa* (San Antonio), April 11, 1939; *El Continental* (El Paso), April 13, 1939; and interview with Eduardo Chávez, Director of the "18 de Marzo" irrigation and colonization project, by Mercedes Carreras de Velasco and Arthur F. Corwin, in Mexico City, July 15, 1971.

77. According to interviews by Arthur F. Corwin with repatriate families in states of Nuevo Leon and Tamaulipas in August and December, 1970, and July, 1971. See also Ramón Beteta al Oficial Mayor de al Secretaría de Relaciones Exteriores, Ernesto Hidalgo, August 6, 1939, ARE, IV/524.5(72-73), IV-744-49.

78. Ernesto Hidalgo al Licenciado Ramon Beteta, June 20, 1939, ARE, IV-744-49, IV-/524.5(72-73) 1939, 3321/Com No. 3391.

79. Beteta, New York City, a Ernesto Hidalgo, May 6, May 10, and May 11, 1939, ARE, IV-744-49, IV-/524.5(72-73) 1939, 3321/Com No. 3391, and attachments.

80. Unpublished research paper on "Mexican Labor and Settlement in Southern California, 1910-1940," by Donald L. Zelman, Department of Social Sciences, Tarleton State University, Stephenville, Texas.

81. Eduardo Hay, Secretario de Relaciones Exteriores, a Ignacio García Tellez, June 20, 1939, ARE, IV/524.5(72:00)2, IV-744-8, 1939, No. 3389.

82. According to interview by Mercedes Carreras de Velasco and Arthur F. Corwin with Eduardo Chávez, Mexico City, July 15, 1971.

83. *Ultimas Noticias* (Mexico City), April 5, 1939.

9/ SOME COMMENTS ON THE MEXICAN MIGRATORY SUBCULTURE

Ernesto Galarza

... I want to thank the chairman for the invitation that brings me here to-day ...

I realize, however, that the subject of this particular hearing—Mexican farmworkers, their culture and their powerlessness in American society—is an area that is strewn with conceptual banana peelings. ... I do not know of any scientific research that has been done on farmworkers in relation to culture and power, as there has been about their wages, housing, and employment conditions. Accordingly, I want to prepare my ground as prudently as I can with some preliminary comments .... Mexican farmworkers in the Southwest today are the product of instability that goes back to their own country. They are people who are ejected from the social system into which they were born and the true culture which they inherited. I make the point in my statement also that this instability is also characterized by dispossession of another kind and that is the dispossession of the wealth which they earn through their labor.

The wage systems in agriculture which I have seen and studied for the last 40 years are wage systems designed to dispossess the farm worker from a portion of the wealth to which he is legitimately entitled. I also make the point that the farm labor group as a group, especially the Mexican sector, is a kind of an escalator system. That is to say, in the last 60 years we have had a generation of farmworkers which grows old on the job in the industry; a second generation of farmworkers who begin to understand that the life of farm labor is not for

Taken by the editor from "Prepared Statement" of Dr. Ernesto Galarza, originally published in U.S. Senate, *Migrant and Seasonal Farmworker Powerlessness. Hearings Before the Subcommittee on Migratory Labor . . . on the Migrant Subculture, July 28, 1969, 91st Cong., 1st and 2d Sess., Part 2* (Washington, D.C.: Government Printing Office, 1970), 460-483.

them, but are not quite able to take it out of there. Then there comes a third generation, which is the generation in which we are today that moves out at the top. They go to the cities and become industrial or service workers. . . .

It is my belief, based on a lifetime of work and study among them, that the Mexican agricultural workers of the South and Middle West exhibit cultural characteristics that may be called Mexican. These characteristics affect in many ways the manner in which they deal with American society and the manner in which it deals with them. These traits are probably in decline, as acculturation proceeds, but they are still sufficiently real to demand our attention. These traits are the Spanish language, intercessory religion, family cohesion, family labor, patron system, a pretechnological view of production and work, a reluctance to act publicly and to act organizationally, education as nonutilitarian, an ethics of verguenza, and moral obligation as a function of palabra.

Let me discuss each of these, very briefly and speculatively, since I am now entering fully on the slippery ground I mentioned before. Within their own group Mexican farm laborers communicate in Spanish. This is undoubtedly the strongest bond between locales, braceros, wetbacks, and green-card commuters. The Spanish speech brought to the New World by soldiers and priests has been stamped, in the course of more than three centuries, with unmistakable Mexican word forms, meanings, and intonations. Until this mark is rubbed out by acculturation, these forms, meanings, and intonations provide an instant key to ethnic identity. In many unnoticed colonias Spanish speech still flows in the sensitive style of true conversation, the platica. One can still hear the platica seasoned with traditional proverbs and folk sayings that convey something even deeper than identity. One who knows these proverbs and uses them discretely and aptly is a Mexican who has tasted the marrow of wisdom of the ethnic group. "Mas pronto cae un hablador que un cojo—sooner a man will fall who lies than one who limps."

However vital this ancestral speech may be, it is of little use in dealing with the alien culture that surrounds and engulfs the farmworkers. Everyday activities for which there are no inherited words but which are identified in English stimulate the invention of half-and-half expressions. We have *locales* for "local laborers," *chanza* for "job," *jale* for "deal," *ganga* for "crew," *raite* for the "day haul," *bonos* for "bonus," *cleme* for the "claim," or allotted work in a field, and so on.

These are, one might say, in-house adaptations of language to deal with the ordinary items of work experience. They are not a vocabulary through which the Mexicans can deal with the outside agencies that determine production, investment, allocations of various sorts, administrative supervision, regulation and the distribution of the wealth created by the industrial operation as a whole. I know of no common and widely understood equivalents in Spanish or quasi-Spanish for "congressional hearing," "wage determination," "Farm

Placement Service," or "referral." In short, the Spanish of the Mexican farm laborers does not have the conceptual tools to deal on equal terms with economic reality in its broadest scope.

This leads me to the next point, which is that the Mexican farmworker still looks upon the family unit also as economic and not merely a cultural unit. That is to say, they tend to think in terms of family labor, which means that each and every member of the family, including the very young, have to contribute not only to the psychological unity of the family, but to its economic survival.

The family is still the principal bond of the Mexican farm laborer to society. The extended family is in his Mexican tradition and he clings to it even though it is becoming more and more the extenuated family. There is a hierarchy within the family and one of its functions is to see to it that the family confronts the world as a unit. To say that in the year 1968 the López family worked for XYZ Corporation picking tomatoes, is in a sense to juxtapose sixteenth-century Mexico with twentieth-century America. As the Mexican farm labor family moves from crop to crop it is abiding by an ancestral custom, and it is reacting to an ancestral need—the need to wring from each member his share of productivity to keep the family alive.

This form of family utility collects a heavy toll, especially from the children. Public schools are located in fixed places, whereas migrant children travel over the face of America; the gap between the two has never been closed. The family can only educate the child in work. It cannot induct the child into a stable community in transit from labor camp to labor camp. A single breadwinner for a farm labor family obviously cannot earn the income necessary for even a low level of living at the wages which have prevailed over the past half century.

This leads us to the reasons for the revival of the *patrón* system in the Southwest. I have no trouble at all in remembering when I was five years of age what the *patrón* meant to us in the little town in Mexico where I was born. The *patrón* was a very vivid figure. He was a man who rode around on a horse with a Winchester hanging from his saddle and a revolver from his belt. Not only was he the authority figure, but the man with whom the campesino made the job connection. If it were not for the *patrón*, you couldn't have a job.

In the Southwest, Mexicans rediscover the *patrón*, but in a different incarnation. He is the labor contractor and the crew leader, and in time he becomes what I call the *patroncito*, the little boss, who accumulates a little capital and is able to play the role of protector and keeper, and a sort of helper; he makes loans to his workers, bails them out of jail, feeds them on credit, lets them live in camp through the winter months until the harvest season and then collects the back rent.

Having been a farm labor organizer for some fifteen years in some ten states of the Union, but particularly with Mexicans, I am convinced that the concept of organized action is not in the culture of the Mexican worker. To join an organization, to take out a card and pay dues, to go to meetings, to go through the whole process of what we know is necessary to the American trade union movement, is really alien to a Mexican fresh out of Mexico and remains strange to him until he has been here at least two generations. The reason is that most of these workers in the last 40 years have come from rural Mexico where the small village is the unit of organization and culture.

In the American Southwest there was nothing quite like this village institution or rural paternalism. The job connection over the border by and large was brought about by the contractor and the crew leader, who, as we said, became *patroncitos*. Just above the contractors another layer of organization was introduced—the association of employers, the contractors acting as brokers between the two levels. In this way the Mexican farm labor market, and, in many respects, the farm labor society, was organized.

One can understand, as a cultural matter, why the farmworker family adapted to this pattern, and why certain historical conditions made it difficult for Mexican field workers to adopt promptly the trade union organization which by the 1940s had become accepted in American life. Those of us who have worked in the Mexican rural community, attempting to organize farm laborers into unions, were well aware of the cultural and practical obstacles we faced. Progress was very slow because of this "cultural drag." While the employer associations were applying organization as a fine art, and while contractors served a fragmented mass of farmworkers, union organization for us was a kind of resistance movement and educational crusade combined.

When I mention education I come to another cultural trait I have frequently found among the older Mexican farmworkers. In their sense of what the word means, education was not instrumental. Education did not prepare one in some practical way to earn a living. Rather education is seen as a social discipline that teaches one the manners and customs that keep the proper or respectful distances between individuals, depending on the circumstances. Thus a man can be *bien educado* and yet be illiterate; he can be a doctor of philosophy and also a boor. How to explain to a group of Mexican farmworkers what one means by a course in labor education? I have often had to grapple with the question. How to induce men in their fifties to accept instruction from a teacher 25 years their junior? How do you overcome the indignity of sitting down in a class on collective bargaining when it is well established that classroom attendance is for children only?

Two other things I want to mention. One is a psycological attitude, the culture trait of the Mexicans so far as technology is concerned. Culturally and given his background as a Mexican, his ancestry, the Mexican does not regard work as anything other than a physiological input. Work is putting your muscle and your nerve into a productive operation. Work is not something that machines do, but that people do. Work is a way of life and not a technology. And some Mexican farmworkers of the older generation have a cultural hang-up, a cultural drawback in that they automatically think of themselves as people born to physically spill their sweat and use up their muscle because this is the only way in which society can produce wealth. And it is very hard for them, but they do learn slowly that wealth can also be produced by machines and that you can also make a living, a very comfortable one sometimes, by owning machines and never doing a lick of work, as they understand it, in your life.

This cultural trait is important because along with it goes a deep respect for putting in an 8- or 9- or 10-hour day, sweating it out and laboring at some kind of a task. And it is an interesting thing. People who consider the Mexican farm laborers lazy and lackadaisical and irresponsible don't know that these people consider people who own machines and who never lift their hands or more than press buttons to make them work, in their opinion, they are the lazy ones. Here you have an almost perfect contrast between cultural traits and cultural attitudes. I bring this into the discussion in order to make the further point that the Mexican does not make a very great effort to become an owner of machines, so that he may live through the labor of machines. . . .

In the Mexican culture originally and as a survival in the Southwest among Mexican farmworkers, especially the elderly, there is a concept of *verguenza*. In its simplest meaning you might say it is a sense of shame, but it is more than that—a very complicated cultural idea. Unless we understand this, we fail to understand why, for instance, it is so difficult to find farmworkers who are willing to appear in public meetings and make known their grievances, distresses and anxieties. They feel *verguenza* in standing up before a meeting, because there is a cultural tendency among other Mexicans to say that this man is showing off, he is pretending to be better than the rest. This keeps these people from legitimately telling a public official (like members of Congress) what is on their minds and what is happening to them.

Mexican farmworkers are overwhelmingly Roman Catholic. The sacraments of the Church still ritualize the high moments of their lives—baptism, communion, matrimony, death. Between these high points are crises in which ritual does not intervene, on-the-spot clutches in which there is an eyeball-to-eyeball confrontation between the believer and his guardian saint. What is demanded of the saint is instant and efficacious intercession to ward off harm. This is the cultural answer which the farmworker invokes in his economic relations with agribusiness, especially if the worker is a wetback or bracero.

I want to tell you of an experience that illustrates this perfectly. I attended a meeting of braceros some years ago where there were a hundred men in the hall—this took place in their barracks—at the front of the dormitory they had erected a little altar. On the top of that they had put a figurine of the Virgin of Guadalupe. They were praying to the Virgin that their contracts might be renewed and that they might receive a wage increase of five cents an hour. I have no doubt that these men deeply and truly felt that the Virgin of Guadalupe was listening to them that very moment. And afterward I made an effort to find out whether their employers and contractors had been listening to the Virgin, because I am sure the Virgin responded to the workers, but I could find no evidence that the employers had responded to the Virgin. This means that from a cultural point of view you have these hundred men reduced to an utter extremity, their only cultural recourse an appeal to their saint, whom they really believed would intercede with them vis-a-vis the employers. So, when you look at the culture of agribusinessmen, they were not in a habit of holding services for the Virgin of Guadalupe to find out what the farmworkers were asking.

This leads me directly to answer the question about Chávez [César Chávez, head of the Huelga Movement that seeks to unionize farm labor]. The Delano movement, among other things, has put together a pattern of cultures and traits which up to now has been very effective and among this is this religious appeal. This symbolism has unquestionably given dignity, hope, and power to the movement. But, of course, I must also point out that an important reason why the Delano people have been able to hold together is that they invoked and received the intercession of the American labor movement and the combination thus far has proved to be effective and very promising. I hope they both remain in the picture, both the Virgin of Guadalupe and Mr. George Meany [President of the American Federation of Labor].

Mexican labor emigration dates roughly from 1910. Within these scant 60 years, the Mexican farm labor class has experienced the worst of all disasters that can overtake a culture—instability. These people have had no permanent and secure habitat. Indeed, cyclical dispossession has been their lot. The land that was theirs before 1848 became an alien land after the Treaty of Guadalupe. Since then they have been dispossessed of the value of their labor by a wage system designed for that purpose. They have been displaced by the advance of technology. They are being dislodged again from rural communities in which they had found refuge by the steady advance of freeways and the lowering upon their heads of the real estate boom.

This has not been all. A culture can be transmitted only in one way. It passes from generation to generation more rather than less intact, more rather than less integral. But among Mexican farm laboring families what has been happening is clear: the sons of the original migrants begin to suspect that laboring for American agribusiness is for their parents. Their sons in turn become convinced that it is "for the birds." The third generation leaves the land for the city. Rural cultural transmission comes to a dead stop when they migrate to the cities. We may speak of this as an escalator routine, in which the young and discouraged are continuously leaving at the top and new migrants from Mexico are continuously getting on at the bottom. And I may add that what I call the top of the escalator is only the threshold of some teeming, poverty-stricken barrio.

I repeat that under these historic conditions the Mexican farm laborers, as a group, have not and could not have developed a culture of their own. They could not and have not acculturated their young in the way that all societies acculturate them and thus survive. They have rather been subject to the special mode of acculturation that takes place when one culture is plumped into the midst of another on unequal terms. To make a living, the members of the culture-away-from-home must accept terms and conditions that enable them to survive and little more. With this type of acculturation there is relegation, of which discrimination and segregation are merely psychological and administrative techniques. We now have a superculture and a subculture.

There is something else I would like to point out in this connection. We can speak of farmworkers in this country as a class but we cannot speak of them as a homogeneous cultural group. Among farm laborers there are Mexicans, Filipinos, Negroes, Indians and Appalachian whites. But there is more than this. Within the Mexican farm labor component there are cultural variations. The self-styled locales are workers who have spent most of their lives in this country and on the land, undergoing the accultural extrusion of which I have spoken. There are the "green card commuters" who, if they are border professionals, have begun to mingle in their attitudes and behavior the Mexican and the American. There are the outcast wetbacks, an underground society drawn from the poorest of the poor in interior Mexico. All of these persons have common cultural origins, if we take them back far enough. But it is important to note that they have very different survival tactics. They are all competing with one another for farm jobs, and when I say "tactics of survival" I mean that locales, wetbacks, and greencarders are more separated from one another by such competition than they are bound by common cultural traits.

I want to again qualify this brief summary of cultural traits. Transported to the American scene they tend to become cultural vestiges doomed in the long run to disappear. That they persist in some degree is explained by the fact that the Mexican emigration is only half a century removed from its roots. I believe that on the whole they are still sufficiently operative to account for some of the helplessness of Mexican farm laborers as a class.

How is this to be explained, in cultural terms? It is to be explained by comparing them with the corresponding traits of the dominant American society. This society is English speaking. Its important business is carried on in that language by right of conquest and of sovereignty. Fluency in English is a condition for holding your own. Lacking such fluency you can be misunderstood in two languages, not just in one. Until he achieves it the Spanish speaker must do all the fumbling. It is he who must pay the penalties of a miscarriage in communication. This is one of the penalties of migration, and I suppose it is imposed under all flags. All that I am trying to point out is that here, in a cultural ambivalence, there is already an enormous loss of social power.

As to religion, we see the Mexican laborer imploring his patron saint. We also see the American employer sending his congressman a telegram. Some

Mexicans may still believe in the efficacy of intercessory religion. No American executive relies on the saints in this fashion. He has devised and perfected very mundane technics for running the show. For some 40 years or more I have observed the test of both systems in corporate agriculture in the Southwest. The saints have lost every round.

There is the same contrast between concepts of the primary social unit. With the Mexican it is still the family. With the American it is the corporation, now fast becoming not only the provider but also the arbiter of style, the molder of attitudes, the keeper of the inheritance, and the giver of values. The object of both of these styles of the primary social unit is cohesion. Both apply it to production. But the life styles resulting from each stand worlds apart. This is so obvious I need not belabor the point. I will rest with the opinion that increasingly in America the securities of corporations appear to thrive as the insecurities of the family increase. Mexican farm labor families are, of course, not the only casualties of this process. They are only a special illustration.

The differences as to work and production ethics are equally sharp. As I have said the only property the Mexican has is the property he works for. It is clear, by contrast, that in the affluent American society the kind of property that counts increasingly is the property that works for you. Do we not have here a cultural difference of very great implications? I believe we do. Given the trend in America in the distribution of the kind of property that works for you it would appear that those who do not grasp the difference are culturally retarded.

Now as to the differences in cultural stress on organization. In the small and relatively compact rural Mexican society the folk life is the social organization. In a society of more than 200 million people living on a vast territory—a society which is, moreover, a quilt of cultures rather than a culture—conflicting interests and cross-grained values, in trying to prevail, make more and more use of better and better organization. The mechanics, the efficiency, of organization become the vital things. Those who do not master them will languish, if indeed they do not perish. The Mexican farm laborers are not experts in this matter. Their employers, the agribusinessmen, are. What expertise the laborers have has been gained in spite of the overwhelming financial and political resources marshaled to prevent their organization.

I want to dispose now of the subject of cultural traits before concluding with some observations on powerlessness.

America is not yet a seamless culture but a texture of many cultures. Upon these there has been superimposed a dazzling civilization. The focus of this civilization is technology. And the command of this technology is in the hands of the arch-azoics. The arch-azoics are persons who abhor "harps diversely framed" and who do not tremble into thought but at the thought that others might think. Their world is not animated nature but nature synchronized, sanforized and computerized. A life style of this kind, to be created and maintained and advanced, requires very great power. We must all be disciplined to pay the necessary tribute to it. Its technique is superb organization. Its instrument is science. Its goal is thrust—thrust into Vietnam, thrust to the Moon, thrust to Neptune—no matter, so long as it is thrust. And its requirement is power.

The farmworkers of the southwest—Mexicans, Filipinos, blacks, white Appalachians—are not exempt from this power. They are peculiarly less resistant to it because of their cultural atavisms. Aside from this peculiarity they are in the same condition as millions of other Americans, nonfarm workers and nonethnics. There is no other way in which I can understand the powerlessness of America's minorities today.

10/ SHADOW LABOR FORCE: MEXICAN WORKERS IN THE AMERICAN ECONOMY
Arthur F. Corwin and
Walter A. Fogel

> The point here is that this exploitation was institutionalized . . .
>
> Jorge A. Bustamante[1]

Some Historic Consequences of Mexican Labor Use

A general history of Mexican labor covering all facets of its long-term impact on the American economy would be a difficult task, since so much of this labor has been migratory in nature and often unreported. Here we intend only to suggest some of the more obvious socioeconomic consequences that have manifested themselves during the past sixty years or more—for example, the phenomenon of labor displacement.

In Texas Taylor found that by World War I Negro labor, which had moved west with the southern cotton frontier, had come to a halt, and incoming peons from Mexico were actually displacing black workers, and some whites, in central and south Texas, thus establishing a new labor frontier that was virtually an extension of Mexico. This process was facilitated by the recruitment of black labor for northern industrial cities during the war and following the 1917 immigration act which had cut off cheap labor from Europe. Significantly, in this same period as cotton moved north to the Texas panhandle and west into the river valleys of New Mexico, Arizona, and California, moving with it were Mexican campesinos, not Negro migrants and sharecroppers. By 1920 the Mexican frontier in agrilabor extended across all the border states, and even into the beet fields of Colorado and Kansas.[2]

In south Texas there occurred another displacement effect that would have far-reaching socioeconomic implications for many states of the union. In this depressed region, as peon families trekked in, more so after World War I, earlier Mexican settlers and their children faced subsistence wages, or, in many instances, displacement from employment in railways, ranches, farms, domestic service, and common labor of many kinds. Many "Tex-Mex people" were pushed into migratory labor streams that foraged deeper and deeper inland in search of better pay; others were recruited by agents of northern agricultural and railway industries. By the mid-1920s south Texas had become the largest migrant labor pool in the United States.[3] Following harvest cycles and Spanish-speaking crew leaders, Tex-Mex migrants swung into California, Oregon, Colorado, Minnesota, Illinois, Michigan, Ohio, and a dozen other states, including Florida, most returning to winter in Texas shanty towns or in east Los Angeles, always some settling out of the stream in other work, their places immediately filled by other displaced persons, or fresh recruits from Mexico—and so to the present day.[4]

During the bracero program, 1942-1964, recorded out-migration of Texas farm workers, nearly all of Mexican origin, averaged around 100,000 a year, but with the end of bracero recruiting, the number rose to around 167,000 in 1967. At that date Texas migrants were working in over thirty states. Since then mechanization in agriculture and anti-poverty programs have reduced the recorded annual job placements to less than 30,000 by 1972.[5] However, it was likely that three or four times that number of south Texas "freewheelers" and wetbacks were slipping into the stream uncounted. In fact, the introverted migratory subculture of the Tex-Mex border region, with its grapevine contacts in Mexico and exploitative middlemen, has always frustrated efforts by farm labor placement services, under federal and state sponsorship since the 1920s, to match supply and demand and prevent the perennial stranding of jobless migratory groups in the nation's interior.

Since 1917 the border commuter—the so-called greencarder who holds a legal immigrant visa and is admitted to work on the American side but resides on the Mexican side—has been a contributer to displacing local Chicano labor, as in California and Texas border counties.[6] Over the years the number of greencarders employed in a given season has fluctuated between 20,000 and 100,000, but in the past decade about 20,000 have been working in California agriculture, compared to around 5,000 in Texas. On the other hand, between 15,000 and 20,000 greencard holders have been working in sales, services, and small industries in Texas border communities, mainly El Paso and Laredo, but also points inland, like Corpus Christi and Houston.[7] In addition, "illegal border commuters," who for decades have crossed on shopping cards, or slipped across, to do day work or seasonal labor in border areas, yet who reside mostly in Mexico, may presently number 150,000 or more.

In California, as Taylor, Fuller, and McWilliams have shown, Mexican migratory labor, often by way of south Texas, replaced not only Orientals as the principal source of seasonal farm workers but virtually all other sources of such labor.[8] During the Depression destitute and uprooted native Americans eagerly grabbed for California farm jobs, but during World War II labor from Mexico once more replaced local labor, so that down to the present Mexican-born persons including immigrants, commuters, and wetbacks, have been the mainstay of harvest labor in that state.

The availability of Mexican labor influenced the pace of mechanization. In the Midwest and Far West labor-saving devices, such as windmills, barbed wire, and steam engines, were rapidly applied, and Webb even suggested that this is how the West was won.[9] Yet southwestern employers of farm labor seemed more inclined, like antebellum southern planters, to defend the necessity of cheap labor than experiment with labor-saving devices. It would appear that the full use and the perfecting of cotton-picking and beet-harvesting machines were deferred for over two decades in California, Texas, and elsewhere, not simply because of technical difficulties, but because growers had easy access to low-cost native labor during the Depression, and then, after World War II, from Mexico. This labor often included women and children in the picking, weeding, and topping crews.[10]

In California, likewise in Arizona, mechanical cotton picking was well underway by the mid-1950s, but in Texas, New Mexico, Arkansas, and elsewhere, Mexican labor, and some Negro labor, was still considered adequate, and planters continued to insist that machines were too costly and "couldn't pick clean." However, by 1960, when it was clear that bracero-contracting faced extinction, that the federal government and the unions were taking up the farm worker's cause, and that wetback crews were nearly eliminated from large farms, growers everywhere in the Southwest turned with remarkable agility to mechanization in cotton and beets. A Texas farmer put it in two words: "Adios, bracero."[11]

Only in the past decade or so have agricultural schools in the Southwest been pressed by agribusiness groups to meet the technological challenge arising from a shortage of common labor and the threat of unionization. Since the 1960s, for instance, the University of California at Davis has been developing and perfecting mechanical carrot diggers, asparagus cutters, orange pickers, tomato harvesters, and so on.[12] These experiments include the cultivation of grapes that can be picked mechanically.

Pioneer studies have shown that abundant stoop labor played a basic role in the projection westward of the southern type of cotton plantation and similar sugarbeet plantation, wherever water could be found or pumped; and that it also facilitated the emergence of corporate agribusiness in the Southwest, and the phenomenon of "factories in the field," especially in the Imperial, San Joaquin, and Sacramento valleys of California. Less known is the contribution of such labor to patterns of economic marginality, like small-scale farm and ranch operations on semi-arid lands considered marginal by agronomists and federal land managers. With low-cost labor available, and also some share-cropping, it was possible for entrepreneurs to press such land into profitable

TEXAS MIGRANT YEARLY
TRAVEL PATTERN

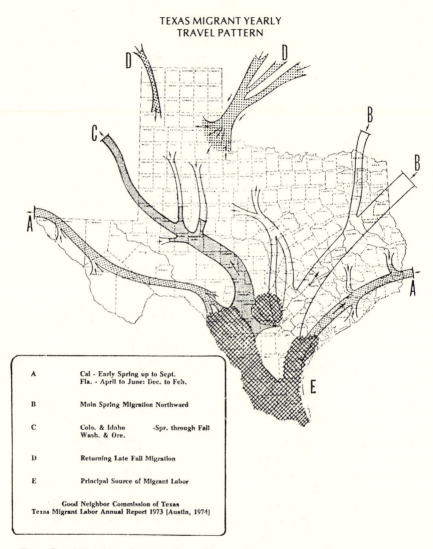

A	Cal - Early Spring up to Sept. Fla. - April to June: Dec. to Feb.
B	Main Spring Migration Northward
C	Colo. & Idaho -Spr. through Fall Wash. & Ore.
D	Returning Late Fall Migration
E	Principal Source of Migrant Labor

Good Neighbor Commission of Texas
Texas Migrant Labor Annual Report 1973 [Austin, 1974]

From Good Neighbor Commission of Texas, *Texas Migrant Labor Annual Report*
(Austin, 1974).

use. Cheap labor made the difference, as in a good part of the "Winter Garden" district of southwest Texas.[13] Unable to compete in the long run with richer farmlands, some of these garden districts have reverted to cactus and mesquite brush since the 1940s.

Elsewhere the broad geographic dispersal of the wetback has enabled many small farmers and ranchers as far north as Nevada, Montana, and Idaho to hang onto low-profit operations. For many years immigration officers have faced the pleas, exaggerated or not: "I can't hold onto this place without Mexicans." Congressional immigration committees have heard such pleading for more than fifty years. Congressmen and agriculturist John Nance Garner said it once and for all: "Mr. Chairman, here is the whole problem in the nutshell. Farming is not a profitable industry.... You have to have cheap labor.... That is the way it is along the border and I imagine . . . anywhere else.[14]

The same pleas perpetuated the emergency labor program of World War II from 1942 to 1965; and gradually, as Mexican labor filtered into other economic sectors, the same touching appeals have been made before immigration officers by small businessmen and industrial subcontractors from Los Angeles to Chicago, who apparently can afford "wet labor" but not heavy capital investment in machinery and union wages, as in garment factories, satellite plants, motels and restaurants, or, earlier, in the million-fingered pecan-shelling industry.[15]

Since the turn of the century American labor unions have been perennially concerned about the displacement effects on native labor, and on unionization and wage levels, posed by unorganized transborder labor. In vain they protested that Mexican nationals were imported as strikebreakers, as in the mines of Arizona and Colorado after 1900, in the steel mills of Chicago-Gary in 1919, and in the great railway strike of 1921-1922 in Kansas City and along the lines.[16] More recently César Chávez, leader since 1963 of the California-based United Farm Workers Organizing Committee, has made such charges repeatedly.

Unable in the 1920s to convince the federal government or the Mexican government to cut off the flow of cross-border labor and unwilling to give Mexico carte blanche reciprocity in union cards, the American Federation of Labor, the Railway Brotherhood, and later the Congress of Industrial Organizations, reached a *modus vivendi* that has endured, more or less, to the present. Certain jobs, such as harvest labor and track work, were simply left to Mexican migrants. Union policy became one of containment: to prevent the spread of Mexican labor into industrial employment or into the more skilled crafts and trades. In fact, until the 1970s unionization of farm labor was considered a lost cause by the AFL, especially since so many industrial sectors seemed to require unionism.[17]

As if to prove the AFL correct, Mexican farm workers in California and Texas in the 1930s made sporadic attempts to unionize with encouragement from Mexican consuls and left-wing American unions, but these efforts failed because of the abundance of cheap labor and hostile legislators.[18] Not until after World War II did the AFL make a half-serious attempt to organize farm labor, and then only in California agribusiness, where such labor was considered semi-factory.[19]

Earlier the American Federation of Labor, under the leadership of Samuel Gompers, and then William Green, had accepted the Mexican farm labor program of 1917-1921, which brought in about 80,000 contract workers, as a necessary wartime measure and worked to close off its perpetuation. Likewise, the bracero program inaugurated during World War II received provisional toleration. The American Brotherhood of Railroad Workers was satisfied when in 1946 braceros were no longer used as track workers. The attempt to extend the use of imported farm labor was something else. When growers sought to make imported labor a permanent labor subsidy and used braceros, as well as wetbacks, to defeat unionism and minimum-wage demands, the AFL, and later the AFL-CIO alliance (1953), began to concentrate less on organizing farm labor and more on pressing Congress to terminate wetbackism and the so-called temporary emergency labor program. Eventually union protests were an important factor in wetback control and in the demise of bracero contracting in December 1964.[20] Since then the AFL-CIO has felt obligated to support Chávez and his Huelga movement, but in the spirit of a nobel and uncertain experiment.

With contract-labor cut off after 1965, and wetbackism reduced or diverted to industrial and service sectors, Chávez and the United Farm Workers (UFW) organized some groups by 1968, and imposed an industrial type of union hiring hall, but unhappy employers faced a constant turnover of split-up crews. The system worked, more or less, where agrilabor approximated factory labor, as in year-round cycles of grape and vegetable production in a benign climate. Even this success, however, owed much to a long-lasting national sympathy boycott against nonunion produce, plus on-and-off subsidies from the AFL-CIO. UFW plans for total victory were frustrated in the early 1970s due to the growing availability of commuters and wetbacks, and, more important, to the loss of contracts to the rival Teamsters Union which guaranteed a more efficient labor force.

Violent contests between Teamsters and Huelgistas over growers' contracts led the State of California to intervene and pass a farm labor bill in May 1975 that provided for secret ballots and a novel State Agricultural Labor Relations Board to supervise elections and review complaints.[21] To make the law palatable to growers, secondary boycotts—such as the picketing of retail stores selling nonunion wine or produce— were restricted. Free of intimidation and under state patronage, the UFW expected to make great gains in winning contracts (even though Proposition 14 to allow unionizing activities on grower property during working hours was voted down in the fall elections of 1976). Meantime, the future financing of the Board, swamped with complaints, has not yet been assured. Nor is it clear that the Huelga formula would work for other groups, like migratory workers. (On March 10, 1977, the two rivals announced a two-year truce in their dog-and-cat fight that would cover other states besides California. Cannery workers, drivers, and some machine operators would remain with the Teamsters, and field hands with the UFW.)

The persistence of migratory subcultures, white, black, and brown, and the seasonal nature of agrilabor, have frustrated for these many years the organization of migrant farm labor. Consequently "powerless farm workers" have become, since the War on Poverty began in 1964, a ward of the federal government and migrant ministries.[22] Since then multiplying but spotty federal, state, and private programs have sought to protect migrant families with health care, housing standards, disability insurance, crew-leader supervision, special schools, minimum wages, and unemployment compensation, as well as food stamps and welfare benefits, as when eligibility based on local residence was struck down by the Supreme Court (*Shapiro* v. *Thompson*, April 21, 1969).

Nevertheless, the part-time nature of harvest work and incentive-pay arrangements have led to countless legislative exceptions; for one thing public officials hesitate to concede a full range of benefits for transient workers and their families, who may work just enough in the fields or packing plants to qualify and then "home it" for south Texas, south Florida, or southern California, where they may collect again, or for Mexico, where by using a postal address in the border state, they can also collect. Hired agrilabor, part-time or full-time, numbered about 2.5 million in 1970, but perhaps only 1 million worked seventy-five days or more, and of this latter figure close to 200,000 would have been migratory (not counting illegals).

Elsewhere unionization of common labor in border industries has been sporadic because of the immediacy of Mexican labor, male and female, including border commuters on a shopping card.[23] The hot battle for union recognition in the Farah apparel plants at El Paso, involving some 10,000 Chicanos and Mexican nationals, was won in 1974 after a two-year siege. Recognition was hailed as a landmark victory by textile unions, but how far such unions can organize "wet labor" in more marginal "sweat shops," as in Los Angeles or San Antonio, remains to be seen.[24]

Undoubtedly Mexican labor has contributed to the development of certain dimensions of the American economy, particularly in the Southwest. During the early part of this century such labor, like other immigrant labor, facilitated the rapid clearing of the land, the development of irrigation systems, and planting and harvesting at a time when power equipment was not always available.[25] Mexican nationals likewise provided unskilled, and skilled, labor for the development of mining and railroads, likewise meat packing, brickmaking, construction, and other industries. They were frequently exploited, according to charges commonly made by Mexican consuls. On the other hand, contractors and employers claimed that they were "exploited" and "taken in" by Mexicans who jumped contracts, after their transportation had been prepaid, in order to explore the American labor market, or who took off with immigrant visas after the ingenuous employer had sponsored their permanent residence.[26]

Taking work as a commodity that is sold to the highest bidder (and made scarce by unionization), transborder labor, generally speaking, has been sold at a low price. As Mexican observers have seen it, and with no little resentment, *la raza* has subsidized and continues to subsidize the Anglo-American economy. Not only have Mexican workers made goods and services more available and more economical for American consumers, they have also contributed to the expansion of *yanqui* capitalism which, in turn, has had—in the eyes of Mexican nationalists—undesirable investment repercussions in Mexico itself. [27] Such considerations, give or take a little, have often been behind the aggressive efforts of the Mexican government to foster unionization (as in the Imperial Valley in the 1930s), and contract programs, and to raise and collect wages for Mexican workers in the United States, beginning in World War I, and running through bracero contracting, 1942-1965, and the present "exodus" of undocumented workers underway since the late 1960s.

The "subsidy effect," an important economic catalyst even in such midwestern industrial centers as Chicago and Milwaukee, has been, not surprisingly, most conspicuous in the border states. Where the standard of living and comfort, if not life style, of countless southwestern families, including Mexican-American, has been resting in good part, as in Mexico itself, on a bottomless supply of cheap labor offered by migrating campesino families. Spacious suburban homes, often built by Mexican construction crews, have seldom been without domestic servants, gardeners, and odd-jobbers from over the border or from across the tracks. [28]

The Mexican "labor subsidy," impossible to measure in monetary terms, has also generated socioeconomic costs equally difficult to quantify. Even before World War I directors of public and private social services were complaining that peon families, jobless during the off-season, presented an increasing burden, not on the employers, who usually waived responsibility for seasonal labor under laissez-faire economic standards, but on winter-haven communities, which frequently found their health and relief services, in the days before federal subsidies, overrun by migrants who wintered in adjacent shanty towns. [29] The pattern was common in the migrant labor reservoirs of southern California, south Texas, and in many cities near sources of seasonal employment, for example, Denver near the beet fields of the South Platte Valley. In such communities special, and usually ineffectual, schools were set up for migrant children. [30]

By the 1920s the "Mexican social problem" was in full bloom, and officials of public charities and health services, along with school superintendents, were compiling dismal statistics on the "Mexican casuals" and their extended families: They formed, as in Los Angeles, around 10 percent of the city's population and 40 percent of its relief problem, 50 percent of the health problem, 30 percent of the criminal problem, and so on. [31] Such data went hand-in-hand with a public outcry in the Southwest to stop the "peon invasion" of the 1920s and influenced the founding of the Border Patrol in 1924, the frustrated drive to put Mexico on the quota, and the State Department's decision in 1928 to cut down on its permissive issuance of visas to semiliterate common laborers.[32] A major objective of repatriation pressures in the early 1930s, in such far-flung cities as Los Angeles, St. Paul, Detroit, and Gary, was to get the Mexican off relief.[33]

Mexican labor emigration resumed after 1942 and the "social problem" of the 1920s became the "wetback problem" of the 1940s and 1950s. Again, southwestern communities compiled distressing statistics and raised an outcry for border control and deportation which culminated in Operation Wetback of 1954, whereby over a million men, women, and children, mainly cotton pickers, were trucked back to Mexico.[34]

During the 1960s increasing numbers of immigrants and *mojados* slipped into the labor market. The ending of the bracero program in 1964 and a closer watch on "stoop labor" increased the immigrants' preference for industrial and service jobs in Spanish-speaking urban areas. Thus they began to compete more in the semiskilled and skilled labor markets with Chicanos and earlier immigrants.[35] With welfare and food commodity assistance more available after the New Deal legislation of the 1930s, displaced local residents increasingly held their ground and sought year-round security on public assistance often in combination with seasonal or part-time work in nearby job markets.

By the late 1960s the cumulative effects of the "wetback problem" had been, in turn, transformed, with the assistance of the anti-poverty bureaucracy and the civil rights movement, into the vastly more complicated and costly problem of an "underprivileged ethnic minority." Thus Mexican immigrants were apparently in need of special funding for health care, rental subsidies, food stamps, free lunch programs, vocational rehabilitation, dependent children, Head Start, adult education, community development, migrant schools, bilingual instruction, the development of ethnic pride, immigrant aid, legal defense, and so on.[36]

Dismal data lurked, as before, just under the surface, to pop up as reports, exaggerations and all, for any legislative hearing or task force research on uninvited aliens and their impact on rising welfare, education, health, and crime costs, as in New York, Chicago, or Los Angeles, or their supposed adverse influence on hard-core ethnic poverty, or even on the nation's dollar drain.[37]

Perhaps the most persistent complaint, supported by wage studies from time to time, is that in southwestern border counties, where most Spanish-surnamed are on substandard wages and some form of social assistance, incoming low-paid workers from Mexico, who are difficult to unionize, continue to push earlier waves of immigrant settlers, willing or not, onto welfare, or toward interior labor markets in search of better pay. Here again poverty-ridden south Texas has deserved special attention from such labor economists as Briggs and Schmidt.[38] The subject is of national importance, for the Tex-Mex displacement cycle has never failed to diffuse an "underprivileged minority" to out-of-state communities. As with the "Negro problem" or "poor white" problem in the South, out-migration has been the "solution" to the "Mexican problem" in Texas.

More so than in other states, Texas communities have in the past manifested marked discrimination against Raza migrant groups, but remarkably little concern about an open border or about the gradual rise of a defensive Chicano folk culture. Unlike those in other states, Texas politicians rarely—until the present—sponsored a movement to cut off cheap-labor migration. Two exceptions were Congressman John R. Box of east Texas who, in the 1920s, wanted to put Mexico on a strict quota, and Mexican-American civic brotherhoods, like the League of United Latin American Citizens (LULAC) and the American G.I. Forum, both of which publicly protested the wetback invasion in the pre-Chicano era of the 1940s and 1950s. [39]

Borderland employers, including Mexican-American and assorted Chamber of Commerce groups, have defended Raza labor for generations as a God-given natural resource like land, water, and sunshine, to be jealously protected against northern labor agents, the Border Patrol, and immigration reforms. Up until World War II and after, even some immigration officers shared this possessive feeling, for in the rough early days of border banditry and liquor smuggling the mounted inspector of customs and the border guards were usually recruited, like Texas or Arizona Rangers, from a tough, local class of farmers and ranchers. Often such a line officer tolerated wetbacks, including domestic servants, especially when they were used by friends or on his own little rancho. Some shared the southern planter's feeling that "damn Yankees" should keep their "cotton pickin' fingers" off the Texas supply of "Meskin help."

Possessive attitudes are reflected in the salty memoirs of John R. Peavey, Texas ranger, mounted border guard, and, later, an immigration officer. He thus described labor-protection needs after the 1917 immigration act:

They were still wet from crossing the Rio Grande . . . a humble, harmless breed of people, eager to find work. . . . Their labor and services were needed by the pioneering Anglo-Americans who were moving into the Rio Grande Valley to carve an agricultural country out of a cactus and mesquite covered pasture land. No other source of labor was readily obtainable and the Mexican people had, for one hundred years, crossed the Rio Grande at will, without any obstruction or objection from anyone. . . .

Then, suddenly, the wet-backs were "discovered" by the big railroad construction contractors of the northern states, and labor agents, whom we called "northern Carpet Baggers," were sent here to entice. . . . These simple people were gathered by the thousands and furnished the best of transportation, including Pullman car service. . . . To a people who had never ridden anything but an ox cart and slept on a bed of straw or weeds and who were raised on Chile, beans, and tortillas, these promises were overwhelming. . . . they were placed in camps . . . expected to work long hours . . . . their wages withheld until the job was finished . . . paid off and released to return home as best they could, and many fell prey to taxi drivers, prostitutes, gamblers and thugs. . . . then they drifted into the cities and towns and became a real problem to the local police.

In many places they were gathered up by Mexican Consuls and sent back to Mexico.

Later it became the duty of the U.S. Border Patrol to gather these stragglers and convey them back to the Mexican border.[40]

To protect its labor supply, the Texas legislature, characteristically, passed a contract labor law in 1929 that provided for licensed agents and licensing fees. (This system regularly pumps fresh labor in from Mexico.) Also, whenever the Border Patrol, "infiltrated by non-Texans," became overzealous in deporting wet labor, as it did in the early 1950s, the patrolmen were denounced as "fascist gendarmes" by Texas grower associations, newspaper editors, and spokesmen for Chambers of Commerce from Laredo south to Brownsville, and they were treated as badly as civil rights workers in Mississippi.[41]

The settlement of campesinos in Texas caused little concern, partly because counties there, like those in the rural South, spent the minimum amount of tax money on the social and educational care of the local labor supply, even after the New Deal created federal subsidies for public assistance. As late as the 1960s, the monthly allowance for a dependent child was around $6 to $8 a month compared to around $40 a month in California, Michigan, Illinois, and other states where migrant families tend to settle out of the harvest cycle. Many semifeudal communities in south Texas simply allowed federal anti-poverty agencies to fund social programs after 1964, as local and state politicians scrambled for patronage, even as more "unspoiled Mexican labor" continued to move in.

Patronage or not, Great Society programs (inspired, it is said, by President Lyndon B. Johnson's youthful experience as a schoolteacher in the miserable south Texas migrant camp of Cotulla) have now become, ironically, the major threat to the borderlands labor supply. Employers' complaints against permissive public assistance and the unemployment compensation racket, here expressed by a Border Patrol veteran, could apply to many American groups, from sea to shining sea:

In town the Courthouse square is covered with Mexican Americans lounging in the sun, gathering the pecans, drinking wine. You could not hire one of them for love nor money. They get their unemployment checks, food stamps, and whatever. Should they go to work for you, they will cause you to fire them the first day so they can draw unemployment. Disgusting.[42]

Thus far, however, Texas employer associations have been more successful in their fight against another imminent threat to labor mobility, namely, unionization efforts in right-to-work state. Undoubtedly, the maintenance there of an open-border labor market and lower taxes, as with unemployment insurance, explains much of the paradox of continuous boom-time prosperity in Texas in spite of federal subsidies for black, brown, and white "poverty cultures," and the job recession of 1973-1977. It's as if Texans had never heard of the crash of free-enterprise capitalism in 1929.[43]

Nevertheless, a century-long era of transborder labor in the Southwest at minimal social costs is over. Now even conservative Mexican Americans, who may shun such names as Chicano or Raza, claim a per capita share (including illegals) of federal and local funds for public education, social services, and community development. Nowhere is this truer than in Texas, where in various towns and counties the militant La Raza Unida Party, founded in 1970 by Anglo-phobe José Angel Gutierrez, has kicked out local politicians, to the delight of the Mexican underclass, and defiantly taken over patronage. The most notable example is at little Crystal City, the "spinach capital of the world," where a small but model Raza self-help community and cooperative farm experiment is underway with a fabulous slush of federal funds.[44]

In response to the threatened political reconquest of the Southwest by La Raza, the present governor of Texas, Dolph Briscoe, a typical Texas ranchero who once took wet labor for granted, and a spokesman for the old Anglo-Latin establishment, has, invoking "the spirit of the Alamo," frequently denounced the emergence of a "Chicano Quebec" or "Red Cuba" in south Texas with federal funding and carpetbagger help. Meanwhile, growing rapidly in political power, Spanish-surnamed leaders, who for their part have likened south Texas to Rhodesia or South Africa, push for amnesty and naturalization measures for the Raza brotherhood. And leaders of La Raza Unida Party seek official intervention by Mexico against cultural deprivation and territorial loss. The pot boils.[45]

All the while south Texas funnels migrants to most states of the Union, where they show up as a needed labor force, and perhaps a "minority problem," as in St. Paul, Milwaukee, Muscatine, Galesburg, Oklahoma City, Ogden, Fresno, Sacramento, Pueblo, Cheyenne, North Platte, South Bend, and Detroit. These and other communities usually have a Virgin of Guadalupe chapel around which social assistance contacts are clustered. The Texas Good Neighbor Commission, founded in 1943 to improve race relations and the socioeconomic condition of Mexican-origin groups, summed up the migrant problem with some sense of despair:

The Texas migrant labor pool . . . is made up almost entirely of Mexican Americans and although the majority of them are native born American citizens, they continue to hold a strong cultural affinity with Mexico and with customs related to their Latin background. Their search for work in the fields and packing plants requires them to travel far and wide. . . . all have tasted the bitter pills of discrimination, deprivation and poverty. An average or composite Texas migrant household head can be described as male and married, about 45 years old with two years or less of schooling, who presides over a family of six-plus individuals (about half of whom work) and who is employed 28 weeks a year. . . . the migrants who have been able to move into non-farm employment have been those who are trainable, employable and adaptable (thus leaving behind the more despairing and difficult cases). . . . it is precisely this group, the chronically and permanently underprivileged, that is most desperately in need of assistance.[46]

Census Data on Mexican Labor

Any assessment of the present significance of Mexican labor in the American economy means groping, today as yesterday, with the same two frustrating questions: What is the absolute and relative size of the Mexican-born work force when so much of it is surreptitious? And what is its geographic, industrial, and occupational concentration?[47] To begin with, as shown in Table 1, the reported Mexican born made up a smaller percentage in 1970 than in 1930, even in Texas and California, the main corridors of transborder migration.

The decennial census has always understated the quantitative importance of Mexico-born and Chicano groups. The illegal aliens mistrust of the census-taker is the principal factor. Some idea of undercounts is suggested by the survey of March 1973 in which the total Mexican-origin population leaped to 6.3 million, compared to only 4.5 million in 1970.[48]

Meanwhile, Mexican immigrants continued to enter at a rapid pace. In fiscal period 1971-1976 some 376,000 were legally admitted.[49] By mid-1976 the Mexican resident-alien population of legal origins numbered somewhere

Table 1   Mexican-Born Population of the United States, 1910-1970
(in thousands)

	United States		California		Texas	
	Mexican Born	% of Total Population	Mexican Born	% of Total Population	Mexican Born	% of Total Population
1910	220	0.2				
1920	478	0.5				
1930	639	0.5	191	3.4	263	4.5
1940	377	0.3				
1950	451	0.3				
1960	576	0.3				
1970*	817	0.4	434	2.2	217	1.9

*The 1970 figures represent the number of persons who indicated they were of "Mexican origin" born outside of the United States. Earlier figures are based on indicated country of birth. The 1970 figure for persons born in Mexico is 760,000.

Sources: 1910-1950, E.P. Hutchinson, *Immigrants and Their Children*, (John Wiley: New York, 1956), p. 6; 1960, *U.S. Census of Population: 1970*, PC(2)-A; 1970, *U.S. Census of Population: 1970*, PC(2)-1C.

between 1 and 2 million. In addition, the number of Mexican persons illegally, or unreported, in the United States might then have been near 5 million, including family members, many of them still concentrated in California and Texas. Such approximations, when transformed into labor force estimates (most illegal and legal aliens are of working age), would indicate a probable Mexico-born labor force of around 2.8 million or more, including perhaps 300,000 or 400,000 seasonal workers. In all, this fast-growing group might have equaled over 3 percent of the nation's total labor force, reported as 88,352,000 in December 1976 by the Department of Labor.

By and large, the relative size of a population group, as in table 2, would be an indicator of its relative size as a labor force, but, of course, would say nothing about patterns of concentration. For instance, the Department of Labor estimated in 1973 that Mexican nationals made up 11 percent of the labor in border counties. [50] This percentage—which varies seasonally—is much higher in gateway cities like El Paso, which also has a large Mexican-alien population (see table 2). Quantitatively more important are the illegal commuters who perform a great variety of tasks, skilled and unskilled, part-time or full-time, in border areas.

Metropolitan Los Angeles—a great center of concentration and commonly said to be "Mexico's second largest city"—had, according to the 1970 census, the largest number of reported Mexican workers—102,000. In fact, sprawling Los Angeles (described as "a hundred towns in search of a city") contained one-fourth or more of all Mexican immigrants legally residing in the United States. Moreover, more than half of all recent immigrants have declared their intent to settle in California, principally in the Los Angeles area. [51]

The census disclosed that in 1970 Mexican-born males were about 10 per-

Table 2   Mexican and Spanish-Origin Populations, Selected Areas, 1970
(in Thousands)

States	*Mexican Born*	*% of Total Population*	*All Foreign Born of Spanish Origin*	*% of Total Population*	*All Spanish Origin*	*% of Total Population*
California	431.1	2.2	591.6	3.0	2,369.3	11.9
Illinois	54.1	0.5	89.9	0.8	393.2	3.5
Texas	217.1	1.9	234.5	2.1	1,840.6	16.4
Metropolitan Areas						
Chicago	49.0	0.8	85.6	1.4	324.2	5.2
El Paso	45.5	12.9	46.4	12.9	181.7	50.6
Houston	20.4	1.0	26.1	1.3	182.1	9.2
Los Angeles	211.6	3.0	307.0	4.4	1,051.4	14.9
San Antonio	35.4	4.1	37.1	4.3	323.8	37.5
San Diego	29.5	2.2	34.0	2.5	121.5	9.0
San Francisco-Oakland	26.4	0.8	60.6	1.9	231.5	7.4

Source: *U.S. Census of Population: 1970*, PC(1); PC(2)-C.

ORIGINS AND ROUTES OF FOREIGN AND DOMESTIC MIGRATORY LABOR AROUND 1976

Note. In 1970 there were in the United States around 2.5 million hired farmworkers mostly local residents but an estimated 196,000 farmworkers were either intra-or .interstate seasonal migrants, chiefly of Mexican origins working out of border labor pools as in Texas, California, and increasingly in Florida where black and Caribbean .migrants have predominated. In 1970 a reported 18,884 Puerto Ricans, 15,470 British West Indians [Jamaicans mainly], and 2004 Canadians migrated to the mainland for agriwork. Unreported agrilabor from Mexico may then have amounted to two or three hundred thousand. As migrants drop out of streams to do other jobs, or settle out on anti-poverty programs, fresh recruits, principally from Mexico, are pumped in.

By 1976 unreported Mexican seasonal and resident agrilabor may have reached 380,000 to 500,000.

Sources: Texas Good Neighbor Commission, *Migrant Labor Annual Reports* (Austin, Texas) Gene Rowe and Leslie W. Smith, *The Hired Farm Working Force 1975* (Washington, D.C.: Economic Research Service, USDA, 1976): *ibid.*, letter of December 12, 1974; and interview sources including district offices of U.S. Immigration Service, and U.S. Consular offices in Mexico.

cent of all (semiskilled) operatives in metropolitan Los Angeles, 7 percent of all laborers, 23 percent of all farm workers who resided, or "wintered," in the area, and small components of all other occupations.[52] The Mexican-born share of employment in these occupations was even greater in the Texas border cities of Brownsville, McAllen, Laredo, El Paso, and, possibly, San Antonio, but this cannot be statistically stated with the available data.

If one bears in mind that census enumerations included a mix of facts for a relatively small proportion of Puerto Ricans, Cubans, and other Latin Americans, employment of Mexicans, male and female, in Los Angeles has been most conspicuous, as measured by the Spanish language-Spanish surname indicators, in nondurable manufacturing. Apparel and other textiles, rubber and plastics, stone and clay products, cosmetics, furniture, food processing and footwear have been the leading employers. In some cases Spanish-surnamed workers were nearly 50 percent of the total work force in the apparel and furniture industries, and most appeared to be Mexican-born. The same would hold for metal manufacturing, laundry, and food services, as well as railroad maintenance, construction trades, and domestic service, most of such labor being unskilled and semiskilled.[53] Greater Los Angeles offered the broadest spectrum of employment for the Mexican-born in 1970, but, to some degree, the pattern would have fitted other metropolitan areas such as Denver, Dallas, Houston, Chicago, or the San Francisco bay area.

After Los Angeles, the largest metropolitan concentration of reported Mexican workers was in the Chicago-Gary industrial sprawl (Table 2). This region has had a sizable Mexican settlement since the 1920s, when border Mexicans were recruited to labor on railroads and in nearby packing plants and steel mills.[54] Lax immigration control, protective coloration offered by Puerto Rican colonies, and a relatively open and high-paying labor market have encouraged a major migration of Mexicans to this region in the past two decades.

The percentage of foreign-born in the Mexican community in Chicago was higher than in any other major city. The 1970 census gave a figure of 50,098 Mexico-born persons in Illinois, out of a reported Mexican-origin population of 160,477. Most of this population was centered in the greater Chicago area. Some Latino leaders at that date were complaining that the census undercount of Mexican-born and Tex-Mex people in that area, including Gary and Milwaukee, may have numbered 300,000 or 400,000, plus other groups of Latin-American aliens. By 1976 estimates of Mexican illegals in the Lake Michigan area were approaching a million, presenting a growing "amnesty problem."[55]

In the metropolitan areas, Mexican workers are commonly found in both heavy and light industries and in building trades, warehouses, and scattered subsidiary plants that often require piecework, or night work, and considerable mobility. Elsewhere, agriculture and food processing industries continue to be major employers of Mexican labor. The phase out of the bracero program after 1964 did not end the use of Mexican nationals as agriworkers in most states west of the Ohio River. Some are commuters, legal and illegal, from central Mexico and the border regions; some have been "immigrated" by employers; untold numbers have slipped into interstate migratory streams; and still others live in on countless farms and ranches all the way to the Canadian border. But California, more than any state, has come to depend on Mexican agrilabor.

From 1956 to 1959, peak weekly employment of Mexican nationals under bracero contracts was an estimated 80,000 to 100,000 with an annual average of about 48,000.[56] These figures represented 11 percent of all farm workers and 26 percent of the seasonal labor force. In 1970 the reported number of all Mexico-origin farm workers was around 114,000.[57] Counting illegals and border commuters, there may have been an additional 60,000 to 80,000 available at peak harvest time.[58] These figures do not necessarily mean that domestic labor has been unavailable. The same might be said of other border states.

Most Mexicans, admitted legally for permanent residence in recent years, have not entered directly into the labor market, for nearly two-thirds of them are housewives, children, or other dependents. Of those immigrants reporting an occupation, most were originally unskilled workers who first entered as wetbacks but who succeeded in building up job skills and family equities—for example, by having a child born in the United States, which exempted the visa applicant from needing a labor certification (until P.L. 94-571, effective January 1, 1977).

An overall estimate of the number of Mexican immigrants and commuters legally at work in the United States for a recent year would be as shown in Table 3.

Some Characteristics of Reported Mexican Workers

According to the 1970 census, the Mexican-born were almost one-fifth of reported Mexican-origin persons in the United States. This fact lowered to some extent the perceived socioeconomic status of the "disadvantaged Chicano population," for distinctions between the two groups have seldom been made, especially in statistics gathered for political-action and civil rights groups. Yet in some cases the newly arrived Mexican immigrant occupied a higher economic—if not educational—status than second- and even third-generation Chicanos, who seem to make little effort, in many cases, to emerge from the Spanish-speaking subculture.[59]

The Mexican-born labor force in 1970 had slightly more men than the total Mexican-American population, and, relatedly, fewer Mexican-born women were employed—30 percent, compared to 37 percent for all Spanish-surnamed women and 41 percent for all women. Also, the median age of an immigrant

Table 3   Rough Approximations of Mexican Immigrants Legally
Employed in the United States Around 1973*

Border Commuters. Various seasonal and permanent jobs in
    agriculture, construction, sales and service in border zones
    performed by so-called "greencarders" admitted as bona
    fide immigrants (INS Form I-151 and I-178), but who are
    permitted to live on the Mexican side. About 40 percent
    are engaged in agro work, principally in California.   45,000

Non-Immigrant Temporary Workers. Certified by Depart-
    ment of Labor and Immigration Service (INS) for tempo-
    rary admission to perform jobs, or job-training. In fiscal
    1973 there were 1,037 workers of distinguished merit or
    ability ("H-1" category); 1,193 semi-skilled or unskilled
    workers, mostly in agriculture ("H-2" category); and 142
    industrial trainees ("H-3").   2,372

Employed Resident Aliens. Admitted as immigrants for
    permanent residence (Form I-151). In fiscal 1973,
    823,325 Mexican aliens reported under the alien ad-
    dress program, including 437,927 in California, 228,785
    in Texas, and 59,805 in Illinois. Apparently no precise
    figures are available on the number of Mexican resident
    aliens employed in the United States, but perhaps half
    of them, including some unreported legal aliens, and
    many admitted as immediate relatives, might have
    been employed in 1973 in predominantly non-agricul-
    tural work.   420,000(?)

                                                    Total   467,372(?)

---

*Excepting conjectures about employed resident aliens, the above data is from INS, *Annual
Report for Fiscal 1973,* Tables 16-A, 35; and *Texas Migrant Labor Annual Report 1972* (Austin: Texas Good Neighbor Commission, 1973). The commuter figure is based on INS count of
45,025 taken in 1971, and does not include about 8,000 Canadian commuters. A count of December 1975 was about the same.

worker tended to be higher; that of the Mexican worker was thirty-eight compared to a national median of twenty-eight.

In general, the educational deficiencies of the Mexican-born have contributed to much of this group's being limited to low-skill sectors of the American
economy. Mexican women averaged about four years less schooling than the
9.6 average for all Spanish-surnamed women. And only 15 percent of Mexican

men, aged sixteen or over, were high school or technical school graduates in 1970, compared to 32 percent for all Spanish-surnamed men.[60] Younger members among Mexican immigrants seem better educated; 31 percent of those between twenty and twenty-four had completed secondary school. Lack of facility in English was a near-universal handicap, as was non-citizenship in a few cases. Two-fifths of the Mexican-born were reportedly American citizens in 1970.[61]

The median income of Mexican-born men, aged sixteen or over, in the Southwest in 1969 was $4,200, compared to $4,850 for all Spanish-surnamed and the national median of over $6,500. The Mexican-born figure was raised slightly by the comparatively large number of men in their prime income age. Mexican women in 1969 had a median income of $1,680, compared to $1,930 for the Spanish-surnamed and a national median of around $2,400.[62]

Family income varied markedly according to regions, and this, in turn, has obviously influenced Mexican migration patterns. The average earnings of Mexican-born families in Chicago during 1969 were over $9,000. This figure was slightly lower than $9,600 for all American families and decidedly higher than $7,500 for Mexican-born families in Los Angeles. Only Detroit offered higher earnings per family—$10,900 in 1969.[63] Mexican family incomes were decidely lower in Texas, usually less than $6,000, and much lower in the border counties, where families who were engaged in migratory or seasonal labor averaged as low as $3,600 a year. However, such a figure should be compared to the few hundred dollars a year earned by migrant labor families just across the border.[64]

Unemployment among reported Mexican males in the Southwest in 1970 was 5.9 percent, slightly less than the 6.2 percent for all Spanish-surnamed men, but higher than the national median of nearly 4.4 percent. Unemployment among Mexican women was 6.9 percent, compared to a national median of 5.5 percent. In border areas, however, unemployment rates for the Mexican-born would have been considerably higher, and those for "subemployment," if it could be measured, would have been higher yet. In such areas, but particularly in southwest Texas, Chicano jobless rates usually range, year after year, from 8 percent to 22 percent.[65]

The comparatively better employment rate of Mexican men, especially in the age group from sixteen to twenty-four, has been partly because most of them have immigrated for a specific job (already held in many cases), and apparently because they have a lower reservation wage than Chicanos; that is, they will take some jobs rejected by the latter. Curiously, after age thirty unemployment among Mexican immigrants tends to be more frequent than among Chicanos, perhaps due to a loss of "job eagerness" once residence has been firmly established, or the inclination to leave the original job once it has served to obtain an immigration document. This may have some implications for the dependency pattern in many southwestern communities.

Occupational categories are suggested by immigration data. In fiscal 1973, for instance, a total of 70,141 Mexican immigrants were admitted. Of this number about a third listed their occupations as indicated in Table 4. (Again many were already practicing these occupations while waiting for a visa call.)

Census data approximates the common visa classification of "reported occupations," such as operatives, service workers, and farm labor. Such occupations employed 87 percent of all Mexican men as reported by the 1970 data. [66] Also, the operative category included two-fifths of employed Mexican women, as in laundries, food processing, electronics, and apparel manufacture; most of the remainder were in service jobs, including domestic service.

Most Mexican workers, male and female, legal and illegal, are employed in small firms. [67] Not being very visible, they have sometimes been referred to as the "shadow labor force" of the Southwest. [68] Put another way, over the years such workers have been most active in the "secondary labor market"—that is, in industrial and service jobs usually providing low compensation, little stability, and few advancement opportunities, and usually requiring mobility more than formal training or education.

Current official data on the occupational and income pattern of legal Mexican immigrants in the aggregate is not available; however, these patterns would probably not differ much from the 1975 current population survey for all Spanish-origin groups in the United States. Such findings show a considerable improvement since 1970 (allowing for inflation and an unemployment rate of 12.7 percent) in the occupational status and median income of these groups, male and female.

Illegal Mexican Labor—Some Approximations

Wetback migration, which virtually ceased during the Depression, resumed in the 1940s, apprehensions swelling from 8,000 in 1943 to a peak of 1,075,000

Table 4

Farm workers, including some foremen and managers	945
Domestic service, mostly unskilled	1,771
Non-farm labor and service workers, unskilled and semiskilled	13,943
Operatives, ranging from unskilled to skilled	1,838
Professionals, technicians, and craftsmen	1,551
Managerial, clerical and sales	1,516
Total	21,564

Source: U.S. Immigration and Naturalization Service, *Annual Report, 1973*, Table 8.

Table 5   Broad Occupation Group of Employed Persons of Spanish Origin 16 Years Old
and Over by Sex and Type of Spanish Origin: March 1975

Broad occupation group	Total, Spanish origin	Mexican	Puerto Rican	Cuban	Other Spanish origin*
MALE					
Total, employed persons (thousands)	2,212	1,358	252	191	411
Percent	100.0	100.0	100.0	100.0	100.0
White-collar workers	26.2	21.4	28.7	37.3	35.4
Blue-collar workers	56.0	60.6	49.5	44.0	50.5
Service workers	12.6	10.4	20.5	18.6	12.5
Farm workers	5.2	7.7	1.4	–	1.6
FEMALE					
Total, employed persons (thousands)	1,299	736	157	129	277
Percent	100.0	100.0	100.0	100.0	100.0
White-collar workers	44.6	42.0	41.9	42.0	54.3
Blue-collar workers	30.7	28.7	35.6	46.1	26.0
Service workers	24.0	28.3	21.6	11.9	19.7
Farm workers	0.8	1.1	1.1	-	–

— Represents zero or rounds to zero.
*Includes Central or South American and other Spanish origin.
Source: U.S. Bureau of the Census, *Current Population Reports, Persons of Spanish
Origin in the United States, March 1975*, P-20, No. 290 (Washington, D.C.,
1976), pp. 8-9. See also Roberta V. McKay, economist, Bureau of Labor Statis-
tics, "Americans of Spanish Origin in the Labor Force: An Update," *Agenda*
(National Council of La Raza), 7:1 (Jan/Feb 1977), 29-32.

in 1954. The farm labor program was enlarged mainly to absorb illegals, who
were then mostly in agriwork, and the number of braceros contracted rose
from 53,000 in 1943 to 438,000 in 1959. By the latter date wetback arrests were
down to 30,196, but as the bracero program was phased out, 1960-1965, apprehensions began a sharp rise from around 49,000 in 1965 to 265,540 in fiscal
1970.[69] By fiscal 1976 apprehensions hit 781,438, even though the American
economy was supposedly suffering a major recession in the period 1973-1976,
with aggregate unemployment rates of between 7 and 9 percent, and much
higher rates for blacks and Chicanos.[70]

Agricultural employment, including food processing and packing, has long
been the destination of the Mexican campesino, and this is still true. Samora
and Bustamante's study, carried out in 1968-1970, found that 57 percent of the
mojados apprehended at work in the United States were in agrilabor.[71] Interviews with 493 deportees revealed the following information: 21 percent said
that they had been apprehended previously, and 25 percent said three times or
more. Approximately 90 percent were under age forty, had less than six years
of schooling, and could not speak English; most were agriworkers in Mexico

Table 6   Income in 1974 of Persons of Spanish Origin 14 Years Old
and Over by Type of Spanish Origin and Sex,
for the United States: March 1975

Type of Spanish origin and sex	Median income	Percent with incomes below $5,000	Percent with incomes of $25,000 or more
MALE			
Total, Spanish origin	$6,507	38.6	1.4
Mexican	6,154	40.8	0.7
Puerto Rican	7,055	33.5	1.4
Other Spanish origin*	7,158	35.7	2.7
FEMALE			
Total, Spanish origin	$3,072	72.0	0.1
Mexican	2,682	76.0	—
Puerto Rican	3,889	67.8	—
Other Spanish origin*	3,469	67.1	0.3

— Represents zero or rounds to zero.
*Includes Cuban, Central or South American, and other Spanish origin.
Source: U.S. Bureau of the Census, *Current Population Reports, Persons of Spanish Origin in the United States, March, 1975,* P-20, No. 290 (Washington, D.C.., 1976), pp. 8-9. See also Roberta V. McKay, economist, Bureau of Labor Statistics, "Americans of Spanish Origin in the Labor Force: An Update," *Agenda* (National Council of La Raza), 7:1 (Jan/Feb 1977), 29-32.

seeking similar work over the border. Of 280 who were able to find work before arrest, 26 percent averaged less than $1 an hour; 56 percent averaged between $1 and $2; 14 percent between $3 and $4; and 3 percent over $4 an hour. [72] These facts confirmed what was already widely believed about the average "repeater" seeking agriwork and other unskilled and semiskilled jobs. Meanwhile, the pattern has become more dispersive, for increasingly wetbacks and alien smugglers head for interior states like Nevada, Oregon, Montana, Iowa, Wisconsin, or Michigan, where the immigration watch fades away.

A study carried out by Mexican Foreign Relations and Migration officials in the fall of 1972, and updated in 1974, involved questionnaire work with more than 3,000 deportees of whom 99 percent were men—61.4 percent between the ages of eighteen and twenty-nine. Their average hourly wage was about $1.40, a reflection of the fact that 58 percent were found in farm and ranch work, and that many were seasonal border commuters who, like their forefathers, peren-

Table 7   Migration of Mexicans to the United States: Immigrants,
Contract Laborers, and Aliens Apprehended,
1940-1976

Fiscal Year	Legal Immigrants	Contract Farm Laborers*	Deportable Aliens Apprehended
1940-44	16,550	118,470	22,320
1945-49	37,740	243,470	795,970
1950-54	78,700	967,010	3,442,240
1955-59	214,750	2,150,400	426,940
1960-64	217,830	1,166,850	172,710
1965-69	215,970	31,427	606,770
1970	44,820		265,540
1971	50,329		348,180
1972	64,210		430,213
1973	70,140		576,800
1974	71,586		709,959
1975	62,205		680,392
1976	57,863		781,438

Sources: U.S. Immigration and Naturalization Service, *Annual Report*, Tab. 14, 27B;
Correspondence with INS, Western Regional Office, San Pedro, California; Di-
rección de Asuntos Migratorios, Secretaria de Relaciones Exteriores, Mexico
City; Leo Grebler, *Mexican Immigration to the United States: The Record and
Its Implication* (Mexican American Study Project, University of California, Los
Angeles, 1965), p. 60.
Does not include several thousand "H-2" temporary workers admitted since
1968.

nially worked in lower-paying areas adjacent to Mexico. The stated destination
of 44 percent of the group was Texas; 25 percent said California; 10 percent,
Arizona; 8 percent, New Mexico; and 3 percent, Illinois. Most had been picked
up in transit and may have been heading for more interior points. Around 80
percent said they were ready to return to the United States. Apparently American wages had either "seduced" or "spoiled" them. Some had never tried
working in Mexico, but followed in the footsteps of earlier generations. For
them the American job market was the only one considered. Those who had
worked in Mexico, mainly in the overpopulated central plateau, reported an
average daily wage of 32 pesos, then equal to $2.56 in American money, and
often this was seasonal work only.[73]

For many years the Border Patrol, which generally does "outdoor operations" along a hundred-mile-wide border fringe, with some checkpoints 300 or
400 miles inland, had regularly apprehended, because of its zone of concentration, four or five times as many wetbacks in agriwork as in industrial or service

jobs. For instance, in fiscal 1973 the Patrol arrested 101,220 Mexican aliens in agribusiness, and 24,996 in trades, crafts, and industry, plus 354,372 others, mostly in transit. [74]

An employment profile drawn from the foregoing statistics, or from interviews with farm-labor campesinos, would grossly oversimplify the present phenomenon of wetbackism. The growing availability of data on the new type of wetback, who leaves Mexico with skills (often learned previously in the United States) or some formal education, or who learns to adjust to the Chicano or Latino subcultures in the United States, shows a different picture: a preference for industrial cities, union jobs, the use of documents, increasing contact with Chicano-run social agencies, increasing use of English, and a growing percentage of female workers (rarely picked up by the Border Patrol). The more sophisticated alien, who may reside in a family group, can pass as *puro Chicano*, or perhaps *Puerto Riqueño*. And frequently his or her wages are from $2.50 to $9.00 an hour, or higher, although these wages may involve kickbacks or payoffs to labor agents, job foremen, and union supervisors. [75]

Since 1974 various cooperative studies, done by both Mexican and American social scientists, such as Bustamante, Cornelius, Villalpando, or Weaver and Downing, tend to confirm an emerging picture of the modern wetback, and throw new light on the nature of perennial migratory movements, in and out of Mexico, and provide fresh information on numbers, comparative wages, motivations, money orders, the use or nonuse of social services, and the like. [76] Although some of these studies are still heavily influenced by the usual samples of seasonal campesino agriworkers (the most easily interviewed), such studies provide a revisionist picture of surreptitious labor migration. (See pages 285-295.)

Meanwhile, in order to substantiate desperate pleas for new federal legislation and increased funding, and to publicize the "alarming dimensions" of the shadow labor force, the Immigration and Naturalization Service (INS), under an outstanding commissioner, Leonard F. Chapman (1974-1976), finally began to accumulate and circulate employment data on all illegal aliens in a consistent manner. For example, investigators who picked up 842 illegals, mostly Mexican women, in Los Angeles in January 1975, found that about 250 were in service industries, such as restaurants and motels, 375 in light industries such as clothing manufacture, and the remainder mostly in construction and heavy industry. Many of those apprehended were already "protected" by the International Ladies Garment Workers Union, for afterall most unions are open to any dues-paying recruit. Since service and garment workers are low paid, the average wage was near the California minimum of $2.50 an hour, but even so, such immigrant women eagerly prefer American sweat shops to similar work in nearby border-zone industries. [77]

INS data confirms that wages are higher for illegals in metropolitan industrial centers, where wetbacks actually compete less with each other, and where union demands, higher levels of public assistance, and unemployment compensation, have combined to create a labor vacuum, even in the inner cities swarming with unemployed ethnic youth, such as Chicago, New York, San Francisco, Dallas, or Houston. In Chicago, for instance, INS investigators in a few days located 2,068 illegals (mostly Mexican), of whom 1,913 were employed: 1,325 were earning $2.50 to $4.50 an hour; 148, from $4.50 to $6.50 an hour; and 61 over $6.50 an hour. [78]

In view of the widespread complaints of unemployment for citizen labor, the illegal alien phenomenon seemed all the more remarkable. By mid-1974 top immigration officials were frankly admitting that the situation was "hopelessly out of control," and shortly after, when two illegals were picked up while painting the Statue of Liberty at $9.71 an hour, the Commissioner declared in exasperation: "No job site is beyond the reach of an illegal alien." [79] (The Commissioner also remarked on several occasions that if immigration officials dined out, they found themselves surrounded by illegal aliens.)

The Ford administration (1974-1976) responded by declaring illegal aliens a "national problem" in a "stagflation" economy, and on January 6, 1975, set up a Domestic Council Committee on Illegal Aliens, consisting of the Secretaries of State, Agriculture, Commerce, Labor, Health, Education and Welfare, the Attorney General, the Director of the Office of Management and Budget, and a presidential assistant, all under a coordinating arrangement with the Department of Justice and its Immigration Service.

The Domestic Council task force initiated, through several federal agencies, fact-gathering studies to determine, if possible, the number of illegals and their "real impact" on the job market and the American economy, including the "dollar drain," estimated to run into billions of dollars. [80] "Social costs" were also to be investigated, for increasingly local officials have been seeking compensation from the federal government for health, welfare, and educational services rendered to immigrant squatters and their families. The cost to the school districts of Los Angeles County alone was estimated at nearly $100 million a year, and the County Board of Supervisors estimated medical care to exceed $8 million for fiscal 1974. [81]

The Domestic Council initiated a major study on employment patterns and wages, which was done under contract to the Department of Labor by North and Houstoun. In the spring of 1975 at nineteen different sites, including Chicago, Detroit, New York, Newark, Miami, Seattle, Washington, D.C., Los Angeles, San Antonio, and San Francisco, researchers interviewed 793 illegals, of whom 481 were from Mexico, 237 from other western hemisphere countries, and 75 from eastern hemisphere nations. Some of them had not been apprehended.

The respondents' average stay in the United States was 2.5 years, there average age 28.5 years (compared to an American work force average of 35), and their average education 6.7 years (with Mexicans averaging 4.9 years). Although some had family members already in the host country, 88 percent of the Mexican respondents said they were supporting dependents in Mexico, sending an average of $129 per month out of an average monthly wage of $424. [82]

The declared occupation of informants at time of entry was distributed as shown in Table 8. However, except for operatives, skilled illegals tended, like many immigrant groups, to lose occupational status on entering an industrialized economy. The percentage of eastern hemisphere and western hemisphere skilled illegals in unskilled jobs increased significantly. On the other hand, the least skilled, those from Mexico, exhibited some upward mobility, especially as operatives in factory work, as shown in Table 9.

Another significant finding was that hourly wages were lower for apprehended illegals, $2.71 on the average, compared to $3.95 for an undetected group still holding jobs. Other averages for hourly wages (which reflected inflation) were: eastern hemisphere illegals, $4.08; western hemisphere illegals, $3.04; and Mexican illegals, $2.33. Average hourly wages in agriculture (where many Mexicans were employed) were $2.11; and for nonagricultural work, $2.83. Wages averaged $1.75 an hour in counties bordering on Mexico, compared to $1.98 for border states generally, $2.60 for a more industrialized California, $3.18 for the Midwest and Northwest, and $3.29 for the East Coast. [83] The minimum wages in those areas ranged then from $2 to $2.50 an hour.

According to another study, contracted by the Immigration Service, various independent researchers consulted by Lesko and Associates, gave an average estimate of 8.2 million for all surreptitious aliens, including perhaps 5 million or more from Mexico. [84] Actually, estimates of illegals holding jobs in the American economy in the period 1973-1976 have run anywhere from 1 million to as high as 5 million and more, AFL-CIO leaders often insisting on the higher estimates. Commonly the INS, under Chapman's leadership, claimed that it

Table 8   Occupational Distribution of Illegals Interviewed

Illegals	*% in White-collar Jobs*	*% in Crafts*	*% Working as Operatives*	*% in Service and Laborers*
E. H.	48	13	27	13 (1.3% in agriwork)
W. H.	34	15	27	24 (13% in agriwork)
Mexican	7	15	13	63 (50% in agriwork)

Source: U.S. Department of Labor, Employment and Training Administration, "Executive Summary" of David S. North and Marion F. Houstoun, *The Characteristics and Role of Illegal Aliens in the U.S. Labor Market* (Washington, D.C.: Linton and Co., 1976).

Table 9

Mexican illegals	% in Mexico	% in U.S.
White-collar workers	7	1.5
Craft workers	15	16.0
Operatives	13	24.0
Service and Laborers	65	58.0

Source: U.S. Department of Labor, Employment and Training Administration, "Executive Summary" of David S. North and Marion F. Houstoun, *The Characteristics and Role of Illegal Aliens in the U.S. Labor Market* (Washington, D.C.: December, 1975).

could free a million jobs for citizens if Congress would increase INS manpower and budgetary resources, and provide something like the Rodino bill (HR 8713) that would impose civil penalties on employers, contractors, and referrers of illegal aliens. [85]

Also, through its field offices the Immigration Service made an overall approximation of the number of illegal workers, as shown in Table 10. For the Western Region (INS) the breakdown was as shown in Table 11.

As a result of the study patterns of illegals promoted by the INS and the Domestic Council, including a "census" of illegal residents, we may in the future have firmer data on numbers, employment patterns, and family members. In the meantime, we here add, in Table 12, some conjectural figures based on a wide variety of estimates from congressional hearings, the *Annual Report* of the INS, reports of other government agencies, and from many interviews, and correspondence, with district immigration officials and Mexican consular personnel in the period 1970-1976.

Possibly 70 percent of the estimated illegals, seasonal or year-round, in agrilabor in 1976 would have been found in Texas, California, Arizona, and New Mexico in that order. Another 15 percent might have been scattered in the Pacific Northwest and Rocky Mountain states. Possibly another 15 percent would have been following harvest cycles in Minnesota, Wisconsin, Illinois, or Michigan, and increasingly in Florida and northeastern states like Pennsylvania, New Jersey, and Virginia. The number of wetbacks in migrant labor streams has been rapidly increasing as federal anti-poverty programs have "settled out" earlier Mexican immigrants and Chicano families. [86]

Of the estimated illegals in other sectors of the economy, perhaps 70 percent were then working in California, Texas, and the Lake Michigan area; possibly 10 percent in Arizona, New Mexico, and Colorado; with the remainder scattered over most states of the Union, including Alaska, but mainly in industrial centers having a previous Chicano or Latino barrio offering congenial and pro-

Table 10   Estimated Totals of All Employed Illegal Aliens by
Immigration Regions and Districts, Fiscal 1976

Eastern Region

New York	840,000	–	850,000
Newark	200,000	–	210,000
Washington	25,000	–	35,000
Other	113,200	–	124,300
Subtotal	1,178,200	–	1,219,300

Western Region

Los Angeles	900,000	–	1,000,000
San Francisco	150,000	–	160,000
Phoenix	30,000	–	35,000
Honolulu	1,000	–	1,500
Subtotal	1,081,000	–	1,196,000

Southern Region

Houston (incl. Dallas)	440,000	–	450,000
Miami	240,000	–	250,000
San Antonio	220,000	–	230,000
Atlanta	60,000	–	65,000
El Paso	45,000	–	50,000
New Orleans	10,000	–	11,000
Subtotal	1,015,000	–	1,056,000

Northern Region

Chicago	270,000	–	280,000
Detroit	40,000	–	45,000
Cleveland	40,000	–	45,000
Denver	20,000	–	25,000
Portland, Ore.	20,000	–	25,000
Other	24,500	–	29,600
Subtotal	414,500	–	449,600
Total estimate	3,688,700	–	3,921,700

Source: Adapted from Senate Committee on the Judiciary, *Immigration 1976, Hearings . . . on S. 3074*, pp. 39-41.

tective coloration, such as Kansas City, Toledo, St. Paul, New York, Newark,
or Detroit.[87]

Table 11   Estimated Number of Employed Illegal Aliens in the Western
Region by Category of Employment and by
Wage Scale Ranges, Fiscal Year 1976

Category	*$6.50 Plus*	*$4.50- 6.49*	*$2.50- 4.49*	*Less Than $2.49*	*Total*
Heavy Industry	333	500	1,167	333	2,333
Light Industry	1,167	4,585	97,189	104,607	207,548
Agriculture	500	7,002	643,482	199,213	850,197
Construction	583	583	3,084	2,251	6,501
Services	583	1,167	13,670	24,672	40,092
Totals	3,166	13,837	758,592	331,076	1,106,671

Source: Robert J. Seitz, Public Information Director, INS. Cited by Vic Villalpando, Project
Director, and others associated with the San Diego County Immigration Council, *A
Study of the Socioeconomic Impact of Illegal Aliens on the County of San Diego*
(San Diego County Human Resources Agency, January, 1977), Table 6, p. 48.

Socioeconomic Costs—a Growing Controversy

Meantime, a new wave of researchers raised serious doubts about restrictionist charges that illegal aliens were, all in all, a socioeconomic liability, and
that most job slots filled by illegals could be filled by jobless Americans. North
and Houstoun concluded from their sample of aliens from both hemispheres
that mostly "illegals are taking jobs that no Americans want."[88]

Villalpando, and others associated with the San Diego County study,
pointed out that in 1975, the depths of the recession in Los Angeles, 2,154 jobs
were opened by the apprehensions of illegals, and the State Human Resources
Development Agency could not fill them. Moreover, when 340 jobs were
"opened" in San Diego County in 1975-1976 under an Employer Cooperation
Program, inaugurated by the INS, the jobs could only be filled by greencard
commuters from Tijuana. Half of those jobs were in the hotel-motel business
and paid $2 per hour (plus tips). A welfare family of five could then receive
about $4,800 annually, tax free (plus other subsidies such as food stamps and
health care), and a family head working alone could not have made that much
at $2 to $2.50 per hour. Therefore, "it is unlikely that persons eligible for welfare benefits would work for the wages that the majority of illegal aliens
receive."[89]

Cornelius, in his field study of long-time "professional migrants" from central Mexico, concluded that their jobs—seasonal work, requiring mobility, at
minimum wages—could hardly be filled by American labor.[90] In a probe of
farm and ranch needs in isolated parts of Nevada and other northwestern
states, Corwin and Hancock found that because of a local labor shortage, ac-

Table 12   Rough Approximations of Mexican Illegals Employed in the
United States Around 1976*

I. Agrilabor

Illegal Commuters. Seasonal farm and ranch hands and odd jobbers from Mexico's border region and central plateau, who avoid inspection or pass as visitors on border-crossing cards	70,000–	100,000?
Migratory Illegals. From same areas, follow wide-ranging migrant streams through many states, working seasonally for large and small agri-business employers	150,000–	200,000?
Resident Illegals. Settled in ones, twos, and threes, often as family units on farms, ranches, dairies, and nurseries, or in nearby Chicano *colonias*, in most states of the Union	160,000–	200,000?
Subtotal	380,000–	500,000?

II. Industrial, Service, and Managerial

Illegal Commuters. Part-time or seasonal migrants in border zone, who do various jobs, avoiding inspection or entering on visitor cards	80,000–	100,000?
Domestics. Crossing as shoppers and visitors to do part-time or full-time housework in all border towns, and placed by employment agencies in many inland cities like San Antonio, Dallas, Phoenix, or Los Angeles	110,000–	140,000?
Service and Maintenance. Unskilled or semiskilled labor in border zones and interior in restaurants, motels, filling stations, garages, car washes, warehouses, dry cleaners, and the like	650,000–	950,000?
Factory and Construction. Unskilled to skilled labor in industrial, assembly, and packing plants, and in building trades, commonly in sprawling industrial zones like Chicago-Milwaukee, Dallas-Ft. Worth, Houston-Galveston, or Los Angeles-San Diego, and smaller cities	900,000–	1,200,000?
Managerial. Those with special supervisory, administrative, or technical skills acquired in factories, shops, stores, agribusiness, or professional schools in the United States and Mexico	80,000–	110,000?
Subtotal	1,820,000–	2,500,000?
Total	2,200,000–	3,000,000?

*These conjectures do not include thousands of illegals picked up on the way to a job or soon after starting one. Figures therefore represent a quasi-permanent labor force, male and female, which in recent years may be growing by 200,000 or 300,000 annually. Moreover, since the Carter amnesty plan of 1977 tens of thousands of seasonal workers and kinfolk have been seeking a non-deportable guest-worker status by either temporary or permanent settlement in the United States. See Chapter 12.

centuated by welfare and food stamps, employers were turning increasingly to Mexican seasonals. A long distance phone call to "Juan" in Guanajuato or to "Jesus" in Chihuahua would send a covey of "needed wetbacks" on their way.[91]

Also, the previously cited surveys by Mexico's Commission on Surreptitious Labor Emigration, as well as the samplings of Mexican sociologist Busta-mante, seemed to confirm a growing interdependence between America's patchwork welfare economy (rather than American capitalism) and Mexico's surplus population.[92]

Piore, an M.I.T. economist, provided a more controversial perspective. By holding wages down, illegals encouraged labor-intensive industries and dis-couraged automation. "In this sense, the presence of aliens serves to preserve native jobs." (Shades of the Luddites!) Moreover, he warned, "any wholesale attempt to end the migration is, therefore, likely to be exceedingly disruptive to the operation of the society."[93] This argument seemed to match the warnings of Cornelius, Bustamante, and Mexican officials that any policelike cutoff of Mexican emigration would threaten economic stability in Mexico and civil lib-erties in both countries. The only justified action, if any, would be a massive work-permit program or some form of amnesty.[94]

To the foregoing, other researchers, and labor leaders, say, in effect, "non-sense!" In a few instances some categories of domestic labor may be unaffec-ted, or even "pushed up," by illegals, but unlike the mix of workers (Spaniards, Italians, Turks, Greeks, Algerians, and others) that migrate to west European countries, the Mexican influx is so massive, so uncontrolled, and so concen-trated in certain economic sectors and geographic regions that even yester-day's wetback is adversely affected. Thus Briggs and Sterling characterized the nonstop Mexican inflow as the largest and most exploitative labor exchange of its kind in the world.[95] And economist Ray Marshall (presently Secretary of Labor in the Carter administration) has rejected the facile com-parison between Europe's guest workers and the Mexican borderland phe-nomenon. In any case, all alien labor tends to settle in and compete for better jobs.[96] Others have pointed out that as alien laborers acquire a sense of secu-rity or legitimation, they appear to lose the virtues praised by employers, such as docility, mobility, job eagerness, acceptance of lower wages, or reluctance to join labor unions and social assistance programs. Moreover, they begin bring-ing in nonworking dependents.[97]

Faced with conflicting data and recommendations from researchers, and Chicano protests against any effort to make the illegal alien the scapegoat for America's unemployed millions, a growing number of legislators and edito-rialists, as well as President Ford's Domestic Council Committee on Illegal Aliens, could not decide whether undocumented immigrants, as a whole, had become a liability or an asset to a welfare-state economy.[98]

Here we will touch briefly on the disputed "macro economy" of illegal aliens, three-fifths of whom were presumed to be Mexican. This issue involves such slippery questions as balance of payments, taxes, welfare, crime, and bicultural education costs. To begin with, North and Houstoun found that nearly 80 percent of their sample sent abroad a monthly average of $151, with Mexican nationals sending only $129. [99] According to the San Diego study, 71 percent of 217 Mexican informants sent home a monthly average of $138. [100] Cornelius found a similar pattern of illegals' sending and carrying home substantial sums. His data included a sample of money orders received by the Banco National de Mexico. [101]

If, hypothetically, there were 2 or 3 million illegal workers each sending to Mexico an average of $130 per month from six months to twelve months per year, the total would range from $2 to $4 billion. How is the money used? Like Taylor in the 1930s, Cornelius confirmed that a certain class of proprietory-minded migrants on Mexico's Central Plateau invested earnings in farms, small businesses, or material comforts. [102] Bustamante confirmed that in many instances the whole village economy depended on American earnings. [103] But apparently some of the money is set aside to pay for the return passage; often it is handled on a regular businesslike basis by a familiar smuggling ring. [104] On the other hand, the San Diego study noted that even if 37 percent of the total earnings of illegals were sent to Mexico, 63 percent of their wages presumably remained to benefit the American community. [105]

Then there is the Mexican side of the argument. As Raza scholars, like Bustamante, pointed out, the expropriation of Mexican surplus labor value in the form of low wages and tax deductions would greatly exceed the so-called dollar drain. [106] In addition, Bustamante and Mexican officials have made abundantly clear to Washington conferees that much of the money sent to Mexico, like money generated there, is spent on American goods, leaving Mexico with an annual trade deficit of between $2 or $3 billion. According to President José López Portillo, inaugurated in November 1976, cutting off border migration is positively not the answer; rather the answer lies in American tariff concessions to help Mexico reduce its peso drain. [107]

North and Houstoun, the San Diego study, Cornelius, and Bustamante all found that about 80 percent of their informants had had taxes withheld from paychecks, whereas only a few had used tax-supported services or applied for income-tax rebates. Perhaps Bustamante's sample of several hundred deportees would be typical: only 3.2 percent had used welfare services, and only 7.8 percent had used public health services. [108] Far from posing a social burden on tax-supported services, do not undocumented aliens contribute more than their share? Chicano scholars, rewriting the history of Mexican labor exploitation, have made much the same point. [109]

However, data from tight-lipped deportees, who often leave a family safely in the United States while going through the revolving door of voluntary departures, and data from illegal family heads who elude apprehension do not enter fully into estimates of social costs. Moreover, the administration of Great Society programs has been so scandalously lax that we cannot say to what extent illegal aliens, or hidden family members, as well as unqualified native groups, including public employees and outreach workers, may be riding on convoluted social programs?[110]

After the federal government subsidized public relief in the 1930s, and after the initiation of the civil rights movement and the Great Society in the 1960s, tax-saving efforts to remove ineligible persons from relief rolls declined remarkably. Removal efforts were hopelessly complicated by administrative regulations and by court decisions tied retroactively to the catchall due process clause of the Fourteenth Amendment: ". . . nor shall any state . . . without due process of law . . . deny any person within its jurisdiction the equal protection of its laws." Accordingly in 1969 the Supreme Court erased historic residency requirements for public assistance. The newly arrived migrant or immigrant family must be granted assistance if there is a *prima facie* need.

California, which probably had over 2 million illegal aliens in 1976, mostly Mexican, plus tens of thousands agriworkers passing for Tex-Mex, struggled during the recession of 1974-1976 to tighten eligibility procedures. In *Varela v Swoap*, a judge decided in a Sacramento County Superior Court in December 1974 that public assistance eligibility could not be terminated solely because the Immigration Service had been unable to find a record of the alien applicant. Nor could persons residing under "color of law," such as certain visa applicants, be excluded. Furthermore, the applicant did not have to certify that he or she was in the country legally.[111] According to welfare officials, the case was another example of the judge in his new role of legislator.

The decision had no impact on general relief, funded by counties, or on food stamps, where qualification procedures have been notoriously permissive throughout the nation. In the latter case, the California Department of Public Welfare determined eligibility, as best it could, without INS verification, under regulations of February 3, 1976.[112]

Revised California regulations of September 5, 1975, led to a new Form WR-6 (Alien Status Verification), whereby the applicant for welfare simply states that he or she is a legal resident, and is not under order of deportation or married to a person who is. Importantly, the California Welfare and Institutional Code (Sec. 11104) was modified to authorize verification of suspect applications through interviews with immigration personnel. According to the San Diego study—a model probe of its kind—with the WR-6 procedure, from May 10 through December 13, 1976, 762 applications were found to be ineligible, meaning a potential savings to the County of some $90,000 per month. [113] In fact, many applications were dropped statewide, so that an estimated $4 million was saved in tax-supported services in 1976. Other states, meantime, have been moving slowly toward similar verification procedures.[114]

Some researchers have pointed out that there has not been an exceptionally high percentage of Chicanos on such programs as Aid to Families with Dependent Children. In California in 1969, a reported 14 percent of Spanish-surnamed families (not all of Mexican origin) received welfare payments. That figure was slightly over the reported Latino population in that state. Texas, by comparison, had been stringent. There, where Chicanos then made up around 18 percent of the population, the comparable figure was 9 percent. Such aid, then, averaged $930 per annum for a Texas family compared to $1,660 in California.[115] Such differentials have long been an important factor in "poverty folk" migrations from one state to another.

Somewhat more recent data on welfare and the Latino population, a prime target of anti-poverty outreach workers, has been given by Barceló and Breiter, who found that Mexican-origin groups made far less use of social assistance than other minorities. Blacks constituted about 14 percent of the national population; yet made up nearly 50 percent of the AFDC case load in 1973. The Puerto Ricans then made up close to 1.5 percent of the population; yet accounted for 6.8 percent of the welfare families. The Mexican-origin groups (then anywhere between 3 percent and 6 percent of the national population) made up 5.4 percent.[116]

Although data has not yet been fully broken down for various ethnic groups, in April 1975, 37.9 percent of the black population was reported to be on food stamps, compared to 11.4 for Latin Americans.[117] Puerto Ricans, who were given blanket citizenship in 1917, would be a major contributory factor in the latter figure, for close to 70 percent of the Puerto Rican population on the mainland and on the island Commonwealth were then on food stamps.

Chicanos have frequently pointed out that members of La Raza, in general, have been reluctant to seek public assistance. It is open to question, however, whether this is principally because of ethnic pride or because of pervasive public-charge fears, dating from the 1930s, that once illegal aliens have been on public welfare they are commonly denied immigration visas.[118]

Welfare statistics alone can be misleading. Public assistance and food stamps enable many legal and legalized immigrants to smuggle in members of the extended family and support them within a subsidized household, even though these dependents have never registered as immigrants or welfare recipients. This has long been a common practice—and a census problem—in American cities like New York, Boston, or Milwaukee and also in the borderland counties where heavy Raza settlements have virtually obliterated the boundary line.[119]

Furthermore, it is now common for legal and illegal immigrants, and native Americans alike, to combine seasonal or part-time work with public assistance for the family group. Migrant workers often do seasonal work strictly for cash without any records or do unreported seasonal work out of state, leaving some family members at home to collect social assistance. Moreover, some families collect from more than one state. But as some welfare directors and some labor specialists, like Briggs, Schmidt, and Fogel, have emphasized, the problem is not so much that newly arrived migrants and immigrants go directly on public aid, but rather that the taking of jobs by free-wheeling workers, domestic or alien, provides not only a handy pretext for employers to ignore local labor, especially union labor, but a justification for local workers, who may be earlier migrants or immigrants, to accept welfare, unemployment compensation, or vocational rehabilitation pay. Thus a multibillion dollar War on Poverty is perpetuated, along with the cyclic pumping in of fresh labor.[120] In any case, according to exploratory studies of Third World immigration by the Comptroller General's Office, immigrant families, who are often legalized immigrants, tended more and more, like native Americans, to go on public assistance and accept other tax-supported services. In 1976, for instance, alien parents in California, New York, New Jersey, Florida, and Illinois collected $72.3 million in Supplemental Security Income because sponsors did not honor sworn affidavits of support.[121]

Some revisionists have overlooked the use that generations of undocumented immigrants have made of a vast array of private social and philanthropic agencies that dispense billions of dollars annually in services and ask few questions. The Catholic Campaign for Human Development, in which Chicano leaders, like Auxiliary Bishop Patricio Flores of San Antonio play a leading role, would be a current example. In general, practitioners of private philanthropy no longer hesitated to put unregistered aliens into tax-supported community development programs, for in the Great Society a clear distinction was never drawn between church and state.

Another sign of erratic social planning was that demonstrators, headed by church and philanthropic leaders, demanded of a new administration both blanket amnesty for their clients and more public jobs and anti-poverty programs for Latino minorities.[122] When President Carter, in response, named Leonel Castillo, a Mexican-American civil rights activist, Commissioner of Immigration in the spring of 1977, the choice seemed somehow dictated by Great Society considerations.[123] The extent to which Castillo's and the Carter administration's broad amnesty proposals might increase social assistance for unskilled alien families has since become one of the most disturbing questions facing congressional reformers and taxpayers in "impacted areas."

The interminable flow of non-citizen Third World children into public schools and into remedial and bicultural experiments for developing "ethnic pride" unquestionably would be the greatest single cost factor in what some alarmed restrictionists see as the "Brown peril." But how to get data? Interview studies of deportees, who rarely reveal that they have a family in the United States, tell us little. And since the INS has for many years followed a *de facto* policy of "hands off" with regard to families lying low in ethnic neighborhoods, no satisfactory data has come from that source. All that immigration officers know for certain is that many "voluntary returns" immediately return to families in the United States.124

Moreover, the federal government itself has, through various legislative and judicial decisions since the 1960s, protected the "invisibility" of non-citizen children in public schools and such programs as Head Start. Various states, however, have been trying, without marked success so far, to minimize the tax cost to property holders, many of whom want "cheap alien labor" without the social costs, as we have seen in the historic example of Texas. In some cases the annual costs of educating the large families of undocumented migrant workers far outrun the families' incomes. But neither the migrant family nor the taxpayer have much choice.

State education codes usually require that every child between the ages of six and sixteen attend an accredited school, public or private. The parent or guardian does not have to provide information regarding the child's immigrant status, only proof of age and local residence. Thus out of a tax fund, resting principally on private homes, most states dutifully spend annually from $800 to $1,200, or more, on each pupil in a public school. By contrast, in other countries, including Mexico, the burden of public education rests not on real estate taxes but on general revenues.

Here again the California experience may be instructive. In 1971 the California Supreme Court in the case of John Serrano ruled that the state's system of financing schools primarily through local property taxes was discriminatory and unconstitutional, for it allowed wealthier school districts, like Beverly Hills, to spend much more per pupil to achieve quality education. As a result California, beginning in 1977, would have to spend over a billion dollars a year in state income-tax money to equalize per capita spending in disadvantaged districts, many of which, like those in Los Angeles and San Francisco, were overrun with illegal aliens. Although in the case of Demetrio P. Rodríguez and others of San Antonio, Texas, the U.S. Supreme Court in March 1973 ruled that the property-tax system of funding public schools was not necessarily unconstitutional, nevertheless, other states, like Texas, Arizona, Colorado, Illinois, and New York, felt constrained to follow California's example.125 Again, as in California, many poorer districts were impacted with invisible aliens. Additional costs in such areas would include federal and state funds for Head Start, free lunches, health care, busing to achieve integration, and bilingual education in a babel of tongues, including American Indian, Tagalog (Filipino), Chinese, Vietnamese, Greek, Portuguese, but mainly Spanish. Some Spanish teachers, moreover, were using bilingualism to promote cultural separatism. By 1977 the federal government had spent about half a billion dollars on bilingualism. (Yet, as the WASP population declined or moved out, the district school bureaucracy seemed to welcome immigrant children as a means to maintain per capita funding allotments from federal and state sources.)

There was virtually nothing that could be done about "undocumented aliens" in public schools. In 1969 the California Education Code (Sec. 6957) authorized the State Board of Supervisors to forward a list of children, legally and illegally in the country, to the Immigration Service. But in September 1975 a judge of the Superior Court voided that section (*Maria de Lourdes v Riles and the El Centro Elementary School District*) on grounds that such lists violated the federal Family Educational Rights and Privacy Act of 1974. Under this ruling, which had a statewide and even national influence, the district superintendent had to submit the names of immigrant children to the Board of Supervisors so that school districts could be reimbursed for per capita costs. But no information could be passed on to immigration officials.[126]

A similar provision for confidentiality was made in a hotly debated school law passed by the Texas legislature in 1975 and upheld by the Texas Supreme Court on May 17, 1978. However, this law also provided that if the school principal reported a pupil as illegally in the district, the state could require the parent, guardian, or local taxpayers to pay the costs. It was intended mainly for the border counties with 70 to 90 percent Mexican-origin population and a low-tax base, where Raza politicians and officials have commonly opened social services to Raza cousins from over the border. In those counties, "where Mexico begins," that law was considered racist, discriminatory, and virtually unenforceable.[127]

Chicano and other revisionist researchers naturally question the generalization—often made by restrictionists throughout the history of American immigration—that unregulated immigration contributes to rising crime costs in port cities and other urban areas. They see exploitation of the undocumented alien as the principal crime.[128] On both sides of this question there has been much tilting with windmills and little precise data. It seems, however, that illegals looking for work in the interior of the country, or keeping a low profile while holding a job or living on public assistance, rarely make a direct contribution to crime statistics and costs. Rather in the case of undocumented Mexicans, the proper focus would be the lawless borderlands.[129]

Most of the crime associated with Mexican aliens has always been a by-product of a rampant, predatory, and degrading wetback business mainly concentrated in the dismal slum areas along the notorious Anglo-Mexican frontier, but with runners throughout the Raza barrios in the United States and Mexico.[130] Passing over how Americans sin on Mexico's side of the line, the reader might consider the following criminal activities on the American side:

(1) An increasing incidence of burglaries, vandalistic acts, and whore mongering committed by vagrants and juveniles who, from border towns like Agua Prieta, Ciudad Juárez, or Matamoros, cross daily and with impunity into adjoining communities like Douglas, El Paso, or Brownsville.[131]

(2) An increasing number of illegals and Chicanos who carry narcotics for smugglers in border counties in order to pay for jobs, transportation, and fake

documents for themselves and family members, as well as for personal profit or to finance La Raza Unida Party's political reconquest of the border states.[132]

(3) Increasing venality in employers, foreman, union organizers, and labor agents who ignore the jobless native worker in search of cheaper labor and kickbacks from docile wetbacks.[133]

(4) Increasing fraud in immigration and civil identity documents and in quickie marriages of "bartered brides" to illegal aliens.[134]

(5) An increasing number of deadly bushwacking incidents leading, as in the 1950s, to dozens of bodies (mostly of Mexicans but also of Guatemalans, Colombians, and others), found floating in the Rio Grande (more than sixty in 1976), or rotting along desert trails, and increasingly involving vicious juvenile "wolf packs" who beat or kill their victims, and even involving greedy Mexican border police seeking to lift money or valuable narcotics from migrants and immigrants.[135]

(6) Increasing deviant behavior among second- and third-generation immigrant and migrant folk who, no longer in fear of deportation and free from the traditional work obligations of the extended family, seem to blossom out in a common profile of juvenile delinquency, as in the "welfare belts" of Los Angeles, Denver, San Francisco, New York, Newark, or Chicago, where black, Chicano, Puerto Rican, Oriental, "poor white," and other ethnic gang lords mark out their turf in violent fashion and steal to support drug habits and subcultural life styles not covered by social assistance subsidies.[136]

The pecking order that naturally results from unregulated migration from rural folk societies into bourgeois communities and the resulting second-rate schools, discrimination, segregation, etc., would of course, contribute to patterns of delinquency, dependency, and alienation in America's inner cities.[137] The West European and Scandinavian experience with its imported "guest workers" has not been much different.[138]

Another incalculable cost would be national job-training programs. The Office of Economic Opportunity and various federal agencies started these programs in 1965 with a view toward abolishing poverty principally among blacks, but the Latino population soon became a major recipient. Among expanding bilingual programs are Job Corps, National Migrant Program, Manpower Development and Training, CETA (Comprehensive Employment Training Administration), and SER (Service, Employment, and Redevelopment). The latter program is administered exclusively by Mexican-American groups, like the G.I. Forum and the League of United Latin American Citizens (LULAC).

"Displaced Chicanos" make up more than half of all enrollees in such programs in the southwestern states and very high proportions elsewhere. Virtually any member of La Raza, documented or not, has had access to learn-for-pay programs. The cost of providing one trainee with several months training has run anywhere from $2,500 to $12,000.[139] The Carter administration has sponsored costly extensions of Great Society or New Deal programs in order to create jobs for unemployed youths and welfare dependents. For instance, in May 1977 Congress approved a $4 billion public works plan that would generate 300,000 jobs, but in a typical comment, Secretary of Labor Marshall expressed the fear that incoming illegals could easily offset all of Carter's job-creating efforts.[140]

Naturally, researchers and reformers have made an overlay of public policy proposals that would solve America's alien dilemma. For lack of space we refer the reader to Chapter 6 and to Vialet's summary account of research findings in conflict.[141]

Here we add only a few observations. There was no significant groundswell of protest against undocumented aliens holding jobs, or sharing social services, supposedly needed by underprivileged Americans. Nor was there any sign that the federal government would ever be pressed into a deportation drive similar to that of the early 1930s. On the contrary, pressures for continuous amnesty measures seemed overwhelming. The reasons are not hard to find. Unlike the 1930s, there now existed a huge social service bureaucracy at all levels of government, trade union security, and a dozen programs to cushion unemployment, including unemployment compensation, which reached an outlay of over $18 billion in fiscal 1976. It appeared that as natives of all ethnic backgrounds were shifting onto these programs and, in many cases, giving up economic mobility, the eager alien arrived on the scene—a "godsend" to employers. A similar welfare-state phenomenon has been reported in England, West Germany, France, Sweden, and other countries characterized by a relatively high level of social security and unionized labor.[142]

Notes

1. Bustamante, "Commodity Migrants," p. 21. See also Stoddard, "Illegal Mexican Labor," 175-209.

2. Taylor, *A Mexican American Frontier: Nueces County, Texas*; likewise his *Mexican Labor: Imperial Valley*; and *Valley of the South Platte Colorado* (1929). See also Luís L. Arroyo and Victor B. Nelson Cisneros, eds., "Special Issue on Labor History and the Chicano," *Aztlán*, 6:2 (Summer 1975), 137-325.

3. Coalson, "Development of the Migratory Farm Labor System in Texas."

4. Texas Good Neighbor Commission, *Texas Migrant Labor Annual Reports* (Austin, 1966-1972).

5. Texas State Department of Health, *Annual Report . . . Migrant Project* (Austin, 1968), pp. 13-14.

6. North, *The Border Crossers.*

7. Texas Good Neighbor Commission, *Annual Report 1972*, pp. 8-9.

8. Taylor, *Mexican Labor in the United States* (Ten parts, Berkeley, 1928-1934); Fuller, "The Supply of Agricultural Labor," pp. 19777-19898; McWilliams, *Factories in the Fields;* also McWilliams, *North from Mexico.*

9. Webb, *The Great Plains.*

10. California, Department of Employment, Farm Labor Service, *Annual Farm*

Labor Reports (Sacramento, 1960-1966); also Craig, *The Bracero Program*, pp. 180-182.

11. John G. McBride, *Vanishing Bracero: Valley Revolution* (San Antonio: Naylor Co., 1963).

12. California . . . *Annual Farm Labor Report 1964.* For current threat to unionist gains of Chavez, see "Machines, 'Villains' of Farm Workers, " *Des Moines Tribune,* February 16, 1978, p. 8.

13. Taylor, *Mexican Labor: Dimmit County*; likewise Menefee, *Mexican Migratory Workers.* See also note 8.

14. U.S. Congress, House Committee on Immigration and Naturalization, *Hearings on Seasonal Agricultural Laborers from Mexico*, 69th Cong., 1st Sess. (1926), pp. 22-24.

15. According to more than sixty interviews by Arthur F. Corwin with immigration and border patrol officers in border states, April-September 1970, August 1972, April-March 1974 and 1975, and in midwestern states, October-November 1973, and May 1974. For earlier use of hand labor instead of machines, see Menefee and Cassmore, *The Pecan Shellers*; and H.A. Shapiro, "The Workers of San Antonio, Texas, 1900-1940" (Ph.D. diss., Austin, University of Texas, 1952).

16. Taylor, *Mexican Labor: Chicago and Calumet Region* (1932); and Levenstein, *Labor Organizations.* Relevant also is Laird's study of Mexican labor on the Santa Fe Railroad, "Argentine, Kansas."

17. Levenstein, *Labor Organizations*; and Reports of the Annual Mexico-United States Interparliamentary Conference, in Archivo de la Secretaría de Relaciones Exteriores, Mexico City (ASRE).

18. For instance, the Mexican labor strike against Japanese growers, in Wollenberg, "Race and Class in Rural California, 155-163; see also Mexican consular correspondence on problems of organizing labor in California and Texas, ASRE, for example, Expediente Personal de Ricardo Hill, 21-6-4, 1/131/4977; or Joaquín Terrazas, Expediente Personal, 21-4-5 (11), 1/131/3880.

19. For problems of organizing farm labor in California see Ernesto Galarza, *Spiders in the House and Workers in the Field* (Notre Dame, 1970); and his *Merchants of Labor.*

20. Levenstein, *Labor Organizations*; and Craig, *The Bracero Program*, Chap. 5: The Demise. Also, Andrew C. McClellan and Michael D. Boggs, "Illegal Aliens: A Story of Human Misery," *AFL-CIO American Federationist* (August 1974), pp. 17-23.

21. Martin Gellen, "A Century-Long Battle to Keep Cheap Labor for California Crops," *Des Moines Register*, November 2, 1973; "Can Chavez Survive?" *Time*, Sept. 3, 1973); "Strikes by Chavez Union Spread When Grape Contracts Expire," *New York Times, July 30, 1973; "More Sour Milk," *Time*, May 19, 1975; and "Rendering to Cesar," *Time*, September 22, 1975.

22. U.S. Congress, Committee on Labor and Public Welfare, *Amending Migratory Labor Laws, Hearings Before the Subcommittee on Migratory Labor* (H.A. Williams, Jr., Chairman). . . 89th Cong., 1 and 2d Sess. July 7, 1965 . . . April 12, 1966 (1966): U.S. Congress, Committee on Labor and Public Welfare, *Migrant Health Services, Hearings . . . 90th Cong., 1 Sess. on S. 2688, Dec. 7 and 13, 1967 (1968); The Migratory Farm Labor in the United States, 1969 Report . . . Pursuant to S. Res. 222 . . . 90th Cong., 2d*

Sess. (1969); U.S. Congress, Committee on Labor and Public Welfare, *Migrant and Seasonal Farmworker Powerlessness, Hearings* . . . 91st Cong., 1 and 2d Sess., June 1969 . . . July, 1969 (Five parts, 1970); and U.S. Congress, Committee on Labor and Public Welfare, *Farmworkers in Rural America, 1971-1972, Hearings . . . 92d Cong., 1 and 2d Sess.* (5 parts, 1971-1972). See also Briggs, Jr., "Chicanos and Rural Poverty, 3-24.

23. Anna-Stina Ericson, "The Impact of Commuters on the Mexican-American Border Area," *Monthly Labor Review* (August 1970), pp. 18-27; North, *The Border Crosser*.

24. *Los Angeles Times*, May 23, 1974, Part I-A, pp. 1-4.

25. Cardoso, "Mexican Emigration."

26. Carrol Norquest, *Rio Grande Wetbacks: Mexican Migrant Workers* (Albuquerque: University of New Mexico, 1973). The author, an employer of Mexican labor, cited examples of employers bringing in one "wetback" after another on immigration papers, only to have the employee leave soon after getting his visa. Immigration authorities readily confirm this pattern.

27. For example, Leal Castillo, "Importancia económica y social," or Jorge L. Bustamante, "Bracero solución en el origen más que en las consecuencias," *Diorama de la Cultura*, suplemento de *Excelsior* (Mexico City), November 10, 1974, pp. 9-10.

28. For example, see series of articles by Aziz Shihab on wetback labor, including domestic servants, in *San Antonio Express/News*, January 27-30, 1974.

29. Some examples: G. Bromley Oxnam, "The Mexicans in Los Angeles: Los Angeles City Survey" (Los Angeles: Interchurch World Movement of North America, 1920); Elizabeth Fuller, "The Mexican Housing Problem in Los Angeles," monograph 17, Southern California Sociological Society (Los Angeles: University of Southern California, 1920); or Anita E. Jones, "Conditions Surrounding Mexicans in Chicago" (Master's diss., University of Chicago, 1928).

30. For example, Taylor, *A Mexican American Frontier.*

31. Much of the periodical literature on the "Mexican social problem" is cited by Lipshultz, "American Attitudes."

32. Neal, "The Policy of the United States."

33. Hoffman, *Unwanted Mexican Americans.*

34. (INS), *Annual Report 1954* and *1955.*

35. Julian Samora et al., *Los Mojados*; Ellis W. Hawley, "The Politics of the Mexican Labor Issue, 1950-1965," *Agricultural History* 40 (July 1966), p. 166; Lamar B. Jones, "Mexican American Labor Problem" (Ph.D. diss., Austin: University of Texas, 1965); and Schmidt, *Spanish Surnamed.* See also Briggs, Jr., *The Mexico-United States Border*, p. 28.

36. Niles M. Hanson, *Rural Poverty and the Urban Crisis: A Strategy for Regional Development* (Bloomington: University of Indiana, 1970), chap. 8.

37. See résumé of recent socioeconomic reports by state, county, and city agencies in Domestic Council Committee on Illegal Aliens, *Preliminary Report* (Washington, D.C.: Department of Justice, December 1976), Appendix A. Also House Committee on the Judiciary, *Illegal Aliens, Hearings*; Inter-Agency Committee on Mexican-American Affairs, *Mexican-Americans: A New Focus on Opportunity* (Washington, D.C., 1968); Senate Special Committee on Aging, *Availability and Usefulness of Federal Programs*

and Services to Elderly Mexican-Americans, Hearings . . . 90th Cong., 2d Sess. (five parts, 1969); and notes 22, and 38.

38. Briggs, Jr., *Chicanos and Rural Poverty*; Briggs, Walter Fogel, and Fred H. Schmidt, *The Chicano Worker* (Austin: University of Texas Press, 1977); "Information on Five Southwestern States and Texas Counties and Cities as to Family Income under $3000 and $2000 per annum," in *U.S. Census of Population, Subject Reports:1960. Persons of Spanish Surname. Final Report*. PC (2)-IB (1963); *Census of Population: 1960,* Vol. 1, Part 45: *Texas* (1962); and Upham and Wright, "Poverty Among Spanish Americans in Texas."

39. Neal, "The Policy of the United States"; and Idar and McClellan, *What Price Wetbacks?*

40. John R. Peavey, *Echoes of the Rio Grande, from the Thorny Hills of Duval to the Sleepy Rio Grande* (Copyright by author, McAllen, Texas, 1963), pp. 257-259.

41. Private files of John W. Holland, former District Director of Immigration Service, San Antonio, and of Fletcher Rawls, Former Chief, Border Patrol, McAllen, containing clippings for period 1950-1954 from such south Texas papers as McAllen *Valley Evening Monitor*, Harlingen *Valley Morning Star*, or *Laredo Times*.

42. Letter from retired Border Patrol agent, San Antonio, April 14, 1977.

43. James Flanigan, "North of the Border—Who Needs Whom?" *Forbes* 119:8 (April 15, 1977), 37-41.

44. For patronage politics in south Texas, see Kenneth Gilmore, "Laredo Learns About the War on Poverty," *Reader's Digest* (January 1967), pp. 44-49; Lester Velie, "Poverty at the Border," *Reader's Digest* (August 1970), pp. 92-97; John S. Shockley, *Chicano Revolt in a Texas Town* (University of Notre Dame, 1973); or John Muir, "Un millonario contra Chicanos," *Excelsior*, January 30, 1977.

45. See statements by gringo-hating José Angel Gutíerrez and others in *La Tribuna de Monterrey*, April 3, 4, and 19, 1976; and in Féderico Gómez Pombo, "En 20 años seremos dueños del sureste de Estados Unidos," *Excelsior*, May 22, 1976, p. 12A; also statements made at Symposium on Immigration and Public Policy: The Humanistic Imperative," sponsored by Chicano Training Center, University of Houston, April 15-16, 1977.

46. Texas Good Neighbor Commission, *Annual Report 1972*, p. 3.

47. See statistical study of migration on both sides of the border by Thomas Weaver and Theodore E. Downing, eds., *Mexican Migration* (Tucson: Bureau of Ethnic Research, University of Arizona Press, 1976).

48. "Persons of Spanish Origins in the United States: March, 1973," and *Current Census Reports*, Series P-20, No. 259 (January 1974).

49. INS, *Annual Report*, Tab. 14: Immigrants Admitted by Country or Region of Birth. See also Tab. 35: Aliens Who Reported Under the Alien Address Program.

50. U.S. President, *Manpower Report of the President* (1973), p. 90.

51. INS, *Annual Report 1972*, p. 46.

52. *Census of Population: 1970*, PC(2)-ID.

53. Ibid.; and Briggs, Fogel, and Schmidt, *The Chicano Worker*.

54. Paul S. Taylor, *Mexican Labor in the United States: Chicago and Calumet Region* (Berkeley: University of California, 1932); and Julian Samore and Richard A. Lamanna, *Mexican-Americans in a Midwest Metropolis: A Study of East Chicago* (Ad-

vance Report 8, Graduate School of Business Administration, Los Angeles: University of California, 1966).

55. Statements by Consul General in Chicago to Mexico's presidential candidate, José López Portillo, "Mexicanos in Chicago . . . ," *La Tribuna de Monterrey*, April 3, 1976; and series of reports on Mexican illegals in Chicago by Robert Suro, *La Tribuna de Monterrey*, February 25-March 2, 1976 (originally published in *Chicago Sun Times*). See also U.S. Congress, Senate Judiciary Committee, *Immigration 1976, Hearings Before the Subcommittee on Immigration and Naturalization . . . on S. 3074 to Amend the Immigration and Nationality Act, March 17, 18, 24, 31; April 1, 7, 8, 1976 . . . 94th Cong., 2d Sess.* (1976).

56. California Department of Employment, *Mexican Nationals in California Agriculture, 1942-1959* (Sacramento, 1959).

57. Letter from B. L. Brown, Deputy Undersecretary of Legislative Affairs, U.S. Department of Labor, to Senator Gaylord Nelson, Chairman, Senate Subcommittee on Migratory Labor, December 12, 1974, in author's files.

58. U.S. Congress, Select Commission on Western Hemisphere Immigration, *Report . . . January, 1978*, Part XVII, "Commuter Problem," 101-130; and U.S. Congress, Select Commission on Western Hemisphere Immigration, *Impact of Commuter Aliens Along the Mexican and Canadian Borders, Hearings* (Three parts, 1968-1969).

59. Fogel, *Mexican Americans in Southwest Labor Markets*; also declarations of Raúl Castro, Mexican-born governor of Arizona, reported in "Chicano Does Not Compete in Society," *Latin American Digest* 10:3 (Spring 1976), 16; and in *El Porvenir* (Monterrey), November 10, 1974.

60. *Census of Population: 1970*, PC(2)-ID, and PC(2)-1A.

61. Ibid., PC(d)-IC. This statistic refers to foreign-born persons of Mexican origin.

62. Ibid., PC(1); PC(2)-ID.

63. Ibid., PC(2)-1A, and PC(2)-ID.

64. See notes 38, 35, and 22.

65. Briggs, Jr., *Chicanos and Rural Poverty*; Briggs, Fogel, and Schmidt, *The Chicano Worker*. See also note 38.

66. *Census of Population: 1970*, PC(2)-ID.

67. Fogel, *Mexican Americans in Southwest Labor Markets*, chaps. 7-8.

68. Fred H. Schmidt, "The Current Economic Condition of the Mexican American," paper presented to the Conference on Economic and Education Perspectives of the Mexican American, Aspen, Colorado, August 28, 1972, p. 5.

69. Julian Samora et al., *Los Mojados*, p. 46.

70. Apprehension data from INS, *Annual Report*, Tab. 27-B.

71. Samora et al., *Los Mojados*, p. 82, and Tab. 7.

72. Ibid., Chap. 6.

73. México, Secretaría de Relaciones Exteriores, Comisión Intersecretarial para el Estudio de la Emigración Subrepticia de Trabajadores Mexicanos, "Informe de Actividades y Recomendaciones" (December 1973; updated October 1974).

74. INS, *Annual Report 1973*, Tab. 30.

75. Interviews by A. F. Corwin with immigration personnel, Mexican workers, and employers in border states, April-September 1970; August 1972; April 1974; and Chi-

cago, November 1974. See also *Los Angeles Times*, June 27, 1973, II-4; "Alien Flood Rolls," *San Antonio News*, October 23, 1974; and Aziz Shihab, "San Antonio Illegal Alien Center," *San Antonio News*, January 21, 1975.

76. Jorge A. Bustamante, "More on the Impact of the Undocumented Immigration from Mexico on the U.S.-Mexican Economy: Preliminary Findings and Suggestions for Bilateral Cooperation," paper presented at conference on Fronteras '76, San Diego, November 1976 (Mexico: Centro de Estudios Sociológicos, El Colegio de México, 1976); Wayne A. Cornelius, with Juan Díez Cañedo, *Mexican Migration to the United States: The View from Rural Sending Communities* (Cambridge, Mass.: Center for International Studies, Massachusetts Institute of Technology, 1976); Manuel Vic Villalpando, Project Director, and others associated with San Diego County Immigration Council, *A Study of the Socioeconomic Impact of Illegal Aliens on the County of San Diego* (San Diego: County of San Diego Human Resources Agency, 1976); Weaver and Downing, eds., *Mexican Migration*. The latter study includes contributions by Mexican anthropologists and demographers such as Fernando Camara and Margarita Nolasco.

77. House Committee on the Judiciary, *Hearings Before the Subcommittee on Immigration . . . on H.R. 982 and Related Bills, Illegal Aliens, 94th Cong., 1st Sess., February-March, 1975. Ser. No. 8* (1975), p. 79. For wider role of Mexican and chicana women in labor force, see Rosaura Sánchez, ed., *Essays on La Mujer*, part 1 (Los Angeles: Chicano Studies Center, University of California, 1977).

78. House Committee on the Judiciary, *Amending the Immigration and Nationality Act . . . Report Together with Additional, Supplemental, and Dissenting Views to Accompany H.R. 8713. Report No. 94-506* (September 24, 1975), p. 7; House Committee on the Judiciary, *Hearings . . . on H.R. 982 . . . Illegal Aliens*, pp. 33-34.

79. Ibid., p. 34.

80. Estimates of dollars exported by illegal aliens run as high as 13 billion annually, Senate Committee on the Judiciary, *Immigration 1976*, pp. 141-143. See also syndicated articles by Holger Jensen, AP writer, "Flood of Illegal Aliens," *Fort Worth Star Telegram*, June 28-30, 1976.

81. House Committee on the Judiciary, *Amending the Immigration and Nationality Act . . . H.R. 8713*, pp. 10-11. See also estimates-of-contract study carried out by IFC corporation on welfare and unemployment costs caused by displacement of local labor and legal immigrant workers by illegals, in Senate Committee on the Judiciary, *Immigration 1976*, pp. 141-143.

82. David S. North and Marion F. Houstoun, *The Characteristics and Role of Illegal Aliens in the U.S. Labor Market: An Exploratory Study*, prepared for the Employment and Training Administration, U.S. Department of Labor (Washington, D.C.: Linton and Co., 1976).

83. U.S. Department of Labor, Employment and Training Administration, "Executive Summary" of North and Houston, *The Characteristics and Role of Illegal Aliens*. (Washington, D.C., December, 1975), pp. 6-7.

84. Lesko Associates, "Final Report: Basic Data and Guidance Required to Implement a Major Illegal Alien Study during Fiscal Year 1976," prepared for the U.S. Immigration and Naturalization Service (Washington, D.C., October 15, 1975).

85. House Committee on the Judiciary, *Amending the Immigration and Nationality . . . H.R. 8713*, p. 7; and *Hearings . . . on H.R. 982 . . . Illegal Aliens*, pp. 123-124.

86. Interview information from Illinois Migrant Council, Chicago, November 26, 1973; Migrant Action, Mason City, Iowa, November 12, 1974; Colorado Migrant Council, Laredo, August 6, 1970, and April 8, 1974; Migrant Affairs, Texas Good Neighbor Commission, and Texas Employment Agency, Austin, December 22, 1974; also interviews and correspondence with personnel in thirteen district offices of Immigration Service in period 1970-1977; and interviews with Mexican consuls and honorary consuls in period 1970-1975 in Laredo, Corpus Christi, Kansas City, Chicago, Phoenix, San Francisco, St. Paul, and Denver.

87. Ibid.

88. North and Houstoun, *The Characteristics and Role of Illegal Aliens*, pp. 162-163.

89. Villalpando et al., *A Study of the Socioeconomic Impact of Illegal Aliens*, pp. 53-61.

90. Cornelius, *Mexican Migration to the United States*.

91. A. F. Corwin, with Charles Hancock, Bureau of Land Management, Reno, Nevada, "A Questionnaire Probe of Farm and Ranch Needs in Nevada and Other Western and Northwestern States," unpublished study carried out in 1975-1976, also with assistance from district offices of Immigration Service. For socioeconomic impact of Mexican squatters on a small town, see Doug McMillan, "Winnemucca's Fast Growing Third Culture," *Nevada State Journal*, February 5, 1978, pp. 1, 10.

92. Bustamante, "More on the Impact of Undocumented Immigration."

93. Michael Piore, "Illegal Immigration in the United States: Some Observations and Policy Suggestions," in National Council on Employment Policy, *Illegal Aliens: An Assessment of the Issues* (Washington, October 1976), p. 28.

94. Ibid.; and Cornelius, *Mexican Migration to the United States*, pp. 44-47; also by Cornelius, "Illegal Mexican Migration to the United States: A Summary of Recent Research Findings and Policy Implications," Unpublished Briefing Paper, Department of Political Science, M.I.T. (April 1977), pp. 17-24. For statements by Bustamante and others, see "Inmigración ilegal, única escapatoria," *El Porvenir*, June 21, 1977, p. 1; and in Alan Riding, "Mexican Says U.S. Alien Program a Myopic Policy," *The New York Times*, reprinted in *The Des Moines Register*, May 26, 1977, p. 6.

95. Briggs, Jr., "Mexican Workers in the United States Labor Market: A Contemporary Dilemma," *International Labour Review*, 112 (November 1975), 351-368; and Richard Sterling, "International Labor Markets: The United States-Mexican Case," unpublished paper (September 1974), quoted by Joyce Vialet, *Illegal Aliens: Analysis and Background* (Washington, D.C.: Congressional Research Service, Library of Congress, February 1977), pp. 109-110.

96. F. Ray Marshall, "Employment Implications of the International Migration of Workers," in National Council on Employment Policy, *Illegal Aliens*, pp. 52-65; and "Economic Factors Influencing the International Migration of Workers," paper prepared for Conference on Contemporary Dilemmas of the Mexican-United States Border, sponsored by the Weatherhead Foundation, April 14-18, 1975, San Antonio, Texas. See also Stanley R. Ross, ed., *Views Across the Border: The United States and Mexico* (Albuquerque: University of New Mexico Press, 1977).

97. Interview information, see note 86.

98. Domestic Council Committee, *Preliminary Report*, pp. 235-244. See also confused editorials in "Illegal Aliens and Scapegoats," *The Wall Street Journal*, May 2,

1977, p. 14; and "Illegal Aliens," *The Des Moines Register*, July 11, 1977.

99. North and Houstun, *The Characteristics and Role of Illegal Aliens*, pp. S-6, 155.

100. Villalpando et al., *A Study of the Socioeconomic Impact of Illegal Aliens*, p. 63.

101. Cornelius, *Mexican Migration to the United States*, pp. 31-35.

102. Paul S. Taylor, *A Spanish-Mexican Peasant Community, Arandas in Jalisco, Mexico* (Berkeley: University of California Press, 1933).

103. Statements by Bustamante, in "Inmigración ilegal, única escapatoria."

104. Information provided by District Director of Immigration, San Antonio, April 5, 1977.

105. Villalpando et al., *A Study of the Socioeconomic Impact of Illegal Aliens*, p. 65.

106. Bustamante, "More on the Impact of the Undocumented Immigration from Mexico."

107. Interviews in Flanigan, "North of the Border—Who Needs Whom?" pp. 37-41; and Carl Migdail, "Time Bomb in Mexico—Interview with José López Portillo, *U.S. News and World Report*, 83:1 (July 4, 1977), 28-30; "Police Not Answer—Portillo Contends," *Fort Worth Star Telegram*, April 25, 1977, p. 1; *El Porvenir*, February 8, 1977, pp. 1, 4.

108. Bustamante, "More on the Impact of the Undocumented Immigration from Mexico," p. 33 and Tab. 6.

109. Arroyo and Nelson-Cisneros, eds., "Special Issue on Labor History and the Chicano," *Aztlán*. See note 2.

110. HEW again reported widespread fraud in major American cities, "Government Pays Welfare to Employees," *The Des Moines Register*, June 24, 1977, p. 1.

111. Villalpando et al., *A Study of the Socioeconomic Impact of Illegal Aliens*, pp. 127-129.

112. Ibid., pp. 135-136.

113. Ibid., pp. 127-129.

114. Information provided by Public Information Office, Immigration Service, Western Regional Office, San Pedro, California, March 18, 1977.

115. Briggs, Fogel, and Schmidt, *The Chicano Workers*, p. 52.

116. Cosmé J. Barceló and Toni Breiter, "Hispanics on Welfare—The Facts and the Figures," *Agenda* (National Council of La Raza, Washington, D.C.), 7:2 (March/April 1977), Tab. 6, p. 33.

117. Ibid.

118. Ibid., pp. 4-6; also Stan Steiner, *La Raza: The Mexican American* (New York: Harper and Row, 1969); and Abraham Hoffman, *Unwanted Mexican Americans in the Great Depression: Repatriation Pressures, 1929-1939* (Tucson: University of Arizona Press, 1974).

119. Interviews by A. F. Corwin with city and county welfare directors in Fresno, San Antonio, Chicago, Mason City, Iowa, and Laredo; and with undocumented Mexican workers in San Luis Potosí, Manzanillo, Monterrey, Dolores (Guanajuato), Arandas, Allende (Nuevo León), as well as in Laredo, San Antonio, Sacramento, Chicago and elsewhere in period 1970-1976.

120. Ibid.; and Briggs, Fogel, and Schmidt, *The Chicano Worker*.

121. Comptroller General of the United States, *Report to Congress. Need to Reduce Public Expenditures for Newly Arrived Immigrants and Correct Inequity in Current*

Immigration Law (Washington, D.C.: General Accounting Office, 1975); and "G.A.O. Says . . . $72 Million," *The New York Times*, November 14, 1977, p. 26C.

122. "Carter puede amnistiar a millones de ilegales," *El Norte* (Monterrey), April 17, 1977, p. 1; Carter Says Aliens Need Amnesty Plan," *Fort Worth Star Telegram* (April 17, 1977), p. 3A.

123. James Reston, "Immigration Policy to Be Dictated by U.S. or by Aliens?" *The Des Moines Register*, May 5, 1977. See also Chapter 6.

124. Interviews by A. F. Corwin with immigration officials and investigators in St. Paul, October 26-27, 1973; Chicago, November 27-28, 1973; Denver, December 18-19, 1974; Phoenix, September 2-3, 1975; Mexico City, April 3, 1975, May 16, 1975; San Antonio, April 21, 1975, April 5, 1977.

125. Robert Lindsey, "New Battles Over School Budgets," *The New York Times Magazine*, September 18, 1977, pp. 17-19, 64-69.

126. Villalpando et al., *A Study of the Socioeconomic Impact of Illegal Aliens*, pp. 145-146.

127. Information from District Director, Immigration, San Antonio, April 5, 1977. See also Flanigan, "North of the Border—Who Needs Whom?" pp. 38-40; and "Texas Schools Battle Tide of Illegal-Alien Children," *The Christian Science Monitor*, December 6, 1977, p. 12.

128. Arroyo and Cisneros, eds., "Special Issue on Labor History and the Chicano"; "Illegals Easy Victims," *Northern California Labor*, Central Labor Council AFL-CIO, Santa Clara County, 26:1 (May 13, 1977), 1. Also some data on aliens and crime costs is given in Villalpando et al., *A Study of the Socioeconomic Impact of Illegal Aliens*, pp. xv-xx, 66-117.

129. Interviews by A. F. Corwin with immigration officers and border patrolmen during extensive tours of border states of California, Arizona, New Mexico, and Texas, April-August 1970 and August 1972. Also visits to immigration offices at Houston, April 12, 1974; Dallas, February 17, 1975; Eagel Pass, January 4, 1975; Del Rio, December 30, 1976. See also note 86.

130. Ibid.; and Peter Arnett's shocking account "West Still Wild Along Border," *Albuquerque Journal*, May 29, 1977, pp. 1B-4B.

131. Orr Kelley, "Border Crisis: Illegal Aliens Out of Control?" *U.S. News and World Report*, April 25, 1977, pp. 33-39.

132. Ibid.; and Victor Dricks, "Heroin War," *Fort Worth Star Telegram*, April 24, 1977, p. 8A. Efforts of Attorney General Griffin Bell and border state attorney generals to stop rampant drug traffic involving illegal aliens are reported in *El Porvenir*, April 22, 1977. The sensational arrest on charges of drug smuggling of Ramsey Muñiz Longoria, La Raza Unida candidate for governor of Texas in 1972 and 1974, is reported in *The Laredo Times*, December 28, 1976; and *Tribuna de Monterrey*, December 28, 1976, p. 6.

133. Interviews, see note 86; and Villalpando et al., *A Study of the Socioeconomic Impact of Illegal Aliens*, pp. 155-164: "Exploitation." The vicious character of alien smuggling rings was dramatized by Chicano actors in a two-hour TV movie "River of Promises," produced by David Gerberkind, and shown on *Police Story* on January 14, 1978.

134. Statements by Commissioner of Immigration Chapman (1974-1976) in Richard L. Strout, "Why a Low Birth Rate Would Not Mean ZPG," *The Washington Star*, May

5, 1976, p. 11A.

135. "Mas de 60 muertos," *El Porvenir*, February 25, 1977; "Judiciales siguen a los mojados," *El Porvenir*, February 14, 1977.

136. Interviews, see note 124; and Donald E. J. MacNamara, *Readings in Criminal Justice* (Guilford, Conn.: Duskin, 1977), pp. 173-180; and Nathan M. Adams, "America's Newest Crime Syndicate—The Mexican Mafia," *The Reader's Digest*, 111: 667 (November 1977), 97-102.

137. See typologies in Raymond Castro, "Chicanos and Poverty: Four Ideological Perspectives," *Aztlán*, 3:1 (1973), 133-149.

138. "Sweden Aroused by Ethnic Problems—Skirmishes with Turkish Newcomers," *The New York Times*, July 24, 1977, p. 7; and Edward R. F. Sheehan, "Europe's Hired Poor," *The New York Times Magazine*, December 9, 1973, pp. 36-37, 70, 72, 74, 76, 80, 82.

139. Walter S. Mossberg, "Manpower Key: New Job Corps Seeks to Swell Output and Slash Its Errors," *The Wall Street Journal*, May 13, 1977, p. 1; and Cathie Carter, "CETA Spends about $5 million to Retrain 2,000 Unemployed . . . in Woodbury County," *The Sioux City Journal*, July 13, 1977, p. 10C.

140. See interview statements in "What Illegal Aliens Cost the Economy," *Business Week*, 2487 (June 13, 1977), 86-88; and for Carter plans, "Jobs—Premium on Youth," *Time*, March 21, 1977, p. 76.

141. Joyce Vialet, *Illegal Aliens: Analysis and Background*.

142. There were an estimated 9 to 12 million alien workers and family members, some of them illegals, in Western Europe and Great Britain around 1975. See Jonathan Powers, with Anna Hardman, *Western Europe's Migrant Workers* (Report No. 28, London: Minority Rights Groups, May 1976); and Henry Kamm, "Immigrant Laborers in West Europe," *The New York Times*, September 26, 1973; Jonathan Power, "The New Proletariat," *Encounter*, 43:3 (September 1974), 8-22.

11/ TWO IMMIGRANT STORIES

edited by Arthur F. Corwin

Migrant, Settler, and Patriot

The life of Guadalupe Salas Villarreal, who first entered the United States in 1907, almost spans the entire history of mass Mexican migration to the United States. He personifies a number of the significant facts about this continuous migration, which are laid out in much more detail in the brief autobiographical sketches by Manuel Gamio, *The Mexican Immigrant: His Life Story* (Chicago, 1931), namely, that the northward drift of Mexican labor along railway lines was a beaten path before 1910; that the migrant worker shifted easily from one seasonal job to another through borderland labor contractors, or through contacts with other Mexican workers; that he usually returned two or three times to the home village in Mexico to visit family and friends, and to size up conditions there before making a decision to move permanently to the American side; that, if he decided in the affirmative, he tended to settle in an extended-family group, usually in a previously established colony of Spanish-speaking; and that as a settler he tended to maintain a deep loyalty to his own people and the mother country, in part because of the hostility or resentment of other social groups against resident Mexican labor. Also, Villarreal speaks for the cultural divergence that has gradually developed between earlier Mexican settlers and their American-born descendants, the Chicanos. Both groups appear to be working for cultural autonomy, but they differ in their concept of the Mexican heritage.

After several migratory adventures in the Southwest, Villarreal found permanent work in 1919 as a steelworker for the Colorado Fuel and Iron Company (CFI) in Pueblo, an industrial city settled by a variety of immigrant groups, most of whom were brought in from southern and central Europe before the immigration act of 1917 to work in coal mines, coke plants, railroads, and iron foundries in southern Colorado. In this city Villarreal became a prominent leader and spokesman for the Mexican colony which was mixed in with Spanish-speaking "Manitos" from northern New Mexico. For many years the New Mexicans tended to call themselves "Spanish Americans," and resented being lumped in with "old Mexico Mexicans." In turn, the Mexicans insisted on their "Mexican-ness" and resented being taken for *pochos* (Americanized Mexicans) by any social group. Yet both Spanish-speaking groups tended to do the same kind of work and to occupy the same socioeconomic status in southern Colorado.

The long-range effect in Pueblo, now a city of about 150,000 inhabitants, was similar to that in other southwestern communities. As the Mexican and the Spanish-American population grew rapidly—relatively more so after the restrictions of 1917 cut off European immigration—the city became polarized into Mexicans and Anglos with few people bothering to make more subtle ethnic distinctions. The city today is considered to be about 50 percent Chicano. It was not a simple bi-ethnic confrontation, such as that between Anglo-Texans of southern folk traditions and Mexican mestizo folk in the borderlands; yet the net effect was much the same. One had to take sides and defend ethnic identity. Villarreal's mission has been to work for the benefit of all the Spanish-speaking in Pueblo but particularly the Mexican immigrant.

Although he reached his ninety-second birthday in 1976, Villarreal, a remarkably vigorous man, has continued to be the mainstay of one of the few surviving *Comisiones Honoríficas*. These committees were established by Mexico's Secretary of Foreign Relations, beginning early in the 1920s, in order to carry on the work of protecting the Mexican colonies in the United States and their cultural identity in towns and cities where it was not possible to maintain a Mexican consul. Villarreal's wife, Cleotilde, originally from a village in the state of Durango, has for many years been a dedicated help-mate in this protective work. The following is from an interview by the editor with Villarreal in December 1974.

Guadalupe Salas Villarreal

I was born in Parral, Chihuahua, which was a small place then. And when I was a boy I never dreamed that I would end up in the United States so far from my homeland. Then the United States was still considered by many Mexican people to be the enemy of Mexico. How I got to this country was this way. I was working on the Mexican Central doing track work. It was good money then, two-and-half pesos a day, when most peons doing farm or ranch work were getting only twenty-five centavos a day. I know because I did peon work too, and other jobs that paid very little. As we were not far from the border, a friend of mine said, "Let's go see Ciudad Juárez, it's just up the line." We had a half-month's pay in pocket. So like a couple of tourists we took the train for a weekend visit. You know how those border towns are, so many taverns, so many girls, so many people after your money, or a free drink, and we just a couple of country boys! Well, in no time at all we were broke, not even having money enough to get back to the job. Someone told us there were all kinds of jobs for Mexicans on the other side of the line. So we walked a few blocks to El Paso. There was no immigration control then, that was 1907, and there were contracting offices right there on the main streets that hired nothing but Mexicans and sent them all over the United States. We were young and had nothing better to do so we signed up to work on the *Sud Pacífico* (Southern Pacific). There were two others so that made four *enganchados* (hooked ones). But, really, I had no idea we were going all the way to Fresno, California! Of course, the ride, and the bread and bologna, was gratis, but they wouldn't let us off the train for they said Mexicans were always jumping off and going to work for someone else. And I think if we jumped off the contractor lost money.

Sure enough when we reached Fresno the other two jumped contract and went looking for work. When my companion and I saw that we decided to do the same thing, for we heard that wonderful jobs could be had anywhere in this country. We found no work in Fresno, but everywhere we found Mexicans who knew their way around, and labor agents that wanted to sign them, you see they got paid by the head. We tried to avoid these *enganchistas*, so we followed some compatriots and hopped a freight south to Bakersfield. We worked for three weeks in a roundhouse there with other Mexicans. It was my first job in the United States and I was making two dollars a day, but my pal heard that there was better work in a stone quarry. After payday we quit. But not finding work there we went to Colton, California, and worked for several months in a cement plant. Then to Fontana, same kind of work for a few weeks, but thinking to do better we took off for Riverside. There I found some hard work as a *barretero*, using a crowbar in a stone quarry which also supplied rock for a cement plant. A lot of Mexicans worked there. You did not have to know English in such places. That was two dollars a day to start, then I worked up to *polverero* (powder man), and put in the charge of dynamite. That was more dangerous work and paid two-fifty a day. Then I got to be a *perforista*, drilling the holes for the dynamite. I had a steam drill and got three dollars a day, that was top money then. A dollar was worth two pesos and a peso could buy a lot in Mexico in the days before the Revolution. Would you believe it? In a few months I sent home more than a hundred dollars to my mother. Then my father was no longer living. This money excited the rest of the family and soon my brother came to California.

I was doing so well drilling those holes by machine that I stayed in that one place until 1910. I even bought a fancy bicycle, and right off had an accident and couldn't work for sometime. When I recovered I went with my brother to Corona, California, and got another job as *perforista* at three dollars a day. After a couple of years we decided that we were money ahead, my brother was then making about two-fifty a day working in the quarries. We thought we should go home and see our people. It was February of 1913, and there was plenty of trouble in Mexico. Yet we took the train to El Paso, Parral being about four hundred miles south of there on the Mexican Central.

Things were uncertain in Parral, and people were frightened, there was no work, so after a few months I went back to El Paso in January, 1914, to get back some money that I had loaned to my *compadres* there. Now because of the revolution El Paso was full of Mexican people, and all the jobs were taken in that city. When I ran out of money I went back to the labor agencies like so many Mexican refugees were doing. By then I wasn't afraid to go anywhere in the United States. It was safer than in Mexico. I signed up to work at Elephant Butte Dam about a hundred miles or so up the Rio Grande, at two-fifty a day. There were thousands of men and mules, and the job was finished by March, 1915.

I went back to El Paso with the intention of signing up for work in California, but I ran into some old friends, and we all went to Villa Matamoros, Chihuahua, thinking that the revolution would soon be over and that we could settle there and maybe go into ranching or something else. But there was much fighting between Villa and other revolutionary leaders and the country was then miserably poor. Once more I went back to El Paso and found work there with the El Paso Smelter which has always hired Mexican people. I worked only a few weeks when some of my friends said, "Let's try Colorado, they say there is good money in beets." In El Paso a lot of people were being hired by the sugar companies, like Great Western of Denver, and being sent north on trains.

So again I went as an *enganchado*, this time to La Junta on the Santa Fe. Man! That was hard work! I had no idea what it was like to do beets. It was piece work and stoop work, planting, thinning, topping, and all that. At first I made very little money. I was exhausted after a few days, and wanted to quit. But somehow I got the hang of it, and believe it or not, I lasted two years in that backbreaking job, averaging two-fifty a day and better. It was hard, yes sir, but we had good times for we Mexicans all worked and lived together as groups.

About then the United States got into war and jobs opened up for Mexicans. It was a good time to look for easier work and I found it in the Santa Fe railroad yards in La Junta. My brother then came. Four of us railroad workers rented a small house in town and did our cooking. We could never get used to the food in this country. We were making close to three dollars a day. About that time my mother died, and my two sisters moved from Parral to El Paso. My brother and I decided that we might as well give up living in Mexico, so we took a train to El Paso and brought our two sisters to Colorado as well as a girl friend of theirs. She turned out to be my wife.

Beets were paying better because of the war, and we figured we could all work like a crew, the women also, and make top money. We went to Wiley, near Lamar, Colorado, that was still 1918. But like I said, the work was hard, and so much depended on the seasons. We couldn't set up a permanent house, by then, you see, I was married and had to think about a family. Then we heard from friends about Pueblo, that there were a lot of Spanish-speaking people from New Mexico and Mexico living there and that jobs were opening in war industries. So we moved there and in January, 1919, I got a job with the CFI steel mill as a laborer at $4.28 a day. I decided that the mill was the place. Later I did more specialized work. When I told them I had experience as a driller I was put to drilling holes in rails, and paid by the ton, making up to seven dollars a day. I did other types of work but always with the CFI, making up to $14 a day, and even more later. For 26 years I worked for them, retiring in March, 1955. Now my wife and I live on a company pension in a house that we own.

We have children, grandchildren, and great grandchildren in this country, some have been in military service and some have become very well educated. One of our sons is an engineer in California. For these reasons my wife and I have never thought of returning to live in Mexico, yet we are Mexican, and we feel Mexican. We could never become citizens of this country. Mexico is still the motherland, and this sentiment we want to keep alive in all Mexican immigrants and their children. The United States is a great country but the true Mexican can never become Americanized. The differences are too great, and the Mexican can never forget how he has been treated here.

I must say that what really opened my eyes and inspired me to seek more education and do protective work was the way Mexicans, and the New Mexicans, were treated in the early days. Pueblo was a much rougher town then, full of immigrant workers from many countries, Poles, Slavs, Italians, Irish, all kinds, but the Mexicans were at the bottom of the heap, along with any Spanish-speaking person. There was a lot of feeling against Mexicans as strikebreakers and as transients who dropped off the railroads and from the coal mines, looking for jobs in Pueblo. Some of these Mexicans were rough types too, no denying that. We Mexicans hardly noticed the feeling against Mexicans when we did migrant work. It was mostly Mexican labor on the tracks, the rock quarries, and in beets. Then we were mostly among ourselves, and no one seemed to resent our taking that kind of job, but this steel town was so different. There was much intense feeling against Mexicans working here especially after the war was over.

Well, in 1920 two Mexicans were hung on a hill in Pueblo without a trial. They were just Mexicans, you see, so nothing was done about it. We collected money in the *colonia* and sent the bodies to their families in Mexico. It was then I realized that if the Mexican was going to stay in this country he would have to defend himself, and that he needed education, and to know the laws, and how to organize his own people. Like most Mexicans I had almost no schooling in Mexico. I set myself to master Spanish, both reading and writing, and I put myself to reading English in order to help my people. I began to read the daily papers, especially the *Chieftain*. About that time I became a member of the *Alianza Hispano Americano* and received its magazine which came from Arizona. Everywhere Mexican workers were trying to organize like other immigrant groups. My wife and I helped organize mutualist societies in Pueblo.

In the 1920s Pueblo had a big colony of Mexicans so the consul from Denver came here and founded a *Comisión Honorífica*. Those who could read and write and had permanent jobs became members of the Commission, and we kept the consul informed about matters requiring his intervention, and we helped celebrate all the Mexican feast days, as we still do. It was not just Pueblo, for then there were dozens of coal mining camps nearby at Walsenburg, Aguilar, Trinidad, Váldez, Morley, and Raton, also toward Salida, that were filled with Mexican workers, and they were in the railroad camps too. We kept the consul informed of all this area. During the Depression we helped repatriate some of our people to Mexico.

We had a lot to do then, those were days of hardship and struggle. Some of us were lucky enough to hold our jobs, and there was still much bad feeling about Mexican workers, even the *pochos* saying that Mexican workers were taking jobs from Americans. Then came the great Franklin Roosevelt, and the second war, and everything changed for the better. Lots of Mexican boys born here in Pueblo fought for this country, and during the war Mexican workers were needed again. Mexico and the United States became allies, and some of us in this country began to feel more at home. In the 1940s braceros came to Colorado to work in beets, then came more wetbacks and immigrants from Mexico, and more New Mexicans, especially when the coal camps were closed after the war. After Roosevelt and the war Mexican people no longer needed the consul to intervene as much, and the Mexican government no longer encouraged the consuls to sponsor the *Comisiones*, and in most places these began to die out, and so did the auxiliary *Brigadas* which were made up of women.

In 1953 I became President of the Commission and my wife became the Secretary, and we have held these offices ever since. We are some of the last people to keep the organization alive. It seems that the young immigrants do not want to take over the Commission so we just stay on because we feel it is a patriotic duty. Immigrants are still coming here but they no longer need the same protective services, and they don't appreciate how easy it is for them now. You see, with Roosevelt the Federal Government of this country began to help people, and now the government does just about everything. Even the immigrant gets help from government programs. Compared to the government what can we do for the immigrant?

Some of the Mexican immigrants are here illegally, of course. And sometimes they come to us for help or advice. All that we can do, or the consul in Denver, is refer them to an immigration consultant. Most of them learn that if they marry a Mexican-American they can stay here. There are church groups that try to help them, pay the legal fees maybe. But there are still important things the Commission can and must do. We try to help the Mexican nationals here with their personal problems, and we keep the consul informed, but mostly we seek to protect the Mexican culture. We try to encourage the younger generations to remember the *madre patria*, to learn Mexican history, to mark the national feast days, like the sixteenth of September, and to speak Spanish. We hold our meetings in the Zaragoza Hall in this neighborhood.

Now we have the young Chicanos who are a mixture of all the Mexican groups in this city. We don't like the term. What's wrong with "Mexican"? We understand their complaints about "second-class citizens," but we older settlers do not always see things the same way. We had to solve our own problems, there used to be hundreds of self-help Mexican societies between here and the border. The Chicanos want political solutions and government money, even if this means taking to the streets. So they have renamed Bradford Park "Emiliano Zapata Park" but this means very little. Many of these young militants know almost nothing of the history of Mexico, cannot speak Spanish, and lack respect for traditional Mexican values.

Right now they are fighting for control of the school system in this city, wanting also programs in both cultures, for most of the kids in school here are of Mexican origins. These youngsters are caught between two ways of life, not being sure of one or the other. Well, at least the older generation knows what they stand for. We are all concerned with protecting Mexicans in this country and cultural identity, always have been, but one difference is that we oldsters, like the Mexican consuls, avoid involvement in political conflicts, and another is that we seek to preserve intact the culture of our Mexican forefathers. But, as I say, who will take over this work now?

Mojado to Inmigrante

The story of José Policarpio Martínez is that of a young Mexican in his mid-twenties who received his immigrant visa in 1974 at an American consulate in Mexico. His was one of some 70,000 visas issued to Mexican immigrants in that fiscal year. According to American consular officials, he would be typical of today's immigrants from Mexico. Initially unable to meet visa requirements for skills needed by the American economy and hindered by the "likely to become a public charge" provision of immigration law, "the typical immigrant" enters surreptitiously and begins building up "equity claims" by acquiring job skills, establishing a family relationship in the United States, or both. He or she then usually turns to legal services, and while the visa application is being processed (which may take many months if the applicant is not a spouse or an immediate relative of an American citizen, or a legally admitted immigrant), continues to work or reside in the United States. When the visa is virtually assured, the applicant returns to Mexico, picks up the document, and reenters as a bona fide immigrant, often bringing in immediate relatives as well. In recent years about 90 percent of Mexican immigration has been of this kind. The following autobiographical account is from an interview the editor had with Martínez at the Monterrey consulate in the spring of 1974.

José Policarpio Martínez

You see, I was working at an early age. That's the custom in Mexico. When I reached ten, my father took me out of school so that I could help with the work on the family *ejido* (small communal farm). That is near the village of Zaragoza which is about thirty kilometers south of the city of San Luís Potosí. When my younger brothers could help with the farm work, then my father sent me to work at harvest time in other states of Mexico during those months when there wasn't anything to do on the *ejido* except pray for rain. That was about 1964, when I fourteen. Usually we went to Sinaloa and Sonora to pick tomatoes, but one year we went to pick cotton at Vallehermosa near the Texas border, and sometimes to other places. We went by third-class bus or were moved on trucks by *enganchistas* (contractors). We made from one dollar to five dollars a day, sometimes more, depending on the crop. Some of this money I gave to my father and mother; also I brought home food and cigarettes. There were always some former braceros and *mojados* in these picking crews, and they were always talking about the fat wages on the other side.

My father had once been a contract bracero and had worked in sugar beets and vegetables in California in the 1950s. He made pretty good money and was well treated by employers, but he never went more than two or three times because he had to pay Mexican authorities a big *mordida* to get his card renewed. I asked my father about going to work *en el otro lado*, but he said don't ever go as a wetback because the *coyotes* would strip me. For some time I went on doing those seasonal jobs in Mexico, seeing the country, having fun, and all the time thinking that one day I would try the United States.

One time when we were doing strawberries near Irapuato for *poco dinero*, one of those *agachados* (stoop workers), who was called El Chango ("Monkey"), threw down a box of berries and cried out: *"Basta!* (Enough!) How many of you *pelados* (worthless ones) want to go with me to work for gringo dollars?" My buddy Julio, who was from my home village, said to me, "That's us, *somos pelados*. Let's go. What have we got to lose?" "Okay," I said. Julio and I were then about age eighteen, that was in 1968. We had saved only a few pesos, so we went to a storekeeper in our village. He was also a moneylender and had a brute of a man to collect for him. This storekeeper never loaned money to *mojados* because he said they never came back. But we convinced him that we needed money for Sonora to pick cotton and that we would be back soon. We got enough from him to buy a ticket on a second-class bus from San Luís, where we met up with El Chango, to Piedras Negras. We also helped pay for his ticket because he was our guide. He was going to show us how to avoid the Mexican *coyotes* at the border, and how to get around the border patrol. Also, he was going to show us how to work our way into the United States.

This Chango was not very *listo* (sharp). He had been deported several times and did little more than farm work in Texas. But we decided to follow him over the border. Julio used to say to encourage me that if a type like Chango could sneak into the United States so could we, besides Julio had relatives in San Antonio. We got rid of our *huaraches* (Indian shoes), and put on tennis shoes because Chango said they were American and good for walking. He also advised us to carry only a small canvas bag with a knife and extra clothes.

We crossed the river a little way north of Eagle Pass, and walked mostly at night. It was early in May and not cold. Walking over two hundred kilometers to San Antonio seemed stupid to me, but Chango said we had to get around *la patrulla*. We kept in sight of telephone poles leading east. At dawn we came to a house of a Texas Mexican who worked for a rancher there. Chango knew him. We got food and water, paying in Mexican money. We slept on the floor of the house, and walked two more nights, sleeping out. All I could think of was stepping on a rattlesnake in the dark. By day we camped under trees and watched a border patrol plane circle around. We ate dry tortillas and sometimes cactus. At another ranch an Anglo owner let us work a day for meals. He said that too many *mojados* had been coming by asking for help, some had been breaking into his buildings, and had killed a calf for food and that he was going to start calling the immigration people, you know, *la migra*.

Finally our path led to the low hills west of San Antonio. There we went to work for a gringo contractor who was building fancy houses. He knew we were wet, but he put us to work mixing cement and carrying flat stones for walls and patios. We lived under a tarp back in the trees, and he gave us food, tobacco and six dollars a day. We worked with three other Mexicans who were paid more. Two of them had green cards, or so they said, but the other was a *mojado*. One day when I had about a hundred dollars safely stuffed in a tin can, Julio said, "we got a nice pile, let's go to San Antonio, and find my uncle. We can always come back to a job like this."

One of the *Raza* workers had a car, and he took the three of us to the city. He said San Antonio was full of Mexicans and that there was not much danger from *la migra*. Maybe he wanted to get rid of us, because he let us off at the bus station to look up the name and the address of Julio's relatives in a phone book. We were about to call the house when two immigration men came up and began asking questions. They arrested us on the spot, and pretty soon we signed a paper. They took us to the border and turned us loose at Nuevo Laredo, for we said we lived there. But they put Chango on another bus and sent him to Mazatlán or San Luís Potosí, or someplace. I never saw him again, but I am sure he is one of the wetbacks who will never be anything more than a *pelado* in tennis shoes.

La migra, just like they said, took nothing from us except the knife. Julio and I still had our sacks and our money. We took a room in Nuevo Laredo thinking ourselves lucky after all. I said to Julio that there must be an easier way. "It's stupid to walk. This is the twentieth century, man!" We went to one of the plazas in Nuevo Laredo and asked a lot of questions of people who had been in the United States. We told them how the immigration people had dropped on us out of nowhere. Some of those people laughed and said, "*ay, que pobres campesinos!*" A man there took us aside an said, "No wonder! You two look like cotton pickers, carrying a bag and wearing tennis shoes. Anybody could pick you out for wetbacks. Now if you have money, you can take a private car to San Antonio to any address you like. I can arrange it, but if you want to stay there, you have got to dress like city boys." As it turned out, this man was good *coyote*, if there is such a thing. He gave me my first lesson in how to make it on the other side. We bought city shoes, slacks, and a sport shirt.

That night we paid about five dollars each to be taken across the river in a flat boat just a few hundred meters from where the bridge crosses to Laredo. It was about ten at night, and simple. There was no fence, and no guards. Not at all like I imagined it. A man on the other side met us, and we walked down a side street to a neighborhood café. All the people there were Mexican or Tex-

Mex. They told us that *la migra* did not always try to stop people crossing the river, but that they did try to stop all *mojados* from going inland, that all the highways as far as San Antonio were watched by *la patrulla*. A man showed up to say that it would cost thirty dollars each for taxi service to San Antonio, eighty dollars to Dallas, and three hundred to Chicago, and so on. We said San Antonio, and had to pay in advance. He sent us to a Mexican rooming house nearby. For the first time I worried that the *coyotes* were going to clip us. But a man showed up around noon the next day. He made a phone call and said the back road was open. We drove toward Corpus Christi and then doubled back to San Antonio. There were four passengers in that car, including two girls going as housemaids.

We stayed in the house of Julio's uncle for a couple of weeks. His uncle had come to San Antonio many years ago and worked in the railroad yards there. Later he brought in his family and got immigration cards for everyone. His family told us to act like Chicanos, like we belonged there, and to learn some phrases in English, like "I was born in San Antonio." They showed us around San Antonio in their car. What a fine city that is! The west side is mostly Mexican and *muy alegre*.

Then Julio's uncle sent us to a labor agency. The man there was a *pocho* (Americanized Mexican) who advised us to go to Dallas, for there were fewer Mexicans there and wages were better. He put us on a night shift in a food-packing plant. The foreman paid the fee, and we were to pay the foreman. Julio's uncle drove us to Dallas, we got social security cards, and went to work for two dollars an hour, paying the foreman fifty cents an hour for the job and because he found us a safe place to stay in the Mexican part of the city. Dallas is like a new city with high buildings, but it wasn't *alegre* like San Antonio. So on weekends Julio and I went by bus to San Antonio. We went to *pachangas* (dances) on the west side and met lots of pretty girls there, who thought that *mojados* were a pretty brave bunch. We dressed right and nobody ever bothered us. This went on for several months, and I had a couple of *novias* (girl friends) in San Antonio. But just our *mala suerte*! (bad luck), *la patrulla* set up a road block north of San Antonio just for a day or two. They had us again. We gave different names, and said, "I born in San Antonio," but they recognized us. We were charged eight or nine dollars for a bus ticket and shipped from Brownsville to San Luís Potosí, which is where they commonly dump *mojados* from Texas.

As I said, San Luís is only about thirty kilometers from my home. So Julio and I went to see our people and tell them of our adventures, and to show off the kind of clothes we used in Dallas and San Antonio. I still owed the storekeeper, and I knew he would have his brute looking for me. Anyway there was nothing in the village to hold me, not even a share of the miserable *ejido*. Everything looked so poor there after Dallas. I told my mother I couldn't stay. My father said, stay, and he dug up some of the money I had sent to him. He said pay off the storekeeper. But as soon as I had the money in hand, I found Julio and said, "let's blow." He also had gotten some money. Now my younger brother ran off with us. He was only seventeen but already married, his wife and kid living in our house there.

Our plan was to go to Nuevo Laredo and get border-crossing cards, for we learned in Dallas how many Mexicans used these to get into the United States. How we envied them. They could even go home for Christmas and get back on that card. Julio and I had to pay the municipal authorities a chunk of money so they would register us as permanent, long-time residents there. We didn't have enough money then for my brother Chuy (nickname for Jésus). The American consul gave Julio and me a crossing card. I tried it a few times. It worked like a key to the front door. I just walked over the bridge and showed it to the *gringos*, and that way I could visit Laredo anytime. But *la migra* there on the bridge were suspicious. They wouldn't give us a pass to go inland to San Antonio, not even to visit Julio's uncle.

Julio's uncle sent him money, and he took off in a private car. Then I used my card to find a job in Laredo in an auto repair shop, at only a dollar an hour but easy work. The owner was a *gringo*, but the manager was a Mexican who had a green card, with that he could work in the United States and live in Mexico. That was his idea of heaven, because he did not want to give up being a Mexican. To hold that job, I had to move over to Laredo and took board and room there. I went back and forth to visit my brother and help him get a crossing card, for he was stuck there in a rooming house. Since Laredo is a dull place and the fun was on the Mexican side, my brother and I would sometimes go to "Boys Town" in Nuevo Laredo; that's where all the women and the night life is concentrated. We spent too much money there.

One day I got a letter from *mi compadre* Julio, who was living with his uncle in San Antonio. He said he had a good job there and could get me a union job at $3.50 an hour. I was fed up with Laredo, so I made arrangements to take off. This included my brother taking over my job in Laredo, and Chuy moved into the same room I had there. You know, he is still there, almost four years now, and he has more money than I do, and a woman friend in Nuevo Laredo. Whether he'll ever go back to his woman in our village, ¿*quien sabe*?

When I got to San Antonio, I sent my *mica* (border-crossing card) to my brother in Laredo, telling him to hold it for me in case I got booted out again. You know, if they catch you working on one of those cards, *la migra* takes it away. Julio left his card with his uncle. In San Antonio I got into a painter's union, not easy, and did painting and construction work. I could afford the payoff, and even sent some money to my folks. Also, I learned a little English working for a gringo boss. For some reason I always worked harder for the gringo. Anyway, I was doing real good, and had my girl friends. But I was a fool, you see. About a year of this good life, and I ran across some Mexicans who had been working in Chicago. They said, "You think $3.50 an hour is good money? You should go to Chicago; for the same work you can get $5.50 or $6 an hour union wage." When one of them offered to take me in his car to Chicago, I said *adios* to San Antonio.

In Chicago I couldn't find a union job unless I paid a pile of money, and then the job was far away from the Mexican colonies. There were lots of wet Mexicans looking for work. I took a job in a warehouse for $2.75 an hour, but it was November and it was really getting cold. We went to the Salvation Army to get heavy clothes and an overcoat. There were about eight of us, all Mexicans, sharing an apartment on the northwest side. That included a woman and her three little kids; her husband had run off someplace. She had welfare and food stamps, and worked part-time in a candy factory. Another Mexican woman came over to baby sit, and do the cooking for everybody. Together we paid that woman ten dollars a day. She was illegal also. We hardly went anywhere for fear of *la migra*. We watched TV and brought in beer. Most wets were there for the money, and they talked a lot about what they were going to do with it when they went back to Mexico. But I couldn't stand it. It was not like San Antonio, where you could move around freely because that city is half Mexican anyway and it has sunshine.

One day I met this Mexican at work who told me all the wonders of California. "You won't freeze your backside there," he assured me, "and you can move around among the Chicanos." Three of us bought a used car and headed for California. It was December and we nearly froze to death in a snow storm in Wyoming. I was amazed to learn that Mexicans were living there. We sold the car in Sacramento and took a bus to Los Angeles.

I lived for almost two years in east Los Angeles, having three or four jobs there. Because I knew a little about machines, I finally got a good job as a machinist in a factory. This involved a little payoff. In the meantime I went in with the two guys from Chicago, and through a Chicano real estate man we rented a small unfurnished house for $150 a month. We filled it with good used furniture, a television set, and all that. We rented one room to another *mojado*. We bought another car and used it to get to work. One of the boys, Felipe, was our driver, for he was once a taxi driver in Guadalajara and learned English from American tourists. He was *muy listo* this Felipe. He had picked up a Texas birth certificate along the way and a California driver's license. Really, that boy had it made! He worked in a plating plant but dropped us at our jobs, for a small fee, of course.

I really liked that factory job and the house. We fixed our own food and had some real fiestas there with tequila cocktails. It was a nice neighborhood mostly made up of Chicano families and Mexican immigrants who had visas and no problems with the immigration. I got to know some Chicanos, and they were always telling me I had a right to live in California. Well, I knew that the gringos had taken the place from Mexico and had set up the immigration service to throw out Mexicans whenever they pleased. The Chicanos said they were working to get *la migra* off of the back of the Mexicans. They told me also of a Chicano immigration counselor who would advise Mexicans free about their immigration rights. So one day after work I went to see him, and he said that probably my employer would not sponsor me, and that even if he did it would take maybe two years to get a visa. He asked if I had close relatives in the United States. I said no. He asked if I were married. I said no. "Well," he said, "you might think of marrying a Mexican-American. There would be no wait then. Do you have a *novia* here?" I thought then of a girl I knew in Los Angeles, but before I could make up my mind that I really wanted to marry her, *la migra* came by the factory and picked me up.

Actually that girl was my downfall. You see, I was making about four dollars an hour clean when immigration got me. I had a union card, a closet full of clothes, a couple of radios, and other things. However, there was this jealous *pocho*. He hated *mojados*, especially when they did better than he could do. Not only did I steal his girl, but I was making more money than him. We had this big argument. I told him off. I said that *puros Mexicanos* (pure Mexicans) were willing to work hard and wanted to get ahead, but that *pocho* Mexicans like him could get welfare if they couldn't hack it. He went away foaming at the mouth, but he knew where I worked. And that very Monday the immigration officers came to the factory and the supervisor pointed me out. Who else could have turned me in?

The immigration people asked me the same questions, like, how many times had I been in the United States. I said it was the first time. That was a mistake. They called in a *pocho* immigration man to break my story. "We know you have been picked up more than once. What's your real name?" They couldn't prove anything because I carried no papers on me and hardly any money. They would have just booted me out again, but I got smart with them. They sent me before a judge. He said, "Why do you keeping coming to this country when you know you are breaking the law? Do you realize that I could send you to prison?" As you have to do, if you want off the hook, I kept my head down all the time and looked miserable. I replied that all I wanted was work to help support my wife and my little *chamacos* (kids) in Mexico. That part wasn't true, of course, but I did tell the truth when I said I had also to help my younger brothers and sisters there. This line usually softens them up. The judge said, "I fine you fifty dollars. Do you have any money?" I said no, the payoffs to hold the job had taken most of it. The judge seemed to believe that. He suspended the fine, but the immigration people said that this time I was a *deportado*, and for the first time they took my finger prints. They said if a *deportado* was caught again he would surely go to the pen for maybe two years. Then they sent me all the way to Mazatlán by bus.

From there I hitchiked to San Luís Potosí, and borrowed a little money from a friend there, telling him to collect from my father, who was holding some money for me. I didn't even stop that time in my home village. I took the bus for Nuevo Laredo, and phoned my brother. He brought me my crossing card and some money, and off I went to San Antonio to see Julio and also to get a Tex-Mex birth certificate like Felipe's. I was then planning to go back to Los Angeles, and maybe marry that Chicana, or someone. There are places, you know, in Los Angeles where you can fix up anything. Also, I wanted to go back there because I had left a lot of things in that house, including hidden money, and I was part owner of a car. You know, a *pelado* like El Chango doesn't mind being thrown out, but when you lose what I lost in Los Angeles, you get damned mad at the immigration people. Still, I had to move with *mucho cuidado* (carefully) because *la migra* had my fingerprints.

I took a job in a filling station as a mechanic and handyman at two dollars an hour, that was on the Mexican side of San Antonio, where wages are low, but it was safe. I figured to work long enough to pay my way back to California. As luck would have it, I soon ran into one of my Mexican-American girl friends, someone I really liked, and after a little while we got married by a justice of the peace. After that we went to a Chicano lawyer who specializes in immigration things and got all our papers in order, you know, birth certificates, and all that. I got a few days off my job and, as you see, was here in Monterrey at the American Consulate getting my immigration papers. Well, maybe soon I can walk right under the noses of *la migra*.

Really, though, I'm in a pretty good mood, not mad at anybody, not even at that *pinche pocho cobarde* in Los Angeles. I have proved that I can make it in the United States, and not as an *agachado*! I want to get along there, and get to know more about the country. From what I have seen I like it. I found that if people get into trouble there, it is usually their own fault. Nor do I want to live all the time in the Mexican colony. I can take English lessons now, find a really good job, no payoffs, get my own car and house. My wife is working as a bilingual clerk in a big store in San Antonio. She can help. We'll have some kids and they'll be *pochos*. They'll have to go school there and learn more about the United States than our *querido México*. But we will teach them Mexican values too. And why shouldn't they mix with the Anglos and the best of both countries? I hope so.

When you are in a country illegally, you do many things *a lo chueco* (crooked), and you are afraid to do other things. And there are all those *coyote* go-betweens. I hardly got to know any *Americanos*, not well, I mean, and that is the way with most Mexicans who go there, because one has to stick close to *la raza*. But *la raza* suffers much from *envidia*. And *la raza* fears the immigration service and the cops. Many Mexicans go there and imagine that the country is hostile to Mexicans. Now I don't feel that way anymore. This doesn't mean I've stopped being *puro Mexicano*. No, señor. With me it's a matter of pride to stay loyal to one's mother country, and to one's own people. For a good Mexican it is shame enough that we have to move to the land of the *gringos* to sell our labor, even if we find many good things here. You see, the thing we never sell—even if we go as an immigrant—is *el alma de México*.

12/ A HUMAN RIGHTS DILEMMA: CARTER AND "UNDOCUMENTED" MEXICANS

Arthur F. Corwin

> A born-again Baptist. . . . In the wake of his conversion experience . . . he viewed his political activity as a form of ministry. . . . Carter's record as governor would seem to bear out his claim . . . prison reforms, civil rights, and programs for the handicapped. In short, his administration was very much a champion of the weak and the poor.
>
> Leslie Wheeler, *Jimmy Who?* [1]

The inauguration of a populist president, James Earl Carter, Jr., in January 1977 added immensely to the controversy and complications surrounding America's alien problem. On-the-job training started for a new Democratic administration. But it was not merely the turnover. "Jimmy," who professed to be a new-born Christian, a liberal Democrat, a continuator of President Johnson's War on Poverty, and a spokesman for the New South, dedicated America to a breathtaking policy of promoting universal human rights, the Good Neighbor image, and a new order of equality for America's minorities and Third World peoples. Needless to say, such goals could hardly be squared with a restrictive immigration policy.

Perhaps Carter, a former Georgia governor, and his New South appointees and intimate advisers, including ol' Georgia friends like Attorney General Griffin Bell, understood the civil rights problems of America's blacks and the dream of Martin Luther King, but they seemed totally innocent of Mexican wetback history—the hypersensitivities and hang-ups of Raza leaders on both sides of the border and the smouldering resentment and infinitude of special claims rooted in the "territorial castration" of 1848.

The perspective that Carter, and Carter people, initially had on the "Mexican problem" was that of the social worker, civil rights campaigner, and bureaucratized poverty fighter. Having "understood the problem" through

320

their support of, or sympathy for, grape boycotts and the underdog cause of California farm workers, they tended, like the saintly César Chávez, to reduce the convoluted question of Chicano rights to simplistic terms: America not only had a moral duty to compensate blacks for past wrongs but an equal—if not greater obligation—to compensate brown-skinned people.[2] Not surprisingly, Carter's Mexican-American appointees felt that, like blacks, they were engaged in a caste struggle to achieve full civil and economic rights in the face of establishment power, exploitation, and racial discrimination, not to mention the colonial conquest of Mexico, the WASP stigma of illegal alien, and the police brutality of an immigration service subservient to the whims of employers.

Less innocent was Secretary of Labor F. Ray Marshall, a University of Texas economist, who had researched migratory labor in the border states and guest worker programs in West Europe. Marshall was expected to be the chief adviser on immigration policy. His approach was less in line with the controversial Third World view held by Mexico and the UN's International Labor Organization that transborder migrant workers, documented or not, should be accorded the same equal-rights protection as native workers, and more in line with the AFL-CIO policy of protecting American labor against foreign competition and with the long and painful efforts of the House Subcommittee on Immigration, headed by Joshua Eilberg, to bring forth a tough employer penalty bill, like that in West Germany, and a revised social security card system in order to shut off the "job magnet" of illegal immigration.[3] But, to a considerable extent, Marshall's knowledge and usefulness were soon offset by Carter's moralistic or Sunday-school approach to Third World grievances and his politicking with national immigration policy.

Partly to conciliate Chicano demonstrators, who claimed to have cast the deciding vote in Texas—the "win state" for Carter—and partly to balance the ethnic coalition interests of the Democratic Party, Carter appointed a Mexican American as Commissioner of Immigration, namely, Leonel J. Castillo, a rising young Tex-Mex politician (age thirty-seven), former Houston comptroller, Peace Corps volunteer, civil rights activist, and community relations specialist. Castillo did not have any experience that would qualify him to administer a national system of immigration standards, but in the new era of ethnic populism, he met the Carter administration's "affirmative action" criteria, for he understood Third World feelings about American colonialism, Chicano grievances against the hated *migra* (Immigration Service), and the seriousness of the border invasion problem. Like Carter's naming Andrew Young to serve as American Ambassador to the United Nations and as America's roving spokesman on the liquidation of imperialism and white supremacy systems, Carter's appointment of Castillo was in line with his sympathy for Third World minorities. The appointment also served his need for a kind of subcabinet minister, or ombudsman, to handle Mexican migratory affairs and complaints and to establish rapport with Mexican officials.[4] Yet even some of Carter's principal advisers felt that Castillo's appointment represented, unfortunately, a glaring conflict of interest between "the welfare of the Mexicans in this country, and the national interest in getting control of the illegal alien problem and reforming the whole immigration system."[5]

As expected, Castillo and other Mexican-American appointees in the Carter government quickly took up a protective stance toward La Raza. The new Commissioner of Immigration pointedly opposed any tough employer penalty bill or identification card that might threaten Raza job holders. And he was ambivalent on enforcement. Speaking before a convention of Texas Mexican-American Democrats, the Commissioner admitted that he was expected to uphold the law, but:

I just happen to believe I ought to be aware of the consequences. If I bring in more patrol officers and manage to cut off the flow [of illegal aliens], I know full well that I am contributing to the pain and suffering of another nation.[6]

Other ambiguous statements followed: "I don't think it practical or philosophically consistent to slam the door shut on these people."[7]

Since Carter insisted that respect for, and protection of, human rights be at the heart of American foreign and domestic policy, Chicano groups, the Commissioner of Immigration, and the Mexican government lost no time in pushing before the Carter administration the flawless candidate for humane treatment—the innocent, long-suffering undocumented alien patiently awaiting deliverance from American exploitation and hound-dog treatment by *la migra*. Carter and most of his advisers eagerly seized on this show-case opportunity to display the new human rights policy and its fruits, which, in turn, led the administration to stand the alien problem on its head: It was now a protectionist problem, not an enforcement one. Consequently, preventing illegal entries and enforcing immigration standards were no longer the top priorities of the federal government's immigration service, but rather the legalization and protection of uninspected aliens and their families.[8] Also, in deference to La Raza complaints that the term "illegal alien," like the "racist" term "wetback," stigmatized people of Mexican descent as lawbreakers and sneaks, the White House adopted the term "undocumented alien," even though most illegal aliens were covered by false immigration or civil documents, and many were involved in the drug traffic.[9]

In addition to the Castillo appointment, Carter named as ambassador to Mexico, Patrick J. Lucey, then governor of Wisconsin and the sponsor of a liberal Wisconsin law to protect migrant workers, legal or illegal, from every form of economic or social exploitation or discrimination. Raza leaders on both sides of the border took this appointment as another confirmation of Carter's protectionism.[10]

Others in the Carter advisory circle, like Marshall, or William Luers, Mexican affairs specialist in the State Department, may not have fully shared Carter's evangelical viewpoint or the "Chávez brown-skinned perspective." Yet they could go along with the protectionist policy, since it seemed like the only diplomatic way to act on a supersensitive question in a divided America. To simply enforce immigration standards would be taken as anti-Mexican, anti-Third World, or racist. If, on the other hand, one could extend legal protection and the rights of labor to all aliens, then employers, finding alien labor no longer cheap and docile, might prefer local labor, and this in turn might serve to protect minority living standards. Under this guise perhaps "enforcement of labor standards" could seem like a humane consideration acceptable to Mexico also.[11]

It was, therefore, with a mix of innocence, politicking, common sense, and evangelism that the Carter administration plunged boldly into a swamp of illegal alien questions. By March 1977 Carter had appointed a task force of top advisers and cabinet officials to come up *pronto* with a neat package of recommended solutions, if possible sometime in May.[12]

The administration should probably have sealed its mouth during task force deliberations, but Chicano and other Latino demonstrators surged forward demanding policy commitments. At a Houston symposium attended by high public officials from the United States and Mexico and academic researchers, Raza spokesmen presented amnesty as a "Humanistic Imperative."[13] Facing other militant leaders from the Commissioner of Immigration's Hispanic Advisory Committee, Chicano Rights Incorporated, Concerned Hispanic Citizens of the United States, The Mexican National Brotherhood of Los Angeles, (Trabajadores Indocumentados), The Bishops Committee of the United States Catholic Conference, The National Committee for the Defense of Immigrants, the Raza Unida Campaign for Civic Action, The Mexican American Anti-Defamation Task Force, One-Stop Immigration, and others, Carter and his cabinet officials prematurely—some said foolishly—announced that some form of general amnesty would be "mandatory" to protect several million innocent people from exploitation.[14] This announcement only increased the amnesty chant, and set off a massive rush of seasonal workers, relatives, and other border crossers who did not wait to hear the qualifying details.

Naïvely Carter officials had hoped to seal off the borders and airports before announcing an amnesty cutoff date of December 31, 1976, but they failed to appreciate the fact that the Immigration and Naturalization Service, on a starvation diet for years, lacked the manpower to seal off any airport or border crossing. A hundred more men—the bottom of the barrel—were desperately thrown like a sandbag into the flood of undocumented aliens pouring through the San Diego corridor, also known as the "war front." Everywhere guards and inspectors were simply overwhelmed by Third World poverty folk seeking amnesty or a possible guest worker status.[15] One cartoonist showed a solitary immigration officer being trampled to death by a horde of aliens rushing toward a factory bearing the sign: "Hiring today: illegal aliens."[16]

Actually little had changed on the Mexican border, where alien smugglers, bandits, drug traffickers, juvenile gangs, and hordes of *mojados, coyotes, pelados,* and sundry peddlers have always maintained a gypsy paradise. As outgoing Commissioner of Immigration Chapman put it: "The most visible battlefront is the Mexican border where 1,720 demoralized Border Patrol agents watch helplessly as thousands of people simply walk into the country each day."[17]

After touring that untamed frontier, Peter Arnett said in amazement: "It's everything except what its supposed to be—the line behind which one country's sovereignty prevails."[18] Washington, noted Arnett, had not only failed to stem the tide of illegals, it had not yet found the answer to the crime and drug smuggling, petty thievery and prostitution that accompany the alien inflow; yet "people on both sides of the border are fighting to preserve the traditional permissiveness." A statement from Ellwyn Stoddard, President of the Association of Borderlands Scholars, seemed fitting: "There has never been an immigration law functioning on the border."[19]

In 1975 a legislative representative for the Border Patrol pleaded:

Mr. Chairman, the employees of the Immigration and Naturalization Service . . . are frustrated. . . . We feel that we are being deprived of a basic human right to go home after duty, warm in the knowledge that we have served our country well. Give us a law we can enforce; allow us the pride of a job well done.[20]

The pleading went on in 1977. An immigration investigator wrote, as a private citizen, to President Carter:

There are millions of illegal aliens in the United States. This does not alarm me nearly as much as congressional and presidential apathy regarding illegal aliens. . . . This is a very lonely and frustrating job because we get no support from Washington or the courts.[21]

At the so-called battle of the black bridge, a notoriously open railway span over the Rio Grande at El Paso used daily by countless illegals over the years, Chicano liberators, seeking an independent Raza state in the Southwest, and Mexican militants from Ciudad Juárez, seeking an open border, swarmed over a handful of border guards who had attempted to stop a unity march. Screaming in Spanish "Death to the Immigration Service!" and "This is our country!" the militants smashed two vans and released two illegals. But for border-state residents whose life style has come to depend on cheap labor and communion with kinfolk, any fence was out of the question. "We don't want a Berlin wall between our two cities," said Ray Salazar, Mexican-American mayor of El Paso, a city whose Spanish-speaking "supporting population" harbored possibly 60,000 or more uninspected aliens in 1977, and continued to serve hundreds of thousands of Mexican and other Latin-American migrants as the "Gateway City" to the United States.[22] After a hard look, one concerned reporter said, "What was a few months ago a border crisis, precipitated by a silent invasion of illegal aliens now shows signs of escalating into an undeclared border war."[23]

Commissioner Castillo tried to inspire the demoralized and helpless immigration officers with a vision of their new mission to protect illegal aliens from abuse by border predators, employers, and enforcement officers. In addressing the graduates of the Border Patrol Academy, he said that border guards were "the front-line soldiers in President Carter's war against human rights violators." And he added, "Possibly no other governmental agency has a greater opportunity to demonstrate to the world our concern for human rights than those of use in the immigration service."[24]

An irate immigration veteran, who witnessed the ceremony, commented:

How does an enforcement officer demonstrate such a concern for a horde of uninspected aliens, *pelados* mostly, who show no concern for American rights and often spit on Border Patrol agents. Failure to enforce the law and condescending respect for the rights of illegals is what led to the present mess. Now what are we supposed to do? Make America totally safe and comfy for illegal aliens? Do we step aside, doff our caps, and say: *Bienvenido* to territory stolen from Mexico? You'll find the job office on your right, the welfare office on the left, and the territorial compensation office straight ahead. And in a moment our green and white patrol car will pick up your wife and kiddies and take them to your low-cost HUD duplex. Over there's the integration bus, and—aw, hell![25]

New protectionist mission or not, the more the presidential task force looked into the bottomless pit of amnesty expectations, the more a scarecrow immigration service was urged to trap alien smugglers and to step up deportations of recently arrived illegals. This move only made the revolving door of non-penalty voluntary departures spin faster. Even so Raza leaders like José A. Gutíerrez, Bert Corona, César Chávez, and José Juárez denounced the "hypocritical effort" to deport deserving aliens while amnesty plans were under consideration.[26]

Meanwhile, Carter and White House staffers, like Stuart D. Eisenstat, seeing an opportunity to please both employers and Chicano groups, moved over to Senator Eastland's camp, where employers' needs came first and no tough employer penalty bill would be tolerated.[27]

Although Carter had given immigration questions his devoted personal attention, it was not until August 4, 1977, that he was able to submit to Congress a task force assessment of the nation's alien problem, together with a package of preliminary proposals intended to provide a gradual legislative solution in accordance with human rights guidelines and certain political compromises. [28] Many modifications were expected, but by that date it was apparent what the Carter administration would try to do:

1. The Immigration Service would be provided with at least a moderate increase in funding, manpower, detention facilities, computer service, sensor equipment, and helicopters. At least it would be a streamlined scarecrow. The task force recommended an additional 2,000 Border Patrol agents. Carter, counting on uncertain cooperation from other federal agencies, would probably halve that figure. Realistically, at least 10,000 to 20,000 field officers—free of paper work—were needed, but then the administration still had to overcome a policy hang-up about a "police solution," since such a solution would be in conflict with the human rights policy and Chicano denunciations of *la migra*. [29]

In this respect one should note that Republican Presidents Nixon and Ford gave no significant financial support to INS, partly because transient and distracted attorney generals—few of them distinguished—had a dozen other major enforcement agencies to look after, and partly because they, like most presidents, had to play coalition politics with, for instance, conservative southern Democrats who dominated key congressional committees, such as Senator Eastland, Chairman of the Senate Judiciary Committee, or Wilbur Mills, until 1974 Chairman of the House Ways and Means Committee. Such defenders of agribusiness were always opposed to increasing INS manpower and funding. Lacking any cabinet level status or clout in Congress, Commissioners of Immigration like Raymond F. Farrell (1960-1974) or Leonard F. Chapman (1974-1976) could only repeat their litany of woes and beg from congressional committees and from the President's Office of Management and Budget, which controlled federal spending and habitually cut another 20 percent off of any INS budgetary allotment. Restrictionists could only hope that budgetary reforms in Congress would finally make the INS an effective enforcement agency. But in the meantime, frustrated immigration officers, charged with sealing off illegal entries, continued to face absurd—some thought a subversive—fiscal situation. The Justice appropriations bill (H.R. 7556), which Congress sent to the White House in August 1977, provided for only 454 additional INS employees and allocated $266 million to the INS for fiscal 1978, a sum merely 5.3 percent larger than the previous budget—and this in the midst of an alien-control crisis and rampant inflation. [30]

2. An employer penalty bill, more like Eastland's earlier S. 3074 than the Rodino-Eilberg H.R. 8713 (or the more current version, H.R. 1663), would be legislated. Mild civil penalties, including injunctions and fines up to $1,000 for each illegal hired, would be imposed on employers who *knowingly* violated immigration laws, while criminal penalities would be reserved only for persons who received compensation for *knowingly* assisting undocumented aliens. Yet—and this said much about coalition politics, AFL-CIO interests, and the

Chávez input—employment agencies and union hiring halls would be exempted.[31]

Although a reliable system of personal identification was needed to determine just who was a "properly documented" job applicant, the Carter administration was opposed to transforming the social security card into a reliable universal identifier. Rather the federal government would "strongly oppose discrimination against Mexican Americans and other ethnic groups that might result from the undocumented alien program." Moreover, federal civil agencies would be ordered "to assure that existing anti-discrimination laws are fully enforced."[32]

Such safeguards were mostly in response to outcries from ethnic and civil rights leaders like California's Representative Edward Roybal, racially-sensitive leader of the Hispanic Caucus in Congress, who insisted that any penalty bill would force an employer to discriminate against brown-skinned applicants: "How's he going to tell the difference between me and them?"[33]

On the other hand, restrictionists were concerned that state and local laws prohibiting the hiring of illegals would be preempted by a mild federal law that would admittedly depend on the voluntary cooperation of self-serving employers and the presumed validity of social security cards and birth certificates for sale anywhere. Others were disturbed that the Carter proposals seemed to ignore past American experience with the wetback business and the European experience with imported guest workers. Asked one editorialist: Is America stern enough?

Failure to enforce immigration laws is a scandal.... A German employer who knowingly hires illegal aliens may face a fine as high as $20,000 or spend five years in jail. ... France has sent back laborers from southern Europe. Germany has given tickets to Turkish labor battalions.... A Gallup poll in April found 82 per cent favored punishing employers who knowingly hire illegals.[34]

3. Full immigrant rights would be pushed for all non-criminal aliens who had taken up continuous residence in the country before December 31, 1970.[35] If this policy were carried out, possibly .5 million to 2 million "invisible aliens," including children, would be legalized. At least half would be of Mexican origin.

At first Carter's advisers had in mind mass amnesty for all law-abiding aliens who had entered before 1972. The cutoff date was moved back to 1970, at least temporarily, after a surge of opposition, mostly unexpected, from congressional leaders, labor spokesmen, and representatives of Zero Population Growth, Daughters of the American Revolution, and other civic organizations, and even from some Mexican Americans. Opponents of broad amnesty charged that it was unfair to visa applicants who played the game by the rules, that aliens fearing deportation would naturally seem law-abiding, that millions more, mostly from Mexico, would come in as immediate relatives of legalized aliens, that amnesty workers would then be free to take better jobs away from American citizens, and that amnesty families would put "an intolerable burden on governmental budgets" by becoming eligible for Great Society programs, such as food stamps and medical and welfare payments, as well as for bicultural programs, remedial education, and "forced busing." [36]

4. More controversial, the amnesty "solution" would offer a protective guest worker status to all other law-abiding alien workers not covered by resident immigrant visas. Formulated principally by Carter, Marshall, Bell, and Castillo (and, one suspects, Eastland), this plan would apply to undocumented workers who entered the country from January 1, 1970, to December 31, 1976. Such workers, numbering anywhere from 1 to 3 million or more, would be allowed to register for non-deportable or temporary resident-alien status. They could then legally reside and work at any job in the United States during a five-year probationary period with the prospect of renewing this guest worker status or becoming full immigrants. And since many were seasonal workers, they would be able to move freely back and forth to the home country. On the other hand, non-deportables would not be eligible for political rights or public social services; nor would they be allowed to bring in family members, and they might still be subject to deportation at the discretion of the Attorney General.

The President rather naïvely reasoned that a double amnesty plan was "necessary to avoid having a permanent 'underclass' of millions of persons who have not been and cannot practicably be deported, and who would continue living here in perpetual fear of immigration authorities, the local police, employers and neighbors." [37] The administration bill bore the title: Alien Adjustment and Employment Act of 1977.

Delighted with the package, Senator Eastland and farm-bloc legislators agreed to sponsor it in the Senate (S. 2252). Rodino agreed to do so in the House, but with many reservations (H.R. 9531). Actually, even before the non-deportable proposal was officially announced, it met with near universal criticism, even outrage. Rodino, Eilberg, and others warned Carter that the proposal went against public opinion and the majority sentiment in the House, that it was full of inequities, administratively unworkable, and made a mockery of American immigration standards, that it would only encourage more illegal entries, more fraud in documenting aliens, and more man smuggling. [38]

The Carter task force hoped that surreptitious aliens offered a protective status as guest workers would emerge, register, be counted, and be placed under documentary control. [39] But how many would report themselves? After all they would still be on a probationary status subject to deportation. [40] And, more important, many had families hidden away in urban barrios or on isolated farms and ranches. What were the Attorney General's real intentions?

Still others pointed out that alien workers with "half rights" were simply a disguised bracero or "gastarbeiter" program like that in western European countries, that since countless relatives of undocumented workers were already clandestinely settled in the United States, the non-deportable proposal, far from eliminating the alien underclass problem, would only compound it. And, anyway, wasn't an offer of second-class citizenship shamefully in conflict with the Carter doctrine of human rights?[41]

Spokesmen for Hispanic minorities, like Congressmen Roybal and Herman Badillo, wanted nothing less than full civil rights and immigrant status for all undocumented residents including family members; and the Spanish Secretariat of the National Catholic Conference of Bishops, objecting to the Carter threat to cut off future undocumented immigration, wanted the federal government, in effect, to subscribe fully to United Nation's resolutions and concede the right of the economic refugee to cross any boundary line in search of work.[42] At best a patchwork compromise, at worst an exacerbation of immigrant and civil rights problems, said legal-aid experts.[43]

In two words, Chicano militants wanted "amnistia incondicional," and chiefly because the original Carter plan made no provision for common "human rights" problems like that of Arturo. With his wife and eight children, Arturo left Mexico behind, crossed the border under false pretenses, and disappeared into the sprawling barrios of Los Angeles.

Currently a bad back has left him jobless. As an illegal alien, he is afraid to apply for unemployment and other benefits. He is in debt, owing $558 to the County Hospital, $800 to a god-daughter and $300 to a friendly grocer.... But despite his troubles, he wants to stay. There is opportunity here that is lacking in Mexico, he says, and his children are getting a good education.[44]

Typically, Arturo harbored amnesty hopes of getting a green card or a guest worker permit. The problem was that a non-deportable status, as originally conceived, would not apply to Arturo's family, even though the children were already placed in the public schools.[45] (For the school control problem, see Chapter 10.)

5. Reacting to threats of even more undocumented aliens unless special Raza grievances were met, Carter proposed, like Alan Cranston, Senate coalition leader, that the current limit on non-preference Mexican and Canadian immigration be increased from 20,000 to 50,000. This proposal was made with the hope of providing at least a small incentive for legal immigration.[46] To many people it seemed that illegal aliens were dictating national immigration policy and more deserving groups, like legally admitted aliens seeking permanent resident status, were being shortchanged.[47]

6. The Carter administration was seeking and would seek more internation-

al cooperation, mainly from Mexico, through yet another top-level interagency committee that would meet with a similar high-level group in Mexico. Also, the State Department would urge Mexico and other countries to take some preventive measures against out-migration. [48] And the administration would lower custom barriers on certain imports from Mexico and other Third World nations, and promote international investments in these nations, particularly in Mexico, in order to stimulate economic development and tourism and thus reduce the surplus labor problem. [49]

7. The administration was promoting and would promote, whenever possible, cooperation between federal, state, and municipal law enforcement agencies and prosecutors on both sides of the border in a combined "super-agency" attack on alien smugglers, drug traffickers, and persons who prey on undocumented aliens. Thus under government reorganization plans, Customs, Immigration, and Drug Enforcement personnel in border areas would be merged into a single administrative agency. The objective was to protect the human rights of border crossers as much as to discourage illegal crossing. [50] The City of San Diego had already established a special Mexican-American police unit (Operación Pollero) to help customs and immigration officers in this double mission. [51] Possibly Mexican border officials and police, some of whom customarily plucked innocent wetbacks (*pollos*) and resented Gringo interference, would cooperate if cooperation were understood primarily as an effort to protect border crossers (rather than an effort to keep La Raza out of former Mexican territory). [52]

8. Federal, state, and municipal agencies would be pressed to enforce, if possible, the Fair Labor Standards Act, the Federal Labor Contractor Registration Act, and other safety, health, housing, work, and tax standards, as a means of protecting undocumented workers and, at the same time, discouraging the alien inflow. [53]

9. Rejecting a binational bracero accord as too controversial, the Carter administration would admit from time to time needed temporary or H-2 workers from Mexico for agriwork. [54] This plan was another compromise, designed to please farm-bloc groups and Mexican critics who felt that dropping the contract-labor program in 1964 to please anti-poverty workers and the idol of the liberal Democrats, César Chávez, was a grievous error: "It worked beautifully until the cry-babies, bleeding hearts and the unions killed it. Now we have the problem of huge numbers of illegal aliens."[55]

Many hoped that Carter would set up another bracero accord, as the best way to assure some Mexican cooperation in border control and to assure that Mexican villagers would return seasonally as needed agriworkers and ranch hands, for otherwise they might be cut off from substandard jobs, or if given a non-deportable status, they might drift toward permanent industrial employment, thus perpetuating the turnover in wetbacks. Cornelius urged that a third of the estimated annual transborder workers, or about 800,000, be given six-month agriwork permits.[56] Raza sociologist Bustamante, who considered Carter's policies myoptic, made similar proposals.[57] After all, as Critchfield pointed out, seasonal migration that improved Mexico's subsistence village economy has also "proved a remarkably efficient and costless form of foreign aid."[58]

However, the legal admission of Mexican H-2 workers was still such a touchy question that it seemed doubtful Carter and Eastland could set up a viable arrangement. For one thing, 7 percent or more of the American labor force, and over 15 percent of the underpriviliged ethnic youth, were still seeking or avoiding work in 1977, and it was generally believed that the country was already saturated with alien labor. The ignoring of this sentiment led to the so-called onion crisis.

In June 1977, still playing coalition politics, the President ordered, as a favor to house majority leader James C. Wright of west Texas, that 809 Mexican seasonals be admitted to save the onion harvest near the desolate border town of Presidio, Texas. Earlier Marshall had refused to certify the request, since employers had not met certain prerequisites. The Attorney General and the Immigration Commissioner ordered the workers admitted anyway at $2.83 per hour. The outcry from labor leaders, including George Meany and César Chávez, was extremely embarrassing for the administration. Both Bell and Castillo were forced to take the absurd position that saving the onion harvest at some spot known only for blistering temperatures constituted a "national emergency," as they understood the provisos of immigration law. Old Washington hands laughed at the administration's fumbling with immigration affairs and public feelings, the split between Justice and Labor, and the spectacle of a Chicano immigration commissioner giving credence to the old hypocritical charge of Chávez (whose Huelga movement harbored wetbacks) that the INS had always been subservient to agribusiness employers. Carter's senior advisers, like Hubert Humphrey, were disturbed at the politicking.[59] *The New York Times* editorialized that one could hardly take seriously Carter's concern for the illegal alien problem if political favors were to be paid in such coin.[60] For Carter it was a stinging lesson in the politics of Mexican labor. Nevertheless, the Department of Labor would probably certify some 40,000 or more Mexican seasonals a year, partly to encourage their cyclic return to Mexico.

Of course foreign-policy considerations played a significant role in the formulation of Carter's initial package of solutions. Carter's advisers hoped that the inclusion of "undocumented aliens" in the new human rights policy, new trade terms for developing countries, and a new Panama Canal treaty would help remove Mexican and Pan American grievances against U.S. colonialism. Mexican President López Portillo, whose country complained of being too far from God and too close to the United States, visited Washington in February 1977 and was thus greated warmly and humorously by President Carter: "The Mexican people know what Yankee imperialism means, and being from Georgia, I have also heard the same phrase used. . . . The proximity to the United States, I hope, will become a blessing and not a curse."61

Soon after, Carter messengers to Mexico City were giving assurances of no mass deportations, stronger cooperative efforts to protect transborder migrants from predators, lower tariffs, developmental aid through international channels, amnesty protection for non-criminal aliens, and a Raza commissioner of immigration. If Carter expected a significant cooperative response from Mexico, he was disappointed.

Mexican officials, who have never quite understood the American evangelical type, were somewhat embarrassed, even vexed, by the sudden unilateral generosity of the Yankee colossus. But López Portillo stood up to it. He coolly repeated that Mexico could not forcibly detain undocumented emigrants. He rejected all "police solutions" and all offers of direct American aid.62

Borrowing a leaf from Carter's open book on human rights, the Mexican President declared a policy of "asentamientos humanos," which, roughly translated, meant that Mexico would attempt to resettle surplus population around rural development projects, yet at the same time would respect the Mexican citizen's right to settle anywhere and travel anywhere, including anywhere in the lost territories.63 López Portillo also announced an "Alianza para la Producción" to promote industrial and commercial development and generate more jobs, but the impatient Americans would have to understand that such policies, like population planning, offered at best a long-range solution.64

Carter advisers were, in fact, learning another lesson. Mexico would take no direct action to detain out-migration. On the contrary, in March 1977 the Mexican government canceled ad hoc arrangements, existing since the early 1950s, by which American bus, train, and airlifts deported Mexican "voluntary returns" to points in central Mexico. Since these points were saturated with surplus labor, future deportees were simply to be left in Mexican border towns with virtually no alternative but to attempt an immediate reentry.65

However, concerned about rampant crime, vagrancy, and deportee problems in the border strip, Mexican officials did agree to pursue alien smugglers, drug traffickers, and predators more vigorously, and offered to transport gratis some of the destitute deportees to interior cities. Efforts were made to prevent Central-American and other Latin-American migrants, illegally in Mexico, from crossing the line, but not Mexican citizens. When a horde of destitute migrants, numbering between 200,000 and 250,000, rushed the border near Tijuana, hoping to come under amnesty plans, Mexican officials could take no action: "If they are Mexican citizens they have a right to travel, as yet they [have] done nothing illegal."66

One of the Mexican government's chief worries was that the Carter promise to enforce labor standards might eventually close off the safety valve and force hundreds of thousands of seasonal and unskilled workers, together with family groups, back upon Mexico's crisis-ridden economy.[67] Having in mind just such considerations, Raza Congressman Roybal proposed (H.R. 6093) that a joint United States-Mexico Presidential Commission on Immigration be established to study and protect the vested interests of Mexican seasonals and immigrants.[68] Carter himself proposed further study of labor needs and immigration policy.[69]

That Mexico, plagued by bureaucracy and its own system of labor exploitation, could absorb surplus labor through long-range investment programs seemed at best a pious hope. As always, a subservient Indo-labor class waited hand and foot on Mexican negotiators, while the latter discussed the shocking "exploitation of La Raza" in the United States. Research on wetback migration by Cornelius, Critchfield, Bustamante, Weaver and Downing, Villalpando, Cardoso, and others had already confirmed that Mexican proletarian emigration, ranging from stoop labor to underpaid skilled labor, had long been an established way of life and adventure.[70] It did not seem possible that Mexico (where allegedly 5 percent of the population owned 95 percent of the wealth) could soon narrow the gap between two national systems of wage standards, social insurance, public and private assistance, and fair-labor practices.[71]

No matter what López Portillo would or would not do, the first year of the Carter government some 9,500 or so immigration people faced an administrative nightmare in handling frantic amnesty and non-deportable alien claims that could cover from 4 to 12 million aliens, chiefly from Mexico and other Third World countries. Commissioner Castillo himself feared that workers and relatives from around the world, hearing of amnesty, would slip in and "melt into communities of illegals that already exist." Then would follow more counterfeiting of rent receipts, payroll stubs, and other documents "that will prove presence in the country for the requisite period."[72]

As amnesty expectations compounded themselves, it seemed that a "non-deportable alien" plan, understood as a "processing pool" by Castillo, was increasingly justified, not so much for human rights considerations as for bureaucratic ones, like "buying time." The INS simply lacked the manpower to patrol a continent and sift out bona fide amnesty claims, even as more amnesty seekers cascaded into the "pool."

In the summer of 1977 apprehension rates for the California front alone were 35,000 per month, representing a fraction of those who made it through. In all, during fiscal year ending September 30, 1977, a reported 1,042,215 aliens were arrested. Mexican illegals alone, captured and recaptured along the border, accounted for 95 percent of the total.[73] Not only was the INS totally unequal to the Carter amnesty rush, but it could not handle the paperwork crisis generated by the "Chicago stays" without pulling men from enforcement duties:

Overwhelmed by paperwork, undermanned and demoralized Federal immigration agents have virtually abandoned their investigations of illegal alien jobholders.... They are drowning in paperwork generated by a Federal court ruling of six months ago.... Agents say ... this is only a preview of what will happen if President Carter's proposal to grant amnesty to illegal aliens becomes law.[74]

Immigration personnel faced not only an enormous accumulation of fraudulent documents but the wily maneuvers of immigrant-aid lawyers, often federally funded. Texas Congressman Henry B. González said of Carter's double amnesty plan: "If I had been preparing a bill for the benefit of lawyers—for a lawyer's Valhalla—I think this would be it."[75]

True, Carter's original task force assessment called for 2,000 additional border guards, but it strangely ignored the pressing need for inspectional, investigative, administrative, legal, secretarial, prosecutive, and detention personnel. To many long-time immigration officials, it all seemed like the worst example of "false economy," with Carter and Congress pumping billions of dollars into public job programs for millions of idle people, while making virtually none of this lavish funding available to the Immigration Service: "If we had more support we could protect American jobs and social services from undocumented aliens."[76]

All the while heavy immigration, legal and illegal, from the Third World seemed to be gaining a fatalistic acceptance. Somehow it seemed "unAmerican" to oppose it, and, unlike the 1920s, restrictionists now faced the dreadful smear of "racism" from hydra-headed poverty fighters. Virtually the only important civic group that dared to push openly for tight immigration quotas—and birth control for the Third World—was Zero Population Growth, Inc.

In the new age of ethnic populism, moreover, the tumble of input from revisionist researchers, academic groups, ethnic lobbyists, and public officials on both sides of the boundary seemed only to smog over fundamental questions of American national interest, such as the economic and cultural marginality of the new immigrants or the sense of racial alienation and entitlements fostered by ethnic militants. Aside from concern about population balance, about the only respectable argument open to restrictionists was that the new immigration contributed to unemployment and heavier taxes for social services. A 1975 study done for the INS estimated such costs at $13 billion, including public assistance extended to aliens, unpaid taxes, money funneled back to the home country, wages lost by displaced native workers and the social aid given to them as a result. But all such estimates were offset by those who argued that low-cost alien laborers paid taxes and subsidized the American standard of living.[77]

Even national publications that editorialized for the business community, like *The Wall Street Journal*, *Forbes*, and *Time*, seemed to accept, tolerate, or condone the new immigration on the grounds that the employer in America's welfare-state economy needed the labor of hard-working immigrants.[78] Others believed that for a free and humane nation built by immigrants, "The choice is between continuing this legacy and standing at the walls to beat back the hordes."[79]

Furthermore, American unionism's monolithic opposition to "cheap alien labor" had cracked open, as local unions run by Teamsters, Garment Workers, United Farm Workers, United Auto Workers, steel and construction workers, and various AFL-CIO affiliates, readily admitted dues-paying aliens and consequently had reasons to defend them. The Carter alien plan had the qualified support of a weakened AFL-CIO confederation under trade-off arrangements that seemed to favor wetbackism and, to some degree, "privileged unionism." Such arrangements included Carter's sponsorship of massive public employment and guaranteed income programs for immobilized groups, escalation of minimum wages to $2.65 an hour by 1978 and $3.15 or better by 1980, and a moderate revision of the Taft-Hartley law in favor of union organizers.[80]

Unless such policies were accompanied by a tough employer penalty bill, or a national identifier card, or a "police solution" of some kind, it appeared that employers would continue to search not for finicky American minority workers cushioned by Great Society programs, nor for aliens protected by amnesty programs, nor for American youth "not worth the minimum wage," but for unspoiled alien labor—Mexican, Guatemalan, Colombian, Dominican, Jamaican, Haitian, Filipino, Taiwanese, Portuguese, and the like—for harvest work, assembly lines, and infrastructural services ranging from medical to culinary.[81]

Apparently western Europe's welfare states had a similar need for guest workers. A visitor to Sweden offered this comparative perspective:

> I found it to be a land of all chiefs and no Indians. All their "menial labor" was done by foreigners. Anyone could see the country was headed for trouble. I never saw a Swedish waiter, bus driver, or street sweeper; they were all Iranians, blacks, Lebanese and Greeks. I asked one of my guides about this, and she replied in amazement, "No one wants to do these things when the government will pay you to go to school. I'm studying for an advanced degree now."[82]

Undoubtedly the Carter administration, in response to widespread public protest, would have to amend its legislative solution to America's alien problem. Yet no matter what Carter might learn on the job or what Congress might do, the terms of an alien-rights debate were set. Carter could hardly retreat from his human rights policy. Moreover, the prospects for cutting down the inflow of uninvited aliens seemed dimmer than ever. The business was simply too

By Ernest G. Garrison

deeply rooted, and poverty fighters beckoned for clients. And as immigration officers often pointed out, the most important deterrent against permanent settlement of illegals—that is, a sense of insecurity—would be removed by blanket amnesty plans. They also doubted that any employer penalty bill or a bigger Border patrol could substantially reduce extended-family immigration, legal and illegal, from Third World regions.[83] Others pointed out that much of this inflow was legally admitted as tourists, visitors, shoppers, and students. Amnesty "solutions" would lead to more of the same.[84]

Colonies of the "new immigration" constituted ever larger supporting populations for more Third World folk, who came not always as job seekers or service seekers but as providers of services for the immigrant subculture such as entertainment, soul food and drink, folk religion and medicine. Commonly the first immigrant fortunes are made by providers of such services, if not in the first, then in the second or third generation. Witness Romana Bañuelos whose "soul food" tamale factory (commonly using undocumented labor) and ethnic politics carried her from a "little Mexico" in Los Angeles County to the post of Treasurer of the United States in the Nixon administration. In the wetback subcultures folk services have also involved uninspected aliens who are self-employed as labor agents, contractors, guides, smugglers, go-betweens, paper fixers, consultants, enforcers, taxi drivers, innkeepers, con men, paid witnesses, hustlers, prostitutes, and in other shady activities none of which necessarily involves employment records. [85]

The Carter administration was mainly concerned with suppressing border smuggling rings, but old immigration hands still believed—if anyone would listen—that the only sensible way to check unregistered folk migration and the mad voluntary departure cycle would be to enforce in exemplary fashion long-standing penalties (since 1929) against illegal entry by "innocent individuals," for all such individuals were, if successful, potential weekend smugglers, guides, or sponsors for kinfolk and *compadres*. (After literally millions of repeated violations of federal immigration and drug laws, there were scarcely 1,800 Mexican nationals in federal and state prisons in 1977.) But such action did not seem likely under the human rights priorities of the Carter administration.

Meanwhile, so many amnesty seekers were arriving after the cutoff date of December 31, 1976, that it appeared the United States faced an age of serial amnesty measures. [86] Would some of the end results be a Spanish-speaking Quebec in the borderlands, or a Puerto Rican problem immensely amplified? [87] Would amnesty measures be accompanied by mass concessions of citizenship, voting rights in foreign tongues, and cultural autonomy for Third World groups? How else could any ethnic minority enjoy full human rights? The central crusade against any strictures in Carter's human rights promise was being led by the National Coalition for Fair Immigration Laws and Practices, which included the American Civil Liberties Union, the American Indian Movement (AIM), PUSH (a black inner-city organization), and numerous Raza or Latino pressure groups, such as the League of United Latin American Citizens (LULAC), American G.I. Forum, PADRES (Spanish-speaking priests), National Council of La Raza, Hispanic Lawyers Association, The Legal Aid Foundation of Los Angeles, and MALDEF. Moreover, the radical International Committee on Immigration and Public Policy, sponsored by La Raza Party in Texas, organized mass protests by Third World minorities against Carter's hypocrisy. [88] All such lobby groups, it should be noted, were in some way involved in, or subsidized by, federal Great Society programs.

In any event, some students of American civilization thought that the new poverty-folk immigration—perhaps 70 percent of it from Mexico—would not pass through or near the Americanization, or melting pot, experience of earlier generations of immigrants, but rather into a paternal patchwork of government-subsidized subcultures similar to Indian reservations, black welfare ghettoes, Crystal City, or other dependent ethnic enclaves under a new national ideology of cultural pluralism. Distinguished sociologists Nathan Glazer and Daniel Bell, both concerned about the direction of the new liberalism, noted that membership in an ethnic group and ethnic entitlements were fast becoming more important and more rewarding than American identity. [89] One might note further that a distinguishing characteristic of Mexican immigration and acculturation promised to be that most of it was arriving—special claims in hand—during the era of Great Society efforts to compensate certain ethnic groups for past wrongs, real or imagined.

Increasingly local governments insisted that a permissive federal government pick up the bills for areas impacted with aliens seemingly entitled to amnesty and compensatory programs. Apparently increased revenue sharing, as Carter proposed, would not be enough. Unhappy Los Angeles County Supervisors hoped to jolt the Carter administration into stronger preventive action:

They are going to sue the federal government, seeking to recover some of the $50 million spent yearly on health, welfare and justice services for those unlawfully in the country. In Los Angeles County alone they numbered 600,000, largely Hispanos. [90]

Relatedly, in August 1977 a charter creating a Southwest Border States Commission, centered in Tucson, was signed by Dolph Briscoe of Texas, Jerry Apodaca of New Mexico, Raúl Castro of Arizona, and Edmund "Jerry" Brown, Jr., of California, all Democratic governors and supporters of Carter. They hoped that the new commission, like a similar Appalachian anti-poverty commission, could tap millions of dollars annually in Title 5 funds and other federal grants to improve employment conditions and promote economic development along both sides of the impacted border, and also to compensate cities, counties, and states for educational and social costs associated with the unregulated settlement of poverty folk. [91] In California alone, as a result of a 1971 State Supreme Court decision on the Serrano complaint, the state, beginning in 1977, would have to spend nearly $1.3 billion annually to equalize per capita spending on underprivileged pupils in poorer school districts commonly overrun with illegal families from Mexico and other Third World countries, like the Philippines and Taiwan. (Presently over 35 percent of the Los Angeles school population is of Mexican origin.) New York and other states faced a similar outlay. [92] But like the Organization of U.S. Border Cities and chamber of commerce groups, the new border-state commission, for reasons of ethnic politics, would probably insist less on enforcement of border control and more on the expansion of anti-poverty and civil rights programs.

Immigration Commissioner Castillo, meanwhile, was pushing his simplistic Peace Corps approach to "positive repatriation." Needy aliens (who are notorious for hiding money, job, and family facts) would be provided with go-home money, medical care, and vocational guidance before being put on the merry-go-round of voluntary departures. [93] At the same time the Ku Klux Klan threatened to take vigilante action to stop the border invasion. In turn, the para-military Brown Berets threatened the Klaners; Mexico moved token troops to the boundary; the diplomatic corps flapped; and border-town priests prayed for peace.[94] Thus in the absence of immigration law enforcement a comic opera unfolded.

Another sign of the new era was a proposal by Senator Robert Packwood of Oregon and various Congressmen from states troubled by Third World immigration, such as John Young of Texas, B. F. Sisk of California, and James H. Scheuer of New York, that a National Committee on Population oversee immigration policy and planned population growth.[95] Carter's package, it should be noted, did recommend more American aid for birth-control efforts abroad with the probability that proud Mexico would accept it—but only through international lending agencies.

As 1978 approached, a less buoyant Carter administration and various congressional leaders were striving to piece together an acceptable compromise solution to the undocumented alien problem, but how to break through a circular phenomenon? Great Society programs continued to maintain millions of underprivileged Americans in idleness or in non-productive activities. This was possible in good part because a continuous supply of aliens provided what compensatory programs could not—namely, a "needed supply" of eager, mobile labor for certain secondary and marginal sectors of the national economy. Unfortunately, however, as alien workers gradually settled in with families, they seemed to compound the minority-folk problems of a patchwork welfare state, and as they settled in, more free-wheeling alien workers were needed. Here, the problem, in a nutshell, for a wasteful welfare state was how to utilize the labor of a foreign guest worker, seasonally or year-round, without taking on his or her family problems and a whole new dimension in human rights and compensatory claims such as those stemming from 1848 and all that.

For Carter the inner-city blacks were problem enough. Here there was reason to believe that social assistance, income transfer payments—and cheap alien labor—served to support regressive subcultures and structural defects in the American economy.[96] Ironically for Carter, a rapidly spreading "brown problem" was immensely complicating his New South attempt to resolve at last the problem of civil rights, social equality, and full employment for blacks.

Meanwhile the more the subject of aliens was researched and debated by countervailing groups, the more legislators and task force groups found that the fundamental issues were hopelessly muddled, and more so by the human rights approach. Little wonder that the esteemed commentator James Reston could say: "This is probably the most complicated human and political problem before the nation today."[97] And there was the disturbing observation of David S. North, Director of the Center for Labor and Migration Studies, Washington, D.C.: "Maybe the worst effect of illegal immigration is that it diminishes pressure on the sending government to do something about their own poverty and overpopulation."[98]

Notes

1. Leslie Wheeler, *Jimmy Who?* (Woodbury, N.Y.: Baron's Educational Service, 1976), pp. 138-140. See also Jimmy Carter's own account of his political ministry and provincial upbringing: *Why Not the Best?* (New York: Bantam Books, 1976).

2. See "Hispanics in the Carter Administration," special issue of *Agenda*, National Council of La Raza, Washington, D.C., 7:4 (July/August 1977), 37-44; and "Young Predicts Mexican OK to Amnesty," *The Des Moines Register*, August 8, 1977, p. 6A.

3. F. Ray Marshall's viewpoints on foreign workers and public policy are reported in "What Illegal Aliens Cost the Economy," *Business Week*, 2487 (June 13, 1977), 86-88; see also his "Economic Factors Influencing the International Migration of Workers," paper prepared for Contemporary Dilemmas of the Mexican-U.S. Border, a conference sponsored by the Weatherhead Foundation, San Antonio, April 15, 1975; and "Employment Implications of the International Migration of Workers," in National Council on Employment Policy, *Illegal Aliens: An Assessment of the Issues* (Washington, D.C., October 1976), pp. 52-65. The gist of Marshall's "Memorandum to the President," submitted on April 27, 1977, is given by Peter A. Schey, legal-aid specialist, in "Carter's Immigration Proposal," *Agenda*, 7:5 (September/October 1977), pp. 8-9. Essentially Marshall would offer amnesty or temporary worker status only to long-term residents with family equities in the United States.

4. Castillo gave somewhat different reasons for his appointment in "Hispanics in the Carter Administration," p. 5.

5. James Reston, "Immigration Policy to Be Set by U.S. or by Aliens?" *The New York Times*, reprinted in *The Des Moines Register*, May 5, 1977, p. 9B.

6. "Flow of Aliens Too Much for INS," *Fort Worth Star Telegram*, July 4, 1977, p. 9A.

7. Interview quote in Richard E. Kipling, ed., "Illegal Aliens the Permeable Line," *Skeptic, the Magazine of Great Debates*, 20 (July/August 1977), p. 46.

8. "President Jimmy Carter's Message to the Congress of the United States," Office of the White House Secretary, August 4, 1977, pp. 1-7.

9. Miller Bonner (AP), "Illegal Aliens," *Stephenville Empire-Tribune* (Texas), August 17, 1977, p. 1B.

10. See editorials: "Benefica ley," and "No más explotación a braceros," *Excelsior* (Mexico City), June 7, 1977, pp. 1A, 9A; also Joe Nash, "Lucey Supports Migrant Workers," *The News* (Mexico City), April 28, 1977, pp. 1-2.

11. James P. Sterba, "Illegal Aliens Pose a Growing Problem," *The New York Times*, April 24, 1977, p. 21L; Fausto Fernández Ponte, "Los Mexicanos en EU," *Excelsior*, May 11, 1977, pp. 1A, 4A; May 13, 1977, pp. 1A, 9A; May 30, 1977, pp 1A, 21A.

12. Fernández Ponte, "Los Mexicanos en EU," *Excelsior*, May 13, 1977, pp. 1A, 9A. For a critical evaluation of Carter's liberal cabinet and the politics of accommodation, see Roger Morris, "Jimmy Carter's Ruling Class," *Harper's*, 255:1529 (October 1977), 37-45.

13. Symposium on Immigration and Public Policy: The Humanistic Imperative, sponsored by Chicano Training Center, Houston, at University of Houston, April 15-16, 1977.

14. "Carter Says Aliens Need Amnesty Plan," *Fort Worth Star Telegram*, April 17,

1977, p. 1; Richard Halloran's account of Carter's amnesty plan from *The New York Times*, reprinted in *El Porvenir* (Monterrey), April 29, 1977, p.1; "Carter promoverá ley," *El Porvenir*, May 11, 1977, p.1; and Fernández Ponte, "Los Mexicanos en EU," *Excelsior*, May 13, 1977, pp. 1A, 9A; and May 30, 1977, pp. 1A-21A.

15. "Illegal Aliens Crossing Borders in Record Numbers," *Stephenville Empire-Tribune*, August 9, 1977, p. 1; Bonner, "Illegal Aliens"; and "200,000 Migrants," *The New York Times*, reprinted in *The Des Moines Register*, August 8, 1977, pp. 1A, 7A.

16. Cartoon by "Lane," in *The Sioux City Journal*, August 5, 1977, p. 4A.

17. Sterba, "Illegal Aliens Pose a Growing Problem."

18. Peter Arnett, "West Still Wild Along Border," *Albuquerque Journal*, May 29, 1977, pp. 1B, 4B.

19. *Ibid.*

20. Statement of Michael G. Harpold, Legislative Representative, INS Council, American Federation of Government Employees (AFL-CIO) before House Subcommittee on Immigration, March 12, 1975, from interview with Harpold, April 24, 1975.

21. Frank C. Dupuy, Criminal Investigator, INS, El Paso, undated letter reprinted in Orr Kelly, "Border Crisis: Illegal Aliens Out of Control?" *U.S. News and World Report*, April 25, 1977, pp. 36-37.

22. For details and photos, see Harry Hurt, III, "The Cactus Curtain," *Texas Monthly* (August 1977), pp. 94-101, 161-166.

23. *Ibid.*, p. 96.

24. "Border Agents," *Stephenville Empire-Tribune*, June 17, 1977, p. 1.

25. Interview with Border Patrol officer, El Paso Sector, June 29, 1977. Feelings of frustrated immigration officers also reported in Hurt, *The Cactus Curtain*.

26. Fernández Ponte, "Los Mexicanos en EU," *Excelsior*, May 13, 1977, p. 9A; "Campaña EU para deportar indocumentados," *El Porvenir*, May 12, 1977, p. 1; "Denuncia Bert N. Corona," *Excelsior*, May 30, 1977, pp. 1A-2A; and other reports in *Excelsior*, July 26, 1977, pp. 1, 12; July 31, 1977, pp. 1, 21; August 2, 1977, pp. 1, 15.

27. Richard Stelle and Eleanor Clift, "Amnesty for Aliens?" *Newsweek*, 90: 1 (July 4, 1977), pp. 16-17. See also Anthony Marro's report on amnesty, *The New York Times*, reprinted in *Excelsior*, May 27, 1977, p. 1A; and "A Flood of Mail on a Hot Issue," *U.S. News and World Report*, July 4, 1977, pp. 31-32.

28. "President Carter's Message to the Congress"; and "Undocumented Aliens Fact Sheet," Office of the White House Press Secretary, August 4, 1977, pp. 1-8.

29. Fernández Ponte, "Los Mexicanos en EU," *Excelsior*, May 10, 1977, p. 1A; May 13, 1977, p. 9A; July 6, 1977, p. 1, 18. See also *El Porvenir*, May 11, 1977, pp. 1, 18.

30. "Bills in Congress," *ZPG National Reporter*, 9:6 (August 1977), p. 3.

31. "President Carter's Message to Congress," pp. 1-2; and "Undocumented Aliens Fact Sheet," pp. 1-2.

32. *Ibid.*

33. "Carter Takes Bill on Aliens to Congress," *The Des Moines Register*, August 5, 1977, p. 2B; see also "Hispanics in the Carter Administration," p. 14.

34. "Opinion-TRB from Washington," *San Francisco Examiner and Chronicle*, July 24, 1977, p. 2B. See also criticism by Representative Joshua Eilberg, Pennsylvania, "Carter Asks Amnesty for Aliens," *The Sioux City Journal*, August 5, 1977, p. 4C. Also Gallup Poll results, showing most persons opposed to amnesty measures, were reported in *The New York Times*, October 30, 1977, p. 22.

35. "President Carter's Message to Congress," pp. 1-2; and "Undocumented Aliens Fact Sheet," pp. 1-2. See also note 14.

36. See note 27.

37. "President Carter's Message to Congress," p. 5; and "Undocumented Aliens Fact Sheet," pp. 2-5.

38. Fausto Fernández Ponte, "Pospone Carter su plan," *Excelsior*, July 28, 1977, pp. 1, 13. See also questions raised by Wayne A. Cornelius, "A Critique of the Carter Administration's Policy Proposals on Illegal Immigration," paper presented to the Carnegie Endowment for International Peace "Face-to-Face" Seminar, Washington, D.C., August 10, 1977, pp. 1-12.

39. Bill Choyke, "INS Head Thinks Aliens Will Register," *Fort Worth Star-Telegram*, August 18, 1977, p. 12A.

40. Cornelius, "A Critique of the Carter Administration's Policy Proposals"; also "Alienating the Aliens: Backlash Against the Plans for Illegal Immigrants," *Time* magazine, September 26, 1977, p. 26.

41. Austin Scott, "A U.S. Plan for a New Class of Aliens," *The Washington Post*, June 11, 1977, reprinted in *San Francisco Chronicle*, June 12, 1977, p. 9; also Stelle and Clift, "Amnesty for Illegals," p. 16; and reports in *Excelsior*, June 12, 1977, p. 2A; July 26, 1977, pp. 1, 12.

42. "Hispanics in the Carter Administration," pp. 14, 37-39, 44. On the other hand, the Migration and Refugee Services of the U.S. Catholic Conference gave guarded approval to Carter's plan. See Donald G. Hohl, "The Catholic Church Reacts to Carter's Proposal on the Undocumented Alien," *Agenda*, 7:6 (November/December 1977), pp. 17-20.

43. See the devastating critique by Peter A. Schey, Director, National Center for the Study of Aliens' Rights, University of San Diego School of Law, "Carter's Immigration Proposal," *Agenda*, 7:5 (September/October 1977), pp. 4-15; and opinion of Mexican American Legal Defense Educational Fund (MALDEF), in "Patchwork Alien Plan," *The Des Moines Register*, August 11, 1977, p. 10A.

44. Hal Lancaster, "Rising Tide Poor Mexicans Flood into U.S.," *The Wall Street Journal*, September 19, 1977, pp. 1, 23.

45. *Ibid*.

46. "President Carter's Message to Congress," pp. 6-7; and "Illegal Aliens Fact Sheet," p. 6.

47. Reston, "Immigration Policy to Be Set by U.S. or by Aliens?"; "Alienating the Aliens"; Kelly, "Border Crisis: Illegal Aliens Out of Control?"; Carl J. Migdail, "Time Bomb in Mexico," *U.S. News and World Report*, July 4, 1977, pp. 26-32; Kem Balani, "Overlooked Aliens," *The New York Times*, September 27, 1977, p. 39.

48. *El Porvenir*, May 11, 1977, pp. 1, 4; *Excelsior*, May 17, 1977, p. 1A; and "Illegal Aliens Fact Sheet," p. 5.

49. Declarations of Leonel Castillo, in F. Juaristi, "Proyecto de Carter," *Excelsior*, June 15, 1977, p. 30A; statements of Patrick Holt, formerly associated with Senate Committee on Foreign Relations, *Excelsior*, May 26, 1977, pp. 1, 18; also "Illegal Aliens Fact Sheet," pp. 5-6.

50. Declarations of Castillo, in *El Porvenir*, May 25, 1977, p. 15A; Fernández Ponte, "Los Mexicanos en EU," *Excelsior*, May 13, 1977, pp. 1A, 9A; and May 11, 1977, pp. 1A, 4A. For reorganizational proposals, see General Accounting Office, *Illegal Entry at*

United States-Mexico Border (Washington, D.C., December 2, 1977).

51. "Braceros deportados," *Excelsior*, August 2, 1977, pp. 1, 15.

52. "Border Gunfight between San Diego, Tijuana Police," *The Des Moines Register*, July 18, 1977, p. 4B.

53. Sterba, "Illegal Aliens Pose a Problem."

54. "Secretary of Labor Marshall in Guadalajara," *El Porvenir*, April 24, 1977, p. 1. See also "President Carter's Message to Congress," p. 6.

55. Jack Pickett, "Editorially Speaking—Illegal Aliens," *California Farmer*, August 13, 1977, p. 4.

56. Cornelius' recommendations reported in "Aconsejan que EU autorice 800 mil Mexicanos," *El Porvenir*, July 1, 1977, p. 1.

57. Jorge A. Bustamante, "The Impact of the Undocumented Immigrant from Mexico on the U.S.-Mexican Economies: Preliminary Findings and Suggestions for Bilateral Cooperation," paper presented to annual meeting of the Southern Economic Association, Atlanta, November 1976.

58. Richard Critchfield, "They Still Come Home to Huecorio," *The Christian Science Monitor*, August 31, 1977, pp. 14-15; and his "Accepting Mexican 'Illegal Aliens,'" *The Los Angeles Times*, reprinted in *The Des Moines Register*, December 18, 1977, p. 3B.

59. Fausto Fernández Ponte, "Permiso especial a Mexicanos indocumentados," *Excelsior*, June 22, 1977, pp. 1A, 17A; June 24, pp. 1A, 9A; also *El Porvenir*, June 24, 1977, p. 1.

60. Editorial from *The New York Times*, reprinted in *Excelsior*, June 24, 1977, pp. 1A, 9A.

61. Richard R. Fagen, "The Realities of U.S.-Mexican Relations," *Foreign Affairs*, 55:4 (July 1977), 685.

62. Migdail, "Time Bomb in Mexico—Interview with José López Portillo," pp. 28-30. Also Alan Riding, "Mexicans Are Vexed By U.S. Migrant Plan," *The New York Times*, August 15, 1977, p. 15L.

63. For the place of resettlement policy in Mexican economic planning, see first annual message of President José López Portillo, in "Texto integro del Primer Informe," *El Porvenir*, September 2, 1977, pp. 1-8, 10.

64. Migdail, "Time Bomb in Mexico—Interview with José López Portillo."

65. Information from District Director, Immigration, Chicago, September 8, 1977. For surplus labor problem in Mexico, see "No hay vacantes," *Visión La Revista Interamericana* (Mexico City), 49:6 (September 9, 1977), 30-34.

66. "200,000 Migrants."

67. Riding "Mexicans Are Vexed by U.S. Migrant Plan." See also Critchfield, "They Still Come Home to Huecorio"; and note 59.

68. "Hispanics in the Carter Administration," p. 44.

69. "President Carter's Message to Congress," p. 6.

70. Wayne A. Cornelius, "Illegal Mexican Migration to the United States: A Summary of Recent Research Findings and Policy Recommendations" (position paper, Cambridge, Mass: Department of Political Science, M.I.T., February 1977); Critchfield, "They Still Come Home to Huecorio"; Bustamante, "The Impact of the Undocumented Immigration from Mexico"; Thomas Weaver and Theodore E. Downing, eds., *Mexican Migration* (Tucson: Bureau of Ethnic Research, University of Arizona, 1976);

M. Vic Villalpando, and others associated with the San Diego County Immigration Council, *Illegal Aliens: A Study of the Socioeconomic Impact of Illegal Aliens on the County of San Diego* (County of San Diego Human Resources Agency, January 1977); and Lawrence Cardoso, "Mexican Emigration to the United States, 1900-1930: An Analysis of Socio-economic Causes" (Ph.D. thesis, Storrs: University of Connecticut, 1973).

71. Lancaster, "Rising Tide Poor Mexicans Flood into U.S."; Hurt, "The Cactus Curtain"; also Vernon M. Briggs, Jr., *The Mexico-United States Border: Public Policy and Chicano Economic Welfare* (Austin: Center for the Study of Human Resources, University of Texas, 1974).

72. "Illegal Alien Amnesty," *The Des Moines Register*, July 25, 1977, p. 7A. See also critique: "Amnesty Plan Weak," *Zero Population Growth National Reporter*, 9:7 (September 1977), 1, 7.

73. Migdail, "Time Bomb in Mexico—Interview with José López Portillo," pp. 31-32; Robert L. Jackson, "Amnesty," *The Washington Post*, July 12, 1977, reported in *Excelsior*, July 13, 1977, p. 1.

74. James T. Sterba, "Alien Ruling Snarls Migrant Job Inquiry," *The New York Times*, August 14, 1977, p. 19. Some 150,000 Cuban "refugees" over the years had been erroneously charged against the non-preference quota for western hemisphere countries, thus reducing the number of visas available to other immigrants, mainly Mexican. Since most Mexican applicants were already in the United States, many with families, they were rushing to apply for papers and a stay of deportation under the court order.

75. Bill Choyke, "Carter's Illegal Alien Plans," *Fort Worth Star-Telegram*, August 14, 1977, p. 17A.

76. Information and statement from District Director, Immigration, Chicago, September 8, 1977.

77. Jim Wood, "Illegal Aliens' Economic Role," *San Francisco Examiner and Chronicle*, September 11, 1977, p. 12A.

78. Flanigan, "North of the Border—Who Needs Whom?" 37-48; "Illegal Aliens and Scapegoats," editorial in *The Wall Street Journal*, May 2, 1977, p. 14; "The New Immigrants: Still the Promised Land," bicentennial article in *Time*, July 5, 1976, pp. 16-24.

79. Stephen Chapman, "Let the Aliens In," *Washington Monthly Report*, excerpt reprinted in *The Des Moines Register*, September 27, 1977, p. 6A.

80. Walter S. Mossberg, "Battle Ahead Over Major Change in Labor Laws, "*The Des Moines Register*, September 2, 1977, p. 6A; "Meany Endorses," *The Des Moines Register*, August 30, 1977, p. 7A; See also Nick Kotz, "Can Labor's Tired Leaders Deal with Troubled Movement?" *The New York Times Magazine*, September 4, 1977, pp. 8-11, 30-31, 42-43.

81. See, for example, Ben A. Franklin, "Jamaicans Are Favored in Apple Capital," *The New York Times*, September 24, 1977, p. 7.

82. "Letter" to the editors, *Time*, August 29, 1977, p. 6. See also "Sweden—Racial Time Bomb," *Time*, August 8, 1977, p. 4; and "Sweden Is Aroused by Ethnic Problems," *The New York Times*, July 24, 1977, p. 7. For a survey of Europe's growing minority problems arising from guest worker programs, see Jonathan Power, with Anna Hardman, *Western Europe's Migrant Workers* (London: Minority Rights Group, 1976).

83. Interview information from office of District Director, Immigration, San Antonio, April 15, 1977; and Chicago, September 8, 1977; also from Public Information Office, Western Region, INS, February 11, 1977.

84. Cornelius, "A Critique of the Carter Administration's Policy," pp. 8-12; Lancaster, "Rising Tide Poor Mexicans Flood into U.S."; and "Amnesty Plan Weak," *Zero Population Growth National Reporter* (September 1977), pp. 1, 7.

85. Roberto Suro, "El Pan de Miedo," series of reports on illegals in *Tribuna de Monterrey*, February 25-March 2, 1976, originally appearing in *Chicago Sun Times*; see also Eugene Nelson, *Pablo Cruz and the American Dream: The Experience of an Undocumented Immigrant from Mexico* (Salt Lake City: Peregrine Smith, 1975); and Ed Idar and Andrew McClellan, *What Price Wetbacks?* (Austin: The Texas Federation of Labor and American G.I. Forum, 1953).

86. See notes 15 and 44.

87. Hurt, "Cactus Curtain"; "OK Bill Making French Quebec Language," *The Des Moines Register*, August 27, 1977, p. 12B; Robert S. Cameron, "Outward Bound: Firms Leaving Quebec—New French Language Law and Independence Policy," *The Wall Street Journal*, September 30, 1977, pp. 1, 26; Epica Task Force, *Puerto Rico: A People Challenging Colonialism* (Washington, D.C., 1977); and David Vidal, "Dream Still Eludes Mainland Puerto Ricans," *The New York Times*, September 11, 1977, p. 6E.

88. "Alienating the Alien . . . " *Time*, September 26, 1977, p. 26; "Response of Hispanic Organizations," *Agenda*, 7:5 (September/October 1977), p. 22; "Antideportation Fight . . . The National Chicano-Latino Conference, San Antonio, October 28-30, 1977," *YS* (Young Socialist newsletter, Jan Jose State University), September 1977, p. 7; "Convention Calls for Amnesty," *The Stephenville Empire-Tribune*, October 31, 1977, p. 1.

89. Nathan Glazer, *Affirmative Discrimination* (New York: Basic Books, 1976); Daniel Bell, "The Revolution of Rising Entitlements," *Fortune* magazine (April 1975), pp. 100-101. See also Nathan Glazer and Daniel P. Moynihan, *Beyond the Melting Pot: The Negroes, Puerto Ricans, Jews, Italians, and Irish of New York City* (Cambridge, Mass.: M.I.T. Press, 1963); and Marvin Stone's biting editorial, "Bring Back the Melting Pot," *U.S. News and World Report*, 83:23 (December 5, 1977), p. 92.

90. Editorial in *San Francisco Examiner*, July 25, 1977, p. 30.

91. "Governors Ask for Swift Border Action," *Stephenville Empire Tribune*, August 9, 1977, p. 1.

92. The importance of the Serrano decision for California and other states is explained by Robert Lindsey, "New Battles Over School Budgets," *The New York Times Magazine*, September 18, 1977, pp. 17-19, 64-69. See also "Los Angeles Schools Plan Busing Amid White Flight," *The New York Times*, October 11, 1977, p. 20M; "U.S. and Chicago Sign Accord for Schools," *The New York Times*, October 13, 1977, p. 16A; "Texas Schools Battle Tide of Illegal-Alien Children," *The Christian Science Monitor*, December 6, 1977, p. 12.

93. Policy speech before Inter-American Press Association, in "Estados Unidos pretende detener un million de extranjeros," *El Porvenir*, October 19, 1977, pp. 1, 4.

94. "El Ku Klux Klan vigilará la frontera," *Excelsior*, October 21, 1977, pp. 1, 10; October 24, 1977, p. 4A; October 26, 1977, p. 1; Miller Bonner, "KKK Calls Carter a Traitor," *Fort Worth Star Telegram*, November 6, 1977, p. 21A; "Troops Sent,"

Stephenville Empire-Tribune, October 31, 1977, p. 1.

95. "Controversia bloquea creación de un comité sobre población," *El Porvenir*, May 19, 1977, p. 1. Carter promised education aid for population programs abroad, "Illegal Aliens Fact Sheet," p. 5.

96. Roger Wilkins, "Historical Tinder for Black Jobless Rate," *The New York Times*, September 21, 1977, p. 58.

97. From editorial "The Problem of Illegal Aliens," *San Francisco Chronicle*, August 8, 1977, p. 40.

98. In Sandy Schline and Carol Palmer, "Chicago Hosts Conference on Illegals," *ZPG National Reporter*, December 1977/January 1978, p. 7.

13/ THE FUTURE OF MEXICAN IMMIGRATION

Paul S. Taylor

"Plus ça change, plus c'est la même chose." In this perspective it may be possible to forecast, at least in general outlines, the future of Mexican immigration to the United States. If the past is any guide, then it would seem that not only Mexican settlement but the use of Mexican migratory labor, one way or another, will continue as before at high levels. For there is good reason to believe that the forces which in the past pushed people from Mexico, and which pulled them toward the United States, will not be radically altered in the near future.

A brief examination of the Mexican side of the border would show that the motive forces behind Mexican emigration have not changed substantially in this century. Before the Revolution of 1910 poverty, land-hunger, starvation wages, and a thirst for adventure pushed the campesino class over the Anglo-American border. Since then living conditions in Mexico have greatly improved. Semifeudalism has been abolished for the most part, millions of acres of land have been distributed to the peasantry, and a heavy investment has been made in irrigation systems and in industrial programs. But, in spite of all this, Mexico is still an underdeveloped country where even now agricultural and industrial wages still maintain about the same relation to U.S. wages as in the 1920s, and as always father, son, and grandson look forward to better wages and adventure *en el otro lado*.

In the meantime, population pressures have nullified the gains made in agrarian reform and in industrial employment. In 1920, when the first Mexican exodus over the border was under way, Mexico's population was less than 15 million, and even then Mexico was relatively overpopulated in relation to economic productivity. By 1976 the population was soaring toward 63 million with prospects of 90 million by 1990 or before. So it is hardly surprising that Mexico now has more angry, land-hungry peasants than in 1910, when the desperate *¡grito!* was first raised; nor is it surprising that half the labor force, urban and rural, is subemployed.

More than ever Mexico's people are close to the United States. The two countries are, in fact, intimately, if not organically, linked by rails, roads, airways, footpaths, and a common border population. Unlike the 1920s several million underemployed people crowd against the American border, and over the years migratory settlement has continuously oozed over the line so that in some areas, like the lower Rio Grande Valley of Texas, it is essentially one folk culture on both sides. Technology, meanwhile, has never ceased to annihilate distances between the population centers of the two countries. Mexico City is now only a matter of a few hours from Chicago or Milwaukee. Given such obvious facts, one can assume that the United States will go on serving as a natural escape valve for Mexico's surplus population.

Furthermore, the Mexican government long ago recognized that Mexican migratory labor was an exportable resource that could contribute to national income. This was not only true of the 1920s, and of the bracero era, 1942-1964, but it seems even truer today. Perhaps as many as 2 or 3 million expatriate workers in the United States (most of them undocumented) are presently sending money and gifts in various ways to the mother country. Given continued economic underdevelopment, gross disparities in income distribution, balance of payment needs, and population pressures, one can expect, all rhetoric to the contrary, that the Mexican government will continue to favor, *sub rosa*, surplus-labor emigration to the United States, and to countenance, however reluctantly, the migration of American industries to Mexico under specified conditions.

American interest in Mexican labor has not really diminished over the years. In the past American employers and the federal government have often regarded Mexico as a labor reserve to be dipped into whenever the need arose. We saw this in World War I; we saw it in the booming 1920s; we saw it during World War II, and during the Korean War; and we see it now in several forms, as when American industries move over the border to take advantage of low-cost labor and special tariff exemptions in Mexico's so-called Free Zone, or when American food-processing companies move into Mexico's interior to cut labor costs and produce a variety of foods for both the American and the Mexican markets. And on this side of the border American employers as always use large contingents of legal and illegal Mexican workers, including commuters, immigrant workers, and wetbacks. As for a possible expanded use of Mexican labor—with official approval—who would doubt that if the United States were to mobilize for another major war, or were to face a serious labor shortage of any kind, that the federal government, under employer prodding, would immediately look to Mexico, and that a new version of the bracero program and a relaxed immigration policy would be forthcoming?

Through the years we have seen many turnovers in interest groups, yet a coalition of interests in one shape or another has consistently maintained pressure on the federal government so that special exemptions might be extended to Mexican workers and their families. Agribusiness, railroads, and other corporate groups are not at the moment pressing hard for an open border or a contract-labor program. Mechanization, union protests (including the Huelga movement), the diminishing influence of the farm bloc in Congress, and access by giant agribusiness and certain industrial groups to cheap labor in Mexico itself are some factors that explain the current relaxing of pressure. But new interest groups have emerged that favor large-scale Mexican migration. For example, Mexican-American groups formerly were aggressively in favor of border control, as in the 1950s when illegal laborers and contract braceros threatened jobs and undermined wages and unionization efforts. Now many of these jobs are unwanted by domestic workers, and, in the meantime, a Chicano ethnic movement has arisen that tends to regard immigration control on the Mexican border and deportation of Mexican illegals as a form of ethnic discrimination. Militants push for special exemptions for Mexican immigration largely on the ground that Mexico once owned the Southwest.

Those who favor special exemptions for Mexican migration find themselves in company with the familiar immigrant-aid societies (now reinforced by the minority-rights movement), certain liberal congressmen, Pan American idealists, philanthropic organizations, evangelical ministers, and a variety of employers running businesses, farms, and ranches—many of them marginal in nature—that depend on the availability of low-cost migratory labor. All of the aforementioned groups, as Carey McWilliams once pointed out, hastily adopted the "poor Mexican" when quota laws cut off the supply of huddled masses from Europe and the Orient. Also, the Mexican consuls have not ceased to defend Mexican residents in the United States regardless of their immigration status.

New legislation pending in Congress raises hopes that at last the federal government is moving toward a confrontation with the illegal alien problem that, as far as Mexico is concerned, goes back to World War I. Various bills to amend the Immigration and Nationality Act, sponsored by Congressmen Rodino, Eilberg, and others, would penalize employers who knowingly hire illegal aliens, authorize the confiscation of smugglers' vehicles, and provide for more cooperation from HEW agencies in locating illegal aliens who use social security cards, or receive benefits under social assistance programs. Citizens who for years have been concerned about loopholes and inequities in immigration law and procedures naturally welcome the passage of such proposals.

But the voice of experience might here offer us a word of caution. Hitherto there have been high expectations that new legislation and budgetary increases would serve to place land-border migration under strict control, as, for example, in 1917 when the general immigration law established qualifications of health, literacy, self-support, and a head tax; in 1924 when the visa control system was inaugurated under consular auspices; in 1925 when the Border Patrol was launched; in 1929 when illegal entry by individuals was made a penal offense and visa controls were tightened; during the Great Depression when laws were passed against aliens on relief and on federal job rolls, and when it was believed by many that an era of dependence on foreign labor had come to an end; in the 1940s when so many safeguards and controls were written into the binational bracero accords; in 1952 when recruiting, concealing, or harboring illegal aliens was made a penal offense; in 1954 when massive drives against wetbacks, together with immigration service reforms, seemed to have promised effective border control for the first time, and so on.

We will here briefly consider, in hypothetical manner, the probable impact of certain commonly proposed reforms in immigration control. For example, the authorization to confiscate smugglers' vehicles—if ever approved by both houses of Congress—is obviously a long overdue and logical deterrent to an old border profession. However, since most illegal aliens from Mexico have always found their own way into the United States over a familiar land border, or, like other aliens, use common carriers, it is unlikely that this blow at alien smuggling would have a major deterrent effect.

More cooperation in locating illegal aliens from agencies funded by the Department of Health, Education and Welfare, again, would be a provision welcomed by most concerned citizens and taxpayers. Yet the possible impact of this cooperation on the flow of illegals would be, all in all, minimal. There are actually dozens of ways whereby a family could—and does—subsidize the maintenance of relatives and friends illegally in the United States without ever reporting or registering the presence of such aliens to social service personnel because of the many overlapping social assistance programs, public and private.

Many families feel an obligation to shelter relatives here illegally. This sheltering may include providing documents to show American birth, and keeping relatives from outside employment or contact with social agencies, precisely to avoid the immigration investigator. Cooperation among federal agencies on alien control seems to make sense, but could "family infiltration" ever be effectively dealt with by a democratic government or a welfare state? The prospect of a house search immediately raises the specter of a police state that quite obviously is repugnant to American traditions. Also, a national identity card for every citizen and immigrant alien seems abhorrent to many Americans.

Proposed reforms would spell out in greater detail the illegal use and falsification of immigration and personal identity documents, and the corresponding penalties. This too seems necessary. Unfortunately, the fabricators of immigration documents often operate outside the boundaries of the country, and most illegal aliens are too shrewd to be caught with false immigration documents on their person. On the other hand, many of the identification documents used by illegal aliens posing as American citizens or legal residents, such as birth certificates, social security cards, and driver's licenses, have been issued in good faith by domestic agencies. Tracking down suspected misuse of such identity papers—which, after all, are not immigrant documents, poses immensely complex problems for administrative personnel at all levels, and for an understaffed Immigration Service. It remains to be seen what effective procedures, acceptable to the courts, could be worked out by administrative agencies. Here one is tempted to observe that the problem of controlling illegal aliens seems to be shifting away from the border and landing ports—the first line of control—to secondary and tertiary lines that would involve an enormous expenditure of time and effort by many public employees, and perhaps by employers.

The various bills that would castigate an employer who knowingly hires, or continues to employ, illegal aliens, might, after these many years, put some bite into immigration law enforcement. But, of course, much hangs on how well such a provision could be enforced. There is a long, dismal history of immigration laws that have never been fully enforced. If one were to assume that an employer penalty bill could be effectively enforced, then one could expect that illegal workers would become even more diffused, invisible, marginal, mobile, or better documented with, say, American or Puerto Rican birth certificates. There would be a natural tendency, already evident, to seek employment with small proprietors rather than with corporate employers. Recruiting, smuggling, job placement, and fabricating of documents would become an even more sophisticated and lucrative business. One should also consider that a law fining an employer perhaps $500 for each illegal employee would not appreciably reduce the legal and illegal entry of family members, who make up most of the immigration from underdeveloped countries.

Legal immigration from Mexico is an impressive figure in itself. In the fiscal period 1972-1976 this immigration averaged between 60,000 and 70,000, a higher level than the late 1920s when alarmed elements within Congress considered a special Mexican quota. Then the alternative was a more rigorous application of visa controls. However, since Mexican immigration today consists more and more of relatives coming in under family preferences, it cannot be so easily reduced by strictures against unskilled or contract labor as in the Depression era.

H.R. 14535, signed into law on October 20, 1976, was the first serious gesture to abandon Pan American preferences and equalize the two hemispheres.

It would impose on all countries a limit of 20,000 immigrants annually, but would not limit immediate relatives. This has important implications for Third World immigration, which tends to be self-sustaining because of extended family obligations. Relatives are sent for and when a visa is denied, perhaps on grounds of public charge, there is a natural inclination to follow the customary backdoor path of illegal entry with the hope of accumulating residential equity and presenting an adjustment-of-status claim.

Here the rapid emergence of a welfare state that includes ethnic minorities is playing, and will play, a decisive role. In earlier decades local charities and relief agencies voiced strong protests against unrestricted immigration in an effort to keep down taxes. Today, however, federal funds provide for the unemployed, low-income, large, or underprivileged family. Now whether a family is gainfully employed or not, it can better afford to take care of unregistered relatives here rather than leave them in the mother country where, as in Mexico, income for a large family may be only a few hundred dollars a year and where social assistance for proletarian groups is virtually nonexistent.

The demographic and political impact of Mexican immigration will be much greater in the future, for American birth rates have dropped to a point where population would be stabilized except for immigration. The Mexican-American population is also following the national trend toward fertility decline. But so long as Mexico's population continues to press toward this country, Mexican minority groups will continue to increase at a rapid rate. Furthermore, mass amnesty proposals excite migratory movements.

Appropriate response is neither clear nor simple. On the one hand, we have humanely motivated amnesty measures or larger immigrant quotas for selected countries. On the other, we find proposals to tighten American controls over admission standards and employment of aliens. These are not mutually exclusive, and a search for a balance between them is natural. In fact, the issue is truly international and appropriate for serious consideration in the Organization of the American States and the United Nations, where responsibilities for solutions can be shared.

Given the present socioeconomic and ideological factors at work on both sides of the border, the future holds a promise that an exceptionally high level of Mexican migration in varying forms, legal, illegal, temporary, or permanent, will continue. Thus we conclude that the control and legitimation of this migration, which became a national issue in the 1920s, will remain a national issue for many years to come.

EPILOGUE:
A NOTE ON ACCULTURATION
Arthur F. Corwin

Perceptive writers no longer ignore the emergence of Mexico-America. This phenomenon has also been labeled "Aztlán," "Chicano Liberation," "La Raza Unida," "The Other Mexico," "A Nation within a Nation," "The Browning of America," "La Reconquista," "MexAmerica," "Chicano Quebec," "The Aztec Curse," and "Santa Anna's Revenge." Whatever the label, Mexico-America is a dynamic, hybrid culture that manifests a symbiotic love-hate relationship between two vastly dissimilar cultures. As an ethnic conscience, it now spreads over the border states and has vigorous transplants all the way to the Latin barrio of Washington, D.C. It has already changed the course of Mexican acculturation and U.S.-Mexico relations. By 1990 it may embrace 30 million Raza folk.

As never before, this Spanish-language soul culture has a flourishing network of educational and indoctrination programs with media pipelines to Mexico. Thanks in some degree to the workings of the American melting pot, Mexico-America is now institutionalized in government and academic bureaucracies, labor unions, legal aid societies, and religious institutions.

For all its vitality and deep historical roots, however, Mexico-America is essentially a foster child of the Great Society. It is very much a political subculture wherein Third Worldism and Raza brotherhood are the dominant ideologies. As such, its present status would have been inconceivable without the Affirmative Action bureaucracy and the daily spread of millions of HEW dollars among underprivileged communities along with matching manna from state and local governments and private foundations. Naturally, the 1980 census, reflecting Chicano and Latino input, sets out to find more ethnic clients. After all, in the political culture of the welfare state, the name of the game is client power.

Many patrons of ethnic programs originally saw the social marginality and the racial complex of the Raza mentality as basically an American assimilation failure. Mea culpas and compensatory programs seemed in order, but those acquainted with Mexico also knew that *el complejo de raza*, much studied by Mexican savants, dated at least from the Spanish Conquest. In this sense perhaps the Raza migration and acculturation experience might be understood as a continuous transfer of the Indo-Mexican's race-conscious struggle, passive or active, against the white man's conquest institutions, whether semifeudal there or corporate here. In any case, Anglo-Americans and other ethnic Americans will have to learn either to live with the imported *reconquista* mentality or to manipulate it as the Mexican elites have.

Perhaps, after all, there would be little justification for "white flight" from the Mexican renaissance or for taxpayer revolts. Many Raza leaders, exhilarated at the swelling ranks of brown power, have promised to be generous with their former Anglo conquerors and patrons, and, moreover, to provide new sources of cultural enrichment and a better cuisine: Just keep the border open, you'll see. Such is the nature of the subject.[1]

Note

1. Suggested reading: Kevin Phillips, "The Balkanization of America," *Harper's*, 256:536 (May 1978), 37-43; Lou Cannon, "Nation Within a Nation: MexAmerica Is Emerging," *Albuquerque Journal*, via Washington Post Service, April 30, 1978, pp. 1B-5B; Elizabeth Midgley, "Immigrants: Whose Huddled Masses?" *The Atlantic*, 241:4 (April 1978), 9-26; John M. Crewdson, "The New Migrant Militancy: Whether They Are Illegal Aliens or Not, They Are Unionizing and Striking," *The New York Times*, April 16, 1978, p. 20E; "HEW—The Beneficent Monster: How to Spend $182 Billion," *Time*, 111:24 (June 12, 1978), 24-34; David R. Maciel, Juan Gómez Quiñones, José Limón, and others, *La otra cara de México: el pueblo chicano* (México: Ediciones El Caballito, 1977); Arthur F. Corwin, "El dilema inmigratorio american, con referencia especial a México," six parts, *Excelsior*, March 23-28, 1978.

APPENDIX

During the period 1970-1976 the principal investigator, Arthur F. Corwin, used parts of the following questionnaire to discuss Mexican migration to the United States with informants who had had experience, or firsthand knowledge, anytime from 1910 to the present. The principal groups interviewed were American immigration and consular officials, active and retired; Mexican foreign relation, migration, and consular personnel, active and retired; American employers and employer agencies, principally in the border-state and midwestern areas; and persons who had written field reports about Mexican migration.

Since much of the early history of invisible migration has to be picked up from oral sources that are fast disappearing, the interviewer made a special effort to locate and interview retired officials and long-term veterans while making tours of American immigration district offices and Border Patrol sectors and during several visits to Washington, D.C., Mexico City, and Mexican border ports.

Complete answers to questions were not expected, but it was hoped that select questions would lead to discussion and helpful commentaries, as well as to suggestions concerning the location of new source materials and photographs.

QUESTIONNAIRE

(1) Why, in view of the literacy, health, visa and contract-labor restrictions established by the congressional laws of 1917-1924, and the rising social protest against the "Mexican problem" in the 1920s, were not more effective measures taken by the federal or the state governments to control illegal border crossings from Mexico?

(2) What reasons or considerations help to explain why the U.S. Immigration and Naturalization Service, or the federal government in general, delayed for so long in developing effective statistical measures for Mexican migration and emigration, especially during the period 1910-1940?

(3) Why, in your opinion, was it so difficult along the Mexican border to enforce the 1929 law making illegal entry into the United States a penal offence? To what extent was this law applied to "smugglers"?

(4) Has deportation of Mexican "illegals" and "dumping" them somewhere south of the border even been an effective deterrent to their re-entry?

(5) Why, in your opinion, was an immigration quota never adopted for Mexico? Would this have been desirable?

(6) Had it not been for the Great Depression do you think a quota would have been adopted for either Mexican immigrants or migrant workers?

(7) Do you think that any quota system or any other restriction by the United States or Mexico (short of a "Chinese Wall") could have been effective against "wetbacks," "coyotes," or "enganchadores" in periods of high labor demand in the United States?

(8) Did the U.S. Border Patrol have sufficient men and means to enforce national immigration laws along the Mexican border before 1942? After 1942?

(9) To what extent is it true that the Border Patrol and immigration officers were indulgent about admitting Mexican migrants during the harvest seasons? If so, in what periods especially?

(10) At any time was the word ever passed along from Washington, D.C., or from the Department of Labor "to take it easy" on incoming Mexican migrants during the harvest season?

(11) As far as you know, was there ever a conscious effort on the part of U.S. employers to build up Mexican labor pools on U.S. side of the border in spite of national immigration laws? For example, did the railroad, mining, or agricultural interests do this?

(12) To what extent do you think individual U.S. employers encouraged Mexican braceros or "wetbacks" to stay in the United States by encouraging them to bring in their families and settle in labor camps or colonies?

(13) Why has it been so difficult to prosecute American employers who

brought in "illegals" or "wetbacks" contrary to national laws? What attempts at prosecution were made?

(14) What, in your opinion, has been the influence of U.S. "vested interests"—politicians, congressmen, employers, and merchants—in preventing more effective border vigilance or legislation?

(15) Give some estimates as to how many Mexican laborers during the period 1920-1940 were living on the Mexican side of the border and working on the U.S. side as "resident aliens" or "commuters."

(16) How many active commuters or "green carders" are there at the present time? What in your opinion is the probable extent of the traffic in falsified "green cards"?

(17) What influence did the American Federation of Labor and other labor groups have on tightening the policy of "administrative control" during the 1921-1942 period? What influence did such groups have on the Bracero Program, 1942-1964? What influence did such groups have in closing the Bracero Program?

(18) When did Mexican migrants, illegal or not, first start bringing in their families on a large scale? It is true that Mexican families at first tended to settle close to the Border?

(19) What are the reasons for Texas' becoming the first major area of Mexican family settlement?

(20) In your opinion, to what extent could the high fertility of "native Mexican stock" or "Spanish stock" already in the United States by 1910 or before be the major reason for the rapid increase of "Spanish-surname" population shown in the censuses of 1920 through 1960?

(21) What have been the most common procedures by which Mexican migrants or "wetbacks" have legalized their residence in the United States? Through relatives? Intermarriage with "native stock"? Children born in U.S.? Employer? Consular application? Other?

(22) From U.S. viewpoint, why have Mexicans, apparently more so than other foreigners settling in the United States, resisted naturalization?

(23) Would the Texas border have been the main area of illegal entry from Mexico in the period 1910-1930? If so, how is this to be explained?

(24) In what years approximately did California first become the goal of most migrant workers from Mexico? Other than higher wages, how is this preference to be explained?

(25) To what extent is it true that South Texas has always been for Mexican migrants a stepping stone to California and other U.S. regions?

(26) How for many years is the internal migration out of south Texas to California and other regions to be fully explained? High fertility rates? Displacement by Mexican "commuters" or braceros? Discrimination? Other?

(27) What do you think of the following hypotheses?

a. that for each legal immigrant from Mexico who settled in the United States during the period 1910-1930, there was probably an equal number of "illegals" or "wets" who later became legal residents of the United States.

    (According to U.S. immigration figures 661,438 immigrants from Mexico were legally admitted in the period 1910-1930.)

b. that for the period 1910-1930 it is probable that for every Mexican who settled permanently in the United States (legal or not), there were at least two more who resided temporarily in the United States as transient laborers.

c. that for the Depression Period, 1930-1940, it is probable that the inflow of Mexican immigrants and migrants slightly exceeded the outflow.

    (The net increase in legal immigration from Mexico during the deade 1930-1940 according to U.S. immigration figures was 27,937.)

d. that during the administration of the Bracero Program, 1942-1964, it is probable that an average of one "wetback" gained entry into the U.S. labor market for every bracero legally admitted under contract. (The number of contract braceros who participated in program— some came several times—during the period 1942-1964 is estimated at over 1 million.)

e. that if a total of 1,279,125 Mexican immigrants were legally admitted during the period 1900-1965 (according to U.S. figures), then it is probable that for this same period an equal number of illegal or unregistered entries eventually settled permanently in the United States.

(Section principally for Mexican informants will be presented in Spanish)

(28) Why has there been so little effective cooperation between Mexico and the United States in controlling illegal border crossings?

(29) Has the federal government of Mexico or the state governments ever had something like the U.S. Border Patrol?

(30) In general did Mexican officials along the border ever cooperate effectively with U.S. officials in controlling border crossings during period 1924-1942?

(31) What degree of success did the government of Mexico have in its official attempts to repatriate Mexicans from the United States during the 1920s and 1930s?

(32) Did the founding of more Mexican consulates in the United States during the 1920s and the instructions to Mexican consuls to do all possible to facilitate repatriation have a pronounced and permanent influence in returning Mexican migrants to Mexico in the 1920s? 1930s?

(33) Did such organizations as the Comisiones Honorífícas (founded in 1921), the Society for Repatriation, and La Alianza Hispano-Americana have marked success in repatriating Mexicans from the United States during the 1920s?

(34) Did the above committees and societies have any influence in causing Mexican nationals to resist naturalization in the United States? Did Mexican consuls have a decisive influence? Did Mexican political exiles and refugees residing in the United States have much influence?

(35) From the Mexican viewpoint, what are the reasons why Mexican residents and workers in the United States have been reluctant to become U.S. citizens?

(36) In general how has Mexican public opinion regarded the exodus of Mexican braceros to the United States?

INDEX